Early
Ibero-Romance

Juan de la Cuesta
Hispanic Monographs

Series: *Estudios lingüísticos*, Nº 5

EDITOR
Thomas A. Lathrop

EDITORIAL BOARD
Samuel G. Armistead
University of California, Davis

Alan Deyermond
*Queen Mary College
of The University of London*

Manuel Durán
Yale University

John E. Keller
University of Kentucky

Robert Lott
University of Illinois

José A. Madrigal
Auburn University

James A. Parr
University of California, Riverside

Julio Rodríguez Puértolas
Universidad Autónoma de Madrid

Ángel Valbuena Briones
University of Delaware

ASSOCIATE EDITOR
James K. Saddler

Early Ibero-Romance

Twenty-one studies on language and texts from the Iberian Peninsula between the Roman Empire and the Thirteenth Century

by

ROGER WRIGHT
University of Liverpool

Juan de la Cuesta
Newark, Delaware

Copyright © 1994 by Juan de la Cuesta—Hispanic Monographs
270 Indian Road
Newark, Delaware 19711-5204
(302) 453-8695
Fax: (302) 453-8601

MANUFACTURED IN THE UNITED STATES OF AMERICA

ISBN: 0-936388-63-1

Contents

INTRODUCTION vii

Part I: Early Romance

1. Complex Monolingualism in Early Romance 1
2. Modern Sociolinguistics and Early Romance 12
3. The Conceptual Distinction between Latin
   and Romance: Invention or Evolution? 21
4. Metalinguistic Change in Medieval Iberia 31
5. The Asterisk in Hispanic Historical Linguistics 45
6. The Study of Semantic Change in
   Late Latin (Early Romance) 65
7. Indistinctive Features (Facial and Semantic) 74
8. Semantic Change in Romance words for "cut" 95

*Part II: Language and Texts in the Iberian
Peninsula before 1080*

9. On Editing "Latin" Texts Written by
   Romance-speakers 109
10. The Non-Existence of "Leonese Vulgar Latin" 127
11. Asturian Texts of the Ninth and Tenth
    Centuries: Barbarous Latin or Written Romance? 135

12.	Sociolinguistics in Spain (8th - 11th Centuries) 155
13.	Logographic Script and Assumptions of Literacy in Tenth-Century Spain 165
14.	The Teaching of Orthography in Tenth-Century Galicia 181
15.	The Purpose of the Glosses of San Millán and Silos 209

Part III: Language and Texts in the Iberian Peninsula after 1080

16.	The First Poem on the Cid: the *Carmen Campi Doctoris* 221
17.	Latin and *ladino* (in the eleventh and twelfth Centuries) 266
18.	Twelfth-Century Spanish Metalinguistics (and the *Chronica Adefonsi Imperatoris*) 278
19.	How Old is the Ballad Genre? 290
20.	Several Ballads, One Epic and Two Chronicles (1100-1250) 300
21.	The Theatrical Nature of the Novelesque Ballads 320

BIBLIOGRAPHY 331

INDEX 353

Introduction

THIS SELECTION OF TWENTY-ONE studies published over the last fifteen years focusses on one topic in particular; the nature of Early Romance in the period between the end of the Roman Empire and the Twelfth-Century Renaissance, concentrating for the later centuries on the Iberian Peninsula. "Early Romance" is the name here given to the language of the Romance-speaking areas of the former Empire in the first part of this period; "Early Ibero-Romance" is the name here given to the Romance language of the Iberian Peninsula in the later part of this period, before it was given geographically-based names such as "castellano." There is no clear chronological boundary between the two.

My interest in the topic began from the viewpoint of Historical Linguistics, and dissatisfaction with the usual explanations of cases of lack of expected phonetic development. This led to a reassessment of a more broadly cultural kind, presented in *Late Latin and Early Romance (in Spain and Carolingian France)*, written between 1977 and 1981, published in 1982. The central thesis was that they did not then, and thus we should not now either, distinguish clearly between Latin and any Romance language until towards the end of the period considered. Gradually, after 1982, it has become clear that this hypothesis involves a reassessment of the data of several separate specialist disciplines. Accordingly, in the ensuing years the consequences of the hypothesis have been considered from a variety of perspectives, as the ideas have been presented and discussed with colleagues in many universities and countries, in many conferences, invited lectures and articles. The results are here collected together, presented in chronological order of subject matter rather than of composition. In each case, there is a brief postscript explaining the paper's original context and relevant later developments.

Thus the hypothesis is here seen from the point of view of sociolinguistics (Chapters 2 and 12 in the present volume), of the metalinguistics of language-naming (4, 17, 18), of modern analyses of writing techniques (13) and the teaching of spelling (14), and of the theory of invention (3); also studied are apparent infelicities of traditional philological practice (5, 9), the textual basis of historical semantic analysis (6) with detailed examples (7, 8), the traditional assessments of Early Medieval Hispanic documentation, including legal texts (10), historiography (11, 18), glosses (15), and hagiography (17), as well as a text from a Catalan context in which Latin and Romance could genuinely be distinguished (16), and the copiously attested, but only in later texts, oral literature of at least the latter part of this age (19, 20, 21). The earliest-composed paper here (16) was prepared in 1978, and the latest (4) in early 1992.

Most collections such as this are retrospective, but this one is an interim report only. Since 1992 several further related studies have gone to press; a *Status Quæstionis* of the present state of diachronic historical studies of Spanish; a general survey and explanation of the lack of Latin-Romance translation before the twelfth-century Renaissance; a consideration of the linguistic situation in the Romance-speaking communities of Moslem Spain; a general study of the relationship between speech and writing within Latin and Castilian, plus another of the relationship between textual changes and linguistic changes; a study of the spelling of the first official undisguisedly Romance text in the Peninsula (the Treaty of Cabreros, 1206), and another comparing its orthography to that of the *Poema de Mio Cid*; a review-article of Michel Banniard's *Viva Voce* (1992); and a syntactic study of the history of the non-agentive uses of *se*. Others are planned.

The most important moral to be drawn is mentioned explicitly in some of the later-written articles; we should stop patronizing the past. The Romance-speakers of the centuries that followed the end of the Roman Empire lived in a versatile and functioning speech-community, with considerable participation in educated culture (when texts were read aloud, as they normally were), and were not obviously less intelligent or linguistically skilled than the Romans before them or modern Europeans. It is possible, advisable, and more generous to assess the surviving evidence in such a light. It is also more plausible.

Late Latin and Early Romance was prepared at a time when the Arts Faculty of the University of Liverpool was a lively and encouragingly interdisciplinary place, where it was possible to discuss aspects of the topic with many specialists. Since then, the Departments of Linguistics, Latin, Italian, Medieval History and English Language have all been abolished. Many colleagues have given help and inspiration in the last fifteen years, but three deserve special thanks: Max Wheeler, now at Sussex, without whose help this enterprise would never have started; Francis Cairns, now at Leeds, without whose encouragement *Late Latin and Early Romance* would never have appeared; and the late Derek Lomax, whose help with the early medieval history of the Iberian Peninsula has proved irreplaceable (not only to me). Derek Lomax died tragically in early 1992. This collection is dedicated to his memory.

R. W.

Part I:
Early Romance

1
Complex Monolingualism in Early Romance

1. Metalinguistics

MANY DIFFERENT NAMES have been applied to various hypothesized forms of language used in the Romance-speaking world after the end of the Western Roman Empire and before the invention of written Medieval Romance languages. Distinctions have been made between Classical Latin, Church Latin, Christian Latin, Late Latin, Vulgar Latin, Medieval Latin, Notarial Latin, Romance, Early Romance, Proto-Romance, Gallo-Romance, Italo-Romance, pre-literary Catalan, pre-literary Galician, pre-literary Italian, etc., etc.. Many of these distinctions have a point (e.g. in Gimeno Menéndez 1988), but their proliferation has come to cloud the main issue. It would be simpler to do what the speakers of the time seem to have done, and to regard the whole gamut of spoken and written usage as being a single language, even though a complex one; thus we should avoid making apparently strict diatopic distinctions between different spoken languages in different areas before the general spread of the fashion for using reformed writing systems (from the eleventh to the thirteenth century); and we should also avoid making apparently strict diastratic or diglossic distinctions before the general spread of the eventually clear conceptual distinction between Latin and Romance, a metalinguistic development which roughly coincides with the spread of the diatopic ones (Janson 1991; Wright 1992b). We can avoid such artificial misunderstandings by calling their language by a single name. It is not immediately obvious what name to use; at the time they still called it *lingua latina*, naturally, in the way that Greek is still called Greek and English is still called English, regardless of diachronic developments, but if we too call the language of that speech-community Latin we run the risk of being thought to imply either or both of two dangerous misconceptions: firstly, that the language of the eighth century was essentially the same as that of the first; and secondly, that they had even at that early time the conceptually separate educated form of speech which we now call Medieval Latin . To avoid confusing this speech-community with either the earlier Latin-speaking one of the distant past or the Medieval Latin ones of the unforeseeable future, I propose that we agree to regard the whole continuum of geographically, socially and stylistically varied speech styles, in the wide area and long intervening period concerned, as being Early Romance.

2. The Myth of Diglossia

There are two main sources of data for the language of the period concerned; the written texts of the time, and the results of reconstruction. Since reconstructed "Proto"-Romance is in some respects not very like the language of the written texts that survive from the time when it is supposed to have been in general use, it has been tempting to regard these two sources as attesting two different languages in a diglossic relationship, either explicitly (e.g. Lüdtke, 1968:ch.5) or implicitly (e.g. Baüml 1980:237). Diglossia, however, as sociolinguists will tell you (e.g. Silva 1988:178; Fasold 1984:36), only works if a conscious conceptual distinction is made between the two languages concerned, and the high version is specifically reinforced by the education system. No scholar can find any explicit reference to such conscious awareness and teaching of a separate non-vernacular high language in the texts of the writers of the time from Romance-speaking areas, despite several occasions where such a distinction would seem to be crying out for a mention if it did indeed exist. There is, for example, no such evidence in the copious writings of the encyclopædically well-informed Isidore of Seville; when Isidore wrote in the seventh century of the requirements of the ideal reader aloud of written texts (the *lector:* in *De Ecclesiasticis Officiis* II.11, quoted in Wright 1982:87-88), he told him not to read too fast or too slow, too high or too low, and to be sure to emphasize the appropriate words and pause at appropriate places, etc., such as is good advice for all readers anywhere, but —despite Fontaine's (1972) and Banniard's (1985) explicit declarations that he did—he seems never to have given any specifically phonetic advice at all; he never said anything, neither explicitly nor in even the vaguest way, to encourage the reader to avoid voicing intervocalic plosives, for example, or to avoid reducing unstressed front vowels to semivowels, or to maintain a phonetic distinction between originally long /ō/ and originally short /ŭ/, etc. On the other hand, he assumed that if the *lector* read aloud with intelligence and care, the audience would understand. Gregory the Great, in Italy, expected his sermons to be largely understood when read aloud to a congregation (see Herman 1988; Banniard 1986 & 1989: 153). So did Cæsarius of Arles in France, whose sermons... were intended to attract large congregations drawn from all classes of society (Wood 1990:71). So did every preacher, for the epoch is full of instructions to preachers to be sure to preach, even to the most unpromising customers. There seems to be no hint in any of the copious early medieval histories, Church councils, hagiographical texts, etc., that in these instructions they were asking for the impossible, as the common modern postulation of diglossia implies that they would have been; we should acknowledge that if they themselves expected their texts to be largely intelligible when read aloud, then it seems only rational that we should also expect that to have been the case.

The first explicit news we have that sermons were not generally intelligible is in the famous edict of the Council of Tours of 813 A.D. By that time the diglossically high Medieval Latin pronunciation for such texts certainly existed, probably as a result of the recent Carolingian reforms of Church Latin. Guerreau-Jalabert's study (1981) implies that for some time these reforms only applied in Church contexts; that is, not only before 800, but also for a couple of centuries after that time, except in church circles, reading aloud was generally intelligible, as McKitterick (1989) deduces on other grounds; given the normal vernacular pronunciation of all lexical items, the archaic syntax and vocabulary found from time to time in the authorized sermons of the Fathers of the Church does not really seem to have caused general confusion, despite the picture painted by Richter (1983) in which the Northern French could not cope with it but the Southerners could. Thus I see the diglossic state as only beginning with the ninth-century reforms, whereas Lüdtke sees it as ending then; despite the fact that he claims to agree with my diagnosis, we do in fact disagree diametrically (Lüdtke 1986, Wright 1991a). My view is much closer to that of Van Uytfanghe (1989; it has changed since Van Uytfanghe 1976); or to that of Ganz (1987:41), who, working independently, refers to it as a reform which separated Latin from the vernacular .

Several studies in an interesting recent collection of historical essays entitled *The Uses of Literacy in Early Mediæval Europe* (McKitterick 1990) suggest an underlying cultural continuity in the Romance-speaking areas from the Roman Empire through to the Carolingians, in which the organization of society still depended to a large extent on the assumption that written texts—letters, laws, instructions, documents of practical kinds—would be intelligible to recipients and interested parties, at least if read aloud to them (see in particular the studies by Wood, Noble, Collins and Nelson; and Banniard 1989). Not many people could write, but several people could read, and virtually everybody, then as now, however illiterate, could understand most written texts when read aloud. That is, the inability to read does not now and did not then necessarily cut people off from literate culture. Each court, each noble house, each monastery, each church, each office, perhaps each village, had at least one person available whose official duties included the reading aloud of written texts to his neighbors, and often also, if necessary, writing on their behalf. Communication wasn't necessarily perfect then any more than it is now, but at least it happened regularly enough for the system to work. The view expressed in such influential studies as Clanchy (1979) and Stock (1983), to the effect that the Early Middle Ages depended more on memory and custom and less on literacy than later times, is currently being modified into differences of degree rather than of kind. The Carolingian and the Twelfth-Century Renaissances increased the proportion of literate people in Europe, but the practical possibilities of running Romance-speaking societies via written documents had existed all along. Furthermore, general sociolinguistic studies carried out in the last few years (such as Graff 1979, Cressy 1980, Stubbs 1980, Levine

1986) suggest that the disastrous effects of restricted literacy have been much exaggerated (e.g. by Goody 1968).

3. Reconstruction

Our problem, the apparent incompatibility of reconstructed Proto-Romance and the language of the texts of the time, cannot thus be solved by merely postulating early diglossia. We need not exaggerate the differences between the two types of data; most of the vocabulary and syntax, and much of the phoneme (grapheme) and morpheme inventory, is the same in both the texts and the reconstructed Proto-Romance, and in any event modern studies of all sorts of monolingual communities conclude there are always considerable statistical differences between the distribution of features in written and spoken usage. Sociolinguists see wide variation as not only normal but necessary. Historical linguists see a scenario based on hectic evolution in one part of a speech community allied to total immobilism in another as highly improbable, and, in this case at least, completely unnecessary. If we can accept that the literate spoke the same language as their neighbors, as happens in almost all literate societies anyway, the monolingual perspective "frees us from having to posit the rather rigidly-defined strata in society which the more conventional view requires us to imagine in order to lend credibility to its notion of linguistic apartheid, even in default of any other evidence that such layers ever existed " (Harvey 1990:181). This is a relief, for now we can evaluate the data provided by reconstruction within a more plausible social framework.

Proto-Romance, as reconstructed by extrapolating backwards from later attested Romance languages, is said to have contained—in comparison with the written texts—no neuter nouns, no ablative cases, no datives and genitives outside pronouns, no synthetic passives or futures, no phonemic length distinctions in vowels, no originally final consonants other than alveolars, and no velar consonants before front vowels other than those that were originally labiovelar; on the other hand, it did include extended uses of prepositions (particularly *ad* and *de*) to replace inflectional nominal suffixes, analytic passives with auxiliary *esse* and tense-indeterminate participles, extended use of grammatically-reflexive *se* with passive meaning, analytic futures (and conditionals) formed with the infinitive and *habeo*, new analytic perfects (including future perfects and pluperfects) formed with activized participles and *habeo*, a multi-purpose complementizer in [ke], extensive use of *ille* and *ipse* with the functions of the definite article, many diminutives in *-iculum* and other newly affixed forms, the use of preposed *magis* or *plus* instead of comparative *-ior*, new palatal affricates and semivowels, and much new vocabulary from, in particular, Germanic sources. (This is just a selection.)

The first thing to say about these plausibly reconstructed features is that the advent of a new feature does not necessarily nor even usually imply nor coincide with the loss of the old feature with similar function. It is perfectly possible that for many centuries there were in wide use both types of future tense, both the older synthetic and the newer analytic, just as there are nowadays in most Romance languages, at least in Europe, where the "going to" forms coexist cheerfully with the synthetic forms evolved from the infinitive and *habeo*; there is no need to postulate that the old futures disappeared at an early date, and even if gradually speakers became statistically more likely to use the analytic than the synthetic, both usages could easily have remained intelligible. The arrival of the analytic perfect, formed with auxiliary and past participle, has still not replaced the old synthetic preterite form except in Northern France, and even here, written texts read aloud with the old preterites are usually intelligible. Then again, the fact that the written forms of later Romance languages reserve dative morphology to third person pronouns does not in itself suggest that the same semantic distinction between direct and indirect object would have been unintelligible if it was encountered incorporated into the nominal morphology of existing texts; on the contrary, it suggests that it would indeed have been understood. The distinction between active and passive competence held good then as it does now. Green's study (1991) of the replacement of the synthetic passive by the grammatically-reflexive *se* does not conclude that they rigidly said *se* and wrote with synthetic passives, but that both were available in different proportions within both registers. As Stengaard (1991:5.2.1) also points out, with regard to the famous Riojan Glosses, even though it is traditional to analyze the glossing of synthetic passive forms by reflexives as being a symptom that they no longer understood the passive, a moment's thought shows us that this analysis is exactly wrong; the presence of the glosses in *se* shows us that they did indeed understand the passive, or else they could not have come up with an effectively synonymous gloss, even if it is also the case that for active use they preferred se. Often, having such alternatives increased pragmatic subtlety; the use of *quod* plus indicative, rather than accusative and infinitive constructions, after verbs of saying, increased pragmatic subtlety by enabling a functional contrast to be established between the two, as Herman (1989) has shown, with the result that in this case the advent of the new seems to have required the concomitant continuation of the old to achieve its purpose. Thus the list of absentees from the reconstructed list of morphosyntactic features in Proto-Romance is not only an unproven but also completely unnecessary part of the reconstructionist hypothesis, for all but the latest part of the period concerned.

Many of the new morphosyntactic usages envisaged by the reconstruction technique undoubtedly did exist at the time we are concerned with, and very probably (as Herman 1990, Varvaro 1991, Lyons 1986 and others have suggested) over a wider area than merely those regions that subsequently chose to incorporate them into their standard. And yet most of these apparent innovations involve the reallocation of existing forms to different functions—in effect, semantic changes—. Such reanalyses as happened to *ad, de, se, esse, habeo, ille, ipse, plus, quod*, etc., were in each case a statistical extension of the distributional frequency of forms that were intelligible in the speech of the Roman empire anyway. For example, using grammatically-reflexive *se* was not the commonest method of expressing passive meaning in the Roman Empire, but it was not unknown, in the same way as the grammatical reflexive occasionally finds itself being used for passive meaning in modern English. Even during the Roman Empire they could have without difficulty interpreted *de* meaning "of," *habeo* as future auxiliary, and also under different circumstances as a perfect auxiliary, *ille* with a demonstrative force sufficiently understated to be analyzable as a definite article, *plus* with an adjective, etc.; and most such usages are not entirely absent from the documentary evidence anyway. Relative statistics of frequency attest changes in progress, as Erica García has taught us (e.g. 1985), but they are irrelevant to the present discussion; if a form is recognizable and intelligible with a particular function, it does not matter whether it appears once a month or twenty times a day, it is still intelligible, and the usages of written texts are not incomprehensible merely because speech tends to use the features concerned less commonly than writing does. Once again, what is being envisaged here is essentially what we would expect to find anyway, on general theoretical grounds; a stylistic difference between speech and writing, based on distributional differences between features which on the whole exist in both modes, even in modern societies with high degrees of literacy and a distinguishable dividing line between the two. I am not the only philologist to take reconstruction with pinches of salt; see for example, Dworkin's recent review (1989) of the handbook by Agard (1984).

The historians' scenario implies that despite the reservations expressed above over syntax and morphology, the pronunciation details as reconstructed for Proto-Romance are largely accurate, even for the reading-aloud of officially-written documents and texts. The written text was nearly always communicated orally by a reader rather than through silent study; this is certainly true of Saints' Lives, sermons and legal documents, probably true of all letters and orders sent from kings to vassals and generals to armies, etc., and even quite likely to be true of official histories such as the *Chronicle of Alfonso III* (Gil et al., 1985). What we can now come to reconstruct is a single wide Early Romance speech community of great diversity, versatility and vitality, where the availability of a wide variety of both older and newer alternative forms, constructions, lexical items, and even perhaps in some cases pronunciations—particularly during the transitional stages of what can be later diagnosed as diachronic sound changes—gave rise in speech to multiple possibilities of pragmatic subtlety and stylistic nuance, such as is anyway characteristic of the oral usage of complex monolingual societies, and also—as Fleischman (1990) has compellingly shown—of at least the unamended manuscript versions of early Mediæval Romance literature. Early Romance was thus in no way inferior to, or merely a corrupt version of, Imperial Latin; Early

Romance is in no way inferior to, or merely an incipient version of, subsequent Romance languages; Early Romance was a fascinating and lively speech community in its own right, which deserves to be studied in itself, regardless of what came before and what was unforeseeably going to come later.

4. Texts.

But if we are to study the language of the period exclusively on its own terms, we have an immediate problem with the written evidence. Not many original texts survive from before the Carolingian reforms, but they certainly existed at the time; in tenth-century Spain, for example, Collins suspects that Leonese legal procedures did produce a multiplicity of written documents in even greater profusion than those of Catalonia (1985:502), at a time when Catalonia had undergone these reforms but León had not. After the end of the Western Roman Empire they were still writing on wax tablets and papyri, which are all too biodegradable. In the 670s the Merovingian Kings switched from papyrus to parchment (Kelly 1990:41), but the Papacy was still using papyrus in the ninth century (Noble 1990:88) and Byzantium in the tenth (Mullett 1990:158). Such early originals as survive are startling; all in capitals, usually without gaps between the words, with many abbreviations, and often requiring an act of faith to be intelligible at all. The famous graffiti from Pompeii, the Vindolanda tablets (Bowman and Thomas 1983), the Visigothic slates from Salamanca province, and the curse-stones from Bath, for example, are not remotely as clear in real life as in their printed editions. If long early texts survive, that is usually because they were subsequently copied onto the more lasting material of parchment. That represents a technological advance for which we must be grateful, but unfortunately the copyists had specific instructions not to copy their originals faithfully but instead to "correct" them according to the anachronistic prescriptions of the fourth and fifth-century grammarians. Surviving texts without such distortions are very few, and even the letters and drafts published by Adams (e.g. 1990) are not phonetic transcriptions of actual speech. In short, many texts as edited today have been significantly altered, and their originals could usually have been less remote from reconstructible Proto- Romance than the modern editions imply. Unfortunately, most modern editors of Latin texts still refuse to allow us to see the earliest manuscript texts without "emendations" (a view most unfortunately supported by Goffart 1987:56), and unamended texts are, of course, what all linguists and philologists need above anything else. Acknowledging these problems, Herman has spent a lifetime minutely analyzing the evidence of tombstones, whose texts cannot be emended.

Written texts were prepared by Romance-speakers in accordance with the detailed requirements of the Grammars. Even at the time of their initial preparation these *Artes Grammaticæ* were at best selective; as grammarians all over the world tend to do, they saw their task in moral terms, choosing some of the many and varied features of the speech of the day as being "correct," and excluding others as "incorrect." As the centuries rolled by, it came to be the case that many of the features positively advocated in the Grammars were rare in active speech. Thus learning to write was getting harder all the time. Important works intended to be kept for posterity therefore went through several drafts; unimportant texts that have survived by accident, such as the Leonese cheeses, have a distinctly less polished air. This fact has the unfortunate implication that in order to know how to interpret the evidence of the written texts composed in our period we need to know how their scribes were in detail trained to write. Not just the script and the physical forming of the letters (as studied by Petrucci 1972, 1986), but of knowing which letters to attempt; that is, orthography. Unfortunately, despite the valuable work of Riché (e.g. 1989), this has hardly been studied at all. For this is not one of the ages when scribes were trying to come up with fairly faithful transcriptions of speech; they were instead trying to disguise their vernacular with a sufficient veneer for it to seem correct according to traditional criteria.

So the conclusion is that this is where research should now be concentrated; we should avoid divisive metalinguistic terminology, we should accept most of the positive reconstructionist hypotheses as being valid for all Romance-speakers, we should look in detail at the surviving unamended texts we have, and then we should attempt to visualize how the scribes who spoke in the way in which we reconstruct their speech learned in detail to reach the practical stage of writing these texts in the way that they did; as in modern

English, that process was perhaps complex, but also essentially monolingual.

1994 POSTSCRIPT.

This paper was originally published in *Linguistic Perspectives on the Romance Languages: Selected Papers from the XXI Linguistic Symposium on Romance Languages*, ed. William J. Ashby et al., John Benjamins Publishing Co., Amsterdam / Philadelphia, 1993, pp. 377-88. It is the text of a paper given to the Symposium at the University of California, Santa Barbara, on the afternoon of Friday 22nd February 1991. This conference was essentially for specialists in Government and Binding, but even so the audience contained many who need to give lectures on the history of the language, and the subsequent discussion was useful. The central thesis of *Late Latin and Early Romance* is in need of rephrasing, in order to allow for a later survival within Early Romance of older syntactic constructions, as a consequence of the idea introduced there, and which I have developed since, that we confuse the issue and cloud the data if we insist on trying to distinguish Latin from Romance in the Early Medieval centuries.

2
Modern Sociolinguistics and Early Romance

THIS PAPER CONSIDERS the sociolinguistic state of the Romance-speaking world between the fifth and eighth centuries. It has often been said that the present-day state of the French-speaking, Spanish-speaking and English-speaking worlds is comparable to that of the Romance-speaking community after the fall of the Western Roman Empire in the fifth century. There is a wide geographical area over which is spoken one sociolinguistically very complex language. Many new features of speech had already arisen during the Empire, and by the fifth century there was a wide range of alternatives of many kinds, which the speakers chose between as they spoke. It is normal for new features to arise without their predecessors necessarily disappearing straightaway. Usually, in these complex communities, what seems to a later observer to have been a straightforward change could last for a long time as a case of variation (cp. Menéndez Pidal, 1926); and in these Early Medieval centuries many ancient forms survived alongside the new ones, without the speakers necessarily knowing, in any particular case, which of the available forms was the older and which was the newer. For example, in the fifth century, they would have had to choose, when pronouncing words whose written form ended in -ITIA (such as MALITIA), whether to give that ending three fully syllabic vowels, or two vowels and a semivowel, or two vowels and a palatalized consonant; and in a community in which all three pronunciations would have been equally intelligible, the unconscious choice between the three available forms would not have been made according to which was the oldest or which was the most evolved form. They would not have known which was which, and if they had known, it would not have been an important consideration; the choice between the three variants would have been made within each individual context for pragmatic, stylistic or sociolinguistic reasons. It is quite likely that they pronounced this suffix in a different way when reading a text aloud (or singing it) from the one they used in formal speech, and both of those might well have been distinct from the way they pronounced it colloquially. For one discovery of modern sociolinguistic theory is that our own pronunciation varies in a more or less systematic way between these separate contexts of use (e.g. Labov, 1972), and that we can understand many linguistic features that we do not ourselves say. Nor is it necessarily the case that the most formal usage is going to be the most archaic. With reference to this particular word, St. Isidore of Seville tells us (*Etymologiæ* I,27.28) in the seventh century that MALITIA is pronounced with a palatalized consonant, and we can probably conclude from this that he spoke it in that way in spontaneous speech, at least, and perhaps at the reading level also. Stylistic and sociolinguistic considerations often mean that it is useful to preserve variation in a speech community; more than that, variation is not only natural, but essential. It would be interesting to discover how far the techniques and discoveries of modern sociolinguistics can help us understand what was happening in these Early Romance centuries.

It will already be clear that I put little faith in the traditional geographical explanations of the multiplicity of available alternatives in the speech of these centuries. It is not easy to believe in the existence of clear boundaries between separate Romance languages at that time; it is not convincing to suggest that we can solve all these problems by suggesting that one alternative was unique to Italian and another to Catalan (etc.) already by the sixth century. The sociolinguist Bailey (1973) has shown that such rigid "genealogical trees" misrepresent what happens in real life. Certainly, statistical differences could have been found between different geographical areas, but at that time these differences can only have been statistical rather than diagnostic, that is, of no necessary importance (even if they happened to be going to be diagnostic later). Many specialists in the field will not agree with this assessment, citing, for example, the supposedly very early separation of Sardinian (e.g. De Dardel,

1982); but we are all aware (with Herman 1965) of the great difficulty that is encountered by those who try to locate the place of origin of a text from these centuries on the base of linguistic evidence alone. For example, Manuel Díaz pointed out (1965) the Romance features which can be detected in the texts of the Visigothic liturgists of the seventh century, but these seem to be general features of Romance rather than specifically Spanish: the femininization of originally neuter plural forms, the regularization of formerly irregular verbs, the activization of original deponents, the avoidance of dative and ablative endings, the addition of a prothetic [e-] before a word beginning in [s-] plus a consonant, the voicing of some intervocalic consonants, the use of compound prepositions, etc. There they are, features of seventh-century Romance to be found in the Spanish liturgy, but they are not particularly "Spanish." Geographical frontiers between separate Romance languages seem to correspond better to the political divisions of the ninth century and later. That is why it seems hard to believe that the choice between available variants in the spoken Romance of the previous centuries can have been made on simple geographical grounds in more than a few cases. The Irish Latinist McManus (1984) has suggested this also for the spoken Latin of the British Isles, which was not in fact as distinctive as has been claimed.

Nor does there seem much point in trying to distinguish clearly between Latin and Romance before the ninth century (an opinion explained at length in *Late Latin and Early Romance*). We should accept that the sociolinguistic situation of these years is far more complex than would be expected if we were merely dealing with a geometrical distinction between two languages, Latin and Romance (in my view, Medieval Latin, distinct from Romance, was a conceptual innovation of the Carolingian reformers of c.800). Before that there was one language, Early Romance, which was getting increasingly complicated sociolinguistically. We can compare this with Modern French, where there are differences between speech and writing, but it is unreasonable to analyze the two as being separate languages. What happens (in both cases) is that spoken language evolves but the rules taught to writers do not. Since we cannot now support the traditional view that there were two clearly separate languages in the seventh century, Latin and Romance, it is worth reassessing from a different approach the texts composed then by Romance-speakers; for it is possible that they can give us clues to the sociolinguistic situation of the time.

This task has to be undertaken with great caution, of course. As we know from modern studies (such as those collected in Coulmas and Ehlich, 1983), and indeed from common sense, texts never reflect spontaneous speech, not even the speech of their author. As regards morphology, there is a great deal to be said for the view expressed by Politzer (1961), to the effect that when we come across suffixes that were spelled perfectly, in a text of these times, we can explain this perfection best if the ending in question was entirely absent from normal speech; for example, the ending -IBUS was more consistently spelled correctly in the seventh century than in the fifth, and the reason for that is that by the seventh century the affix had disappeared from normal spontaneous speech, so the scribes could learn the ending written -IBUS and reproduce it exactly without any interference from a spoken form in (for example) [-eßos]. This has an equivalent in Modern French; many writers always spell totally correctly the verbal affix for third person plural verbs -ENT, but none ever pronounce it at all, neither as [-ent] or as anything else. The endings of the French preterite tense, which is only used in writing, are normally spelled correctly, and can be pronounced without any hesitation when reading aloud, even though not used in colloquial speech. In the same way, we need to be aware that texts of those centuries, if written by a speaker of Early Romance, represent one stylistic level of that Early Romance. It is normal in every language for some features of texts, even when read aloud, to be ones that would never appear in spontaneous speech, and in Early Romance as in the complex speech-communities of modern times this is a normal sociolinguistic phenomenon.

It is also worth pointing out that nowadays the differences there are in the normal spelling of texts from different geographical areas do not usually correspond to phonetic distinctions. For example, the spelling differences that there are between the written English of Britain and the USA occur in words that are pronounced more or less the same on the two sides of the Atlantic. That is, spelling variation is not direct evidence of spoken variation. For example, the

British forms *centre, programme, marvellous, catalogue, defence* and *through* are of words that are pronounced with the same phonemes corresponding to the different letters of North American *center, program, marvelous, catalog, defense,* and *thru.* If there is any kind of analogy to be drawn between the two speech-communities, we have to conclude that it is not always valid to deduce the existence of geographically-based variation in speech on the evidence of geographically-based variation in texts in the seventh century either.

It is possible that the errors made in inscriptions and public notices might be more reliable, but they do not in fact give us clear evidence of syntax or vocabulary now. Constructions and words are used on posters and public signs that would never be used in normal speech, because they too are on a separate stylistic level. For example, there is in English a word ALIGHT; in speech this is an adjective meaning "on fire," in public notices it is a verb meaning "get down" (usually from a train). This latter meaning for the word is hardly ever heard in real life, but even so we understand the word when we see it, and we would be able to read it aloud if need be, and even though it is now an archaism we would read it with the normal evolved phonetics of the late twentieth century. That kind of phenomenon is found in all modern languages, and could well have occurred also in the sixth and seventh centuries. Words and forms that were falling out of colloquial usage could easily stay alive on the sociolinguistic level of public notices, and could have been understood and read aloud without difficulty by people who would never have used them otherwise. And the same applies to morphology; in the Iberian Peninsula, most nouns were probably used in speech almost always only in the form that was originally only accusative, whatever the syntactic context, but for centuries the speakers would have been able to recognize and read aloud the other case endings, with their normal evolved phonetics; and even (if it were necessary) write these latter forms not used in speech, if they had been professionally trained to write. For example, one word which is found in a number of legal texts contains the word VOLUNTAS. In normal speech, in eighth-century Spain, the population, including the lawyers, would probably have used the form [boluntáde]. When reading aloud, that is, operating at that stylistic level, perhaps they would not have read it exactly the same as they would have spoken it colloquially; and if they happened to read it as [boluntás], or perhaps [boluntá], that is, without the normal final syllable, that would not have struck anyone as wrong, because in all societies we know that lawyers are liable to speak in an esoteric manner in their work but speak more or less normally when they get home from the office (cp. Crystal and Davy 1969: chapter 8; and *Late Latin*, pp. 166-71). In short, all the variations, alternatives and confusions that we can reconstruct for the Romance-speaking world are phenomena which modern sociolinguistic theory tells us that we would expect to find there anyway.

But although sociolinguistic theory can help Romance philologists to get the general problems into focus, it seems unlikely that the detailed investigative techniques used by the modern researchers will be appropriate for use when we consider the details of the Early Romance centuries. Lüdtke (1968), for example, has applied the modern concept of "diglossia" to the Early Romance world (as the word was used by Ferguson, 1959); but this cannot be accepted, for Fasold (1984) (and others) have established that the existence of "diglossia" depends on the general recognition within the speech community of the existence of two separately distinguishable languages, not merely of different stylistic levels, and this recognition cannot be identified for the period preceding the Carolingian reforms. Labov (1972) and Trudgill (1974) have developed complicated techniques to illuminate complicated data collected from the modern United States and Great Britain, but it seems improbable that we will ever have enough data, or any clear data at all, concerning linguistic variation in seventh-century Toledo, comparable with the data available to Labov and Trudgill. Nor do we have enough available data to exploit the theory of variable rules; that is, that observable variation is the result of internalized rules of statistical variation, of such a kind that at a given stylistic level 60% of our relevant utterances would be of one type and 40% of another, for example. Romaine (1982) has used this idea, among others, in her excellent historical study of Scottish English of the 15th Century even in the absence of spoken data. But in the seventh century, everything would be guesswork. Lesley Milroy (1980) has used the theory of "social networks" to explain some of the diversity there is in Modern Northern Irish speech, and she and Jim Milroy have recently (1985) explained the implications that these networks have for our understanding of modern linguistic changes; but this theory, and the "Wave" theory preferred by Bailey, depend on a detailed analysis of who knows who in the community, which is also out of our reach for the Early Romance world. Even so, there are specialists in the "Late Latin" texts of the age who understand sociolinguistics; in particular, the works of Van Uytfanghe, Itkonen and Richter should be mentioned here.

Thus although it would hardly be feasible for modern investigators into Early Romance to make use of the detailed techniques developed by recent sociolinguistic theory, it would certainly be valuable for us to acquire a general sociolinguistic understanding of how and when people nowadays vary in speech and in reading aloud; and to realize that people can understand all sorts of uses that they would rarely actually say themselves, that variation is usually explicable according to other criteria than the merely geographical, that the same person can vary in speech according to social and stylistic parameters, that educated people vary along the same stylistic scales as the uneducated, and that textual variation does not inevitably indicate variation in speech between the authors of the texts. Such realizations should at the least prevent Romance philologists from descending into nonsense. Several of the assumptions of the Romance philological manuals now in use would probably seem absurd to a modern sociolinguist. For example, some of them still say that periods of wide contacts and communications, such as the Roman Empire, favor linguistic change less than periods of comparative isolation between communities, such as the seventh century; but the Milroys, and Trudgill, have established that the opposite is true, that linguistic innovations increase at times of mobility and good communications. It is absurd to continue to tell our students (if we do) that Latin only began to change much after 600.

It is also absurd to keep telling our students that the spelling of the Strasbourg Oaths was designed that way to help native speakers of French Romance. As we all know, reading (and writing) phonetic transcriptions to which we are not accustomed is much harder than reading (or writing) normal spelling. In the modern world, phonetic transcriptions are only useful for foreigners who can read their own language but do not know how to pronounce the language in question (as in tourist phrasebooks); phonetic transcriptions are no help to those who speak the language anyway. That is why I suggested (in *Late Latin*) that the Oaths were written the way they were for the benefit of a Germanic-speaker who did not know Romance well; and (at the Aix-en-Provence conference) that the famous 11th-century Riojan Romance glosses were written the way they were to help a foreigner who did not know the local speech but wished to read aloud there in an intelligible manner.

To conclude: it may be true that modern sociolinguistic theory cannot help us greatly in the reconstruction of detail, partly because New York and Norwich are not very like seventh-century towns, but it can help prevent us from talking nonsense. A general reorientation of our perspectives along these lines will allow us to realize how very improbable are some of the traditional explanations of aspects of these Early Romance communities. At least we can now prepare to carry out the new kinds of research that this perspective implies; for the moment, it is a case of "reculer pour mieux sauter."

1994 POSTSCRIPT.

This paper was originally printed as "La sociolingüística moderna y el romance temprano" in *Actes du XVIIIe Congrès International de Linguistique et de Philologie Romanes,* ed. Dieter Kremer, Vol.V, Tübingen, Niemeyer, 1988, pp.11-18. The conference was held at Trier. That was the unamended text of the contribution to the *Table Ronde* entitled "Les Langues romanes—champs exemplaire pour le développement de la sociolinguistique et de la pragmatique," held on the morning of Wednesday 21st May 1986. I had been invited to contribute to the Round Table after submitting the abstract, and had no time to rewrite it; thus its early historical bias was alien to the interests of most of the audience, and, being in Spanish, of little interest to the central Franco-German axis that dominates these conferences. So far as I know, the paper has aroused almost no interest. The point about British and American spelling reflecting different teaching conventions rather than different pronunciations has eventually led to some of the other studies in the present volume, and others I have prepared more recently. Since 1986, the idea seems to have spread that Lüdtke and I agree about diglossia; but as the next paper in the present volume shows, we in fact disagree diametrically, for Lüdtke sees Latin-Romance diglossia as ending with the Carolingian Reforms, and I see it as beginning then. Romance historical sociolinguistics has occasionally been practiced since; Lloyd (1992), for example, has reconsidered its general potential, and Penny (1992) has applied social network theory to the history of Judeo-Spanish. My views have not changed since 1986 as to the conclusion: just a little sociolinguistic understanding is all that it would take to inhibit some of the elementary misrepresentations that still get printed within our field.

I should have given in full the quotation from Isidore's *Etymologiæ* I.27.28, because it illustrates the point about the non-phonetic nature of spelling conventions in a startlingly direct manner:

> 28. Y et Z litteris sola Græca nomina scribuntur. Nam cum iustitia sonum Z littera exprimat, tamen, quia latinum est, per T scribendum est. Sic militia, malitia, nequitia et cetera similia.

The word MALITIA eventually becomes Spanish *maleza*, "weeds." Instead, as an appendix to the original paper I added the text of the first Strasbourg Oath and of *Glosa Emilianense* 89, neither of which seems really necessary to reproduce here.

3
The Conceptual Distinction between Latin and Romance: Invention or Evolution?

Several historians have recently been arguing that early developments in human society, such as agriculture, were often consequences of human inventiveness rather than of any kind of automatic evolutionary process (cp. Van der Leeuw and Torrence 1989). I have argued before (Wright 1983) that historians of language need to pay more attention to the philosophy of history, and this distinction between evolution and invention seems a crucial one to make within our own historical discipline.

Some diachronic linguistic developments certainly occur in an evolutionary manner, without any speakers particularly willing them into existence. But several other developments are the consequences of a decision made by one or more speakers, and these changes can sensibly be regarded as in origin cases of invention. The latter are sometimes assumed to be peripheral to historical linguistics. Lass, for example, accepted without argument that change does not involve (conscious) human purpose (1980:82). Chomsky has also exiled such phenomena from consideration *a priori*: 'each actual "language" will incorporate a periphery of borrowings, historical residues, inventions, and so on, which we can hardly expect to—and indeed would not want to—incorporate within a principled theory of Universal Grammar' (1981:8). Fortunately there is no compulsion for us all to be necessarily interested exclusively in universals, and even if we are, linguistic inventiveness can plausibly be seen as being as much of a human universal, in the sociohistorical development of languages, as is the linguistic creativity that Chomsky himself has so often stressed, despite the fact that not every individual invention exists in every language community. This paper suggests that one such conscious decision concerns the separate establishment of systematically different levels of language for different social purposes; specifically, that it still seems most likely that the conceptual distinction between Latin and the contemporary Romance Languages of the Early Middle Ages can only have been the result of an innovation made on purpose in a particular historical context, that of the Carolingian renewal of Christian intellectual life, rather than the inevitable result of a gradual evolution. I disagree, therefore, with R. A. Hall's explicit view that 'A diglossic situation would have arisen anyhow, Carolingian "reform" or no "reform" ' (1986:215); there was nothing inevitable or evolutionary about the arrival of the eventually clear diglossia between Latin and the Romance languages in the later Middle Ages. The Carolingian scholars did not merely become conscious that Romance and Latin were different (Michael 1988), as has often been suggested; they invented the difference.

Some historical developments can only have been invented on purpose, the creations of an individual genius rather than the result of unconscious evolutions by the mass of the human community. The wheel, the rowing boat, coinage, the bow and arrow, the internal combustion engine, for example; and within linguistic history, writing. Ong (1982:83-85), Harris (1986), and others argue that writing can only have been an invention. Historical linguists have tended to shy away from this conclusion, using some non-committal and indeterminate phrasing such as the 'development of writing' (as in Jeffers and Lehiste 1979:161), but writing cannot just have turned up unasked and unpremeditated. The idea of writing at all was a giant step for mankind, comparable to the invention of the wheel, and so subsequently were the successive elaborations of ideographic script based on the lexicon, syllabic and then phonemic scripts based on the phonology, punctuation, diacritics, the establishment of spaces between written words, shorthand, written tone curves, the International Phonetic Alphabet, the initial teaching alphabet, word processors, voice synthesizers, modems, etc. They were all inventions, which would not be here at all if some enterprising character had not thought of the idea. One inventor is enough, though: we can watch, in a historical atlas, how the idea of writing spread geographically from its Sumerian origins of c.3500 B.C. (e.g McEvedy and Woodcock 1967:26, 36, 44, 56). Subsequently, new systems of recording a language do not just emerge unbidden either; for example, the distinctively non-Latinate spellings of the Romance languages were intentionally elaborated for a practical purpose (as were shorthand and the International Phonetic Alphabet, etc.). In *Late Latin and Early Romance* (Wright 1982) it was suggested that the new writing system which we now call written Old French was consciously first elaborated for a particular purpose in a specific context; that is, to assist those speakers of Germanic who knew how to read Medieval Latin aloud to use that knowledge to read aloud in a manner that might be intelligible to speakers of Old French. Here too, as Elcock showed long ago (1961), we can see on a map how the initial invention, in this case of writing in a manner intended to give rise to an intelligible Romance reading, was imitated successively in geographical areas spreading outwards from its north-eastern French origins; one inventor followed successively by adjacent imitators.

Sinclair's 1987 article entitled 'Language: a gift of nature or a home-made tool?' suggests reasonably that language is both. Many linguistic developments are undoubtedly of an unpremeditated type that cannot seriously be thought of as invention. Most sound changes are unintentional. Indeed, if teleology is consciously invoked by speakers during the course of a sound change, the aim seems generally to be that of preventing the change taking place at all. Some phonetic changes, however, have proved to be explicable by appeal to conscious or semi-conscious phenomena such as phonosymbolism (e.g. Malkiel 1987), to conspiracies to conform to intuited phonetic templates (Pharies 1986), or to desires to escape from undesirable homonymy, and people of unusually explicit metalinguistic awareness may perhaps initiate these on purpose. But these changes are a minority, and Pagliuca and Mowrey (1987) could well be right to see most sound changes as being simply the consequences of unpremeditated relaxation of muscles round the mouth. It is thus understandable that such phenomena as the precise conditions of a conditioned change, or the detailed strength hierarchies that determine the chronology of related changes (as in Harris-Northall 1990; Cravens 1988), need to be painstakingly unearthed by specialist linguists long after the event, for they are neither the conscious inventions of a human mind nor accessible to native intuition.

Many grammatical changes are similarly unintentional. The replacement of the Latin case system with Romance prepositions, changes in statistically preferred word orders, the creation of compound prepositions from adverb + preposition sequences, for example, seem to be probably, though not necessarily, best regarded as unintended and evolutionary. And yet Ridruejo (1988) has argued rationally that morphosyntactic innovations can easily be intentional. Many semantic changes are also gradual and evolutionary; those that involve a shift in prototypical reference points, for example (e.g. Wright 1985), or those that occur when a superordinate term comes increasingly to be used with the reference of one of its hyponyms (e.g. Wright, 1990). Some semantic changes can be established on purpose, however. Scientists, philosophers or social reformers often have recourse to the establishment of their own definitions of words that are already in use with a related but slightly less clear or defined meaning, and if they have sufficient authority they can in time succeed in changing the meaning of the word thereby. Einstein did not invent the word *relativity*, but he invented the definition of it that is now its central meaning. New words, that is, lexical change, are generally conceded to be, at least sometimes, inventions. The only time the word 'invention' is used in Jeffers and Lehiste is in this connection (1979:130: 'the vocabulary of a language is continually being enriched by the invention of new words'). Borrowing of foreign words is similarly also in the first place an individual initiative.

Individual initiative, in short, has a higher place in most types of linguistic development than it is sometimes given credit for; as the Milroys say (1985:345), 'it is not languages that innovate: it is speakers who innovate.' For every systematic feature of language, however obvious it may subsequently appear, there must have been a first time. Hurford's (1987) discussion of the psychological history and present basis of numerals is illuminating in the present context. Numerals seem a natural linguistic feature to us now. But they were not always there in language. Only up to the number three can the human brain perceive number without calculating it. Above that number, humans have invented their systems of counting, in a long sequence of successive small progressions whose complexity and rationale vary from community to community (and thus from language to language). Above three, all numeral systems are in origin invented, as was the wheel. The method of counting in tens, the *hundred*, the *thousand*, the *million*, are all inventions, and simultaneously conceptual and linguistic inventions. Hurford does not come up to date, but in our own time both the concept and the lexical item of the *light year*, the *parsec*, the *googol*, are all human inventions of the same kind. In a millennium's time the concept and the word *googol* (a 1 followed by a hundred zeros) will seem as commonplace to English-speakers as the *hundred* does now. They were individual inventions once, but once invented anyone can learn them, and they come to seem self-evident.

New linguistic standardization of all types, not merely the orthographic, requires a conscious standardizer (as Marcos Marín has demonstrated for Spanish: Marcos Marín 1979, Marcos Marín and Sánchez Lobato 1988). The prescriptiveness of all prescriptive rules is invented by grammarians who think they perceive a moral order in grammatical details; the demanding peculiarities of the Latin rhetorical cursus, metrical poetry, and indeed, as Norberg (e.g. 1958) has shown, Latin rhythmical poetry, are examples of this. The detail of the morphology required of written Latin was prescribed by grammarians (especially Donatus); and so, I suggest, were the details of the peculiar and artificial Late Medieval system used for reading written texts aloud even in Romance-speaking areas, that is, producing one specified sound for each already-written letter (or digraph). All reading involved reading aloud. It seems obvious and natural to read Latin that way now, as obvious and natural as it is to count in tens. But such a method of reading aloud one's native language is totally unnatural. Anglo-Saxon speakers, however, at least since Bede, had learned to read the same texts, in what was to them a foreign language, aloud in that way; they brought this system with them to the Continent, and there, as a result of using such pronunciations in speech as well, they were at times unintelligible to Romance speakers (as Boniface was to the Pope). Whenever and wherever this reading system began to be required of native Romance-speakers, its prescriptive rules must have been in origin introduced from some non-evolutionary source. Most modern sociolinguists, including Schlieben-Lange (1982) on Romance, suggest that systems of diglossia need not only to be intentionally set up, but also to be continually reinforced subsequently—mainly by teaching the high variety in the education system—in order to exist at all, and do not arise naturally otherwise. What exist otherwise, and do indeed evolve unplanned, in a single wide speech community, are complex patterns of sociolinguistic variation.

Such patterns as modern sociolinguistic theory would lead us to expect to find anyway, particularly as concerns the relationship between speech and writing (e.g. Tannen 1982; Traugott and Romaine 1985; Pellegrini and Yawkey 1984; etc.), seem to be sufficient to explain attested phenomena from pre-Carolingian Romance Europe, largely reconciling reconstructed Romance with the (unamended) manuscript evidence. Fontaine (1981), Varvaro (1984) and others have recently been in essence envisaging such a state, in which the many and varied registers of spoken and written language were still even so part of the same language, and read texts such as sermons were given vernacular phonetics in the ordinary way, as they always are now. Sabatini (1983:170) picked up this interpretation of the evidence with enthusiasm, since in this way the many conscientious pre-Carolingian preachers can be at last thought to have been intelligible to their audiences, the scholars who continually urged priests then to preach can be absolved from the charge of asking for the impossible, and hundreds of thousands of Early Romance-speaking individuals can recover their linguistic self-respect, their voice, their ability to understand their priests, indeed, their very participation in society in pre-Carolingian Romance Europe; as opposed to the idea, still widely held—e.g. by Coleman (1987:50)—that, 'of course,' pre-Carolingian Christian congregations found their services incomprehensible. The monolingual view of Early Romance Europe seems to be confirmed, for example, by two recent independent studies on Gregory the Great (Herman 1988, Banniard 1986) which both conclude that, unlike some of the Carolingian scholars, Gregory had no clear conceptual distinction between Latin and Romance in his mind, of the kind required for diglossia to exist; the question just did not arise, and he cheerfully wrote sermons intended to be read aloud intelligibly to the illiterate. This question apparently never arose in the mind of Isidore of Seville either (cp. Fontaine 1981:776). If Gregory and Isidore did not know about such a distinction, it cannot have existed in the sixth and seventh centuries.

The hypothesis of Romance monolingualism also solves the problem that worried Bullough (1985:285, 287), concerning what language Charlemagne spoke with the Italian scholars at his court in the 780s: they all spoke Romance, in a mutually intelligible, if not similar, manner. Versteegh (e.g. 1986:426, 447) is the only historical sociolinguist I know of explicitly to disagree with this view. Versteegh, unlike most historical linguists (cp. Wright 1987: 621), sees lack of change as normal, and thus not in need of any explanation, and change therefore as necessarily externally caused. In his view high status, within a postulated nascent state of diglossia, accrues inevitably to those speakers who remain unaffected by the externally-caused deviations which lead to what he sees as pidginization in the speech of the socially less prestigious, such that this high level, reinforced by grammarians, naturally survives in formal situations even when the spread of the pidginized (in this case, Romance) variety means that the correct variety is hardly anyone's native speech any more. Hence, to Versteegh, many societies are *de facto* diglossic, without anyone having willed that diglossia into existence. But the supposed inevitability of the survival of a Latinate level of speech alongside evolving Early Romance speech, which seems to have been based on an assumption that educated people do not get involved in sound changes, has been untenable as a supposition ever since Labov and others established that (in the words of the Milroys, 1985:343) 'speakers who lead sound change are those with the highest status in their local communities as measured by a social class index.' That is how archaisms get stigmatized (cp. Silva 1988:164); *pace* Versteegh, archaism rarely has automatic high prestige. (Diez rejected Versteegh's approach in 1826, in fact; see Diez 1975:277-82.)

The tradition of reading Latin aloud as an artificial language, a sound for each written letter, in the Romance-speaking world as everywhere else, has the air of being obvious, and as though it had been forever present. But someone, somewhere, had to establish that as a standardized norm, for it could not arise naturally in a native Romance community. There was a kind of continuity through the years between Carolingian and Imperial Latin in the vocabulary and syntax of the educated, for these could always be resurrected from Classical books by antiquarians (Fontaine 1981:786), but what we now think of as traditional Latin pronunciation had no such direct continuity with that of the Empire (cp. Lüdtke 1988:63, on [-m], for example). That is why the invention of the need for what we now call Latinate pronunciation (with the sounds determined by the spelling) is the key issue here. As the historian Hobsbawm (1983:1) pointed out, 'traditions which appear or claim to be old are often quite recent in origin and sometimes invented.'

In *Late Latin and Early Romance* the chapter which recounted the details of the suggested source of the Latin-Romance distinction, located in the latter years of Charlemagne's reign, was entitled "The Invention of Medieval Latin." This use of the word *invention* has been criticized (e.g by Godman, 1985:146). But I shall stick by it. That chapter argued in detail that the Carolingian scholars established the phonetic distinction around the year 800 A.D. as part of the educational reforms, in order initially to standardize the performance of the Church offices, and that the Latin-Romance distinction is only clearly felt subsequent to those innovations. Charlemagne and Alcuin knew they were introducing something revolutionary with their edict *De Litteris Colendis*, which added the study of *litteræ* to the requirements of the already revolutionary *Admonitio Generalis* of 789 in order that clerics should impress their hearers by speaking well (*bene loquendo*) when reading or singing written texts (*in legendo seu cantando*) (Wallach 1959:204), and such reading proficiency becomes a requirement of the *litterati* thereafter (cp. Stock 1983:27). The onus is on Godman and Versteegh, and any other scholars who are sure that the clear conceptual distinction was established earlier, to suggest who else did it, when, where, how and why.

The elements that came to constitute Medieval Latin existed before Alcuin's arrival at Charlemagne's court—the writing system existed everywhere, the reading aloud system existed in Anglo-Saxon England—but their combination and conceptual opposition to vernacular was something new and positive. In Hurford's words (1987:12), invention typically involves a creative act of putting together existing elements (which may or may not be physical) in some novel way (also Schon 1967:87, 192). The concept and combined attributes of Medieval Latin were thus invented out of pre-existing ingredients. Rabin's study (1985) has shown how the same kind of conscious invention of a diglossic system happened also in ninth-century Byzantine Greek, in eighth and ninth-century Arabic, and in the Hebrew written in Moslem countries in the 10th century. This was an internationally felt psychological need; not confined to the Latin-Romance civilizations but consciously pursued in culturally less peripheral areas also. In other sociolinguistically comparable societies, diglossia has only existed if it was consciously established, in a particular historical circumstance, and was then educationally reinforced, as with katharevousa Greek, and does not exist in any society if nobody has invented it there (see e.g. Silva 1988:178; Rotaetxe 1988:60-61). The subsequent, and probably consequent, emergence of distinctively and intentionally non-Latinate writing systems for recording Romance vernaculars were—can only have been—experimental inventions by enterprising and innovative linguists, even if they were based on some existing approximations, and even if we do not now know who the inventors were. Perhaps they were Nithard at Strasbourg for the elaboration of the Oaths and Hucbald at St. Amand for the *Eulalie* sequence; but even if not, those advances must have been made by someone, in the same way as shorthand was invented by Isaac Pitman. The Riojan glosses were also elaborated for a purpose, and perhaps it was to aid a Catalan visitor to read aloud in local phonetics (Wright 1986). In any event, they did not just evolve.

CONCLUSION

Probably at all levels we have linguistic innovators of the past to thank for the invention of some of the structural distinctions that are subsequently taken for granted. Few people have the capacity to invent, but some do, and the capacity that we all have to learn from others is more plausibly seen as innate than is the actual concept demarcated by the inventor. After all, even a language acquisition device can only acquire things that already exist. Socially purposive language planning is the result of an intentional initiative. It continues to seem probable that the Latin-Romance distinction of the later Middle Ages was created through such language planning, and that it would not have existed if it had not been invented. I entirely take the point made by McKitterick (1989:12-22) that through the ninth and tenth centuries the distinction took a long time to become generally felt (maybe at first it was only at Tours and centers influenced by Tours); but this is how it began.

1994 POSTSCRIPT.

This paper was first published in *Latin and the Romance Languages in the Early Middle Ages*, ed. Roger Wright, London, Routledge, 1991, pp. 103-13; reproduced by permission of Routledge. It is a very slightly emended version of the contribution to the "workshop" with the same title held at the Ninth International Conference on Historical Linguistics, at Rutgers University, New Jersey, U.S.A., on Thursday 17th and Friday 18th August, 1989. The way in which such a workshop came to be organized, and the remarkably wide, intellectually stimulating and mutually illuminating nature of its contents, are explained in my introductory chapter to the same volume, "Latin and Romance: a thousand years of incertitude" (pp. 1-5), not reproduced here. The present paper probably suited an audience of historical linguists better than it fitted into the resultant volume (one surprising reaction was that it had "caught the Zeitgeist"). Reviewers, however, have tended to interpret this chapter as a mere rehash of the hypotheses expressed in Chapter 3 of *Late Latin*, an assessment which seems to miss the point in the other direction, in that the purpose of this paper was to illuminate those hypotheses from previously unconsidered general historical linguistic viewpoints. The role of individual initiative, of scribe, teacher and chancery, in the earliest *scripta* in the Iberian Peninsula, is a topic I have developed since.

4
Metalinguistic change in Medieval Iberia

WHEN DID THE DIFFERENT languages in the Iberian Peninsula first become different? The answer to this apparently simple question is far from obvious. Several criteria have been suggested for the establishment of this kind of conceptual distinction, but in the end the ones that turn out to be most important are political rather than linguistic; and the best answer to this question seems to be to place these metalinguistic divergences, for the Iberian Peninsula at least, in the thirteenth century.

We cannot rely on the criterion of mutual comprehensibility. Granted, if two individuals are totally unable to understand each other, then it is likely that they are not speaking the same language. But political decisions can invent distinctions of this kind between forms of speech that on the whole are indeed mutually comprehensible. Even now, the speakers of the separate Iberian Romance languages can sometimes understand each other, each of them speaking their own language, but we should not deduce from that that they all have the same language now. We can hardly deny that Portuguese, Castilian, Catalan, and now also Galician, are conceptually separate languages. It follows from this that the criterion of mutual comprehensibility is not the only one to be used when we are trying to decide if different forms of speech are in fact different languages or not.

These distinctions have been placed at the other chronological extreme; it has been suggested that some of the differences between the modern Hispanic languages go back to the times of the earliest colonization by the Romans. Under this view, the linguistic diver-

Diagram adapted from Hall (1976), 14-15.
("PR" = Proto-Romance; "DD" = dialects)

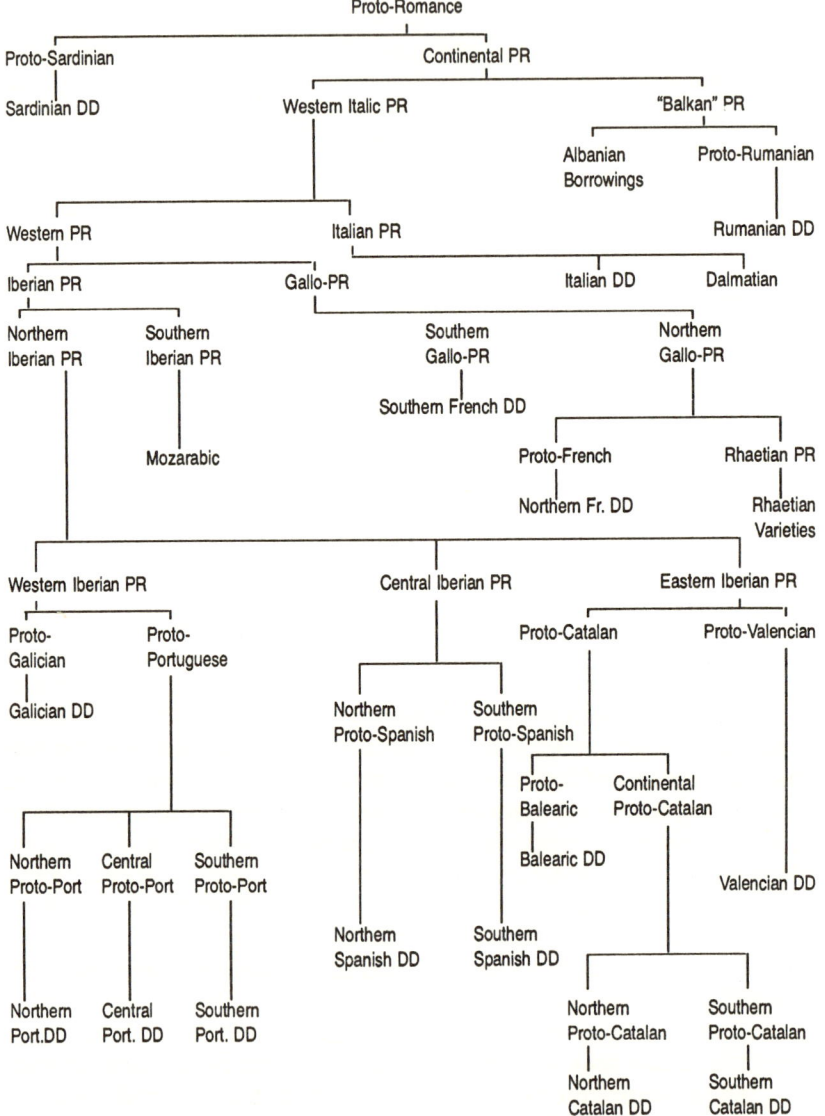

sity of the Peninsula can be traced back to seeds sown at that time, either as the result of the pre-Roman "substratum" languages or because different colonists came from Italy already speaking different dialects; and the geolinguistic frontiers that were established then would have remained, in this theory, ever since. But although there is no reason not to accept the validity of some of the differences that can be reconstructed for that time, these do not justify the postulation for that early period of a conceptual differentiation between whole separate languages of the kind that we are looking for (within the whole Roman Empire, not just in the Peninsula).

Our first task, then, is to consider the diagrams presented in the works of Robert A. Hall Jr. Here I reproduce an amalgamation of relevant diagrams from his *Proto-Romance Phonology*. Hall presents his diagrams to us as being the results of comparative reconstruction. Diagrams of this kind were originally designed on purpose to look like genealogical trees. They have often been criticized, and for a variety of reasons (e.g. recently by Craddock 1989). For example, the earliest distinction made in the diagram is shown to be that which separates Proto-Sardinian from the rest, supposedly more than two millennia ago; but it could well be that, if we want to reconstruct the time of the separation of Sardinian at all, we will come to a different answer if we consider morphology and syntax from that which we get from concentrating (as Hall does) on phonetics. Besides, the distinctively Sardinian feature, whether it is a new one or a surviving old one, could well have coexisted for centuries on the island with features which we now categorize over-definitively as being mainland Italian and not Sardinian. Sardinians and Romans were in continual contact throughout the Empire and the medieval period, and on the whole it is often possible for Sardinians and Romans to communicate successfully even now. There can be no doubt that many (or all) of the reconstructed differences between the speech of the two areas are genuine; the problem lies in the date of the conceptual metalinguistic distinction between two different languages, and the conclusion drawn from these reconstructed differences that two conceptually separate languages need to be represented at such an early stage in the genealogical tree-diagram.

These diagrams have also been criticized for a more aesthetic reason; that this tree image distorts the data in that it gives the impression that each of these separate speech entities, once it has diverged from the rest, has continued to evolve as a separate unit in its own delimited geographical area, rather than forming part of a larger synchronic speech-community. This leaves no room for the possibility that a later innovation could have spread across the geographical frontiers implicit in the diagrammatic representation. Yet it has long been realized that at least some changes take place in such a manner, which could be better represented metaphorically through the image of a wave; if you throw a stone into a lake, you can see the waves rippling outwards to affect parts of the lake that are quite a long way from the stone. Malkiel (1983) and others have appreciated the problem of combining these two images into a single metaphor, because a tree is not very like a lake; even Hall mentions this problem, without solving it (1950:23).

In addition to criticizing these diagrams for their misleading chronological implications, and for the artistic inappropriateness of the inherent analogy, we can also criticize them for the conceptual vagueness of the labels attached to each node or branch of the tree. What sort of ontological or conceptual status should we grant to, for example, this "Western Proto-Romance" that gave birth to this "Iberian Proto-Romance"? How are we to define this "Northern Iberian Proto-Romance" which derives in turn from it? How do these three entities differ from each other, on the vertical (chronological) axis? How did each one differ clearly from its "sister" languages on the horizontal (synchronic and geographical) axis? We can also reverse the implied direction of these questions and ask, for example, if this diagram is meant to suggest that there was no appreciable internal variation within each of these separate postulated entities. If there was no linguistic variation within the same geographical area, why not? For today, at least, there is linguistic variation inside every speech community. If such variation did indeed exist then, how are we meant to distinguish between (a) the internal variation that existed within each of these separate individual units and (b) the geographical variation which encouraged the reconstruction theorists to make a conceptual distinction, between each of these supposedly separate linguistic entities on the diagram, in the first place? The more we consider such questions, the more we are likely to conclude that these diagrams, for all their apparent neatness and clarity, raise more problems than they solve. Walther von Wartburg proposed similar theories with greater subtlety and more success, but there have been criticisms even of his fundamental opposition between Western and Eastern Romance. The same kinds of problems have been seen in the work of Robert de Dardel, usually for metalinguistic reasons of the type adumbrated above.

The new element that has arisen ever stronger in the last fifty years, as the work of Alberto Varvaro in particular exemplifies, is our increasing understanding of sociolinguistics. The theory of early dialectalization—which in Hall's perspective began some time before Jesus Christ, and in that of Wartburg began in the third century A.D.—has been giving ground gradually to the realization that language-internal variation is inevitable and always to be found; a more satisfying hypothesis can now include the undoubted individual discoveries of the separatist tradition within a general picture of greater versatility and flexibility than a two-dimensional geometrical figure. For one thing, in general it now seems probable that a majority of variation phenomena, in any language, can best be explained sociolinguistically rather than merely geographically. This is partly because the new features whose presence may be going later to distinguish one daughter language from another tend to arise in other areas as well as those of the later daughter's geographical home; and also because they arise long before the disappearance of the older features that fulfilled the same function previously. Green (1991) traced the sociolinguistic and stylistic nature of this coexistence in the case of the increasing use of reflexive grammar with passive semantics, in all areas of the former Empire; this use coexisted with the old synthetic passives for centuries (and with the analytic passives still today). In the same way, all over the former Empire, future tenses formed by the combination of the infinitive with an auxiliary verb were used in some sociolinguistic levels and some stylistic registers for several centuries before the old synthetic futures disappeared entirely from speech. Outside France (and much of Catalonia) the new perfect tenses created with the auxiliary and the past participle still coexist quite cheerfully with the older synthetic preterite forms. Clear diatopic and diastratic distinctions arose late; some of the features that seem now to distinguish Old French Romance from Old Iberian

Romance, for example, actually existed in both areas for several centuries before the speakers made a subconscious choice of which one they preferred to perpetuate in the new local Romance standard; this comes out clearly, for example, from the fascinating studies by Lyons (1986, 1992) on possessive adjectives. In this way, the diversity discovered by the Reconstruction theorists can be preserved, but the theory of early dialectal divergence in separate clearly definable geographical areas between conceptually distinct languages is unnecessary. At the very least it is anachronistic to postulate such divergence actually within the Roman Empire. The results of the epigraphic analyses of Herman (and many of those by Gaeng) lead to a similar conclusion: that the Roman Empire indeed saw evolution and linguistic variation, naturally, but without there being any clear differentiation between the speech of different places.

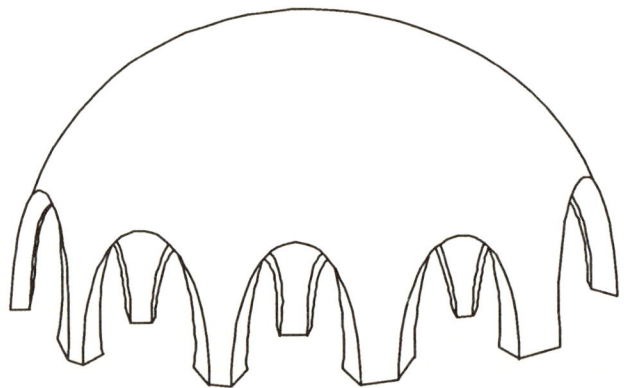

Speech: The Romance area (8th Century) with its universal "dome" (Varvaro 1991).

The conceptually monolingual nature of Early Romance lasted much longer than the Empire did. If we feel the need to have artistic representations of what happened in that speech-community in the post-Imperial centuries, we can recommend, rather than any kind of tree diagram, the image proposed by Varvaro (1991). Varvaro does not visualize trees nor waves; he refers to the "dome" of standard (but not archaic) Latin which had social prestige, and which remained spread out over and above the forces which were leading to greater differentiation between geographical areas. So far as I am aware, Varvaro has never attempted to draw this image, so I have tried to do that myself here.

In this picture we see Romania from the sixth to the eighth centuries as if it were a building. It is a single building, but each part of its dome is held up by a geographically separate column, representing the speech habits of one region. Each part of the area covered has a direct link, therefore, with the "universal" dome that unites the whole speech-community. We could, if we really wanted, give a label to each of the supporting columns, calling them "Northern Iberian Early Romance," "Southern Italian Early Romance," or names of this type, but only with the proviso that nobody should interpret these columns as being entirely separated from each other at least before the ninth century, and in many cases later still. There is geographical variation but there is also a metalinguistic unity, as each regional column provides for access to the central and higher dome. That is, every Early Romance speaker was still able to keep in linguistic touch with traditional educated culture. Another advantage of this pictorial representation is that we can preserve the normal sociolinguistic metaphor of regarding standard and geographically extensive registers as "superior" to those of lesser geographical and social extension.

Another advantage that this metaphor has over the tree (as Varvaro points out) is that between the fifth and the ninth centuries we can propose that the dome (representing the sociolinguistically "prestige" register) gradually crumbles and fragments, for practical reasons such as the decreasingly urgent necessity in speech for shifting style into that universal register, without the building thereby ceasing to seem to be a single conceptual unit within the semantics of the speakers. We can propose, for example, that the Early Romance-speaking Byzantines (speakers of "Danubian Romance," perhaps, in Hall's categorization) who came to settle on the southern Iberian coasts around the year 600 A.D. still managed to communicate successfully with the natives of the Peninsula. We can suggest, though, that by the ninth century, at least, some of the different columns were beginning to find that they had no direct communicative link with each other as a result of the crumbling of parts of the dome that had connected them for centuries previously. The Rumanian column, for example, seems more likely to have lost these links at an early date than does the Sardinian one. Thus between the ninth and eleventh centuries some of the separate entities postulated by Hall in his diagrams for a very much earlier time (a millennium earlier) at last begin to find themselves standing as separate, conceptually distinguishable, entities. By the eleventh century, not much of the dome is left in active speech; within the Iberian peninsula it seems reasonable to suggest that although non-Catalan Ibero-Romance still has a conceptual unity, we can glimpse by then the existence of some kind of a frontier between this Ibero-Romance and the Romance of Catalonia, a frontier which coincides more or less with the border of the "Spanish March" of the Carolingian Empire. From the Carolingian era onwards, but only in the areas touched by the Carolingian reforms, we can add to our metaphorical building the image proposed by Muljačić of a newly invented "roof," to represent the conceptual innovation we now call "Medieval Latin," which was introduced into Romance Europe at the end of the eighth century; in this way the new roof can be seen to have replaced the crumbling dome in its role as a universal prestige register.

All these metaphorical representations have only been applied to speech, of course. If we still insist on pictorial metaphors, we can take a different perspective on the dome to include writing also within the same image. We can see it from the air, as in the second picture here. This is an adaptation of the image of a "nebula" which has been put forward by the French linguistic historian Michel Banniard. Banniard uses this image to represent his plausible view of the role of writing in the Early Romance communities up to the ninth century, and it is not meant to have any geographical implications. For writing, of course, there is no possibility of conceptual fragmentation at that time. From our aerial view we can see the center shining brightly, like the central part of a nebula; within our metaphor, that is the highest and most central part of Varvaro's dome.

Further out from the center we can see less brilliant areas which are even so linked directly to the shining traditional cultural centre; further out again are Romance-speakers of lesser cultural brightness (and education) who nevertheless are a part of the same nebula, of the same "ensemble." More specifically, even in the ninth century, traditional culture was still generally accessible to all if the texts were read aloud sympathetically (cp. the studies in McKitterick 1991).

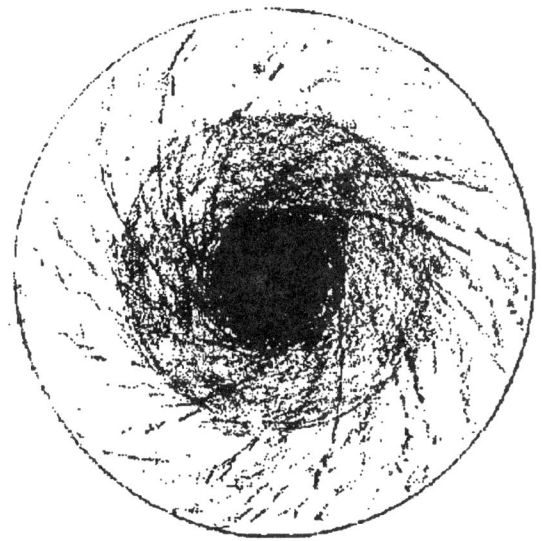

Writing: Aerial view of the dome:
= Banniard's "view."

Before the age of the Carolingian renewal of intellectual life, any pictorial image that preserves the metalinguistic unity of the early Romance area—with the exception that may have to be made for Rumanian—has greater value than an image of a tree with separate branches (or roots). The Romance world had a conceptual unity; it was monolingual. Of course, this monolingualism was heterogeneous, evolved, socially and stylistically complicated; but, being a single unit, we should use one name to refer to it (I prefer "Romance," or "Early Romance"). There is little to be gained by doing now what they did not do then, erecting clear but anachronistic theoretical distinctions between Late Latin, Vulgar Latin, Christian Latin, Romance, Iberian Proto-Romance (and Northern, Central, Southern, Eastern and Western Iberian Proto-Romances), pre-literary

Catalan, and so on, unless we are entirely clear and explicit in our own minds that with these labels we are referring to interconnected styles within one single language, and no more than that. Zumthor, 1984, and Gimeno Menéndez, 1988, are, for example; but there are also scholars who are multiplying these entities more and more. In addition to early and improbable geographically based distinctions, De Dardel (1983) postulates five separate chronological stages for Proto-Romance; and within these five stages there were, according to a later analysis by De Dardel (1987), no fewer than four separate successive Basic Word Orders. Historical distinctions can have validity, naturally (if we avoid the red herrings of typology, as Pinkster, 1991, points out). St. Isidore of Seville himself made such diachronic distinctions between successive stages of his own language (*Etymologiæ* IX, 1.6-7). He did not make them between geographically separate Latin/Romance languages of his own time; the only geographical distinctions he offered concern minute details such as some agricultural words of his native Bætica, but even Hall has stopped short of inventing a separate Seville Proto-Romance for the seventh century. The inhabitants of the Peninsula did make clear distinctions for centuries between their own language and Greek, Arabic and Hebrew (and, we must presumably suppose, Basque), but erected no such internal distinctions within their own Early Romance. (It is pleasing to note that the recent excellent book by Clavería Nadal makes no such internal distinctions either for these early medieval centuries).

What interpretation should be given, then, to the discoveries made with the techniques of reconstruction? Firstly, we should be happy to accept the validity of the reconstructed phonetic practice of all speakers in each area more or less as these techniques have suggested it was. We can suspect, thanks also to research from several historians, that texts read aloud could normally be generally understood, then as now. But this very fact also has implications for their morphology, syntax and vocabulary; we need to accept that within this conceptually monolingual Early Romance of the Peninsula there coexisted (a) old words, morphemes and constructions that were destined to seem archaic later, but which were still alive then in the sense that most people could still recognize and understand them when they heard them read aloud from written texts;

with (b) other words, morphemes and constructions more characteristic of active speech, which had been introduced comparatively recently, being ones we can reconstruct as forming part of Early Romance; and we should further accept that the whole apparently disparate "ensemble" was still a single conceptual unit, in the Iberian Peninsula even as late as the eleventh century. This is a millennium later than the strictest reconstructionists, such as Hall and De Dardel, prefer to believe. (The speakers of Early Romance tried to bar many normal features of their speech from their own written texts, not so much because they were new as because they were not recommended for use in the grammatical tradition deriving from Ælius Donatus; cp. Wright 1991b; Zumthor calls this filtering process a "prisme formulateur"). For present purposes, the important fact is this; at that time they did not think of their language as being a mixture of an older one and a later one (of "Latin" and "Romance"). It was their own synchronic system. Early Romance served them as well in their lives as modern Spanish serves modern Spaniards in theirs (cp. Alarcos 1982). Every synchronic state of any language could be analyzed as at least in part made up of archaic and innovating features, but is nonetheless a state of its own; there is nothing adventurous in suggesting that this applies to eighth-century Iberian Early Romance as well.

Early Romance in general was beginning to suffer geographical divergence by the ninth century, but within the Peninsula there was still unity in what had been one of the supporting columns, that is, non-Catalan Early Ibero-Romance. They did not give it such a distinctive name themselves, though; that is, it does not seem to have had yet solid conceptual independence; the most we can perceive is that at times they were aware of a distinction between the speech of the Peninsula and that of other areas, at least in some details of vocabulary and perhaps pronunciation. As I have pointed out before (Wright 1992b, 1993), it looks as though the more precise metalinguistic geographical distinctions, between Galician, Castilian, Aragonese, Leonese, had not formed in the Peninsula even by the twelfth century, and quite possibly not until the thirteenth. At the end of the thirteenth century it looks as if it is possible for us to begin to refer sensibly to Castilian, Galician, Aragonese, and Leonese, as conceptually distinct entities; although it still seems rather unfortunate that we have to operate with labels of such an exclusively geographical origin, as if this were the only kind of variation there was. Nor should we give the impression to modern students that there was no variation at that time within each of these units. There was, of course, even in Old Castile. For thirteenth-century France we are lucky to have available the excellent studies of Dees and the Van Reenens; these show the existence of such variation with considerable clarity, which they are able to represent pictorially in simple annotated maps of Northern France, indicating the separate provinces. In these studies, variation comes over as statistical, and also as varying according to local rather than regional political units. If we look at data, rather than politics, variation usually does seem to be in this sense local rather than regional, but metalinguistic labels do not normally arise from dispassionate analysis of the data so much as being administratively imposed from above. As Janson (1991) showed, identification of separate languages tends to happen at the same time as, or even some time after, official decisions to reform writing systems. We could say that as many languages are thought to exist (in literate communities) as there are official writing systems. That is, in this case, the idea that Castilian, Gallego, Leonese and Aragonese were separate languages was inspired by the fact that each administrative area had acquired newly elaborated spelling systems in the thirteenth century. An earlier perception of these geolinguistic distinctions is not visible to us, not even, so it seems, between the Romance of Al-Andalus and the Romance of the Christian-ruled areas. I proposed (in Wright 1993) that before 1100, disregarding Basque, Arabic, Hebrew, and any surviving Berber languages, there was in the whole Iberian Peninsula (perhaps with the exception of Catalonia) a metalinguistic state similar to that of the modern English-speaking community in Britain; that is, a single language, Early Ibero-Romance, containing a great deal of variation; and that by the end of the thirteenth century there had arisen a very different metalinguistic state, more like that of late twentieth-century Spain, in which several newly-identified languages, named on a geographical basis, are coming to be thought to be different, a perception allied to and catalyzed by the invention of new spellings. For example, the modern distinction which some wish to make between the Catalan of Valencia and that of Barcelona is reminiscent of the distinction that was made in the thirteenth century between the speech of Catalonia and that of the Occitan area, and in each case the distinction is reinforced by the elaboration of official orthographical differences. These are all political decisions, both in the thirteenth and the twentieth century. For similar reasons, the distinction between Galician and Portuguese was invented in the fourteenth century. There were differences, mostly merely statistical ones, that we can reconstruct for earlier times, but they were felt as language-internal within Romance rather than as symptoms of the existence of separate languages.

1994 POSTSCRIPT.

This paper is a translation of "Los cambios metalingüísticos medievales," in the *Actes du XXe Congrès de Linguistique et Philologie Romanes*, Editions Francke, Tübingen and Basel, 1993; that was the exact text of the paper given to that conference, in Zurich, on Thursday 8th April, 1992. The diagrammatic representation of his "dome" caused Varvaro, who was there, to give a broad smile, but he has still not told me how closely it fits his own image. Banniard has never drawn his own image of the "nébuleuse" either, so far as I know. All these diagrams are merely visual aids, of course, not meant as exact counterparts. The subsequent discussion was, inevitably, dominated by linguistic politicians from Spanish "autonomías" with local bones to pick. I gave the same paper the following month at the University of Valencia; the audience there fell about in laughter at Hall's diagrammatic representation of Catalan; if there is any sense in distinguishing separate "Catalans," the basic dividing isoglossic line runs North-South, that is, it is between East and West, whereas Hall (without apparently investigating the subject) regards North versus South (that is, with East-West isoglosses) as the default case. I was glad to give this paper close to the centenary of the invention of the concept of the isogloss; it has long been suspected that the individual isogloss is more real than the dialect frontier, but even many of those are now appearing as transition zones, and perhaps dialect boundaries need politically established separate standards on each side to pull the inhabitants separate ways when they are style-shifting. Perhaps the image of competing magnets could be elaborated.

5
The Asterisk in Hispanic Historical Linguistics

YAKOV MALKIEL (1989) HAS pointed out that the use of the asterisk in diachronic Romance studies has become ambiguous. It is in danger, indeed, of becoming misleading, and Malkiel's desire to see standardization in the field should be supported. To this end, I have extended several of the arguments initiated in Malkiel (1989), and also studied what a number of specialists in Romance and Hispanic Philology have actually meant by using the device. The focus here is exclusively diachronic; specialists in synchronic syntax use the asterisk in a different way from historical linguists, in order to indicate unattested concatenations of individually attested forms (as neatly explained by Rosen, 1987), although that habit has its critics as well: most notably the scholar who claims to have started the practice (Householder 1973). The twenty authors whose works are scrutinized for the present purpose should not construe any of the forthcoming observations as being hostile—or at least, in so far as they are, please note that one of the books to be criticized is my own.

The twenty-three studies considered here are listed in chronological order at the end of this article (Appendix A). Of these authors, seven explain what the use of the asterisk is intended to convey in the study concerned; one explains why the asterisk is not used; the other fifteen give no explicit guidance to the reader on the matter. These explanations are reproduced on the next page:

1   Rickard (1974: 9): '*: postulated (i.e. unattested) form.' (44/49)

2   Elcock (1975: 32): 'the linguist would indicate by the convention of an asterisk that it is a reconstructed form.' (308/334)

3   Macpherson (1975: 91): 'when the Vulgar Latin form has to be deduced from the evidence of the Romance Languages but is not documented, the postulated root is prefixed by the abbreviation V.L. and an asterisk: e.g. *culebra* < V.L. *COLŎBRA. (75/89)

4   Hall (1976:1): 'Forms ascribed to a Proto-language are usually marked with an asterisk and are therefore often called "starred forms," e.g. Proto-Romance */abantjare/ "to go ahead." In this work, however, the label PRom. (=Proto-Romance) always refers to a reconstructed form, and hence renders unnecessary the use of an asterisk or star.'

5   Cano (1988: 293): '*: forma lingüística no documentada pero exigible en la evolución.' (81/85)

6   Maiden (1991: 285): 'Words preceded by an asterisk are the reconstructed Proto-Italo-Romance or Proto-Ibero-Romance base of the modern forms.' (100/106)

7   Stengaard (1991: 315): 'el asterisco usado [.../ por no conocer una documentación.' (27/37)

8   Penny (1991: 5): 'an asterisk indicates the lack of confirmation from written sources, and therefore the hypothetical (but not necessarily doubtful) status of the word concerned.' (137/190)

The numbers in brackets at the end of these quotations refer to the proportion of uses of the asterisk in that book which actually seem to fit the definition given. Thus for example, Rickard (1974)'s definition holds for forty-four of his forty-nine uses, but two of his asterisks accompany forms whose existence is in fact being denied, and the three other asterisked forms are in fact known to be widely attested; of Elcock (1975)'s 334 asterisks (excluding the seventeen in his hypothesized first draft of the Strasbourg Oaths), 308 fit his definition, six accompany forms whose existence is being denied, and twenty asterisked forms are attested; Macpherson (1975) uses the asterisk for purposes other than those proclaimed on fourteen of his eighty-nine occasions, including seven that immediately follow after the definition; Hall (1976) announces at the start that he is not going to use asterisks, so the function of the twenty-seven that turn up later in that volume is thus initially baffling; Cano (1988) follows his intelligent and slightly different definition eighty-one times out of eighty-five; Maiden (1991) follows his proclaimed practice 100 times out of 106; Stengaard (1991)'s definition is presupposed rather than asserted, and applies twenty-seven times out of thirty-seven, the existence of the other ten being indeed undocumented but also denied (disregarding fourteen uses for footnotes and one to indicate a corrupt manuscript); Penny (1991)'s definition is skillfully phrased, yet his 190 asterisks include thirty-nine for forms that are known to be attested and fourteen for forms whose existence is being denied. All relevant statistics are summarized in Appendix B.

When Malkiel or I refer to an asterisked form which is in fact attested, that is not primarily because the investigator has disregarded documentary evidence (although that is so in at least one case; Harris-Northall's *CAPU- (1990: 62) is actually attested in both the Visigothic liturgy and the Visigothic laws, as the infinitive *capuisse*; Díaz y Díaz 1965: 71). The references are to forms that are indisputably attested but with a different morphological case usage from that required by the etymologist's (ultimately neogrammarian) theory (Malkiel 1989: 25). Several writers, for example, give an asterisk to *LUMINE, the etymon of Sp. *lumbre*. Yet LUMINE is a normal attested form from Imperial times, being the ablative singular form of LUMEN. The asterisk is there to hypothesize a function rather than a form, because some scholars wish to bar *a priori* the possibility that a Romance noun could descend from an originally ablative form; what is being hypothesized is not the form itself but the functional use of the form as a direct verbal object. In this way using the asterisk begs an important question. Penny wrote a persuasive article (1980) arguing that the original case-functions of forms are not necessarily relevant to the choice of surviving member of a reducing paradigm; so it is surprising to see that he too stars *LUMINE (1991: 108). It would perhaps seems more logical to write *LUMINEM, with the accusative-marking -M. Asterisks have also occasionally been used to mark explicitly attested forms as being non-standard, although Romance Philologists have not usually done so; Malkiel also points out (1989: 43) that Ernout and Meillet's etymological dictionary often stars non-classical forms while repeating an actual written attestation; e.g. (example chosen at random), *fānō is given an asterisk when being quoted from its written source in Varro (1951: 384).

When an asterisk is used in historical linguistics to deny the existence of a form at all, the scholar is adapting the device from the practice of modern synchronic syntactic study. This seems a natural thing to do (there are four such cases in Wright 1982) but it provides great potential for ambiguity and is surely inadvisable. For example, Lloyd (1987) stars 211 forms altogether, of which fifty-one are forms whose existence seems to be specifically being denied; Dworkin (1985) uses 150 starred forms altogether, of which thirty-two seem to be being denied; etc. Malkiel has made the proposal on a number of occasions (1970, 1979, 1989) that if we accept the use of the traditional superscript asterisk for undocumented forms whose existence we positively wish to postulate, then in order to avoid confusion we should use instead a subscript asterisk for undocumented forms whose existence we do not wish to postulate (e.g. '*MANS' as plural of MAN, 1979), yet it seems that neither Malkiel nor anyone else has actually followed this advice. Pensado, however, regularly uses a double asterisk and italicization for forms whose existence is being denied; in the two 1991 studies considered here, she double-stars **zato (1991a: 203), **seze, **alvierto and **doice (1991b: 66, 73, 79) as denied forms, and her other eighteen single-asterisk italicized uses are all for forms postulated as existing. This use of double asterisks to deny a form's existence is an admirable practice. Henceforth I propose to follow her example.

We can thus begin to clear the air by not starring those forms such as LUMINE that are attested but whose morphological analysis offends our preexisting etymological theory, and by double-starring forms of whose existence we wish to deny the possibility. There still remains even so a great residue of ambiguity and, indeed, fog. Some of the confusion is a consequence of the fact that the device was not invented for the Romance field at all, but for pre-literate languages. The use of the asterisk for this purpose was made generally known by Schleicher, although, as Koerner (1989: 179–84) has shown, Schleicher did not actually invent it. Schleicher was not a Romance philologist. When used by those studying prehistoric stages of a language, the implication of the use of the asterisk and the nature of the form it accompanies is unproblematic; the asterisk suggests that a lexical item of more or less the phonemic form implied by the manner of the accompanying transcription, however broad or narrow that is, existed at a period in the past for which we have no contemporary written evidence. Romance philologists mentioning languages other than Latin and Romance are at liberty to use it that way too, naturally, for reconstructions in prehistoric Indo-European, Old Germanic, Old Celtic, Old Basque, unspecified pre-Roman or what Hall calls "Mediterranean," as well as Italic or occasionally 'Ancient Latin' lexical items. In such cases what is being postulated, by definition, is a spoken form, for writing was not used in the prehistoric societies referred to. Even so, the implications of the asterisk attached to non-Latin etyma in the work of Romance Philologists can be unclear; when scholars attach asterisks to postulated etyma of Germanic or Celtic provenance, it is rarely if ever made explicit whether the words are equally unattested in both Germanic (Celtic) and Latin, or unattested in Latin but attested in Germanic (Celtic); and conversely, when they do not attach asterisks to such etyma, it is similarly unclear whether they are attested in both languages or attested only in one, and if so which.

When Romance philologists use the asterisk for reconstructable forms in Late Latin / Early Romance / Proto-Romance, they are referring to a historical period when writing indeed existed, and the lack of written documentation is therefore significant, with different implications from those of a written form's inevitable absence in pre-literate societies. We need to appreciate that enormous confusion has been and is still being caused by the failure in our discipline to distinguish clearly between three separate phenomena: (1) a lexical item in a speaker's mental lexicon; (2) the written form of a lexical item; and (3) the spoken forms of a lexical item. (As a subset of lexical items, bound morphemes have come in for the same confusion on our part.)

Diachronic linguists from other areas of study might assume that the Romance philologist's asterisk usually postulates the existence of an item unattested in writing. But this is not the case. If we set aside the reconstructed etyma from languages other than

Latin, and those whose existence is being denied, and confine our attention for the moment to asterisked forms in capital letters (leaving for later consideration the asterisked forms printed in italics, in ordinary script, in phonetic script, in phonetic script between slashes, in phonetic script between square brackets, in bold type, in phonetic script in bold type, or between inverted commas), even then, we discover that totally unattested items form only a tiny minority of the asterisked forms (see Appendix B1). Entwistle (1936) presents five out of his twenty-one asterisked capital forms in this category, Corominas (1961) seven out of his fifty-six, Menéndez Pidal (1972) four out of his sixty-two, Elcock (1975) three out of his 296, Macpherson (1975) one out of his sixty-seven, Wright (1982) three out of seven, Dworkin (1985) none out of his forty, Lloyd (1987) none out of his 143, Meier (1987) thirteen out of his 238 (mostly, like Menéndez Pidal's, presented in elongated type rather than in capitals), Cano (1988) none out of his seventy-four, Ariza (1989) none out of his five, Harris-Northall (1990) none out of his forty-three, Pensado (1991) one out of her thirteen, Penny (1991) two out of his 126; total, thirty-nine out of 1191. Roughly, only one in thirty asterisked capital forms are asterisked in order to indicate that these are unattested items. (These statistics are not necessarily precise, for there is often a lack of clarity in the text as to why a form is asterisked, and there might be disagreement over the precise categorization of some of these examples). It would be preferable to propose that in future the asterisk is confined only to these one in thirty: that is, for use with lexical items, both words and morphemes, that are indeed unattested and whose existence is being postulated. The etymon for Romance words for 'small' might be a good case in point.

The other approximately 96% of asterisked reconstructed forms in capitals (Appendix B1) fall into two main further categories (in addition to those like *LUMINE, or the unattested combinations of attested words that receive the asterisk they acquire in modern syntactic studies). The largest category concerns unattested lexicalized combinations of individually attested morphemes, very nearly always of a free lexeme plus one or more reconstructably productive bound, usually derivational, affixes. In such cases, the component parts are attested, and what is being hypothesized is the lexicalization of their potential union. Yet the question of whether a particular combination of live lexeme and productive affix counts as a lexical item at all is a thoroughly problematical one even in synchronic study; lexicographers vary widely over which combinations to include in Modern Romance dictionaries. The use of an asterisk to indicate that a particular combination of attested morphemes is not itself attested in lexicalized form in texts of the Late Latin / Early Romance / Proto-Romance stage would be entirely acceptable if the analyst ever stated that that was what he or she was using it for. Several scholars have intuited the awkwardness of this practice; Malkiel (1989) prefers to insert a plus sign between the morphemes in such cases, and Meier a minus sign (or hyphen), implicitly thereby demonstrating unease about using an asterisk to mark such unattested combinations of attested morphemes on the same level as totally unattested and thus far more hypothetical items. The late Professor Meier made a career out of postulating affixed forms in capital letters (or elongated script), and used the asterisk for this purpose most of the time (183 out of 238 such uses in Meier 1987); e.g. *v i d - i n - i a r e as the postulated root of Sp. *guiñar*, Fr. *guigner*, It. *ghignare*, Old Oc. *guinhar*, formed off *uidere* plus two attested suffixes (1987: 47); or sometimes without the hyphen, e.g. *p e r u s t i c a r e off *ustus* as the root for the subsequently deverbal *brusca* ('kindling', 1987: 23); etc. The asterisk accompanies the hyphen, in effect, even if he refrains from inserting one. Meier never seems to have proposed in these reconstructions the existence of either a totally unattested affix or a totally unattested lexical root. Indeed, Meier gave the impression of being constitutionally unable to prefer a non-Latin etymon, whether hypothetical or not, to the unattested combinations of attested morphemes that he almost invariably recommended (cf. Meier 1989). That is, he used the asterisk liberally, while at the same time explicitly preferring not to postulate the existence of any unattested morpheme, a conjunction of approaches that borders on the self-contradictory. A further complaint that can be made against the use of asterisked capitals for such reconstructed combinations of lexeme and affix, adduced also in passing by Malkiel (1989: 66), is that there is no need to postulate a Latin etymon from an early period in the many cases where both the lexical root and the affix survive into the relevant Romance languages and no further phonetic change consequent to their lexicalization need be accounted for. For example, given Sp. *apagar* ('extinguish') and Italian *appagare* ('satisfy'), it is easier to propose that the lexicalizations happened after the separate phonetic developments of pre-consonantal AD > *a* and PACARE > *pagare*, for a separate semantic purpose in each case, rather than reconstructing an unattested, but nonetheless polysemic, asterisked capitalized *ADPACARE. The capital letters D and C in this asterisked form imply the existence of the sounds [d] and [k] in the reconstructed verb at the time of its initial lexicalization, but there is no advantage or need to reconstruct them.

This case (adduced among others by Penny, 1991: 11) demonstrates in passing the potential confusion that can be particularly caused by the other main category of asterisked capital forms; one which Malkiel (1989) refrains from mentioning, but is the most misleading of all. A surprisingly large number of asterisked forms printed in capital letters are lexical items whose existence is certain and generally agreed to be attested; the reason for the asterisk is that the form adduced (by the philologist) has been given (by him) a spelling which is not attested. Twenty-two of Lloyd (1987)'s 143 asterisked capital forms, twenty of Penny (1991)'s 126, fifteen of Macpherson (1975)'s sixty-seven, sixty-five of Elcock (1975)'s 296, and forty-two of Cano (1988)'s seventy-four, for example, fall into this category (called 'intermediate' in Appendix B1). The following examples come from Cano (1988): *PRIMAIRU (compared with attested PRIMARIU, p. 71), *VERECŬNNIA (compared with attested VERECUNDIA, p. 78), *CAIPA (compared with attested CAPIAT, p. 158), etc. Twice adduced is *COLÒBRA (Cano 1988: 81, 208), compared with COLŬBRA, which was also the example used in Macpherson (1975)'s definition of what an asterisk is for (see above). These lexical items are not unattested. The spellings produced by the modern author seem to be; but it should be elementary linguistic practice to distinguish carefully between a lexical item (which is constituted with phonemes, and exists in the mental lexicon), an orthographical form (which is constituted with letters, and exists in writing), and a phonetic form (which is constituted with sounds, and exists as vibrations in the air); and in this common practice of inventing unattested spellings, the three entities are being hopelessly confused. This habit, of inventing and then starring unattested spellings of generally-known lexical items, struck me as so peculiar that at first it seemed not only pointless but even deliberately baffling; then a ghastly suspicion dawned, which is still with me. Some of our colleagues, and not only in the distant past, believe—or behave as if they believe—that Latin spelling was an exact phonetic transcription of the writer's speech, regardless of his time and place. This is in itself a grotesquely implausible hypothesis, but it seems that it must be the hypothesis which underlies this practice. For example, several of the scholars investigated here (including Malkiel 1989: 68) invented, starred and capitalized a form *COMPERARE, as in (here quoting Lloyd 1987: 201) '*COMPERARE "to buy" (C.L. COMPARĀRE) > *comprar*'. The implication of Lloyd's phrasing really does seem to be that the usual spelling with an 'A' (COMPARARE) can at all times and in all places only have represented a pronunciation with an [a], so that if the modern scholar wishes to postulate a different spoken vowel he needs to invent a different written form. This idea is not only strange but unnecessary. Phonetic script had not yet been invented, and even if we were to think it might have been, we know for other reasons that Proto-Romance probably had a schwa [ə] but no symbol ever biuniquely allotted to that sound in writing.

The Schleicher tradition sensibly used asterisks to reconstruct spoken forms of postulated lexical items in preliterate times; but the Romance philological tradition has developed that habit further: the asterisk is now used when mentioning lexical items whose written form, as attested, is not exactly the same as a phonetic transcription would have been of the pronunciation we wish to reconstruct for that lexeme at a Late Latin / Early Romance / Proto-Romance stage. The presence of the asterisk here thus confuses a simple issue. We might as well transcribe Modern English *ORINDZH in asterisked capitals as though it was a hypothetical entity. *orindzh* is indeed unattested in writing (other than in my own metalinguistic work, Wright 1982: 50), but asterisked capitalized *ORINDZH—written that way, as in Romance philological practice—would merely be a written representation of a pronunciation [ɔɹɪndʒ] of a lexical item that is indeed commonly attested in writing, as *orange*, and does indeed exist. For what our colleagues mean by asterisking *COM-

PERARE (with a letter E after the P) is not that this is a hypothetical, but reconstructable, lexical item, but that it is a reconstructable pronunciation of a lexical item commonly attested in a different form, with the invented orthography designed in this case to represent a proposed [e] (or [ə]) in the second syllable. In all the many cases in this category it is not the lexical item itself, but a particular phonetic representation of that item, which is being postulated in the reconstruction, so it is surely preferable—if we wish to write this reconstructed phonetic form on paper at all—to write this reconstructed pronunciation in the same way that we write all other phonetic entities in scholarly study, that is, in phonetic script, and preferably in the International Phonetic Alphabet. Written forms in phonetic script, of course, are never attested at all in the years before the initial invention of phonetic script, and are extremely uncommon even now, so even if we use phonetic script ourselves for such forms the use of an asterisk with the phonetic transcription of a lexical item of the past seems (as Hall says, see above) an unnecessary piece of typographically redundant hypercharacterization. What Cano means, for example (1988: 71), by asterisking *BAISU is that at some point in Late Latin / Early Romance / Proto-Romance the lexical item traditionally written BASIUM was pronounced with the offglide [i] (or [j]) preceding the sibilant [s] (or perhaps [z]). It would be simpler and less misleading simply to write here 'BASIUM [bájsu]'—if indeed that is the pronunciation he is wishing to hypothesize, for among the demerits of the practice here being criticized is its lack of precision. Malkiel himself does not discuss this explicitly, but seems to prefer to asterisk italicized forms for such intermediate phonetic reconstructions, writing (1989: 40) *abodega for the form intermediate between apotheca and bodega, and *alicer rather than alacer as the etymon for Sp. alegre (1989: 86).

The asterisked form, then, is often meant in this way to refer to an intermediate pronunciation. Intermediate, that is, between that of ancient Latin, presumed (perhaps justifiably) to be represented isomorphically in the traditional orthography, and the earliest Romance forms, also presumed (in part justifiably) to be isomorphically represented in the Old Romance orthographies. That meaning for the asterisks in this category, however, is a deduction on my part. None of the studies investigated here phrases the purpose of their asterisks in this way, although Cano's definition comes close. The fog caused by the failure to make this clear, and the conceptual confusion between the lexical item, its phonetic form and its written form, can lead and has led to baffling habits and comments. Consider, for example, the very common practice (which astonished me even as an undergraduate) of writing nominal etyma intended to be accusative singular in capitals without their final -M (whether or not the form is accompanied by an asterisk): POPULU as the etymon of *peuple, povo, pueblo, popolo,* etc. These forms of second declension nouns are not normally attested at all; POPULU, with a final letter -U, is not the traditional spelling of any morphological case, and may never be attested as such. For the sake of consistency, the form might thereby seem to be prima facie deserving of the asterisk which should never have been allotted to *LUMINE, being in the same 'intermediate' category as *CAIPA (etc); in late manuscripts where the accusative indeed often lacks a letter -*m* (or the tilde) the final written letter is usually -*o*. The purpose of this is sometimes understandable in that the etymologist wishes to refer to a lexical item without committing himself to any particular case-form; but nearly always, at least among Hispanists, it is only intended to represent the originally accusative singular. This dropping of the written -M in capitalized etyma is still common among etymologists; Lloyd half-realized that it was inconsistent, for he devoted a note to it (1987: 72, n. 3): 'When Latin words are given as the etyma of Romance words, the usual practice will be to give them in the accusative singular form of nouns and adjectives, minus the final /-m/.' Unfortunately, this manner of explaining the habit compounds the confusion, for the Latin words were never found in texts with a final '/-m/' in phonemic slash brackets, but instead normally with an orthographic -M, and the suspicion returns; can even the intelligent, meticulous, hard-working and near-omniscient Paul Lloyd actually believe that traditional spelling was a phonemic script? For the reason the letter is traditionally omitted from these accusatives is that we can feel sure in most cases that the final -M corresponded to no sound. Yet if philologists feel justified in reshaping the etyma unasterisked for that purpose, why not do it for all purposes? It would be best then to avoid not only the capital letters but also the asterisk, and present the pronunciation of all etyma in unasterisked phonetic script, unless the lexical item is indeed totally unattested.

It seems likely that other laborers in this field have probably had a similar thought to this. For seven of the twenty authorities consulted in the present exercise do not use asterisked capitals at all (Hall, Rickard, De Dardel, Pharies, Ariza, Maiden, Stengaard), while nine of the twenty, at least occasionally, do indeed use asterisks with phonetic script: Hall, Lloyd, and Penny between phonemic slashes, Rickard, Elcock, Lloyd, Harris-Northall, Maiden and Penny between phonetic square brackets, Macpherson and Harris-Northall in bold type, Ariza and Maiden usually in ordinary unbracketed type (see Appendix B, 4-8). Hall's use of asterisks with phonetic script is interesting. At the start of his *Proto-Romance Phonology* (1976), as quoted above, he states that he will not use the asterisk, but in the event he does, with phonemic slashes: nineteen times to hypothesize the existence of the accompanying pronunciation, and four times to deny it. In his *External History of the Romance Languages* (1974) he uses the same device for fifty-eight Germanic etyma, one Norse etymon, and seven postulated Latin-Romance forms, plus one form whose existence is being denied. In his *Proto-Romance Morphology* (1983) the asterisk and the phonemic slashes similarly accompany fourteen Proto-Indo-European reconstructed forms, eight other reconstructed forms, and three whose existence is being denied. Presumably his asterisk is meant to imply that the form is not found in any written form at all at the time for which Hall is postulating its initial existence, although his habitual chronological vagueness makes this a far from illuminating presentation. Macpherson uses phonetic script in bold type to hypothesize the existence of six forms and deny three ('*λaxa, *nexár, *rwéxa', which 'clearly did not happen', 1975:157). Harris-Northall (1990) uses an array of devices with phonetic script both to postulate and deny a form's existence; starred square-bracketed forms to postulate eight forms and deny two, bold type phonetic script to postulate six and deny seven, bold type in square brackets to postulate four, and unbracketed phonetic script to postulate two and deny two. In general, the hypothesized pronunciations represented in phonetic script are much more often than not intermediate between those attested in what is assumed to be an isomorphic manner in Latin and in Romance orthographies, as in the 'intermediate' category of asterisked capital forms, but at least there is in the case of phonetic script no doubt about what is being postulated; the pronunciation of a lexeme which we know to have existed, but which was written then in a manner different from what its form would have been had the scribes been clairvoyant experts in the modern Phonetic Alphabet. That lack of correspondence applies to all the spellings and pronunciations of the time, naturally, whether asterisked by modern philologists or not, so this asterisk is as unnecessary with phonetic script as it is with capital letters, but at least what we have here is the redundant laboring of an intelligible point (a hypothesized phonetic form) whereas the previous category (asterisked capital forms) involved the muddling of three separate points (phonetic, orthographical and lexical phonemic forms). There seems to be no nuance of meaning to correspond to the way in which asterisks are occasionally placed inside rather than outside the brackets.

One proposal that Malkiel put forward in his 1989 study seems uncharacteristically unhelpful: that is, to star forms in which a vowel has changed quantity, e.g. from Ī ([i:]) to Ĭ ([i]); he offers (47) *glĭris (in italics, in this case) as opposed to the original glīris, the original genitive form of the word for 'dormouse'. Such quantitative deductions can often be made from verse, but Latin texts were not normally written with the macron and the micron. Probably neither form is attested with the diacritic. *Gliris* is attested, and we cannot presume that the first letter *i* never represented a short [i]. There seems little point in adding an asterisk to mark forms as undocumented if they could not have been expected to occur in that written form at all (such as in phonetic script before it was invented, or with usually absent diacritics). Let us write instead that the written form *gliris* came in time, particularly in this case in France, to represent a pronunciation with a short [i] rather than a long [i:] in the first syllable.

Philologists often use asterisks with italicized forms (Appendix B2). Hall's *Phonology* (1976) and Harris-Northall (1990) are the only works studied here not to use that practice at all. As with the capital forms, the implication is sometimes that a pronunciation is reconstructed to have existed in a form similar to that which would be implied were the accompanying form written in italics actually written in phonetic script; and, as before, sometimes the existence of such a phonetic form is emphatically being denied. Rickard (1974) and Stengaard (1991), who use no asterisked capital forms at all, use italics for the purposes fulfilled elsewhere by capitals—that is, for unattested combinations of genuinely attested morphemes (such as, passim in Stengaard, *essere*—which in fact is copiously attested, but in what we now call, as a result of a change in naming practice—see Janson 1991—'Italian'), for intermediate pronunciations, and in Stengaard's case for eight denials (out of thirty-seven uses overall). Lloyd (1987) uses asterisked italics on eleven occasions to hypothesize, and on fifty occasions to deny, a form; Wright (1982) twice to hypothesize and four times to deny; Pharies (1986) forty times to hypothesize and fifteen to deny, and twice where even a specialist reader cannot be sure whether affirmation or denial is intended (it seems to be both at once: *noño*, twice on p. 15); Dworkin (1985) eighty-seven times to hypothesize and twenty-two to deny: etc. Lloyd is again here half-aware of the ambiguity, as to what is or is not being hypothesized with an asterisked italicized form, without resolving it: e.g. 'the absence of any evidence in writing for Early Castilian forms like *faço*, *yaço* or *plaço* or *teno* and *veno* merely indicates that these changes all took place at a very early stage, before there was any need to write Castilian' [sc. 'to write Romance in a new and distinctively Castilian manner'] (1987: 295).

Starred italicized forms are also used for unattested concatenations of individually well attested items, as by the synchronic syntacticians. This is the only role De Dardel (1983) gives to the asterisk, that is, for items which are indeed attested. In its way, this apparently perverse decision is as it should be, for almost everything else in his book (apart from the medieval quotations) is hypothetical and reconstructed but presented without an asterisk. Asterisked italicized forms in these twenty-three studies are also found for hypothesized pre-Latin forms (Hall, Pensado), Germanic forms (Entwistle, Hall, Macpherson), Celtic forms (Entwistle, Rickard, Elcock), Basque forms (Corominas, Menéndez Pidal), and even, very inappropriately, for an Arabic form (Wright). In such usages the distinction between italics and capitals has broken down; but generally that distinction—in the work of writers who present forms in both scripts with asterisks—seems to concern the target orthography that would have been aimed at if this postulated form had in fact ever been written. The chronological distinction between Latin and French (etc.) is an administrators' fantasy, of course, but the distinction between trying to write in the old way and trying to write in a new way, once new ways had been invented, is a real distinction, and if for some perverse reason modern scholars do not want to use phonetic script when discussing pronunciations, that typographical distinction has at least some raison d'etre when followed consistently.

Asterisks are also used to accompany words in inverted commas by three writers (Dworkin, Meier, Penny), unambiguously to refer to a meaning which a particular word does not have. A number of the works also use asterisks as footnote signs, which seems tempting fate in an etymological study.

CONCLUSION

As a result of this investigation I feel exactly as Malkiel (who refers to 'downright whimsical armchair reconstructions', 1989: 26) says that most people in the field come to feel over time; that the asterisk should only be used sparingly, if at all, in diachronic study. In addition, it is surely preferable to use phonetic script, rather than any other, for pronunciations, of the past exactly as it is for those of the present, and if the lexical item in question is attested in any orthographical manner at all then no asterisk need accrue to its phonetic version. In this way we can preserve the essential theoretical consistency of phonetic developments by postulating early etyma for Romance forms to derive 'regularly' from, without thereby postulating more than we need; compare Orr's distaste (1948: 82) for the 'application of sound laws to those forms of words which some literary document had happened to consecrate. Instead of writing, for example (Macpherson 1975: 109) 'LAXIUS > V.L. *LASSĬUS > O.Sp. lexos', we could write 'Late Latin' (or Early Romance or Proto-Romance, to taste) '[lássjus],' (if that is indeed the proposed pronunciation—it is not clear) 'written *laxius*, > Old Spanish [léʃos], written *lexos*', without using an asterisk at all. (We will then need to reconstruct the pronunciation of a whole word, rather than just one of its constituent sounds.) Then we can keep the asterisk for genuinely unattested but reconstructable lexical items (such as 'O.Sp. *losa* < *LAUSA', Macpherson 1975: 122—unless it is indeed attested after all), and its function is perceptibly unambiguous. Even then, though, what is reconstructed is a phonetic form, and the red herring of what its orthographic form would have been remains an unnecessary complication, so it would be preferable to write OSp. *losa* < *[láwsa] (in phonetic script). In both cases, a phonetic representation is usually what is reconstructed, therefore best presented in square brackets. In addition, the double-asterisked forms whose existence is being denied should also ideally be presented in phonetic script, unless it is specifically a written form whose existence is being denied. Whereupon the remaining uses of the single asterisk would be for the phonetic form of totally unattested items. Such a restricted use of the device would give it the advantages it at present does not have, of having clear reference and of neither representing nor precipitating conceptual confusion.

Appendix A

The works investigated here (in chronological order), and the abbreviations used in Appendix B, are as follows:

En   Entwistle, William J., 1936. The Spanish Language (London: Faber).
Co   Corominas, Juan, 1961. Breve diccionario etimológico de la lengua castellana (Madrid: Gredos), words beginning with M-.
MP   Menéndez Pidal, Ramón, 1972. Orígenes del español, 7th ed. (Madrid: Espasa-Calpe).
Hl   Hall, Robert A. Jr., 1974. External History of the Romance Languages (New York: Elsevier).
R   Rickard, Peter,1974. A History of the French Language (London: Hutchinson).
El   Elcock, W. D., 1975. The Romance Languages, 2nd ed. (London: Faber).
Mc   Macpherson, Ian, 1975. Spanish Phonology (Manchester: UP).

H2   Hall, Robert A. Jr, 1976. Proto-Romance Phonology (New York: Elsevier).
W   Wright, Roger, 1982. Late Latin and Early Romance (Liverpool: Cairns).
H3   Hall, Robert A. Jr, 1983. Proto-Romance Morphology (Amsterdam: Benjamins).
DD   De Dardel, R., 1983. Esquisse structurale des subordonnants conjonctionnels en roman commun (Geneva: Droz).
Dw   Dworkin, Steven N.,1985. Etymology and Derivational Morphology: the Genesis of Old Spanish Denominal Adjectives in -IDO (Tübingen: Niemeyer).
Ph   Pharies, David, 1986. Structure and Analogy in the Playful Lexicon of Spanish (Tübingen: Niemeyer).
Ll   Lloyd, Paul M., 1987. From Latin to Spanish, I (Philadelphia: American Philosophical Society).
Me   Meier, Harri, 1987. 'Nuevas anotaciones al Diccionario Etimológico de Corominas/Pascual', Verba, 14: 5-74.
CA   Cano Aguilar, Rafael,1988. El español a través de los tiempos (Madrid: Arco).
A   Ariza Viguera, Manuel, 1989. Manual de fonología histórica del espanol (Madrid: Síntesis).
HN   Harris-Northall, Raymond, 1990. Weakening Processes in the History of Spanish Consonants (London: Routledge).
Ma   Maiden, Martin, 1991 'On the Phonological Vulnerability of Complex Paradigms: Beyond Analogy in Italo- and Ibero-Romance', RPh, 44: 284-305.
S   Stengaard, Birte, 1991. Vida y muerte de un campo semántico (Tübingen: Niemeyer).
Pn   Pensado, Carmen, 1991a. 'How was Leonese Vulgar Latin read?', in Roger Wright, ed., Latin and the Romance Languages in the Early Middle Ages (London: Routledge), pp. 190-204.
     ———, 1991b. 'Un reanálisis de la "l leonesa"', in Raymond Harris-Northall & Thomas D. Cravens, eds, Linguistic Studies in Medieval Spanish (Madison: Hispanic Seminary of Medieval Studies), pp.63-88.
Py   Penny, Ralph, 1991. A History of the Spanish Language (Cambridge: UP).

APPENDIX B

1 *CAPITALS

Postulation of:	En	Co	MP	H1	R	El	Mc	H2	W	H3	DD	Dw	Ph	Ll	Me	CA	A	HN	Ma	S	Pn	Py
Unattested Lexeme	5	7	4			3	1		3						13						1	2
Unattested sequence of attested lexemes			3			2																
Unattested combination of attested morphemes	12	35	32			176	49		2				22		105	183	32		28		12	60
Different morphological analysis of attested form		2	1			20									2	1			7			36
Intermediate form (between 'Latin' and 'Romance')	3	3	12			65	15						1		22	9	42	5	8			20
Ancient Latin form		1	1			2									8	1						
Ancient Basque form		1				1																
Pre-Roman form						1																
Indo-European form													3									
Old Germanic form		5	1			3			1				6		3	29						6
Old Celtic form		2	5			23			1						2							1
Greek form	1						2															1
Romance form			1																			
Denial of existence of:	En	Co	MP	H1	R	El	Mc	H2	W	H3	DD	Dw	Ph	Ll	Me	CA	A	HN	Ma	S	Pn	Py
Latin form			2										9									
Unattested sequence of attested words													1									

2 *italics

Postulation of:	En	Co	MP	H1	R	El	Mc	H2	W	H3	DD	Dw	Ph	Ll	Me	CA	A	HN	Ma	S	Pn	Py
Unattested lexeme	2		1	1																		
Unattested combination of attested morphemes						15													19			
Different morphological analysis of attested form		1			2	3							1									3
Intermediate form (between 'Latin' and 'Romance')						11									3					2		
'Mediterranean' form				6															1			
Germanic form	7			1			7															
Celtic form	2				17	3																
Arabic form									1													
Basque form		2	3																			
Unattested Medieval Romance form	5	18	21			14	2		1				87	39	11	18	6			5	2	20
Denial of existence of:	En	Co	MP	H1	R	El	Mc	H2	W	H3	DD	Dw	Ph	Ll	Me	CA	A	HN	Ma	S	Pn	Py
Medieval Romance form	6		10		2	6	4		4	2			22	14	38	1	4	1		5		8
Unattested Latin sequence of attested forms																				3		
Modern form														12								2
Modern sequence of forms				1					5	1				1		2	1					

The Asterisk in Hispanic Historical Linguistics

	En	Co	MP	H1	R	El	Mc	H2	W	H3	DD	Dw	Ph	Ll	Me	CA	A	HN	Ma	S	Pn	Py
Modern meaning of a form																			1			

3 ***italics**

	En	Co	MP	H1	R	El	Mc	H2	W	H3	DD	Dw	Ph	Ll	Me	CA	A	HN	Ma	S	Pn	Py
Denial of existence of Medieval Romance form																			4			

4 ** / /* (or /* /)

Postulation of:	En	Co	MP	H1	R	El	Mc	H2	W	H3	DD	Dw	Ph	Ll	Me	CA	A	HN	Ma	S	Pn	Py
Old Latin form				1				3	1													
Proto-Indo-European form									14													
Germanic form				58																		
Norse form				1																		
Proto-Italic form								1														
Proto-Romance form				3					1													3
Medieval Romance form				3				11	6		3											16
Conceivable Medieval Romance form								4			2											2
Denial of existence of:	En	Co	MP	H1	R	El	Mc	H2	W	H3	DD	Dw	Ph	Ll	Me	CA	A	HN	Ma	S	Pn	Py
Proto-Romance form								1														
Medieval Romance form								2			1						1					
Modern form				1				3	1													1

5 **[ ]* (or [*])

Postulation of:	En	Co	MP	H1	R	El	Mc	H2	W	H3	DD	Dw	Ph	Ll	Me	CA	A	HN	Ma	S	Pn	Py
Latin form				1																		
Medieval Romance form						15								1			8					6
Denial of existence of:	En	Co	MP	H1	R	El	Mc	H2	W	H3	DD	Dw	Ph	Ll	Me	CA	A	HN	Ma	S	Pn	Py
Proto-Romance form																		2	3			

6 *phonetic script (without brackets)

	En	Co	MP	H1	R	El	Mc	H2	W	H3	DD	Dw	Ph	Ll	Me	CA	A	HN	Ma	S	Pn	Py
Postulated proto-form																		100				
Denial of existence of form																		1				

7 *bold phonetic script

Postulation of:	En	Co	MP	H1	R	El	Mc	H2	W	H3	DD	Dw	Ph	Ll	Me	CA	A	HN	Ma	S	Pn	Py
Medieval Romance form			1					6									6					
Denial of existence of:	En	Co	MP	H1	R	El	Mc	H2	W	H3	DD	Dw	Ph	Ll	Me	CA	A	HN	Ma	S	Pn	Py
Medieval Romance form						3											7					

8 *[ ]

Postulation of:	En	Co	MP	H1	R	El	Mc	H2	W	H3	DD	Dw	Ph	Ll	Me	CA	A	HN	Ma	S	Pn	Py
Medieval Romance form																		4				

9 *ordinary type

Postulation of:	En	Co	MP	H1	R	El	Mc	H2	W	H3	DD	Dw	Ph	Ll	Me	CA	A	HN	Ma	S	Pn	Py
Proto-Romance form																		1	1			
Denials						2												1	2			
(Assorted uses by Ariza)																		7				

10 *' '

	En	Co	MP	H1	R	El	Mc	H2	W	H3	DD	Dw	Ph	Ll	Me	CA	A	HN	Ma	S	Pn	Py
Denial of a meaning													1		1							3

11 * for footnotes, etc.

	En	Co	MP	H1	R	El	Mc	H2	W	H3	DD	Dw	Ph	Ll	Me	CA	A	HN	Ma	S	Pn	Py
			1	7		17		4	3		18							15				

1994 POSTSCRIPT.

This paper was published in the *Journal of Hispanic Research*, 1, 1992, 1-16, as the journal's inaugural paper. It is reproduced here by permission of Impart Publishing Ltd, to whom we are particularly indebted for permission to reprint the final appendix neat. That published paper was a slightly expanded version of one delivered (under the title "*") to the annual Romance Linguistics Seminar in Trinity Hall, Cambridge University, in January 1992, and later in Spanish to audiences at the Universities of Valencia (May 1992) and Oviedo (January 1993). Despite the presence in some of these audiences of practitioners referred to in the paper, it met with general approval. Two of the linguists investigated have gently pointed out that I slightly misrepresent them, and I am glad to apologize here: Robert De Dardel announces explicitly on p.31 that "Dans le texte et dans le tableau, les formes du latin et du roman commun sont données en capitales (QUANDO), sans astérisque pour les formes reconstruites (BENE-KE)," deliberately wishing not to distinguish typographically between the attested and the unattested; and Birte Stengaard indeed makes it clear in connection with her use of *ESSERE that it is only being postulated thereby as hypothetical within the Iberian Peninsula. It is probably too much to expect that the advice contained in this paper will be generally followed, but it has certainly sharpened up my own usage.

6
The Study of Semantic Change in Early Romance (Late Latin)

The history of the development and divergence of the Romance languages out of the Latin of the Roman Empire is the most fully documented case of language change that we possess. This ought to mean that the development of the discipline of historical linguistics is closely interwoven with the theoretical and practical advances made by Romance philologists; that the proponents of theories of language change which are meant to have universal validity check with care the attested details of the development of Latin into the various Romance languages; and, conversely, that Romance philologists take account of the accepted discoveries of historical linguistics when interpreting their evidence. But some of them have been happy to work with assumptions that seem absurd to a general historical linguist. For example, specialists in Late Latin texts, that is, those written between the end of the Roman Empire and the Twelfth-Century Renaissance, once tended to regard the language of those texts as some kind of direct transcription of speech. It was partly a reaction to the weaknesses in this approach that encouraged the application to the Early Romance languages of reconstruction techniques originally designed for languages with no documentation at all. By working backwards from the Romance languages, scholars created a hypothetical entity called Proto-Romance, postulated to have existed at the same time as surviving Latin texts were written but not to be identified with Latin. This did lead to occasional illuminating reexaminations of the textual evidence, as in the brilliant article by Politzer (1961), but some scholars never looked at the texts, in effect priding themselves on not taking into account the copiously available evidence that is the envy of those who study other language families. Specialists in Bantu or Athapaskan languages, for example, would be delighted to have a seventh-century text, wouldn't they? At the very least, they wouldn't ignore it.

These barriers are not impermeable. At our conference at Stanford in 1979 I pointed out that lexical diffusion theory demolished the phonetic evidence that had bolstered the view that Late Latin and Early Romance were totally separate languages. Esa Itkonen in Helsinki, Michael Richter in Dublin, Marc van Uytfanghe in Ghent and others have been working simultaneously on Romance historical linguistics and Late Latin texts. Romance historical linguists quite often now consider together Late Latin and subsequent Early Romance documentary evidence without erecting an artificial barrier between the two; e.g., among others, Timo Riiho's work on Spanish prepositions, Mario Saltarelli's paper on syntactic diffusion at the Stanford conference, Dieter Wanner's paper to this conference and Suzanne Fleischman's book on the future. But there are still scholars who ignore the Late Latin evidence entirely; for example, Saussol wrote an interesting book on the use of the Spanish copulative verbs *estar* and *ser* in the *Poema de Mio Cid*, and then included in the book's title the phrase "Origins of their functions," as if nobody in Spain had talked at all until the twelfth century, or as if their Latin etyma STARE and SEDERE had never existed.

The Romance Reconstructionists are of course right to be wary of some of the Mediæval Latin texts: texts written in England, Ireland or Germany, because these were probably written by native speakers of languages other than Romance. In addition, texts written after the ninth-century educational reforms in France and much of Italy, or after 1080 in most of Spain, are likely to be written by authors who did regard Latin as a conceptually entirely distinct language from their own spoken Romance; but texts from before those dates in Romance-speaking areas were probably written by speakers of Old Romance, who were using the only written mode they knew for recording their language (cp. Wright, 1982). This was not a direct transcription of speech any more than modern written French or English is a direct phonetic transcription of spoken French or English. This lack of direct correspondence means that some phonetic and morphological reconstruction is necessary, but it is even in these fields a good idea to look at texts and see if genuinely attested spellings appear in a chronological order compatible with the order required by the simplicity metric. And in lexical studies, the appearance of a new word in written form is precisely the evidence we need (as when Moralejo discovered the source of Spanish *jerigonza* written in a seventh-century text as *Ihericuntina lingua*).

In many respects the language of Late Latin texts seems to us archaic. But there is no reason to assume that the apparent coexistence of an attested, but archaic, usage in a Late Latin text with a convincingly reconstructable spoken form in the coetaneous Proto-Romance implies necessarily that the older usage did not also exist in the speech of the time. A new linguistic phenomenon can arise long before the eventual disappearance of the old form which it seems in retrospect to have neatly replaced; the author of the text, rather than indulging in antiquarianism in using an older form, might merely have been favoring one competing variant over another, the favored one being one which we know now, but couldn't have known then, was destined to die out. I've argued before (Wright, 1983) that new and old uses could regularly coexist in Early Romance until the eighth century or so. This comment is pertinent to morphological and syntactic change in Romance because, for example, of the probable lengthy coexistence of the use of old and new methods of rendering the passive (recently studied by Codoñer); it is pertinent to phonetic change, since for stylistic and sociolinguistic reasons old pronunciations are under no compulsion to die out merely because new ones have come in; and it is particularly pertinent to semantic change, since words regularly acquire new meanings without losing the old.

In general terms, the survival of the old despite the arrival of the new is not without interest. For another perspective which has shifted over the last thirty years in historical linguistics concerns the theoretical status of features that have not changed. Once upon a time it was presumed in a vague sort of way that if it were left to itself a language wouldn't change at all, so that the only interesting objects of study were taken to be those aspects which indeed had changed. More recently, people have realized that it is natural for all languages to evolve, so that what has not changed is potentially significant. Hence the recent interest taken by historical linguists in Classical Arabic and Hebrew, Katharevusa Greek, Post-Carolingian Mediæval Latin, etc, as artificially maintained invariant systems. Hence also the realization that sounds that have not changed might have as much theoretical significance as those which have, with the resulting elaboration of theories of consonantal strength hierarchies (as in Cravens's excellent paper to this conference); hence also the interest shown by lexical diffusion theorists in words that have not undergone phonetic changes as well as in those that have. This too applies to semantic change. For example, the fact that the eye is the only part of the face whose normal lexical item has not been involved in a semantic shift in the history of the Romance languages is of considerable interest, and could be interpreted as indicating that the eye has semantically real psychological boundaries in a way that other parts of the face have not. For in Spanish, for example, the word for "mouth" used to mean "cheek" (*boca*), the word for "chin" used to mean "little beard" (*barbilla*), the word for "eyebrow" used to mean "eyelids" (*ceja*), the word for "nose" used to mean "nostril" (*nariz/ces*), and the word for "cheek" used to mean "jawbone" *(mejilla)*, but the word for eye has not changed (*ojo*). And now, at last, I'll turn to semantic change directly.

Semantic change in lexical items is often intelligently discussed by etymologists whose primary focus is on the phonetic: e.g. Malkiel's paper to this conference; but in general it is an underdeveloped branch of historical linguistic theory. This is not because it is in itself a small subject. Countless lexical items have acquired new meanings. Yet historical linguistic textbooks, while occasionally mentioning it, rarely even give it a separate chapter (and even these conferences average only about one paper per conference on the topic). Writers on semantic theory, at least within the European tradition, have been more likely to discuss change; Ullmann, Vilches Acuña, Waldron and Baldinger, for example; but specifically diachronic semantic principles seem not to have been elaborated in the last twenty years. Perhaps this is because of Gilliéron's famous motto, which is certainly true, that each word has its own history. Since historical linguistics, like other branches of linguistics, has recently been dominated by believers in universals, the generally accepted presumption that there are no universals in semantic change may have led some linguists to assume that it is of no interest. This is to put the cart before the horse. There can be no objection to looking for universals, but there are strong objections to the assumption that if universals are not found the whole investigation must therefore be pointless. Roger Lass's realization that in diachronic linguistics there are no rigorously predictive principles was a great step forward; no matter that many European linguists have always taken this for granted anyway, it is an advance for an instinctive seeker after clear universals to admit that there may not be any. In diachronic semantics, no scholar has seriously been tempted to claim that there are.

How and why does the modern Spanish word *verdugo*, "executioner," come from a mediæval word meaning "sapling"? Schulte-Herbruggen's article will tell you how. It is hardly a predictable development. Nobody wants to predict that the English word *sapling* will mean "executioner" in 700 years time. But the change is explicable if we understand the difference between sense and reference, if we know a little semantic theory, and, above all, if we look at the textual evidence. In that article the intermediate stages of the semantic change are helpfully documented in chronologically intermediate texts. I am not now going to tell you what those stages are, because my point is that it is not easy to guess, simply by using general techniques of reconstruction, but that it is easy to follow if we look at the texts. My point today is that we can do the same for semantic changes known to have taken place in the Late Latin - Early Romance period.

López Pereira, of the department of Latin at the University of Santiago de Compostela, has recently explained a baffling semantic fact of Mediæval Spanish and Catalan by looking at a Late Latin text: Old Spanish and Catalan *civil* undoubtedly come from Latin CIVILEM, "civil," but why should they also be able to mean "cruel"? In the *Crónica Mozárabe* of 754 A.D. López Pereira found attested *civiliter* meaning "in civil war"; a ruler who behaved *civiliter* was treating his opponents cruelly. No amount of guesswork and reconstruction could have established that as the route of change; but because the Santiago Latin department is building up a vast filing system of attestations in seventh and eighth century texts, López Pereira could.

The development of Latin MAXILLA "jawbone" into Spanish *mejilla* "cheek" is clarified for us by Isidore of Seville, who, in his seventh-century *Etymologiæ*, regards the two *maxillæ* as still being bones, but distinguished from each other as left and right, as cheeks are, rather than as upper and lower, as jawbones are; he says there are four canine teeth in the human mouth, two in the right *maxilla* and two in the left *maxilla* (sequentes canini vocantur, quorum duo in dextra maxilla et duo in sinistra sunt). Semantic changes in Spanish words for parts of the face are discussed at length in Wright (1985), and one of the interesting things to come out of that investigation was that even a writer as hyper-literate as Isidore of Seville could use his words this way with their developed meanings, often—as in this case—of a kind that we might be able tentatively to guess at, but without our otherwise being able to reconstruct the chronology or the precise semantic nature of the intermediate stages. As it is, we can see from this sentence that the ninety-degree shift in the perception of *maxilla*'s sphere of reference happened before that sphere of reference moved away from the bones outwards to the flesh.

If we can find semantic development in Romance attested even in the vocabulary of the scholar Isidore, does this mean that a word used by Isidore without the reconstructable developed meaning implies conversely that the semantic change in question has not yet happened in Spanish Romance? In phonetics and morphology, because all the scribes were taught from the *Artes Grammaticæ* to follow the old norms, the presence of such unevolved forms in the texts of these times tells us little about pronunciation or spoken morphology. Semantics, however, was not covered by these *Artes*; yet Isidore had read many ancient works, and it is possible that he used words with an archaic sense more often than most of his contemporaries. That is a professional hazard of his being a lexicographer. But it is also true that in general semantic changes seem to take longer to complete than phonetic ones, particularly in that the old meaning can often coexist happily with the new meaning, and fail to drop out at all. So in such cases Isidore may be just favoring one meaning current in the community rather than another. Even so it is sometimes possible to deduce that a development cannot have got far yet, if we find a sentence where the new meaning, if it was available to the contemporary reader, would have stultified the sense of the sentence. For example, Spanish *colgar*, "to hang," comes from CONLOCARE, "to place." When we find in the seventh-century prayer-book the request that we be placed by God's right hand on the Day of Judgment (*ut... a dextris tuis tempore iudicii conlocemur: Oracional*), we can provisionally assume that the liturgists did not consider it possible for the ordinary Christian to misunderstand that as being "hung by your right hand." Since other contemporary uses of this verb all seem not to mean "hang," we can for the moment date that development as starting later than the seventh century. This is what a reconstructionist would probably guess, from the fact that Catalan and Occitan *colgar*, and French *coucher*, from the same etymon, have specialized in a different way to mean "put to bed"; but it is comforting to have some documentary support.

More examples of useful attestations. Spanish *madera* and Portuguese *madeira*, "wood," come from Latin MATERIA; to follow this shift it is helpful to see Isidore say (XIX.19.4) that all pieces of wood which are destined to be made into artifacts are known as *materia* (materia inde dicitur omne lignum quod ex ea aliquid efficiatur). Spanish *llegar* "to arrive" derives from Latin PLICARE "to fold." It was once suggested that this development arose from ships folding their sails. In fact, the oldest Spanish vernacular texts also have *allegar*, from ADPLICARE, and the seventh-century evidence shows *adplicare* used with the meaning of "arrive": e.g. the Visigothic Laws 8.2.3, *qui in itinere constitutus in cuiuscumque forsitam campo adplicaverit* (whoever is going on a journey and comes into someone's lands); the older meaning of "put together" is also attested. Since there seem to be no uses of *plicare* in these texts, the evidence supports the view put forward by Corominas that the direct development of these words was that of *allegar* from ADPLICARE, which could in Imperial Roman times be used of ships coming into dock (not of folding sails); we could add now that the subsequent back-formation of *llegar* is not surprising, since many Old Spanish verbs have two forms, one with a prefix *a-* and one without. Corominas (1980) quotes Classical uses, the early fifth-century *Peregrinatio Ætheriæ*, and eleventh-century Mediæval Latin uses, but the seventh-century ones would have helped him considerably.

Spanish *querer*, "want" and "love," from Latin QUÆRERE, "seek," is copiously attested meaning "love" in the seventh-century Visigothic prayerbook, where the congregation are described simply as *te querentes* (as opposed to those who hate the Lord: e.g. *Oracional* 765, Ne obliviscaris, Domine, vocem querentium te, ut superbia eorum qui te oderint ..); it can also mean "seek" (1117: et querere et invenire), or both at once. Spanish *domingo* "Sunday," comes from the adjective DOMINICUS: in seventh-century texts this can still be a general adjective connected with any lord, any *dominus*, but there are also six uses as a noun meaning "Sunday" in the Visigothic prayerbook, and eight in the full phrase *die dominico*; we can suggest that the new nominal use had arrived without implying that the old more general and adjectival use had dropped from speech yet. We also find *feria* used for "weekday," as in Modern Portuguese *feira*, developed away from the original "holiday." Other new Christian meanings include *missa* as a noun meaning "mass" in *Oracional* 550; *sermo* meaning "sermon" as well as the older and less specialized "speech"; *communicare* and *communio* with both new specialized and older general meanings; whereas there is no sign yet, for example, of the development of *incensum* from a participle meaning "burnt" to a noun meaning "incense." It has also proved possible to use this documentary evidence (Wright, 1992a) to argue that a word often thought to have undergone a semantic change did not in fact do so; Mediæval Spanish *ladino*, meaning "vernacular," comes from LATINVM; but rather than changing from meaning "Latin" to meaning "Romance," this lexical item always meant "vernacular," in the Roman Empire, in Isidore, in the ninth-century Christian writers of Moslem Spain, and in Old Spanish.

Scholars have been looking at the usage of Isidore since his own lifetime, of course: the work of Sofer and Fontaine, for example, is essential. All I want to do today is to point out that both general and Romance students of diachronic semantics have got documentation available for a long period, documentation which they tend to ignore but which might well be more helpful than reconstruction. Rothwell has pointed out that discussing semantic change in Old

French from a basis of theoretical reconstruction has often led to published analyses that can be simply disproved by actually looking at Old French texts; in essence I want to move that argument five centuries earlier.

1994 POSTSCRIPT.

This paper was printed in the *Papers from the 7th International Conference on Historical Linguistics,* John Benjamins Publishing Ccmpany, Amsterdam / Philadelphia, 1987, pp. 619- 28; it is an exact reprint of the lecture given at that conference in Pavia, Italy, on Thursday, September 12, 1985. It has aroused no interest at all, in part because semantic change is still an undeveloped area of Romance linguistics. As regards the present paper, the only point that should be clarified is that the quotations from the Visigothic texts are not meant to be taken as necessarily the first attestations of the developed meaning, merely as illuminating data; it is, of course, entirely possible for a change to have begun at an earlier date than that.

7
Indistinctive Features (Facial and Semantic)

FILLMORE (1975) MADE A neat distinction between two kinds of semantic theory, those involving the "checklist" and the "frame." The former has been the type most commonly used by generative linguists, who like to represent necessary conditions for the appropriate use of a lexical item as a combination of semantic units within square brackets; this technique has been at times elaborated into networks of considerable sophistication (e.g., by Kay and Samuels, 1975). The "frame" idea, on the other hand, suggests that a language has semantic structures which impose an artificial framework onto intrinsically undifferentiated aspects of human experience. This approach (which is traditional in Europe) does not construct groupings of logically necessary conditions that have to be met for an item to be used appropriately; instead, Fillmore suggests, there is at most an exemplary "prototype" in the center of each part of the frame. Other scholars following Fillmore, including Verschueren (1981) and Coleman and Kay (1981), have developed this notion, applying the word "prototype" to features which are "more or less" rather than plus or minus; Comrie (1981:101) even used it for his definition of the linguistic notion of *subject*. In cases where the outside world offers no clear boundaries, it may indeed be artificial for linguists to postulate them in semantic structure, and the data to be examined here also suggest that in such cases a frame may be all there is.

This note concerns semantic changes in Spanish words for parts of the face. The face seems at first sight to be composed of a number of distinguishable parts; the chin, jaws, mouth, cheeks, nose, eyes, eyelids, eyelashes, eyebrows, ears, temples, and forehead, say. Such entities might plausibly be thought to correspond to acceptably distinctive components in a "checklist" theory of semantics; if the *cow* can be allotted the unit [+ BOVINE] on its list of logically necessary conditions for use, the word *mouth* ought to be able to require the unit [+ORAL], or something similar. We would no more predict that the word for e.g. 'cheek' would change its meaning to 'eyelash' than that the word for 'cow' would change its meaning to 'hornet.' The theory of semantic change in a checklist model finds it easy to describe the acquisition of new [...] material (semantic specialization), or its loss (semantic generalization), but it is uneasy about the replacement of such material with some apparently incompatible relative; in practice, attested changes are rarely described by these theoreticians (but see the admirable study by Werth [1973] for one of the few attempts to categorize in such a manner changes that have actually occurred, in this case using the trees of generative semantics). So what should we think of the Rumanians, who indeed have developed Latin GENA 'cheek,' 'cheekbone' into *geană* [dʒánə] 'eyelash'?

Such a development must surely be regarded as unpredictable. It would not be surprising to discover that this change has never happened in any other language. But one of the lessons a student of semantic change has to grasp is that explanations cannot be expected to be predictive. Lass (1980), for one, has correctly diagnosed that the study of language change is unable to follow the strict principles of natural sciences (as many European scholars have been pointing out for decades). Lass finds this conclusion depressing. Other historical linguists (e.g., Samuels 1973) seem not to expect predictability. Many people would find it exhilarating to see proof that speakers are not in the grip of inexorable logical necessities; one of the ways in which human unpredictability in linguistic activity can be demonstrated is through the presentation of data that show semantic boundaries to be porous. The meanings of words for parts of the face are so often altered in the history of Romance that it suggests that perhaps many of them are never rigid at all, and certainly not logical necessities; words for one part of the face can with apparent ease come to be used for another. This fact suit the 'frame' approaches based on Gestalt theory and field analysis (e.g., Baldinger 1980, Ullmann 1962; some of the data here discussed were presented in Zauner 1903:355-433).

Latin had three words for 'cheek,' that is, 'the side of the face below the eye.'[1] None of their descendants mean 'cheek' in Romance. BUCCA was borrowed into other languages from Latin with the meaning 'cheek' (e.g., Welsh *boch*, Greek βοῦκκα, Breton *boch* and Berber *abeqqa*: Corominas and Pascual 1980-, 18603), but its Romance descendants do not have that meaning. In Western Romance they mean 'mouth' (It. *bocca*, Sp. *boca*, Fr. *bouche*, etc.; even the earliest attestations in Western Romance are indisputedly 'mouth'—see e.g., Smith 1977:255-61). In Rumanian *bucă* means 'buttock.' Apart from *geană* mentioned above, GENA and MALA do not survive; these disappearances may be partly due to formal similarity with a number of other words. GENA (ultimately related to English *chin*, Germanic *kinn* 'cheek,' and Sanskrit *hanu* 'jaw') may in addition have been the victim of excessive ambiguity, apparently being usable for any area between the eyelid and the chin (inclusive). The usual Latin word for 'mouth' was ŌS, ŌRIS; but the meaning of this word was also capable of spreading out beyond its boundaries. Even in ca. 200 B.C. Plautus used the phrase *ore rubicundo* to mean 'red face' (not 'red lips'):

> rufus quidam, ventriosus, crassis suris, subniger,
> magno capite, acutis oculis, ore rubicundo, admodum
> magnis pedibus. (*Pseudolus* 4.7.115-17)

It seems that OS could as easily be used to mean 'face' as 'mouth.' Ambiguity may not have often arisen, but if it did it is understandable, if not predictable, that in some circumstances BUCCA might have been considered an acceptable alternative, inasmuch as the inside of the cheek is indeed part of the mouth. OS might also have been gradually affected by impending homonymy with several words; in particular, once the neuter gender fell out of fashion, the accusative would be likely to be *OREM in speech, and

---

[1] This is the definition given in the indispensable *The Advanced Learner's Dictionary of Current English* (Oxford, 1963).

in every case except the awkwardly imparisyllabic nominative the form might have appeared unacceptably close to AUREM 'ear.' As Ullmann (1957:293-94) argued, change through "contiguity" of sense (as has happened to BUCCA) is a means of change not an explanation, for the initial impulse often arises in some perceived deficiency in the previous lexical unit. [aw] > [o] is probably quite a late change, but even before it occurred there were forms of speech in Italy that had [o] where Latin had [aw]—as in the celebrated case of *plaustrum/plostrum*—and in words with close semantic relations even near-homonymy can inspire therapeutic reactions, as Malkiel (1979) suggested has happened to Sp. *hasta* and *hacia*. Something similar is happening with the English homonyms *oral* and *aural*, both normally with [ɔ:]; it seems that in cases where the distinction is important, the form [ɔ́:ɹəl] is usually understood to be *oral*, and the word *aural* has either to be replaced (by e.g., *auditory*) or given an ad-hoc spelling-pronunciation [áωɹəl]. The combination of occasional homonymy, potential ambiguity, and the availability in many cases of an intelligible substitute in BUCCA for 'mouth,' might suffice as a reasonable explanation for the loss of OS and the downward shift of the southern part of the frame for BUCCA.

The definitive adoption of BUCCA for 'mouth' probably postdates the end of the empire and predates the end of the general Old Western Romance community, in view of the Welsh and Rumanian evidence. This is also likely to be the period of the surprising adoption of a Greek word to mean 'face'; Spanish and Occitan *cara*, and Fr. *chère* were borrowed from (probably Byzantine) Greek κάρα. Corominas and Pascual (1980-, 1:839-42) cautiously accept this etymon; a Byzantine dating helps allay some of their doubts. This borrowing is intrinsically unpredictable enough to suggest that there was some kind of lexical uneasiness or deficiency that it was able to relieve (cp. Goddard 1980). If the definitive shift in BUCCA and the adoption of κάρα can be seen as roughly contemporary 6th-c. developments, perhaps the problems of OS can be seen as a contributory factor to them both. Other words for 'face' seem not to have been acceptable; VULTUS has not survived in Spain, although it has in Italian *volto* (*bulto* being a 15th-c. Latinism in Spanish, meaning originally 'image'). FACIES might have been felt even less unambiguous than OS for 'face' in view of the width of its semantic range ('shape,' 'form,' 'appearance,' 'character,' 'surface,' as well as 'face'). The availability of BUCCA for the 'inside of the cheek,' i.e., 'mouth,' is occasionally attested from Classical times: a cliché *quod in buccam venerit*, meaning originally 'whatever comes into your mouth,' even developed to apply to writing as well, as in *quod in bucam venerit scribito* (Cicero, *Atticus* 1.12.4).

The diminutive form of AURIS 'ear,' AURICULA, is attested as a lexicalized form with no apparent diminutive meaning from Classical times. The suffixed form becomes the normal word for 'ear' in most Romance languages (e.g., Sp. *oreja*, Ptg. *orelha*, It. *orecchio*, Fr. *oreille*). Probably this is partly because that form was unambiguous, but AUREM in speech was often not (with HORAM and AURUM in the lexicon as well as *OREM). In writing the form continued normally to be AURIS, unaffixed. St. Isidore, in early 7th-c. Spain unhelpfully links both AURIS and AURICULA separately with AUDIO, rather than with each other; discussing a supposed relationship between LAURUS 'laurel' and LAUDES 'praise,' he adds in passing *ut in auriculis, quæ initio audiculæ dictæ sunt* (*Etymologiæ* 17.7.2; Lindsay 1962); elsewhere (11.1.46) *aures* is said to be a corrupted form of *audes*. *Auriculæ* are not mentioned in this latter chapter, which discusses parts of the body. The meaning 'mouth' could not have similarly transferred to a diminutive form of OS, since OSCULUM already meant 'kiss' and the rarer OSCILLUM meant 'mask.' In Rumanian, where BUCCA did not move in this way, OS disappeared nonetheless; the word for 'throat' shifted, GULA >*gură* 'mouth,' with the eventual result that 'throat' acquired a Slavonic neologism in *gît*. This implies that the process was a drag-chain rather than a push-chain; i.e., that the impending loss of OS led to the shift in BUCCA or GULA respectively, rather than vice versa.

If there were always strict logical necessities for the use of words, such shifts as that in BUCCA would be hard to envisage. But it could be that such distinctive semantic features as words possess tend to have been sharpened factitiously by academicians, lawyers, grammarians, and allied pedants; in their natural state the meanings of many words do not have strict intrinsic borders so much as transition zones, since the edges of the relevant frame can be shifted if the speaker wishes. The 'cheek' is an instructive example of this lability. It seems likely that during the shift in BUCCA from 'cheek' to 'mouth' there was a period when the word could mean either or both, as if the border had been suspended; it may have been at that time that suffixed forms arose to refer unambiguously to the 'cheek,' like Portuguese *bochecha* and Corsican *buccella* (Bonfante 1951:372). *Buccella* in Latin had meant 'morsel'; the diminutive in the Corsican form is lexicalized out of significance. The Portuguese are able to use *face* (< FACIEM) as well as *bochecha* for 'cheek,' but *face* can still also mean 'face' (or 'front'), so there are no distinctive edges to the cheek there either. In general, though, once BUCCA had moved to 'mouth,' and 'mouth' had come to be considered as its primary meaning (or, in European terminology, the center of the word's semasiological field; cp. Baldinger 1980:289), the meaning of 'cheek' seems to have been left in as unsatisfactory a position as the 'mouth' had been before, having no unambiguous word available.

This indistinctiveness seems to have been the impulse for the extraordinary activity in this semantic area, both neologizing and shifting, that took place in the period before the emergence of naked written vernacular. French (*joue*) Occitan (*gauta*) and Catalan (*galta*) borrowed a Celtic word (*GAUTA), Rumanian a Slavonic word (*obraz*, which can also mean 'face'; Manoliu 1974); the Italian *guancia* is in origin a Germanic word (WANKA), and *ganascia* a Greek word (γνάθος) borrowed from the Byzantines. Italian dialects, in fact, according to the maps in Kahane (1941), have amassed a total of fifteen different etyma for their words for 'cheek.' Old Spanish did not borrow. Early Medieval Spaniards seem to have considered moving the reflex of TEMPORA, the word for 'temples,' downwards; Dworkin (1982) has pointed out that there is no obvious extralinguistic upper boundary to the cheek, so that the shift from 'temple' to 'cheek' that seems to have been initiated in North-West Spain (e.g., *tenllera* < TEMPORA) and also in Old Castilian (*tienlla*; cp. Alvar 1980) was a simple one to perform. Castilian, however, eventually preferred instead to move the sphere of reference of MAXILLA upwards.

In Italy MAXILLA (the Latin for 'jawbone') has derivatives meaning 'cheek' as well as 'jaw,' but Standard Italian has decided to keep the word *mascella* as 'jaw.' The use of *mascelle* in Dante's *Inferno* XXXII 107, for example, can only mean 'jaw,' since they chatter;

> quando un altro gridò: "Che hai tu, Bocca?
> non ti basta sonar con le mascelle
> se tu non latri? qual diavol ti tocca?"

(*Bocca* here is the man's name). In Classical Latin the word first meant the lower jaw-bone, but Pliny referred to crocodiles' upper jaws with *maxilla: maxillas crocodilus tantum superiores movet* (*Natural History* 11.159), and that distinction between upper and lower may not have applied colloquially. The Rumanians pulled MAXILLA in a different direction, so that *măseà* now means 'molar tooth' (although this may also involve nominalization, via ellipsis of the adjective MAXILLARE). In the West, however, Late Latin seems to be beginning to spread the domain of MAXILLA upwards and outwards. In the Vulgate, for example, the non-Classical *mandibula* is used to clarify *maxilla* in the following passage where the translator wishes specifically to refer to the 'jawbone of an ass' in Judges 15.15: *inventamque maxillam, id est, mandibulam asini, quæ jacebat, arripiens*. This renders a phrase using one Hebrew word that could mean either; the same bone is referred to four times in the next four verses, twice with each word; the implication of the phrasing is that *maxilla* is insufficiently precise, needing to be clarified with the more technical *mandibula*. *Maxilla* is used to translate the Greek σιαγών 'jaw,' in Christ's advice in Luke 6.29; *et qui te percutit in maxillam, praebe et alteram*. It may seem from this that Christ was not advising us to "turn the other cheek" but "offer the other jaw," i.e., that if the attacker removes some of your lower teeth you should offer him the upper ones as well. The Vulgate version of St. Matthew (5.39), however, also translating σιαγών, specifies the *dextera maxilla; quis te percusserit in dexteram maxillam tuam, præbe illi et alteram*. Here the *maxillæ* are distinguishable on either side of a vertical line, 'left' and 'right,' rather than of the horizontal line envisaged by Pliny, 'upper' and 'lower'; the change has already progressed quite a way.

Isidore comments (*Etymologiæ* 11.1.44-46):

> Malæ sunt eminentes sub oculis partes ad protectionem eorum suppositæ. Vocatæ autem malæ sive quod infra oculos prominent in rotunditatem, quam Græci appellant, sive quod

sint supra maxillas. Maxillæ per diminutionem a malis; sicuti paxillus a palo, taxillus a talo. Mandibulæ sunt maxillarum partes, ex quo et nomen factum.

This seems to be evidence comparable to Kahane's diagnosis (1941) based on Italian dialects: that in 7th-c. Spain *maxillæ* covered at least the jaws and the fleshy part of the cheek. Perhaps, since *mala* is likely to have been absent from the vernacular, it covered the cheekbones as well. Elsewhere Isidore refers to the *dextra maxilla* and the *sinistra*, as being the place for two canine teeth each, which suggests that *maxillæ* here are distinguished as in St. Matthew, by a vertical barrier (like 'cheeks') rather than by a horizontal one (as 'jaws' are), but still include the jawbones within their reference; *Sequentes canini vocantur, quorum duo in dextra maxilla et duo in sinistra sunt* (11.1.52). The three uses of *maxilla* in the Visigothic liturgy suggest that the word may mean both together there too;[2] they echo the Biblical requirement to offer the other *maxilla* to your attackers, although only the third repeats it lexically. All three are from the Sacramentary (Ferotin 1912):

774 ...dorsum utique ad flagella ponens, maxillas vero ad palmas constituens, faciem quoque tuam a confusione sputorum non retrahens
803 ...Iesu...qui passionis tuæ tempore dorsum ad flagella, maxillas ad palmas ponens, nec contumax, nec contradicens, inventus es
809 Jesu, Deus Noster, cui (=qui) maxillam prebuisti <percus>soribus tuis...

---

[2] The Visigothic Latin texts are currently being given a manual concordance by the Latin department of the University of Santiago de Compostela; the huge corpus of Laws and Liturgy is completed, and the other texts have begun to follow. Since Spain is the main centre of 7th-century literacy, the concordance is of great help to Medieval Latinists and Romance linguists alike. I am very grateful to the *fichero*'s organizer, Manuela Domínguez, for letting me use it; she wishes it to be known that any Romance scholar is welcome to do likewise.

It looks as if the transition period is over, and the jaws have slipped out of the potential reference of MAXILLA, by the 10th century. One of the 10th-c. Silos glossaries published by García de Diego (1933) offers MALAS: *maxillas*; the Silos glossary published by Goetz (1984: 116), the unpublished San Millán glossary (*Em* 46), and the allied glossary in Goetz (1984:83), all offer *Manas. malas. maxillas*; although glossary equivalents can often be inexact, since they derive from the original context of the manuscript gloss, such a bald correspondence suggests that the distinction between *mala* 'upper cheek' and *maxilla* 'lower cheek,' postulated by Isidore, is not widely felt in the 10th c. even if it was in the 7th. The slightly later use of a word transcribed from Arabic script as *maxšilla* (Corriente 1980: 185) in the Hispano-Arabic poetry of Ibn Guzmán apparently means 'cheek'; the lower edge of this part of the frame has gradually moved upwards. By the time of the early 13th-c. graphical reforms, which make vernacular usage easier for us to assess (cp. Wright 1982: Chap. 5), the Castilian word seems only able to mean 'cheek.' The pregnant abbess in Berceo's *Milagros de Nuestra Señora* 508*b* (Dutton 1971) is said to have freckles on her *masiellas*, which cannot possibly be her 'jawbone': *fuéronseli faciendo peccas ennas masiellas*, apparently a symptom of pregnancy. The mother of the converted Jewish boy in *Milagros* 364*b* is said to have torn her *massiellas* with her nails, and that too cannot refer to the 'jawbone': *tenié con sus oncejas las massiellas rompidas*. In the *Libro de Alexandre*, 50*d* young Alexander lets his feelings appear in his *maxiella: parecies' la rencura del cuer en la maxiella* (Canas 1978: 104; Nelson 1979: 162). This use of the item for 'cheeks,' now apparently the norm in Castile (and borrowed with that meaning in Basque *masaila*), is occasionally also visible to us in the Latin written by Medieval Castilians, since before Nebrija (as Rico 1978 points out) it was normal for even well-educated Castilians to write "Latin" as Castilian in Latinizing disguise. In the 14th c., St. Bridget saw a vision of the Virgin Birth, which was put into Latin by her Spanish confessor Alfonso (formerly Bishop of Jaén); after the baby was born, *quem tunc mater suscepit in manibus et strinxit eum ad pectus suum, et cum maxilla et pectore calefaciebat eum cum magna leticia et tenera compassione materna* (Bergh 1967:7.21.16; cp. Bergh 1981). We cannot imagine that Mary comforted her baby by pressing him to her jawbone: she pressed him to her cheek, her *mejilla*, thinly cloaked with a Latinate form in *maxilla*.[3] Vernacular Bibles translating Luke 6.29 now suggest that Christ told us to turn the other cheek. (The Authorized English Version of 1611 gives "to him who strikes you on the cheek, offer the other also"; English *cheek* by then means 'cheek,' although *cheek* too in the past had meant 'jawbone').

Mejilla, it seems, no longer meant 'jaw' in the 13th c. By this point, the Castilians had decided instead to use for 'jaw' metaphors taken from the construction industry. *Carrillo*, as Dworkin (1982) argued, originally meant 'pulley,' 'block and tackle,' as indeed it still does; and by the 13th century it had been borrowed for originally figurative, and subsequently literal, use as 'jaw' (presumably comparing the pulley to the joint of the lower jaw). Corominas (1954-57; *s.v.*) and Alarcos (1973) both commented on this meaning as attested in Alfonso X's *General Estoria* 1:222: *en el Nilo a una bestia que llaman cocadriz...quando come muerde, e non mueve el carriello de yuso si non el de suso solo...en amos los carriellos a muchos dientes e muy fuertes*. The reference to upper and lower *carriellos* assures us that it meant 'jaws' (cp. the comment in Pliny 11.159 above and Spitzer 1924). This is also the probable meaning in the *Libro de Alexandre* 469c (Cañas 1978: 151; Nelson 1979:264), where Hector tells Paris that in war it is no good looking pretty, you need strength and determination:

> Non se faz la fazienda por cabellos peinados
> nin por ojos fermosos nin çapatos dorados;
> mester ha puños duros, carrillos denodados,
> ca lanças nin espadas non saben de falagos.

Paris is being told, with *carrillos denodados*, to grit his teeth and take the fighting seriously.

---

[3] *Maxilla* here might also be a scribal error for *mamilla*, Latin "nipple." On the use of Medieval Latin as an indicator of vernacular vocabulary, see now the excellent article by Rothwell (1980).

It was no good. *Carrillo* could not remain within its boundaries; it soon changed to mean 'cheek.' In Nebrija's Spanish-Latin dictionary of ca. 1495 (Macdonald 1973), Spanish *carrillo de cara hinchado* is translated as *bucca*, i.e., 'cheek,' for BUCCA never meant 'jaw' despite its wanderings. *Carrillo* (*como rodaja*), 'pulley-wheel,' is a separate entry, translated as Latin *vertebra* (which, to add to the fun, meant 'joint' in Classical Latin rather than 'vertebra'), although *rodaja* is rendered as *trochlea*. Nebrija translates *mexilla de la cara* into Latin as both *mala* and *maxilla*, and (*"antiguamente"*) *gena*. The Academy Dictionary now offers the thought that the *mejilla* is the top part of the cheek and the *carrillo* the lower; if so, the words are moving upwards in sequence, but although Lang (1887:72) agreed with this it seems very doubtful whether many Spanish-speakers are aware of such a distinction. This looks like a case of the Academy trying to impose a clear boundary between two words where there is none. (There may be a register distinction though; *mejillas* are more appropriate, for example, in love poetry).

Nothing daunted by the loss of *carrillo*, the 'jaw' took on another constructional metaphor. Modern Spanish *quijada*, Old Spanish *quexada* and *quexar*, Portuguese *queixo* (which meant formerly 'jaw,' but now also means 'chin'), Catalan *queix*, and *queixal* 'molar tooth,' all seem to come from an originally adjectival derivative *CAPSEUS of Proto-Romance CAPSA 'box' or CAPSUS 'framework'; their history is complex enough to have appealed to Malkiel (1945) . (Perhaps the affixed form *quixada* or *quexada* was the preferred form to avoid confusion with *quexo* [< QUASSIO] and *queso* [< CASEUM].) The Latin-Romance glossaries of ca. 1400 edited by Castro (1936) offer *quixada* as the Romance gloss for all of MALA (*Escorial* 1478), GENA (*Toledo* 745, *Palacio* 131) and MANDIBULA (*Toledo* 843, *Palacio* 132). This seems to imply that the meaning of *quijada* was in the process of following its precursors up the side of the face, but if so, that climb was reversed during the 15th century, for Nebrija offers only *mandibula* as the Latin counterpart for *quixar* (*o quixada*) . Other items for 'jaw' adopted from an original meaning of some kind of 'framework' turn up in Italy (Bonfante 1951:383). The conclusion from all this movement—also adumbrated in De Witte (1950:121-27)—is that the cheek knows no boundaries, and such distinctive virtue as exists in its lexical items works by means of polarity alone; the semantic structure of Spanish wanted to fit a framework with more or less distinct boundaries, but the external world provided no such boundaries to guide the positioning of the frame.

Affixation in these cases seems to be one of the lexical resources available for differentiation of meaning, rather than involving the addition of any intrinsic sense in the affix to the meaning of the lexeme. An *auricula* was not smaller than an *auris*, nor a Corsican *buccella* smaller than a *bucca*. In Spanish, the old form for 'heart,' *cuer*, has grown to *corazón* (perhaps to forestall confusion with *cuero* or *cuerpo*?), but the apparent augmentative force in -*azón* does not prevent the word being applied to hearts of all sizes (though Corominas claims that it originally applied to the hearts of warriors or lovers!). The 'head,' Latin CAPUT, has acquired a distinctive -*eza* (<-ITIA) ending in Spanish *cabeza*, to distinguish it from *cabo* (<CAPUT), now generally meaning 'end'—and, indeed, if applied to the anatomy, it can as easily mean the other end, so ambiguity is more possible here than it is in the normal extensions to other applications of words for 'head' to be found in all languages (cp. Cravens 1982:54-55)—; the -*eza* ending, which was usually used to form post-adjectival nouns (see Pattison 1975: 147), has here no semantic content. It may indeed be merely a reflex of a variant plural form CAPITIA for CAPITA (see Corominas and Pascual 1980-, 1:711), although CAPITIA as attested was the plural of CAPITIUM, 'head-covering.' (The Italian *cappezzolo*, 'nipple,' does, however, preserve some semantic point in the final extra affix).

Noses are also of interest (as Lang 1887:69-70 and others have observed) . Outside Iberia NASUM survives (It. *naso*, Fr. *nez*; also Cat. *nas*). Non-Catalan Iberian noses lose NASUM for a conflated form derived from both NARES 'nostrils' (or 'sense of smell') and its late derivative NARICÆ; *NARICES is the postulated etymon of Sp. *narices*, originally meaning 'nostrils,' but now in the singular *nariz* meaning 'nose' (in both Spanish and Portuguese). Perhaps there also existed in Very Old Spanish a non-palatalized form (i.e., < NARICAS rather than *NARICES) off which to coin *narigudo* ('big-nosed'). *Narices* still means 'nostrils' as well as 'nose' (and 'noses'), but whereas other languages have kept the singular form with the meaning of 'nostril' (e.g., Cat. *nariu*, It. *narice*), Spanish now has no singular word for 'nostril' and has to say 'window of the nose,' *ventana de la nariz*. This sequence of events seems perverse; the sensible distinction between NASUM and NARIS was lost in Spain, and both forms were replaced by the ambiguous derivative NARICÆ/ -ES, which eventually comes to have different meanings in the singular and plural. Perhaps the first stage lay in the expansion of the meaning of NARES to include 'nose.' NASUM is not used in Isidore 11.1.47, where NARES is the whole 'nose' as well as the 'nostrils.' Chindaswinth's Law 5.6.4. 3-4 (also from Gothic Spain) twice has NASUM and NARES co-referring in the same sentence: *qui in naribus si sic percussus est, ut nasum ex integrum perdat, C. solidos percussor exolvat...si vero nasus ita conlisus est, ut pars turpata narium pateat*. Another of these codes prescribes that women who carry out circumcision should (in theory) be punished *naribus abscisis*, which can only involve cutting off their noses, since nostrils cannot be cut off. Perhaps it was during the stage when NARES meant both 'nose' and 'nostrils' that the suffixed form came into general use, to create a semantic contrast between NARICÆ or NARICES 'nostrils' and NARES 'nose'; one of the glosses in Goetz's anthologies (1894:573) suggests that *narices* was thought to be the plural of *naris* (Cp. Corominas and Pascual 1980-, 4:213). Both the loss of NASUM in the first place and of NARES subsequently remain inexplicable. It would be desperation to see the replacement of NARES by the affixed form as in some way analogous or connected with the loss of AURES for AURICULAS.

There are other cases of meaning-shift across the Castilian face. *Barbilla* 'chin' is in origin the diminutive form of *barba* 'beard,' but even this sensible distinction is lost when *barba* is used, as it now often is, to mean 'chin.' In the *Poem of the Cid* it was unambiguously 'beard': see Bly (1978) and Smith (1977:261-62). *Barbilla*, consequently, would now be an inappropriate choice for either 'little beard' or 'little chin.' CILIUM was classically 'eyelid,' and still so to Isidore (11.1.42); its Spanish derivative *ceja* is 'eyebrow,' just as *sobrecejo* < SUPERCILIUM 'eyebrow' moved north to become the Spanish word for 'frown,' but other Romance derivatives of CILIUM, such as It. *ciglio*, Fr. *cil*, and Ptg. *celha*, mean 'eyelash.' Latin seems not to have had a lexicalization for 'eyelashes' other than merely being part of the 'eyelids,' *palpebræ*. Pliny is said by Lewis and Short to have used *palpebræ* for 'eyelashes' rather than 'eyelids,' but the most eyelash-like example can be reasonably interpreted to mean both together: *capnos fruticosa* (a plant)...*eadem evulsas palpebras renasci prohibet* (*Natural History* 25.99). In any event, Romance derivatives of PALPEBRA, although often phonetically peculiar, such as Sp. *párpado*, succeed in referring to the 'eyelid' alone. For 'eyelash' Rumanian took over GENA (see above); Spanish *pestaña*, Portuguese *pestana*, Catalan *pestanya* and Gascon *pestane* borrowed the Basque *pizta* (although Corominas and Pascual 1980-, 4:506-9 point out that early Castilian uses could also mean 'eyebrow,' and regional Catalan forms include both brow and lid as well). *Pizta* did not mean 'eyelash' in Basque, but 'blear in the eye' (and might originally have been an Indo-European borrowing). Isidore just calls eyelashes *capilli*, 'hairs,' in *Etymologiæ* 11.1.40: *in summitate autem palpebrarum locis...extant adnati ordine servato capilli tutelam oculis ministrantes;* Sp. *cabellos* (< CAPILLOS), and even *pelos* (< PILOS), would be unsuitable now for 'eyelashes.' One of the ca. 1400 Latin-Spanish glosses (Castro 1936) offers PALPEBRA *por pestanna del ojo;* and Nebrija's Spanish-Latin dictionary (ca. 1495) offered the converse in *pestaña*, (*pelo del ojo*): *palpebra*, which might mean that the meaning of *pestañas* was threatening to creep inwards onto the eyelids in the 15th century; if so, *párpados* has effectively repelled them, for there is a clear distinction in Modern Spanish between the two words. *Párpado del ojo*, however, is rendered as Latin *gena* by Nebrija; GENA could once be used for the 'eyesocket,' but Nebrija's evidence collectively suggests uncertainty on his part. This would in a sense be entirely appropriate, since medieval uncertainty is the clearest feature of the phenomena being here examined.

The forms here examined so far collectively suggest that uncertainty about the boundaries of words for parts of the face in Spain has led to a variety of therapeutic reactions: the loss of some polyvalent words (OS, GENA, MALA); the acquisition of derived forms (*barbilla, cabeza, nariz*); the limitation of the reference of a word to only a part of its semasiological field, which can either correspond to the original meaning (*pestaña, quijada*), or the extended (*mejilla, boca, carrillo, ceja*); and the acquisition of originally metaphorical uses into literal terms (*quijada, carrillo*; cp. also *coronilla* 'crown of head,' *muela* 'tooth' < MOLAM 'millstone,' Ptg. *testa* 'forehead' and

Fr. *tête* 'head' < TESTAM 'pot'—Cp. Cravens [1982] and German *kopfe* < CUPPA). Other expedients include: the humanization of animal terms (Sp. *rostro* 'face' < ROSTRUM 'beak'; the reverse happened in CRINEM > *crin*, `woman's hair' > 'horsehair'); the adoption of onomatopoeia (*garganta* 'throat' is apparently such, although the presence in other Romance areas of cognate forms meaning 'gland,' 'molar,' 'jaw' and 'cheek' [Bonfante 1951:380-81] does not inspire confidence in this word's value as a clarificatory term); and the possibility of recruiting foreign words. Source languages in this last category include not only Basque (*pestaña*) but also Arabic (*nuca* 'nape'), Byzantine Greek (*cara*), Technical Latin (*mandíbula*, in the 18th century), and French (*mentón* 'chin,' borrowed at the end of the last century, perhaps intended to be a clearly shaven alternative to *barba* or *barbilla*). If Dworkin (1982), following Covarrubias, is right to derive *sienes* 'temples' from SENES 'old men,' as a reaction to the southward creep or incipient desuetude of *tienlla*, the source used for that acquisition seems little short of desperation as a remedy to preserve distinctiveness in linguistic features where facial features have proved to lack it.

The above data come from standard Castilian. Other Spanish dialects offer us comparable developments. Borrego Nieto (1981) for example, studying the vocabulary of Villapera de Sayago (in the province of Zamora) finds that there *rostro* only means 'cheek' (300); that for several speakers *pestaña* does include the 'eyelid' and even the 'eyebrow' (305); the pupil of the eye has metaphorically attracted the word for 'oak-apple,' *bogayo* (179); and *quijada* has been confined to the jaws of animals, with *mandibula* being generally available for the human 'jaw.' Penny (1978), studying Tudanca, finds a regular use of *picota* for 'nose' (augmentative of *pico* 'beak'), *garguelu* rather than *garganta* for 'throat,' and an apparently neat distinction between *barba* 'chin' and *barbas* 'beard.' Penny (1969), studying the Montes de Pas nearby, finds *papos* for 'cheeks' (rather than 'double chin,' as in Standard Castilian), and both *quijas*, unaugmented, and *carrieras*, probably a variant of O. Cast. *carriellos*, for both human and animal 'jaws,' with *mandíbulas* also available for human jaws. (These three works exemplify a welcome trend for dialectologists to group extensive vocabulary data into onomasiological sections, without ignoring those forms that happen to correspond to standard Castilian.). Iglesias (1981) has also pointed out a colloquial Spanish liking for using proper names for parts of the body, although the head is not particularly favored with this device. A recent study on dialectal French words for parts of the body (Bimson and Thurman 1980) offers the following semantic shifts within the head, in different areas of France: *bouche* meaning 'lips'; *gaugno*, 'fish gills,' also meaning 'lip,' 'jaw,' 'mouth' or 'cheek'; *goule* moving from 'throat' to 'mouth' to 'lip,' and *gueule* from 'throat' to 'mouth' or 'jaw'; *gorge* changing from 'windpipe' (GURGULIO) to 'throat' to 'mouth'; *baras* shifting from 'beard' to 'jaw'; *visage* from 'face' to 'cheek'; etc. The distribution of isoglosses in that study supports the idea of changes occurring in chain-shifts, as proposed here; this is to be expected in a "frame" theory, since a shift in part of the framework simultaneously affects both sides of the relevant border.

Amidst all this turmoil stands firm the eye itself. OCULUS is still with us as the Romance word for 'eye.' No other word has seriously crossed into its territory (and LUMEN has left it). Nor does it mean 'earlobe' in Meglenitic. Nonetheless *ojo* is a net exporter. Ramón Trives (1979) analyzes 32 lexicalizations of *ojo*, based on six central semes; among other things *ojo* means 'keyhole,' 'eye of a needle,' 'hole in cheese,' 'skylight,' 'porthole,' a 'spring of water,' 'round church window,' and even within the body it is not only 'callus on the hand' but a common word for an aperture at the other end of our anatomy, the connotations of which, combined with the literalization of originally metaphorical uses—may eventually lead to another word than *ojo* being preferred for the 'eye.' It seems to be losing the abstract sense of 'sight' to *vista*—in Old Spanish *ojo* was used this way (e.g., see Smith 1977: 253-54), but now the closest equivalent to the English 'with the naked eye,' for example, is probably *a simple vista*; prominent sights *nos saltan a la vista* whereas only an insect can appropriately *saltarnos al ojo*. (The same applies, perhaps even more so, to *oreja* 'ear' and *oído* 'hearing'). Possibly this makes *vista* the current favorite if any word is to take over the meaning of 'eye' from *ojo* (a statement of possibility, not a prediction!). Classical poets could apparently use GENA to mean 'eye,' but otherwise words for other facial features have succeeded in remaining outside these particular borders.

This suggests that the facial boundaries of the eye are semantically more real than most; maybe this corresponds to extralinguistic reality. The internal parts of the eye, however, attract metaphor. *Pupila* dies out from the vernacular, and is subsequently borrowed from Latin into most Romance languages; *pupila* and *niña* 'pupil' (literally 'girl') in Spanish (cp. Nebrija: *niñilla del ojo*) are examples of what Corominas proposes (art. *niña*) is a near-universal linguistic tendency to use a word that originally represents the reflection perceived in the pupil (mentioned also by Isidore, *Etymologiæ* 11.1.37). Fr. *prunelle* is, however, taken from 'sloe.' English and Spanish *iris* were taken from the Renaissance Latin *iris* 'rainbow,' ultimately from Classical Gk. ἶρις; in Greek it seems not to have meant 'iris of the eye,' and in Classical Latin the 'rainbow' was *arcus (pluvius)*. Isidore did not use *iris* (for the iris of the eye) but *corona* (11.1.38), although in the event *corona* was adopted higher up as *coronilla* 'crown of head.' (Spanish now combines both classical words in *arco iris* 'rainbow'). *Niña* and *iris* still seem intuitively to be live metaphors; it is not clear why the adoption of a form for use as a literal word has been avoided, unless the center of the eye (as 'evil eye') attracts the same unease as weasels or other traditional recipients of euphemism.

One conclusion to be drawn from all the turbulence may be that it is worth considering whether semantic fixity is more rigid at some times than others. Times of comparatively wide education and high literacy (such as the present) may encourage professionals to impose clearer distinctions than naturally exist otherwise. The continental European tradition of semantic analysis, as represented in the work of Baldinger and many others, sees the function of the lexicon as an attempt to impose some kind of anthropocentric rationality on a reality which initially comes into the brain as a confused flux of only slightly differentiated impressions; in order for us to be able to talk intelligibly at all some kind of criteria have to be set up to enable us to be as unambiguous as necessary about whether we are referring, for example, to the 'cheek' or the 'jaw,' the 'night' or the 'day,' etc. Without the intervention of self-conscious logical semanticists, the question of whether there is an exact boundary line, and if so, where, is not likely to seem important. Baldinger's section on legal language, for example (1980:42-61), shows that even though we all know what 'day' and 'night' mean, the precise border depends on artificial conventions such as lighting-up times and case-law. To this extent, semantic boundaries seem comparable to dialect boundaries. Left to themselves, cognate dialects have transition zones rather than strict diagnostic lines between competing variables; they do not bundle the zones in the same place, and it requires some kind of artificial boundary to move the isoglosses (heteroglosses) closer together as each side of the transition zone acquires a separate prestige norm as a model for approximation in style-shifting (see Trudgill and Chambers 1980:10-14). Similarly, if lawyers, teachers, members of the Academy feel the urge to do so, they can decide to superimpose rigid lines on the semantic transition zones that occur between the prototypical areas of reference; so the Academy Dictionary tries to distinguish the meaning of *mejilla* as being intrinsically higher up the face than that of *carrillo*, and may have had sufficient authority to affect the usage of some people, although most Spaniards seem unaware of the distinction. Similarly, *mandíbula* has probably kept its strict meaning in Castilian only by being largely restricted to the usage of anatomists. Such scientific attempts to standardize the fit between our semantic framework and the outside world are rare, however, between the end of the Roman Empire and the Renaissance. Isidore attempts it, but his attempts are not often convincing. Many surviving glosses from that period imply the acceptability of considerable semantic leeway. Kohler suggested (1954) that Spanish is still in this state, citing *barba* 'chin' (505) as one example of several words that are often used to mean something close to, but different from, what might be expected (in this case, 'beard').

Rothwell (1962) argued that it is unproductive to apply logical semantics to Medieval France, since "in a language untrammelled by grammarians and academies the development of the vocabulary can often be quite undisciplined" (30); in an area where time, weights, coins, and other apparently objective units varied from place to place, it is hardly likely that there was sufficiently rigid agreement on other matters to permit clarity in general "structure." "Frame" Theory is less inappropriate under such circumstances in that it is only the existence of a rough boundary that is postulated, rather than the ability to draw it precisely or position it exactly. In Medieval Spain, words of many kinds seem to have surprisingly unfixed edges in the 14th-c. *Libro de Buen Amor*, in meaning as well as in form (particularly as regards derivational morphology; cp. Adams 1970). A research task that is crying out to be done is an investigation into whether or not semantic distinctions became rigid during the Alfonsine standardizations of the late 13th century at the same time as much of the spelling and some of the grammar. Now that we have to hand the Madison Concordances (Kasten and Nitti 1978), such an investigation might be possible to carry out. My guess is that before the arrival of dictionaries they were not so standardized. If Spanish words from the same etymon (*EXCURTIONEM) can mean 'toad' (Castilian *escuerzo*), 'hedgehog' (Mozarabic *uxcurchón*), 'scorpion' (Aragonese *escurzón*), 'viper' (Catalan *escurçó*) and even perhaps 'worm' (in the *Libro de Buen Amor* 1544c; although Hook [1979-80] argues persuasively that it means 'toad' here[4]), we need not find the gyrations of facial features surprising.

Semantic change often plays only a small part in modern discussions of historical linguistic theory (e.g., Bynon 1977). This is not because it is a small subject; a glance at any etymological dictionary shows that a surprisingly large number of words come from an undisputed etymon with a different meaning. Nor is it often discussed seriously in synchronic generative studies on semantics, although many European writers on semantics such as Ullmann (1962), Waldron (1967), Baldinger (1980:277-309), and specifically on Romance, Cremona (1959), consider it intelligently and show that it is possible to be rational and even "scientific" if we have sufficient data. Ullmann, for example, sets up a category of Semantic Change through "contiguity," which is what we have examined here. The reason for the shyness among generative theorists must be, at least partly, the difficulty in describing this kind of semantic change in easily annotated form such as could be used for an algorithmic input. But linguistics has grown out of the behaviorist belief that language has no meaning; it is currently

---

[4] Hook and I find our approaches interconnect here (Wright 1976:18).

growing out of the assumption (sponsored by those wishing to acquire funds from bodies wishing to invent translation machines) that natural language has the precision of computer language; with any luck it can soon grow out of the idea (despairingly proclaimed by those who instinctively want linguistics to be a natural science) that language-change runs according to some kind of predetermined typologically-induced "drift" (see Matthews 1982, Wright 1983, etc.); as part of the same tendency, checklist theories of semantics will give way to less logical varieties. "Drift," algorithmic syntax, and semantic rigidity have been ideals in the minds of linguists. If we wish to study language as it is rather than as we wish it were, we have to accept that the oppositions inherent in distinctive linguistic features at times have distinctive virtue by means of potential contrasts within the Gestalt rather than by logically necessary and referentially-precise content with fixed square-bracketable edges. This applies not only to colors. The history of Spanish words for the face suggests that facial features (other, perhaps, than the eye) have this kind of indistinctiveness, and it is probable that the history of other semantic fields in Romance may lead to comparable conclusions. Sampson (1979:59ff.) suggested that the facts of semantic change argue against the existence of semantic structure; but it would be fairer to see them as counterarguments to "checklist" theories alone, for they are easy to explain as the results of minor shifts in the fitting of a "frame" onto human perceptions.[5]

1994 POSTSCRIPT

This paper was published in *Romance Philology*, 38, 1985, 275-92, and is reprinted here by permission of the Regents of the University of California (copyright 1985). It represents the results of the first serious research carried out after the preparation of *Late Latin and Early Romance*, and at the time I had the intention (which may even one day be realized) of preparing a whole book on Semantic Change. It was delivered orally in provisional form to the

---

[5] I am grateful to my colleagues, Max Wheeler and Andrew Hamer, for their comments on an earlier draft of this paper; their views do not necessarily connect with mine.

annual Romance Linguistics Seminar at Trinity Hall, Cambridge, in January 1983; later, subsequent to its acceptance by the journal, but before its appearance, it was delivered in slightly shortened form at the Universities of Oxford (May 1984), Dublin (November 1984), and, in Spanish, Santiago de Compostela (April 1985). Many colleagues have sent me interesting pieces of extra data as a consequence, some of which I here repeat for interest: that Romanian *bucă* can in fact be used to mean "cheek"; that Spanish *carrillos* can be used to refer to "buttocks" but *mejillas* cannot; similarly, it is possible only to *bufar los carrillos*, "blow out one's cheeks," rather than the *mejillas*; that the supposed mozarabic form *maxšilla* is in the MS actually the equivalent (in the Arabic alphabet) of *makhshall*, of uncertain meaning, and thus hardly a clear case; that in Portuguese "to have something in one's eye" can be *ter alguma coisa na vista*, and the speaker's own face tends to be *cara* but someone else's tends to be *rosto*; that Celtic borrowings from Latin *gena* include Welsh *gen* "jaw, chin," Medieval Breton *guen* "cheek," Old Irish *gin, giun* "mouth"; that in English all is Germanic except *face*; that, with reference to *naribus abscissis*, a princess referred to in the "Aragonese" *Cronica de Morea* had her *rostros* cut off ("lips"? Possibly "nose"); with thanks to Rodney Sampson, Lynn Williams, Ralph Penny, Richard Hitchcock, Norman Lamb and Fred Hodcroft. I have also discovered that Spanish *juanetes* "high cheekbones" really is a diminutive of the proper name *Juan*; that Berceo's *Signos del Juicio Final* tells us of serpents and/or scorpions who bite and/or sting with their *rostros* (*meterlis an los rostros fasta los corazones*, 39c); and that in *Patrologia Latina* Vol.112, cols. 1575-78, there is "B. Rabani, Glossæ Latino-Barbaricæ de partibus humani corporis," in which the majority of the glosses are Latinate, or both Latinate and Germanic, rather than Germanic alone (e.g.: "*Palpebræ* sunt sinus oculorum a palpatione dictæ augbrauua").

There is still wide and unexploited scope for pan-Romance consideration of the diachronic evolution of semantic fields of this type; much of the data were elaborated years ago (as in Zauner's article in this case), but an updated global vision of the diachronic dynamics is uncommon.

8
Semantic Change in Romance Words for "Cut"

WE CAN ILLUMINATE SEVERAL semantic changes at once if we visualize some parts of the vocabulary as structured wholes, where changes in the criteria for the use of one word can have consequences for others. Intrinsic links between lexical items arise partly because one early stage in the cognitive process that prepares us to be able to talk about the world is that which identifies separate entities as being distinct from each other; Wright (1985) studied changes that can be located at this stage (in Spanish words for parts of the face). Today I consider linked changes located at a subsequent stage: if we wish to choose a word with which to refer to one of these separately delimited potential referents, one of our next tasks is to decide on the appropriate level of generality or specificity (a decision that is usually made on pragmatic grounds). For much of our vocabulary structure is organized according to scales of increasing specificity. The standard examples of these scales are terms of natural history, sometimes represented on paper as in Table 1.

			Thing						
			Creature						Object
Animal	Insect	Fish	Bird						
			Duck				Owl	Crow	etc.
			Mallard	Teal	Wigeon	Shelduck	etc.		

In this theory (e.g. Lyons 1968: ch.10) a term is said to be the 'hyponym' of the ones directly above it on these scales, and the 'superordinate' of the ones directly beneath it; the English words *duck* and *owl* are thus hyponyms of the word *bird*. Hyponyms of the same superordinate are said to be incompatible with each other; e.g. any bird describable as a *duck* cannot also be described correctly as an *owl*. The vertical lines in these scales correspond to our criteria for choosing between the hyponyms of a superordinate term, and these distinguishing criteria are based on some perceptible difference that we have learned. It seems most likely that in our search for a word with which to refer to our intended referent, we usually enter the vocabulary from the most general end, if.only because it is easier for lazy speakers to find the word *thing* (*thingie, whatsit*) than *wigeon*; and then we are faced with increasingly specific choices to make, until we find the most pragmatically suitable place to stop searching. In this way we can find words for referents which we haven't seen before, and changes in the world do not necessitate a change in the semantic structure. For example, when the Spaniards first met pineapples in the New World, they called them *piñas*, as they still do, which till then had only been used for "fircones"; the perceptual criterion distinguishing fircones from other fruits also worked to separate pineapples out as part of the same category, and no Spanish-speaker finds this polysemy confusing. Choices from the hyponymic scales are not the only ones that need to be made, of course; words are always chosen by the speaker from several possible available items, and even though these choices are normally unconscious they are never forced on us by logical necessities in square brackets inherent in our intended meaning.

The hyponymic scales are the scene of two of the standard categories of semantic change: generalization and specialization. Generalization occurs when a word moves up the scale to a higher level. One example is the Spanish word *argolla*. In Spain that means a "large ring," as on a quayside, or at the smallest as a bracelet, as opposed to an *anillo*, a "small ring" as on a finger; but in parts of America the criterion of size is lost and *argolla* can be used for an engagement ring, which sounds daft in Spain. The converse is specialization: where a word only survives with a specialized sub-part of its original potential reference. An extended case involving several words is the semantic structure of words meaning "cut" in the Romance languages.

The English word *cut* can be defined as "strike a successful blow with a sharp edge"; that is, it is a hyponym of the word *strike* with the criterion of "successfully with a sharp edge." In Latin the word for "cut" was SECARE, and in a few parts of the Romance-speaking world, including Sardinia (*segare*), that word still means in general "cut." There are many different kinds of cutting operation, each of which might require a separate lexical hyponym of its own. One of these is to "cut corn," that is, "reap," "harvest." With a specific direct object, SECARE could naturally always be used to refer to this. But in some areas, notably the Iberian peninsula, *segar* came to mean specifically "reap" even when used elliptically without a direct object; for example, in the thirteenth century the Riojan poet Gonzalo de Berceo intended the phrase *tiempo del segar* to convey unambiguously "harvest time" (*furtávalis las miesses al tiempo del segar, Vida de Santo Domingo* 420a), and the translator of St Matthew's Gospel used the agent noun *segador* to mean the only thing that it has ever meant, "harvester" (*La miess es mucha e los segadores pocos*: "the crop is heavy but the laborers are scarce" in the *New English Bible*, 9:37; also 9:38 and 13:30). This is specialization: SECARE, *segar*, has moved to occupy a slot to which it was originally superordinate. At this point you will be wondering whether this journey was really necessary; didn't Latin already have a perfectly good word for "to reap"? It did: METERE, which is common in the Vulgate Bible. That word survives in standard Italian *mietere* with that same meaning (and Occitan *meire*). In Spain METERE itself has gone; perhaps because of potential confusion with MITTERE > *meter*, METIRI > *medir* or METUM > *miedo*, when the rhizotonic '-ERE paradigm disappeared in Spain (as it did not elsewhere); but the so-called frequentative form, MESSARE, survived, formed off the past participle of METERE. In Sardinia it is this form that means "reap," as also in some Northern Iberian valleys; elsewhere in Spain *mesar* specialized further to mean "pull out" - that is, a form of harvesting but specifically without using any sharp-edged instrument - and then extended its referential criterion slightly so as to be applicable to pulling out hair from the head as well as grass or corn from the ground. In the *Poema de Mio Cid* (of c.1200), *mesar* is used on five occasions, all referring to pulling pieces out of someone's beard (lines 2832, 3186, 3286, 3289, 3290), and the point would there be lost if any connotations of using a razor, knife or scissors lurked still. The result was that "cutting corn" was becoming a vacant slot, a potential squat ripe for colonization by something else. And yet the noun MESSIS, "harvest," both the action and the result of reaping, survived into Old Spanish with its meaning unchanged, as *mies* (cp. the Berceo quotation above); so *mies* came to be semantically the nominalization of *segar* rather than of its formal cognate verb *mesar*.

In France, however, the derivative of SECARE, Old French *seier*, Modern *scier*, usually means to "saw," that is, "cut with a saw," although in some areas it can also mean "reap" as in Spain. Latin hadn't had a separate hyponym of SECARE for "saw," using SERRA SECARE to convey the meaning merely syntagmatically. In Spain, Sardinia and parts of France a derivative verb *(a)serrar(e)* was formed to fill the gap; for words created via affixation can fill apparent lexical gaps as much as can semantic change or neologism—the processes are intimately linked. In Northern France the coining was in the reverse direction; they eventually created a noun *scie* off the verb, unambiguously meaning a "saw." Modern Italy is similar to France: Italian *segare* usually means to "saw," and the noun *sega* was originally only a "saw" (*segatore* being a "mower"). In France METERE disappeared, and MESSARE may well never have existed, but another verb formed off the cognate noun, in this case MESSIO, -ONIS rather than MESSIS, took that place: French *moissonner*.

Meanwhile, SECARE itself had acquired a frequentative form *SECTARE, which, where it survived, in Old Portuguese and Asturian *(as)seitar*, meant "reap." The Castilian equivalent, if it existed, would have been *sechar*, and Malkiel (1947) was surely right to argue that *cosecha*, which has in modern times become commoner than *mies* for "harvest," has some kind of connection with SECTARE, despite Corominas's disagreement (1980:121).

To sum up so far; where SECARE survives it has, outside Sardinia, specialized, that is, acquired extra criteria for use concerning the nature of the cutting concerned; where METERE has survived, mostly in Italy, it has kept its meaning of "reap," so that SECARE has there not slid down the scale to occupy that particular hyponymic slot.

SECARE seems thus not to have been determined to "push" its way into any particular lower slot, but we could reasonably call these developments a "drag"-chain; where a hyponym (e.g. METERE) is falling out of use, for whatever reason, its superordinate (here SECARE) can always be used instead, by definition. Eventually this pattern of choices can shift the distributional pattern of the reference of the original superordinate term, and, as Erica García has been arguing persuasively, such distributional shifts can lead to semantic change. In this case it has. In most of Spain *segar* came usually only to be used if the referent cut was grass or corn. The superordinate slot for "cut" was not left as a vacuum, since it was still possible to use *segar* for referring to other types of cutting; but it would have increasingly felt metaphorical to do so, as if we were now to talk in English of barbers "harvesting" their clients' hair. So it was not logically necessary, but it was nonetheless convenient, to consider using something else as the superordinate.

The French for "cut" is now *couper*, formed off the noun *coup*. French *coup*, Italian *colpo*, Spanish *golpe* and Catalan *cop* all mean "blow"; they derive from Late Latin (Early Romance) COLAPHUS, which was originally borrowed from the Greek κόλαφος, meaning "punch," but COLAPHUS had semantically generalized to mean a "blow" of any kind, losing the criterion of "with a fist." This had thus came to fill the slot being vacated by the Latin superordinate terms; the noun ICTUS was falling out of general use, and PLAGA only survived with the sense of "wound" (the results of the blow rather than the blow itself), in Spanish *llaga*, Portuguese *chaga*, French *plaie*. The superordinate Latin verb CAEDERE, "strike a blow," also fell out of use. The Old Spanish verbs *colpar, golpar* and *golpear* (the form that survives), Catalan *copejar* and Italian *colpire* kept close semantic contact with their cognate noun, similarly generalizing to mean "strike a blow" of any kind. In France, however, they then chose to specialize the verb, *couper*, with the new criterion of "with a sharp edge" which distinguishes the meaning of "cut" from "punch," "slap," "kick" and other fellow-hyponyms of "strike" (Cp. Lehrer 1974). The French word meaning "strike" is now *frapper*, of uncertain etymology, which had previously meant "to hurl oneself onto"; the timing of the semantic changes shows the change in *frapper* to have begun at a slightly later stage than that in *couper*, but the change may not yet be complete. (*Frapper* has certainly become the superordinate for most of the hyponyms of "strike," but not all French-speakers seem to see *couper* also as a modern hyponym of *frapper*.) The change in French *couper* happens to none of its cognates in other languages, and can for this reason plausibly be dated to a late enough time for it to be seen as an intermediate stage there in a drag-chain, as the superordinate *couper* slid down to where *scier* would have been if it had not itself specialized, and then the loss of *couper* from the "strike" slot dragged *frapper* across in turn.

Italian *tagliare*, Catalan *tallar*, Portuguese *talhar*, Rumanian *tăià* and Old Spanish *tajar* all came to be normal superordinate words for "cut." They came from Late Latin (Early Romance) TALIARE (or TALEARE, [-lj-]). This word has generalized from being once a hyponym of SECARE, for it was formed off the noun TALEA, which was originally a "cutting," a small section cut off a bush in order to be independently planted. French *tailler*, on the other hand, from this root, remained on the same level of the hyponymic scale but enlarged its criterion for use, being now suitable for any careful cutting such as shaping precious stones, carving wood, pruning trees and cutting out clothes. In Spain, TALIARE > *tajar* has since respecialized, but it seems to have been the superordinate term in at least Early Mediaeval Spain. In a tenth-century document from León it appears to be used for slicing cheese (*quando la taliaron*: Menéndez Pidal 1926:25; Wright 1982:173). In the *Poema de Mio Cid*, *tajar* is used for cutting down orchards (line 1172: *tajavales las huertas*) rather than taking cuttings off them, and also for cutting hair (1241, *Nin entrarie en ella tigera, ni un pelo non avrie tajado*). King Alfonso X's *Siete Partidas* I.IV.99 has the phrase *mesabanse los cabellos et tajabanlos*, "they pulled out and cut their hair." The agent adjectives *tajador* (5 times in the *Cid*) and *tajante* (as in the *Libro de Alexandre* 1347d, *todos eran tajantes como foz podadera*) both meant "sharp." *Tajante* still means "sharp," mostly in a metaphorical sense, "trenchant," but the verb itself, *tajar*, has since, in Spain, specialized again, to mean usually "chop into pieces," implying strong action as with an axe, and now unsuitable as a word to use for referring to cutting hair, or to cutting a finger without cutting it off.

There are two possible reasons for the decision to respecialize the reflex of TALEARE in Castilian, unlike elsewhere. One may lie in the potential confusion, at places and times where TALEARE preserved the lateral consonant, with *talar*. *Talar* comes from a Germanic root (*talan*) and originally meant "devastate"; it tends now to be like the English *fell* and be confined for use with trees. The noun *tala* could already be used to refer to the peaceful right to cut firewood from trees on common land in eleventh- and twelfth-century law. Thus both *tajar* and *talar* came to be hyponyms of "cut." For "felling" trees Latin had tended merely to use CAEDERE, "strike," the general superordinate of SECARE, in the absence of a specific lexicalized hyponym. Later, in the sixteenth century, the Italian *tagliare* was borrowed into Castilian as *tallar* with only the meaning of "engrave"; this is a combination of borrowing and specialization that need cause no surprise, given the shape of the slot it was borrowed to fill. Thus now a Spanish tree can be felled (*talar*), chopped into sections (*tajar*) and those sections be given an engraved carving (*tallar*); a phonological minimal trio of three hyponyms of "cut."

But Old Spanish *tajar* may have been losing the battle to fill the superordinate slot anyway, to its rival, *cortar*. The origin of *cortar* was a fairly rare Latin word CURTARE, meaning "shorten, reduce," semantically related to CURTUS, "short." Latin CURTUS could mean "castrated" and "circumcised," so even then could be used to refer to the results of some cutting actions, but the adjective survives in Romance with the meaning of "short" and no cutting connotations; Spanish *corto*, Catalan *curt*, Portuguese *curto*, French *court*, Italian *corto*. Rumanian *scurt* comes from a form with the prefix EX-. So does the Rumanian verb *scurtà* and dialectal Italian *scortare*, "shorten," and French *écourter*, "cut short," that is, "shorten with a sharp edge." In thirteenth-century Spanish the verb means specifically "cut": for example, the five uses in the *Poem of the Cid* (lines 751, 767, 2423, 2728, 3652) are for cutting through helmets, waists and heads with a sword. The semantic structure of "shorten" and the semantic structure of "strike" are separate. Yet it happens at times that words with a precise hyponymic criterion in one part of the vocabulary can be adopted for use elsewhere, with the same criterion under a different superordinate. It is possible that by Very

Early Mediaeval Spanish the normal use of CURTARE was still for "shorten," but usually now specifically "with a sharp edge" (as EXCURTARE means in the Merovingian Salic Law); and that eventually a need for a word with that specific criterion under the superordinate "strike" led the word to override structural boundaries and come to mean "cut," whether or not the cutting also involved shortening the object referent. With the subsequent specialization of *tajar*, the Spanish "cut" structure has come to be filled now as in Table 2.

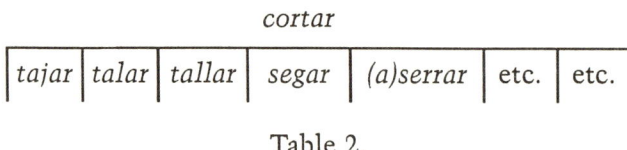

Table 2.

(The etcetera in Table 2 include such words as *afeitar* "shave," *amputar* "amputate," *podar* "prune," *hender* "split," and so on.)

Once Spanish *cortar* had come to have "cut" as its central literal meaning, it could no longer be used to refer to shortening that did not involve a sharp edge, e.g. shortening sail or debates. There was emerging another potential gap. Derivational morphology came to the rescue again: the Spanish superordinate for "shorten" has always been *acortar*. *ADCURTARE did not exist in Latin, but there was nothing adventurous in this invention: many Old Spanish verbs had forms both with and without an essentially meaningless prefix *a-* (cp. the coexistence of *serrar* and *aserrar* mentioned above, or *allegar* and *llegar* referred to in Wright 1987). In this way *corto* and its semantically related verb *acortar* have both broken off semantically from *cortar*; thus to "shorten sail" is *acortar la vela*, in which the sail remains uncut. *Acortar* is the only one of the words in this paper to come early enough in the alphabet to be in the ongoing *Diccionario Histórico de la Lengua Española*; one of its four thirteenth-century attestations (Vol.I:522-24) probably involves shortening with a sharp edge (of a wooden beam: Berceo, *Vida de San Millán* 227b), but the other three do not (shortening life-expectation and law-suits, and limiting damage in general).

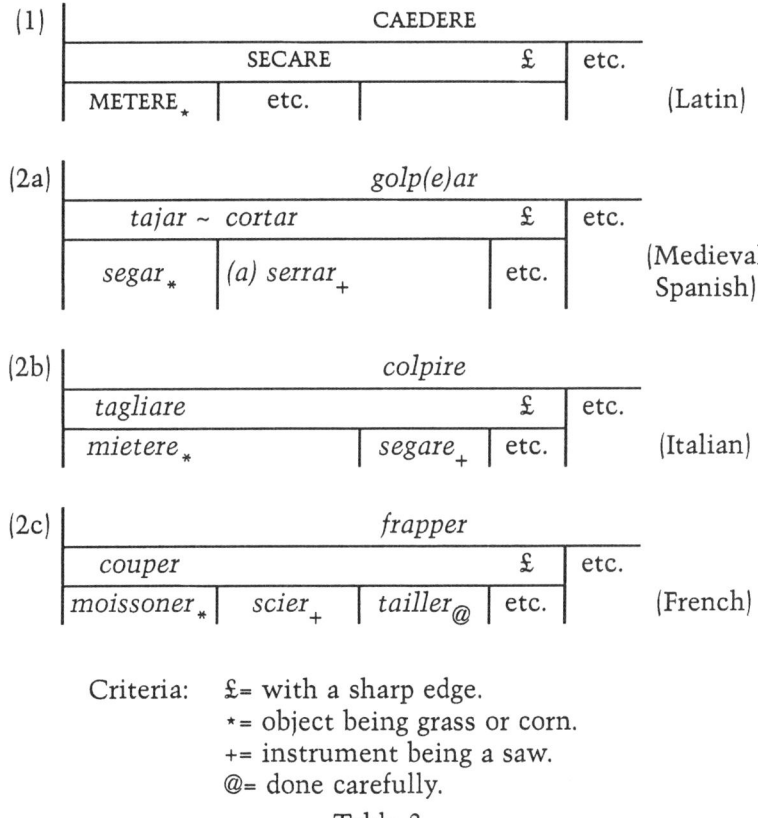

Criteria: £ = with a sharp edge.
* = object being grass or corn.
+ = instrument being a saw.
@ = done carefully.

Table 3.

CONCLUSION

We have been looking at the data of Table 3. The rigidity of these diagrams should not be taken too seriously; not everyone in the same area at the same time need have the same detail in their lexical structures, and words are used non-literally all the time. Even so, as a generalization, we see the survival of a more or less consistent substructure, intended to contain a word meaning "strike" and a hyponym thereof with the specific criterion of "successfully with a sharp edge"; this word, in turn, is superordinate to an indeterminate number of hyponyms of its own; the structure is roughly constant, though the words filling the slots have, at least in some cases, moved. It looks as though in Spain, for example, over time some words fell out of use (METERE, CÆDERE) and also the number of hyponyms at the bottom of this scale increased, for social rather than linguistic reasons (education tends to involve progressively complicating, filling and lowering the more specific end of the hyponymic scales). Newly required hyponyms have sometimes been acquired from other languages, as *talar* from Germanic and *tallar* from Italian, but often by specializing the criteria for the use of the superordinate term which has always been available for use to refer to these referents anyway (by definition), as has happened with Spanish *segar* and French *couper*. For a while the word so specialized can uneasily remain available for referents incompatible with its new literal sense, but to do so sounds pointlessly metaphorical, and there is a search for a new literal superordinate. This can involve generalization of another hyponym, as with the Late Latin (Early Romance) words TALEARE and COLAPHUS; or the adoption of a word that happens to have the required criterion for use, from another substructure of the vocabulary, as with *cortar*. Thus not only is semantic change part of a wider process that also includes borrowing and affixation (cp. Wright 1985), it can also be similar to that type of phonetic change describable in terms of drag-chains. This is only one kind of semantic change in lexical items, of course; and all I really want to point out now is that semantic change in several lexical items at once can be studied rationally from a structural perspective.

1994 POSTSCRIPT

This paper was first given at the 8th International Conference on Historical Linguistics, in Lille, France, on Wednesday morning September 2nd, 1977, under the title of "Semantic Change: logic, perception and theory; semantic change in Romance words for 'cut.'" It was published in a slightly revised form as "Semantic change in Romance words for 'cut,'" in *Historical Linguistics 1987: Papers from the 8th International Conference on Historical Linguistics*, John Benjamins Publ. Co., Amsterdam/ Philadelphia, 1990, 553-62. It was given again in a much expanded form at the annual Romance Linguistics Seminar in Trinity Hall, Cambridge, the following January, but this shorter version is the more satisfactory. At Cambridge it emerged that in Sardinian *segare* has also acquired the meaning of "break," and the noun *thadza* (< TALEA) means "slice," although in the absence of a cognate verb. Tagliavini (6th ed., 1972:27-29) uses words for "cut" as the central example in a section entitled "La geografia linguistica: deduzioni metodologiche," mentioning reflexes of *resecare*; similarly, the present paper fails to mention that even though *caedere* fell out of usage, several prefixed forms did not. Other such prefixed forms in Old Spanish include *entallar* ("engrave") from the *Primera Cronica General*, quoted by Cano 1989:284, and *trastajada* quoted by Varvaro 1987:167. It could also have been pointed out that *Els Segadors*, the Catalan Anthem, is as unambiguously "harvesters" in Catalan as *segadores* was in Berceo. (Moore and Carling, 1982:136-37, 179, also use *cut* as a example of semantic flexibility in the English phrase *cut the sandwiches*; but they seem to have missed the point; even if the phrase is used to mean "prepare the sandwiches," literal cutting is still understood to be involved in that process.)

Part II:

Language and Texts in the Iberian Peninsula before 1080

9
On Editing 'Latin' Texts Written by Romance-speakers[1]

EDITORS OF EARLY MEDIEVAL texts need to be continuously aware of the difference between *Grammatica* as used by Germanic- (or Celtic-) speakers and as used by Romance-speakers in the Early Middle Ages. The theme of this article is that modern editors of such texts from Spain are too often inclined to act as if the authors were not Romance-speakers, and follow a depressing and unhelpful tradition of seeing the early medieval Romance/Latin relationship as being analogous to the Germanic/Latin relationship. It was not.

1. For Romance-speakers, *Grammatica* = Writing

The differences derive from the fact that *Grammatica* was taught in different ways in different language communities. The historical origins of the difference need to be appreciated. All early Medieval Education was based on the teaching and learning of *Ars Grammatica*. The words *Ars Grammatica* were originally connected specifically with writing. The *Ars Minor* and *Ars Secunda* (or *Ars Maior*) of the fourth-century Grammarian Aelius Donatus were compiled for the benefit of people who spoke as their native language fourth-century vernacular Latin; what philologists of some schools call 'Proto-Romance.' These works, plus the commentaries based on them, became the basis for linguistic education for

---

[1] This is the revised text of a lecture given at the Warburg Institute, University of London, in June 1990, and also at the University of Oslo, Norway, in September 1990. I am grateful for comments made by participants at these occasions.

centuries afterwards. The fifth-century grammarians, such as Consentius, Pompeius, Servius and Sergius, worked within the same atmosphere, still essentially considering the formal registers of a language which they and their readers already spoke. These grammarians were thus, in modern terms, not specialists in the teaching of Latin as a foreign language, but specialists in Linguistics, with particular reference to the demands of writing. In sixth-century Italy, Cassiodorus maintained, in his work on language, a similar focus on deciding which were the supposedly 'correct' forms to be used in written texts; his grammatical works were intended to help copyists at Vivarium, who were also native speakers of the language. In sixth-century France, Caesarius of Arles tried hard to encourage his flock to be literate in the language which they already had. In the seventh century, the first chapter of Isidore of Seville's *Etymologiae* was essentially a derivative grammar based on the fifthcentury African commentators on Donatus. He too, and his successors such as Julián de Toledo, were teaching their readers about the smart and formal way to operate and analyze the language they already spoke, that is, seventh-century Spanish Early Romance/Late Latin (in this period we can as justifiably call their language the one as the other).

The grammarians mentioned hitherto, and others, were writing for the benefit of students who were native speakers of the language in question, training them in the arts of writing, reading, and to some extent analysing, the language they already had. The students could already be expected to pronounce it, use the normal grammar of speech, and know the basic vocabulary, and did not need to be taught that; features which had by and large slipped out of spoken Latin, however, such as many of the noun inflections, did need to be taught, which is why so much of the Grammarians' attention lay precisely there. But all, including the Grammarians, spoke the language of their time and place, and the techniques of writing professionally (*Ars Grammatica*) were aimed at producing respectably traditional-looking forms of that same language. Recent historical research suggests that in early medieval Romance communities few people could write, more could read, and almost everybody (then as now) could understand written texts read aloud with care. To the Romance speaker, Latin texts were not in a foreign language.²

2. FOR NON-ROMANCE SPEAKERS, *GRAMMATICA* = ANOTHER LANGUAGE

The teaching of Latin-as-a-foreign-language only began, naturally enough, where there was a community of non-Latin speakers who wished to learn to read written Latin texts. It is in eighth-century England that we begin to see a change in the nature of grammarians' texts; everything about Latin had to be taught there from scratch, for the students there had no advance native expertise.³ The Anglo-Saxon scholars had some knowledge of the works of the Visigothic writers of Spain, and also some personal contacts with speakers of Early Romance from France and Italy. It is possible that there were native Romance-speakers around in Anglo-Saxon England who were able to demonstrate personally (in *Grammatica* classes) linguistic features that were taken for granted in the preexisting continental works of linguistics. This could be parallelled today, if a non-English-speaking community wished to learn English but only had the works of English-speaking theoretical linguists such as Halliday to guide them; the books are not totally useless for the purpose, but the students would need considerable extra guidance from native speakers who already know the language well, or they do not even get to square one. Yet the influence of Early-Romance speakers in Anglo-Saxon England was, so far as we can see, not decisive in the establishment of the nature of Anglo-Saxon Latin. In pronunciation, for example, the phonology of eighth-century Anglo-Saxon Latin owed more to the phonology of Anglo-Saxon than it did to the phonology of the native speakers of any part of the former Roman Empire. We can deduce this, at least, from the nature

---

² These arguments were developed at greater length in the first two chapters of Wright (1982).

³ The best work on the use of *Grammatica* in non-Romance countries is Law (1982). As she shows in another study (1987), these Grammarians were actively reshaping the received tradition for their own community's different needs.

of the alliterative and rhyming techniques of Early Medieval Insular virtuoso poetry.

There were other Anglo-Saxon intellectuals with pedagogical linguistic interests, but the key initial figure is Bede. He kept a notebook of useful points that had come up in his pedagogical experience, covering orthography, grammar, inflectional morphology, derivational morphology, lexis and semantics, and even phonetics, although it seems only in connection with syllable-division in the choir. This work is practical and pedagogical, although essentially addressed to other teachers rather than to his students, and collectively has the air of being an aid to the 'Latin as a foreign language' teacher. When he adapts details from his sources, he does so for the practical purposes of his own community. It is unfortunate that this work has come to be given the misleading title of *De Orthographia*, for it is not especially concerned with spelling.[4] Bede established personally a tradition of eighth-century Insular Latin learning, which was in a number of ways rather different from that current in contemporary Romance-speaking Europe. Eighth-century written texts followed the same models, and ostensibly the same grammar, wherever they were written. But in the case of Germanic-speakers, including in due course those on the Continent speaking varieties of Germanic other than Anglo-Saxon, they were writing a foreign language that was self-evidently not their own vernacular. They were bilingual; and this foreign language was uniquely defined for them by the Grammarians (and their commentators).

They had to learn everything from teachers. This included pronunciation. The way the Anglo-Saxon speaker learned and was taught to pronounce was on the basis of written texts. They knew, as they learned, the written form of a word right from the first moment that they encountered it. The teachers offered it to them in written form, and they based their pronunciations on that preexisting written form. This had one significant consequence in particular; in the Germanic-speakers' *Grammatica* classes, every written letter in a word gave rise to a sound. There were to be no

---

[4] Dionisotti (1982:122) sees it as "a reference work for the Library."

silent letters. This was a natural consequence of the general inability of the Early Medieval Grammarians, just like first-year language students today, to distinguish letters from sounds. Not only that, but each written letter (or digraph) was meant to give rise to the same sound in every circumstance, wherever it appeared in the written form. Thus, in the British Isles, the spelling determined the pronunciation. This is, of course, completely the opposite of what all people (including speakers of Early Romance) do with their own native language, where they pronounce the words first in speech, and only write them much later, if at all. Isidore's clientele knew their language anyway, having learned it in the ordinary manner as children, whether or not they ever learned later to read or write. Morphological features such as the paradigms demonstrating the endings of nouns (*declinationes nominum*), however, would have been useful in both traditions; in seventh-century Spain they were needed, and explicitly taught, because they were largely unused in speech, but encountered in reading and needed for writing.

3. EARLY ROMANCE

It is worth reminding ourselves of what the linguistic situation of seventh- and eighth-century Western Romance-speaking Europe was like. It was (mutatis mutandis) rather like that of Modern English or Modern French; a huge geographical area whose language, Early Romance, contained within it a wide variety of linguistic alternatives; there were alternative items of vocabulary, different grammatical ways of expressing the same idea, different phonetic ways of pronouncing the same word, but it still remained in essence a single speech-community.[5] All such wide single speech-communities have within them enormous variety, not only geographical but also stylistic, sociolinguistic, contextual, and even variation between young and old, male and female, rich and poor, etc. Such variation within a single language is not only normal but useful for all sorts of practical purposes (what linguists now call

---

[5] On this see several studies in Wright (ed., 1991) and McKitterick (ed., 1990), Herman (1988), Banniard (1989).

'pragmatics'). A large number of innovating linguistic features had arisen over the centuries, in the way they always do, for no spoken language has ever been fixed, unchanging and static, not even fourth-century Latin. Some of the old Classical forms and constructions were no longer in active use. But it seems reasonable to deduce that the old linguistic features had in several cases not yet dropped out entirely; they would still be understood by those listening to written texts being read aloud, and even active seventh-century Romance speech, for example, could well have included both the old-fashioned accusative and infinitive constructions and the new *quod* plus indicative constructions which seem in retrospect to have neatly taken their place, both the old-fashioned genitive endings of nouns and the new-fashioned equivalents with the preposition *de*, both old words such as *equus* and new words such as *caballus*. In general, then, the Romance language of the time contained both old and new grammatical features, but only the reconstructably evolved phonetics; writing and talking involved statistically different proportions of the relevant competing morphosyntactic and lexical forms (as in modern English) rather than any rigid apartheid between literate and illiterate, which (as Harvey and others have pointed out) is otherwise unattested and thoroughly improbable on many grounds.[6] This was essentially the nature of Iberian Romance until the second millennium.

When speakers from this pulsating, lively, versatile, flexible, rich, complex, but monolingual Early Romance speech community came to learn to write—if they ever did, for most of them did not—they were hit at once by the artificial restrictions of the old Donatus tradition. Early Medieval Romance was—to the eternal disappointment of all Romance philologists—not permitted to appear neat on parchment as in an exact phonetic transcription. Prescriptive Grammarians, then as now, are always restrictive. They always interpret their function as that of specifying as 'correct' in a written context just some, out of the wide existing variety, of the forms, expressions, constructions and words available in the wider community. They see their job in moral terms; variations are not

---

[6] See Harvey (1990), Herman (1990), Alarcos (1982), Wright (1991b).

merely formal versus informal, innovating versus archaic, characteristic of one geographical area rather than another, and so on, but—in writing, at least—as 'correct' or 'incorrect.' Whereas Latin for the non-Romance speaker was uniquely defined by the *Grammatica*, the Romance-speaker's language had a much wider range of usage of which the *Grammatica* only prescribed a sub-section as being acceptable in writing. The same happens today; native English-speaking University lecturers in Spanish-as-a-foreign-language usually have a considerably narrower idea of what is permissible Spanish than the native Spanish-speaking *lectores* who are their colleagues. As Franco (1985) has pointed out, for example, the rules that we teach students concerning the need to use *estar* rather than *ser* in locative senses are not always followed by native speakers (who can at times be heard saying *¿dónde es...?*).

This debilitating tendency to see a moral order in grammatical details hamstrings later generations of Romance-speakers who depend, when writing, on the earlier grammarians' prescriptions which have by then become traditional. The eighth-century spoken Romance community in general, and continuing to the twelfth century in the Iberian Peninsula, is alive and sophisticated, capable of communicating and interacting orally as well then as people are now, but Romance-speaking scribes were told in their training that in writing they ought to follow the traditional prescriptions and only include on paper those linguistic features that had been blessed as 'correct' in the fourth century A.D. (with in practice the addition of some declensional subtypes of ecclesiastical words taken from Greek). This limitation was by then doubly restricting, because several of these forms deemed 'correct' in the Late Empire had largely disappeared from most active speech four hundred years later (ablative cases of nouns, synthetic passives, etc.), and the proportion of available eighth-century variants that coincided with the fourth-century moral perceptions was lower than it had been originally. And yet, in Romance Europe, people did succeed in writing; the 'Renaissance' of Visigothic Spain had made Spain the most educated area of the seventh century, and its intellectual traditions continued, both in nominally Christian and nominally Moslem Spain, to flourish well into the tenth century, producing a large number of written works, some of which survive. Collins deduced that tenth-century Leonese society was just as dependent on documentation as that of tenth-century Catalonia, despite the fact that Catalonia was, and León was not, an area where the Carolingian Latin-Romance distinction operated.[7]

4. THE PRACTICAL PROBLEM

Here we get to the serious practical problem. The original works of Isidore, Ildefonso, Eugenio de Toledo, Julián de Toledo, Eulogio de Córdoba, Alvaro de Córdoba, the ninth-century Asturian historians, and so on, were written by speakers of Early Romance; their speech was more versatile than were the written forms that they were taught were acceptable, and, although they knew their *Grammatica*, features of their ordinary speech habits are at times observable in the early manuscripts, including such erudite productions as those of the greatest scholar of the age (Isidore) and the texts of the mozarabic liturgy. So we find there, for example, *se* used instead of synthetic passives, prepositions used instead of case endings, theoretically neuter plural nouns used as the feminine singulars that they had become in speech, theoretically third-conjugation verbs used with the fourth-conjugation endings that they had often acquired in speech, etc., etc. The writers had been taught according to an already ancient tradition about which features of speech could and could not be included, but as time had gone on more and more normal spoken features theoretically could not be written, and they were not always successfully kept out of the texts.

The problem is that subsequent editors have misunderstood the essential distinction that we need to make. These Early Medieval Romance-speakers were writing the language they already spoke, following ancient restrictions; unlike the Germanic-speakers, they were not trying to write in a foreign language. Those modern editors, from Ambrosio de Morales in the sixteenth century, who 'corrected' the voluminous original work of Eulogio de Córdoba out of all authenticity, up to the recent editors of Isidore's *Etymologiae* who scorn the readings of the early manuscripts, do an enormous

---

[7] Collins (1985); cp. also, Collins (1989).

disservice to scholarship, assuming that these Romance-speakers had been taught Latin-as-a-foreign-language in the same way as the Germanic-speakers were, and that the Romance-speakers were trying to write in the restrictive foreign language rather than in an archaic but nevertheless 'correct' style of their own language which they had been led to believe was morally preferable. In short, I would plead with all editors of early medieval texts from Romance Europe—as do most of the contributors to the special issue of *Speculum* for January 1990 (on 'The New Philology'), and Law (1982)—not to emend their early manuscripts at all. Oroz Reta's comments at the start of his recent edition of the *Etymologiae* are little short of grotesque:

> ...creemos que el texto isidoriano que ofrece la Bibliotheca Oxoniensis, en muchos pasajes, podía corregirse sin dificultad...en modo alguno podíamos pensar en realizar un estudio o análisis de los numerosísimos códices isidorianos...para ofrecer un texto más puro y correcto...hemos tratado de uniformar las grafías variadas...hemos corregido...creemos que hay que uniformar...

He is, in short, proud to have distorted the original and rendered his edition useless for linguistic research. There is, however, one scholar above all who has aimed to edit these texts professionally: Juan Gil of Seville. As an antidote to the above, note his comment:

> Normalmente, al editar la obra de un escritor visigodo, se suele modificar la grafía al uso clásico. Esta corrección, con todo, entraña no pocos peligros; falsea el aspecto externo de un texto, regulariza grafías que no regularizaron nunca sus propios autores, encubre fenómenos fonéticos y en ocasiones atenta contra los mismos usos ortográficos visigodos.

Gil is referring here not only to spelling but also to morphological features. This important article came out in 1973, but seems not to have had the effect it deserves.[8]

5. How the Romance West was lost

Unfortunately, nowadays, in the Romance-speaking world, people do not think of themselves as Latin-speakers any more, and (like Germanic-speakers) they do now think of Latin as a foreign language, different from their own Portuguese, Catalan, Venetian, etc. The way in which this conceptual distinction arose is at the forefront of debate in contemporary Romance philology. I have long expressed, and still hold, the view that this conceptual distinction began at the point where the two traditions clashed; where the Germanic view of Latin as a foreign language, whose grammar was defined uniquely by the prescriptions of Grammarians and untouched by the enormous vitality of eighth-century spoken Romance, came into startled contact with the versatility and liveliness of that speech; and recoiled in horror. That is, to be more precise, the appointment of Alcuin of York to reform the Carolingian education system. The distinction between Latin and vernacular was obvious to a Germanic-speaker, naturally, and Alcuin and his group wished to introduce that distinction into the education system of Romance Europe as well. So they presided over the conscious invention of a new conceptual distinction, between Latin and Romance, and Romance-speakers in at least some of the Carolingian cultural centers of the ninth and tenth centuries began to be taught, on Anglo-Saxon lines, Latin as a foreign language, with a grammar, a vocabulary, and even a pronunciation distinguishably separate from even the most formal styles of their own native language as spoken in France, Catalonia and Northern Italy. (Incidentally, I do not wish to be accused of fostering a 'great man' view of history; the consequences of Alcuin's prejudices were almost

---

[8] These quotations are from Oroz's edition of Isidore (1982:258-59)—of which Díaz y Díaz's Introduction is excellent—and Gil (1973:193), which is relevant for all texts up to the twelfth century (and sheds also an interesting light on the *Historia Roderici*, p.223).

totally pernicious.) Eventually this invented conceptual distinction spread out of the Carolingian Empire into the rest of the Iberian Peninsula, Italy, and elsewhere, and in due course it came to seem so obvious and natural and normal that Dante, in his *De Vulgari Eloquentia*, thought it had always existed. But the distinction, even in France, took time to become generally accepted and spread beyond progressive Church circles; on the whole it seems that students in France were not generally taught to make a conceptual Latin / Romance distinction till after the millennium, still previously on the whole being taught to write in a particular style of the language they had rather than being taught from scratch a whole foreign language.[9] As suggested above, in Spain, this stage probably lasts until at least 1080 and for most purposes until after 1200; that is, in Spain, as in France, the eventual triumph of the dead hand of restricting Germanic pedagogy over the preexisting complex Romance monolingualism took a long time to be generally accepted. My own recent studies of the *Vita Dominici Siliensis* (of the 1080s) and the *Chronica Adefonsi Imperatoris* (c. 1147) suggest that the Latin-Romance metalinguistic distinction which seems so obvious to us now, as if it had always existed, was not consciously felt then (and, as Niederehe pointed out, was not entirely clear even to Alfonso el Sabio).[10] This means that all texts from pre-12th century non-Catalan Spain, and quite possibly most of those from the 12th century as well, are in written Romance, rather than, as usually stated, corrupt and barbaric Latin.

I have discussed the implications of this reevaluation at some length elsewhere with reference to the *Chronicle of Alfonso III*. Fortunately this Chronicle (originally from the royal court of late ninth-century Oviedo) has been luckier in its modern editors than has poor Isidore; Bonnaz's edition (1987) is stultifyingly classicizing, but the editions of Prelog (1980) and above all Gil et al. (1985) are intelligently and accurately presented in such a way that we can watch how successive adaptations of the text gradually formalized

---

[9] See McKitterick (1989), Van Uytfanghe (1989, 1991), and the long Introduction to Guerreau-Jalabert (1982).

[10] The references are to Wright (1993), Wright (1992b), and Niederehe (1987:102).

an original that began essentially in written Romance.[11] In France, the textual evidence of pre-reform compositions was often doctored ('emended') into apparent respectability by Carolingian and post-Carolingian scholars. They did this themselves to the Benedictine rule, for example, as well as to many of the texts of the early Fathers of the Church, and to their own *Annales Regni Francorum*; and almost certainly to large numbers of other earlier texts that only now survive in post-Carolingian manuscripts. And from being taught that this 'correction' was what they were supposed to carry out, gradually students and editors came to be taught that the original writers must have got it 'right,' and that everything which Donatus would not have approved of must have been introduced by careless copyists because they could not have been there in the original; hence Ambrosio de Morales' assumption that he was right to distort the evidence of his manuscript, as if Eulogio de Córdoba was a closet Anglo-Saxon, as if Eulogio had been writing a non-vernacular foreign language defined only by the *Ars Grammatica* tradition rather than writing a formal style of his own speech, such that Ambrosio de Morales presumed that all the non-Grammatical features must be the fault of incompetent manuscript copyists. But we know, particularly as regards twelfth-century Spain (and later), that copyists were more likely to distort their originals by making 'corrections' of their pre-Reform originals, rather than by introducing errors. There is no need for us to do the same.

6. AFTER THE SEPARATION

We have seen that before 800, and in many cases later, Romance-speakers, if they were taught to write at all, were taught how to write acceptably the language which they already spoke, according to an ancient tradition which ruled out of acceptability a large number of features of their speech. Germanic speakers, on the other hand, were taught only that limited and limiting tradition, Latin as a foreign language, not usually including knowledge of how the language was actually spoken at the time. After 800 the two systems coexist in Carolingian France until eventually—perhaps

---

[11] Wright (1991b) considers this in more detail.

after a couple of centuries in several places—the view of Latin as being a foreign language became normal; in due course this conceptual separation became normal in the whole Romance-speaking world. In Spain the definitive dissociative process accompanied the invention and general spread of undisguised vemacular writing and the Latin-teaching reforms consequent on the Lateran Council of 1215 and the Council of Valladolid of 1228.

It was a Pyrrhic victory. For it was precisely in places where Latin was taught and learned and conceived of as a separate language from native vernacular that works were also written in a new form based on that vernacular; this explains why works in Germanic vernaculars seem to appear in written form before those in French, Provençal, Catalan, Sicilian, Castilian, etc. But this apparent precedence of Germanic texts is a mirage. Before the change in perspective in Romance areas, Romance indeed had a written form, but to us, looking back from much later, that form appears to be 'Latin.' The texts in consciously reformed nontraditional spelling and morphology that we call now 'Old French,' 'Old Provençal,' 'Old Castilian' (etc.) emerged from centers of expert Latinity only after this metalinguistic change, in places (such as St Amand, Fleury, San Millán, Palencia, Toledo, San Fernando's chancery, etc.) where it seems probable that Latin had recently started being taught and learned as a foreign language from the normal Romance vernacular, and as a result the vernacular came in due course to appear to need a new separate written guise. It cannot be pointed out too often that the earliest 'Romance' texts were in fact elaborated by expert Latinists in progressive cultural centers; the reason for that was that nobody else saw any point in making such a distinction until Latin (*Grammatica*) was generally conceived of as being a different language from normal speech. It is time to discard forever the ridiculous idea, still apparently current, that early texts in written vemacular form were produced by and for the illiterate; on the contrary, by definition, the illiterate could not write at all, and those that could read or write would (as in the modern English-speaking world) find a phonetic script harder to use than the traditional forms. (The practical mechanics of the changeover in the Iberian Peninsula have been illuminated by Emiliano (1988, 1991)). Eventually, in this new guise, written medieval Romance languages were able to capture their own oral spontaneity, vitality and life (as we see in their literature)—which had been there in speech all along, but impermissible in writing—, whereupon the dead hand of reformed *Grammatica* could be left to the pedants.

7. AN UNSCIENTIFIC ANALOGY

Consider the following analogy. In the year 2000 a reform of the United States education system is entrusted to a politically powerful group of Arabs, who have only learned English as a foreign language uniquely defined by the Grammar books, use in speech as a result only the most formal grammar, and pronounce every written letter (such as to be often unintelligible to the natives), but write it according to the same rules as the English-speakers in the U.S.A. The Arab scholars' leader (Mohammed Al-Kwin) is empowered to insist that everyone in the best Universities should speak as he does (at least, in formal situations), and indeed, within a century or so this artificial system comes to be normal in U.S. higher education. This system, already normal in the non-English speaking world, effectively excludes the majority of English-speakers in the U.S. from understanding what used to be merely the written form of their own language. So eventually someone thinks of the idea of writing spoken U.S. English according to a reformed writing system—for, say, oaths sworn in court, sermons, popular poems. The new vernacular writing systems are taken up in the rest of the English-speaking world, until eventually, after another century, the distinction between English-as-a-foreign language (Grammar) and regional vernaculars (formerly seen as variants of English, but now separately called e.g., Australian, Indian, British, etc.) comes to seem natural everywhere. Meanwhile Arab and Arab-trained scholars rewrite the text of the works of American writers of pre-2000, in order that they can fit their preconceptions of how they `ought' to have been written (excising *didn't* for *did not*, *gonna* for *going to*, *thru* for *through*, etc.).

Under such circumstances, would it be right for subsequent scholars to regard the surviving original versions of works by J. D. Salinger, Philip Roth, etc., as being in barbarous Grammar rather than merely in the written mode of their own vernacular? Would it not be preferable to edit them without such emendation? Let us not, therefore, in the real world do the same to early Spanish medieval texts, for they too were originally in the written mode of their author's vernacular.

8. NINE CONCLUSIONS

1. All Spanish texts from before 1080, and most from before 1200, need to be edited without any emendation at all from the earliest manuscript(s), rather than changed as a result of what anachronistic preconceptions lead editors to think 'ought' to have been written instead. This applies not only to Histories, but all varieties of legal documents, including *fueros*, Church Councils (such as the 1055 Council of Coyanza), hagiography, and indeed everything else. Ideally, facsimiles of the manuscripts would be available (as the latest editors of Merovingian documentation realize: see the comments of Ganz and Goffart, 1990), but they are often not clear enough in themselves. Conversely, García Larragueta's (1984:123-46) attempt at a typescript facsimile of the *Glosas Emilianenses*, for example, clarifies Olarte Ruiz's photographic facsimile (1977), but would be misleading on its own (in that it resolves some abbreviations and is not free of misprints).

   This is in no way a revolutionary suggestion. It is, for example, what is prescribed by the *Asociación de Lingüística y Filología de la América Latina* for its forthcoming publications of documents. Quoting Gil again (1973:208): 'la tarea es difícil; pero la única manera de cumplirla es respetar al máximo—no me cansaré nunca de repetirlo—las grafías de los manuscritos.'

2. This fidelity should include a resistance to any temptation to resolve abbreviations at all, for in practice the way abbreviations are resolved begs many questions. Abbreviations were intended to be recognized, but the unit to be recognized was meant to be the lexical word rather than the omitted letters; that is, for example, whether we resolve *nro* as *nostro* or *nuestro*, or *tēs* as *testis* or *testigo* (etc.), our decision probably results in giving a misleading impression.

3. Since the texts in question are written in the formal version of Spanish Romance, rather than a barbarously unsuccessful attempt at another language entirely, we should stop insulting

their language and their authors. We cannot seriously explain the language of the Rotense version of the Chronicle of Alfonso III simply with the theory that the Asturians were all barbarously stupid and corrupt; for we know from historical research how enterprising and resourceful ninth- and tenth-century Asturians actually were. Similarly, the present nature of the *Fuero de Valfermoso de las Monjas* is better described as the result of a serious attempt at formalizing the vernacular than of a crass attempt at writing another language entirely.

4. Etymologists should realize that all the texts in question are evidence for Spanish vocabulary. It is inappropriate that Corominas should adduce the first attestation of a Spanish word (in his etymological dictionary) as of necessity being one that is spelled incorrectly in cases where the same word 'correctly' spelled is attested earlier. *Camisa*, for example, is given by Corominas a first documentation date of 899, despite being attested as *camisiam* in Isidore's *Etymologiae* XIX.21.1. (Corominas & Pascual 1980:787)

5. The computerized dictionaries should therefore extend their corpus further back in time also. Not to do so is misleading. For example; the fact that *rege* appears in the late tenth-century *Nodicia de kesos* and also in countless documents and histories, etc., should not be hidden from the enquiring philologist who might otherwise think that the thirteenth century invented the lexical word itself rather than merely the orthographic form *rey* (and *rei*). Oelschlager (1940) glimpsed this truth.[12]

6. Likewise, the exciting CD-ROM project of all old Spanish texts (ADMYTE), sponsored by Professor Faulhaber, would ideally start earlier than it will, since its initial cut-off point depends on an anachronistic dichotomy.

7. Ideally, also, the Madison medieval Spanish publication enterprises should include all such texts (before, let us say, St

---

[12] Wright (1982:173) reprints the *Nodicia*; *rei* is the form used in what may be the first official document in "written Romance," that is, the Treaty of Cabreros of 1206.

Martin of León) as within their brief.¹³ A chronological line has, however, for practical reasons to be drawn somewhere: I suggest 500 A.D.
8. Let us altogether appreciate that (from the point of view of the authors) there is a greater linguistic continuity between the *Chronicle of Alfonso III* and the Chronicles of Alfonso X than between the former and Lucas of Tuy, despite its greater textual similarity with Lucas; that is, both Alfonsos (or their ghosts) formalized their vernacular in the currently prescribed manner.
9. It is thus up to the philologist to work out how notaries in (for example) tenth-century Galicia, speaking in the way that we can reconstruct tenth-century Galicians did, in practice learned to write their texts in the way they did (in particular as regards orthography and morphology). By a strange coincidence, that is exactly what I am currently investigating.

1994 POSTSCRIPT

The earliest version of this lecture was not specifically intended for a Hispanic audience, being delivered to a seminar on Medieval Education at the Warburg Institute, London, in June 1990, and then to another audience of medievalists in the University of Oslo, Norway, in September the same year. The invitation then came to contribute to the Festschrift volume for Dennis Seniff, who died in November 1990, so this paper was then expanded and made more specifically Hispanic; thus it was first published in *Linguistic Studies in Medieval Spanish*, ed. by Ray Harris-Northall and Thomas D. Cravens, University of Wisconsin (Madison), Hispanic Seminary of Medieval Studies, 1991, 191-208. The "unscientific analogy" is close enough to make the point clearer, but not, naturally, an exact parallel. Even so, the analogy was used again in a plenary lecture to the 28th International Congress of Medieval Studies in Kalamazoo, Michigan, on May 7th 1993, and seems to have a suitably illuminating effect. The recommendation to

---

[13] For St Martin of León, and why he deserves to be considered exceptional, see McCluskey (1989).

Hispanic medievalists to treat all non-Catalan texts from between 500 and San Martín de León as Romance is for practical purposes unlikely to be accepted, but the intrinsic point remains.

10
The Non-Existence of "Leonese Vulgar Latin"

I RECENTLY ELABORATED IN DETAIL (Wright 1982) the theory that the pronunciation of medieval Latin, as we have known it for twelve hundred years, was invented around the year 800 A.D. at the Carolingian court for the original purpose of establishing a fixed standard pronunciation of the offices of the Roman liturgy. According to this view, spoken medieval Latin was based then on the technique (which is still the one generally used today) of pronouncing one specified sound for each written letter of the correct orthographic forms, as if the spelling were also a phonetic script. This technique of spoken medieval Latin was not generally introduced into the Iberian Peninsula until after the adoption of the Roman rites, a process initiated at the Council of Burgos in 1080. Before then the local vernacular Romance was the only language spoken, although when it was written it tended to adopt more archaic morphology and vocabulary. In these centuries I suggest that they did not speak the Latin of the empire, nor the "Leonese Vulgar Latin" envisaged by Menéndez Pidal (1926, 1970: paragraphs 95, 109; subsequently renamed "latín popular arromanzado" by Lapesa; 1980: paragraph 40); all that they spoke was Romance, although naturally this contained within itself all the stylistic, sociolinguistic and geographical variation that all the vernaculars in the world normally do. This perspective, which has the virtue of being simple, and has solved some problems, does however raise further questions that need to be considered; for texts from the Iberian Peninsula, written between the fourth and the eleventh centuries, can hardly be taken to be exact transcriptions corresponding to spontaneous speech. If it is indeed the case that all the Leonese of the ninth century spoke ninth-century Leonese Romance, why did they write in such an antiquated manner, so unlike their own native language (as we can plausibly reconstruct it)?

As far as spelling is concerned, there is no problem. The "correct" orthography is always the one taught, whatever it may be like. The tenth-century Leonese were taught the traditional orthography. Whether or not it corresponds closely to pronunciation, all such traditional orthographies can function in practice precisely because they are indeed traditionally taught, since the only practical function of any kind of orthography is to aid identification of the corresponding lexical unit. We can hardly believe that in those centuries they understood about or practised phonetic transcriptions in the modern sense; not even the Romans had managed to make clear distinctions between spoken sounds and written letters.

For Menéndez Pidal, the presence of correct orthography was a symptom of a Latin-speaking writer, and the presence of semi-Latinate orthography was a symptom of a similarly "semi-learned" one; but it is safer to limit ourselves to deducing that correct orthography merely indicates a well-taught writer, and semi-Latinate orthography indicates a less skilled writer, without either type of spelling being appropriately taken to be a phonetic transcription of the writer's pronunciation. They were trying to write as they had been taught, and some of them managed that better than others.

Their training had been based for centuries on the *Artes Grammaticæ* of the late Roman Empire; and these also included all the morphological inflections that were needed for correct writing, whether or not they were used in speech. In addition to this, notaries had at their disposal several formulae, and technical legal terms and phrases, which they had learned by heart and could use every day. This means that the formulaic parts of a legal document cannot be used as evidence that their constituent linguistic features belonged to the normal speech of the writers, neither in León in the year 900 nor now. (This distinction between the language of the formulaic and "free" parts of legal documents was cogently made in Sabatini 1965). In every country, the differences that there usually are between notarial language and normal vernacular are internal differences of style rather than between separate languages.

We can expect, then, that the "semi-Latinate" appearance of many texts (as of the one printed here) is caused by the professional training of the notary. The same happens today; lawyers do not want to write in a colloquial style, but neither do they have to learn a wholly different language in order to compose their documents. All they have to do is become skilled in the legal style of their native language. A millennium ago, Leonese lawyers similarly had to learn no more than a particular style of Romance vernacular. As a result, we now find many documents such as the following (taken from Floriano 1951, Vol.I, no.76, pp.314-15, slightly corrected to agree with the photocopy Floriano also supplied):

In dei nomine ego daIldi una cum marito meo daui placuit nouis ad*que* conuenit bono animo et propria nouis fuit uolumtas ut uinderem*us* uob*is* argemundo et uxori tue recoIre uinea sicuti et uendim*us* In uilla q*ue* uocatur piasca In loco ubi dicit*ur* Illa clausa ad Illo salice medietatem In Ipsa uinea et In Ipsa terra uacabile q*ue* Ibi est I*us*ta Ipsa uinea medietatem. de termino in termino. ad Integritatem Ipsas medietates et In terra. et In uinea. cu*m* sua. clusura de giro In giro adpreciatu*m* In solido et quat*uo*r. modios et tu dedisti nob*is* pro Ipsa uinea et pro Ipsa terra precium q*ui* nobis plahcuit. Id est boue colore nigr*um* In solido et duos modios et karnarium In tria quartaria. et zibaria trja quartaria et oralem. In semodio et de ipso precio aderato aput uos deuitus non remansit ut ex odierno die et tempore abeatis Ipsa uinea et Ipsa terra uobis p*er*petim abitur*um* et q*ui*tquit de Illut facere u*e*l Iudicare uolueritis sit. uob*is* de nos concessa potestas. si q*ui*s aliq*ui*s. an nos. aut eredes u*e*l quoliuet omo de parte n*os*tra contra unc fact*um* n*os*tr*um* uenerit uobis ad Inrumpendum qod non possitis Ipsa terra et Ips uinea post nomine n*os*tro uindicare qualiter Inferam*us* uob*is* Ipsa uinea et Ipsa terra duplata quantum de uos fuerit meliora(ta) Facta kartula uenditjonis die. XIII k*a*l*endas* Iulias In era dccc...Et principe ordomio sede*n*te In asturias ego daildi a*n*c scriptura uenditjonis a me facta manu mea I-I-I feci d. dauit. cognomento. amorellus anc scriptura uenditjonis q*ui* fieri uolui manu mea I-I-I f*ec*i et testib*us* tradim*us* roboranda.

ermoIgius scripsit   (Signa)

Abbreviations have usually been resolved in my reproduction here as they would have been in the "correct" orthography, but *nr̄o*, for example, could as easily be resolved when reading aloud into [nwestro] as [nostro]. It was texts like this that encouraged Menéndez Pidal to hypothesize the existence of "Leonese Vulgar Latin," which in his view would have combined Latin grammar and medieval Leonese phonetics. This bill of sale seems to have been prepared on the 19th June 862; the date is unclear at the end, but from the photocopy it looks as if there is only room for one more *c*, or *ci* at most (although Floriano suggested 861, that is, an additional *LX ^{V} VIIII*). Here Daildi and her husband David are selling a vine field to Argemundo and his wife Recoire; Daildi and David wrote a cross and *feci* (or just *fe*) and Ermoigius wrote the rest. (These same people reappear in Floriano's documents nos 66 and 72).

This document includes mainly "correct" forms in the formulaic sections such as *In dei nomine*, the date, the final formulae, etc; but even here we can find the usual uncertainties, e.g. as between *b* and *u* in *nouis*, and the lack of a tilde over *scriptura* at the end. But neither in these parts nor in the free sections can we conclude that the details of the written form are close to being transcriptions of the speech of either Daildi or Ermoigius. This is not a transcription, but a stylized version intended thereby to be legally acceptable. Daildi told Ermoigius the relevant details in Leonese Romance, and the notary then "legalized" it. Lawyers in all communities polish their clients' speech in a similar way.

Even so, it is worth considering the further question of how this document would have been read aloud subsequently. Brian Dutton has pointed out—as we would anyway have expected—that legal documents were read aloud, and comprehensible when read aloud, even to illiterate interested parties. The lawyers cannot, obviously, have read the texts aloud as if they were written in phonetic script. That would in any event be extremely difficult, even for modern experts in phonetics. As soon as they recognized the written word, they would say it in its usual Romance phonetic shape, however it happened to be written in the text. Thus those words of this text that existed in normal vernacular in León in 862 would have been read aloud with their normal phonetics. For example, diphthongization of original [ɔ́] and [ɛ́] had long been normal, and so when they were read aloud the words *loco* and *boue* automatically contained [we], and the words *terra* and *inrumpendum* contained [je], as in their normal vernacular. Intervocalic consonants that were originally unvoiced had voiced centuries earlier, and so *loco*, *placuit* and *iudicare*, once recognized as lexical units, were automatically given a [g] ([lwego], [plogo], and in León probably [ʒulgaɾe]), and *duplata* both a [b] and a [d] ([doblada]). The same happens to American English -*t*- (*tomato* [təmejdə], etc.) What had been [tj] and [kj] in the Latin of the Roman Empire had become palatal affricates, and so *precio* (and *pretio*, if it was written correctly) would have been read aloud as the normal vernacular [pretsjo] and *adpreciatum* as [apretsjado]. For the same kinds of reason, *ipsa* would have been recognized as the written form of [esa] and automatically read aloud as such, *karnarium* as [karnejɾo], *salice* as [sawtse], *dedisti* as [diste], *facta* as [fejta] (or in Castille [hetʂa]), *quatuor* as [kwatro], etc. There is no problem at all in this; the English now read the word written *stationer* as [stejʃnə] and *could* as [kud], etc., and modern French readers recognize and produce *noeud* as [nø], *quand* as [kã], *hameau* as [amo], etc. The problem would arise if we had to read them aloud as [stationer], [could], [noeud], [kuand], [hameau], [loko], [plakuit], [adprekiatum], [ipsa], etc., and—obviously—when reading it does not ever occur to us to read these words in such a strange way. It is essential not to be misled by spelling; in English the words *you*, *too*, *do*, *shoe*, *grew* and *through* all end in [-uː], whether read aloud or in spontaneous speech; in the same way, there is no reason not to envisage that in tenth-century Castille the written letters -CUL- (as in *oculum*), -LI- (as in *filium*) and G- (as in *gentes*) all represented [ʒ] ([oʒo], [hiʒo], [ʒentes]).

Words that did not survive in the normal vernacular Romance would have been read aloud by analogy with other words spelled in the same way. In this way, *aput* (that is, *apud*) would have been read as [abo], in the same way as *caput* was recognized and read as [kabo], even though it seems likely that the word *apud* was no longer used in spontaneous speech; and we can plausibly suggest that *k͞ids* would be read with a diphthong, as was *inrumpendum* ([enrompjendo]). (Lange 1966 discusses the vocabulary of two

Portuguese documents of 882 and 897; for *cibaria*, see p.108; for *medietate*, *modios* and *quartaria*, see p.249).

The same applies to the inflectional suffixes, which form a special case within the general vocabulary. They had no problem in reading *-um* as [o], *-i* as [-e], *-am* as [-a], etc. They may perhaps have had more difficulty with some nominatives such as *uoluntas*, in which the vernacular form in [-ade] (< -ATEM) came from the accusative case of an imparisyllabic noun; but I suspect they in practice used when reading aloud the usual Romance form [voluntade] in ninth-century León; this is, after all, closer to the written form *uoluntas* than are many spoken and written forms of the same word in Modern French, for example. Disyllabic nominal suffixes are interesting cases; *-arum* and *-orum* could have been read as [-aro] and [-oro]. These endings almost certainly no longer existed in normal Leonese Romance; but here we are not considering normal vernacular but an archaic register written and then read aloud. In any event, to some extent they avoided these forms in writing; there are none in this text. *-ibus* could have been read aloud as [-iβos] or [-eβos], but I suspect it was read aloud simply as [-es], as in the normal plural of the vernacular word, which by now lacked any such distinctively dative or ablative form: *testibus* as [tjestes], say, or *nobis* as [nos]. (Politzer 1961 argues cogently that *-ibus* would have been spelled best by those who never used it in speech.) In my view, neither lawyers, nor monks, nor anyone else, is likely to have produced [-bu-] or [-βu-] here, neither in speaking, nor in reading aloud a word whose written form ended in *-ibus*. English lawyers do not pronounce an [l] in *could*, nor French ones [llent] in *veuillent* ([vœ:j]).

Verbal affixes could be read in a similar way; *-auit* as [-ó] (or conceivably still [-óđ] in the ninth century), *-etur* as [-édor], *-erit* as [-jere], etc. The few words whose form when read aloud like this did not correspond exactly to normal vernacular (for example, synthetic passives), in some cases as a result in changes of word order, would have been thought of as peculiarities of the legal style, as the Spanish future subjunctive (in e.g. *viniere, fuere*) is thought of today. Spontaneously, [-edor] was not normally heard. Similarly, if a modern Spaniard reads Berceo aloud, he or she reads the letters *-iere* as [-jere], without that necessarily meaning that the future subjunctive is a feature of their usual speech, and without our referring to them as users of "Ancient Vulgar Castilian."

From documents like this (and no other evidence), in which there are spelling mistakes attributable to vernacular phonetics (for example, here, *precio, zibaria*; other documents are "worse"), Menéndez Pidal deduced the existence of a distinct "Leonese Vulgar Latin," spoken by semi-learned people. For him, such forms represented the "voluntary yielding to a common language halfway between the Latin of the schools and the popular Romance" (1970:456, paragraph 109), rather than just being mistakes. In his view, this language had essentially Latin grammar with medieval phonetics (although the famous *Nodicia de kesos*, 1970:24-25, did not even have outdated morphology). This same combination of essentially "correct" grammar with evolved phonetics seems to me to be a distinctive feature of the reading aloud of written texts, and no more than that (see the extensive discussion in Wright 1982:165-73). Menéndez Pidal built up a whole linguistic system, distinguishable both from the normal Romance and from Latin, which belonged to a large number of people who happened also to be experts in phonetic script; but it is simpler just to see them as scribes of average ability who spoke the vernacular of their time and place. In Ninth-century León they spoke Ninth-century Leonese Romance. This Romance was not homogeneous, and naturally included stylistic and sociolinguistic variation, but was no more than one language. This is not a revolutionary idea in itself. In any elementary sociolinguistics textbook we can see that this is the usual situation, and that if the near trilingualism postulated by Menéndez Pidal had existed, that situation would be little short of miraculous. We can at last discard the hypotheses of Leonese Vulgar Latin, of spoken Medieval Latin in Spain before the reforms that were accelerated in 1080, and of the existence of many experts in phonetic script, and indeed of a whole bundle of venerable but unlikely explanations.

1994 POSTSCRIPT

Late Latin and Early Romance came out in 1982, just after the end of the Falklands-Malvinas War. The editor of *Incipit* had the admirable idea of extending possibilities of reconciliation through inviting British contributors to the journal's forthcoming volume, and was kind enough to include me in the invitation. Thus the Spanish original of this article first appeared in *Incipit* (Buenos Aires, Argentina) 3 (1983), 1-7 as "La no existencia del latín vulgar leonés." The same volume carried a lengthy review of *Late Latin* by José-Luis Moure. For the article, I had no time to do more than elaborate one of the most important sections of the book, but other reviews have shown that that section was also one of the least well understood, so this exercise was worthwhile then and its reprinting is worthwhile now. The article had unexpected consequences; that, and the review, were the first news that scholars had in Spain of this kind of analysis, and while it repelled some (and still does) it helped considerably in the success of the proposal to produce a Spanish translation of *Late Latin*; and also led to friendships that I value among the Asturian and Leonese scholars interested in texts such as that of Ermoigius. Many of the ideas mentioned in this little article are expanded in later ones in this collection; the more that detailed analyses and general considerations can be undertaken together, the more we are likely to see clearly what actually happened in this fascinating period before the Europeanizing reforms of the late eleventh century.

11
Asturian Texts of the Ninth and Tenth Centuries: Barbarous Latin or Written Romance?

ARMANDO COTARELO VALLEDOR CALLED the second half of the ninth century in the Iberian Peninsula "a time of total literary decadence" (1933:583). Manuel Gómez Moreno called the text of the *Crónica Albeldense* "classic for its barbarism" (1932:565), and the "Rotense" text of the *Chronicle of Alfonso III* "barbarous in style" (1932:585). The language of this text has also been called "barbarous" by Valdeavellano (1952:480), Sánchez Alonso (1941:111) and others. Miguel Stero referred to its "clumsy latin" (1946:126). But King Alfonso III and his Court were neither barbarous nor clumsy nor totally decadent, and it is about time we began to reexamine in a more generous and sympathetic perspective the evaluation which we give to the texts prepared there. That is what this paper aims to achieve.

1. THE CHRONICLE OF ALFONSO III.

The two versions of the *Chronicle of Alfonso III* have been edited three times recently; by the German scholar Jan Prelog (1980), by Juan Gil of Seville (1985), and by the French scholar Yves Bonnaz (1987). As is generally known, the language of the earliest surviving version of this Chronicle, the late ninth-century version known as the "Rotense," is not very classical. Prelog edited it more or less as we find it in the oldest manuscripts, a procedure which did not commend itself to Bonnaz:

> Although it is considerably better than earlier editions, it is accompanied by rather an unwieldy apparatus criticus, and the text has not been sufficiently cleaned of the incorrect forms and altered spellings found in the oldest manuscripts, whose preservation is not always justifiable. (viii)

Bonnaz does not follow this practice in his own edition:

> So I have chosen in my own edition to print the classical Latin variant wherever that seems possible...I have, in short, made my own emendations. (xliv-xlv)

That is, Bonnaz prints what he thinks ought to have been written, even though, as he realizes, in this way he does not always reproduce the original text; he still presumes (as most editors used to think some time ago) that every non-Classical usage can be blamed on bad copyists, even though it is now widely realized that copyists are more likely to "correct" than deform their originals. Referring to the "extreme corruption" of the language of the oldest copies, Bonnaz asks the following question, which he wishes us to regard as rhetorical:

> Should I have kept all these incorrect forms on the grounds that they come from ancient manuscripts, and their latin would have been more like the Latin used in the ninth century? In reality, the fact that they are not systematically repeated in these manuscripts and that they cooccur with impeccably classical forms leads me to think that they are not always very significant . . (xliv)

Juan Gil, on the other hand, would reply that it is indeed best to keep the original details as far as possible, pointing out that:

> The reader is going to be confronted with a text that will at times appear to him to be barbarous and chaotic, very unlike the tidy classicizing editions that are usually produced...in this way, in its supposed barbarousness, the text seems stranger, and leads us into a quite different world...(59-60)

Thus even Gil refers to the supposed barbarousness, although he reproduces it.

Linguists, of course, prefer manuscripts to be edited without any emendations at all. We need all the authentic details, however insignificant they may seem to historians. This need is being expressed in ever more explicit and vociferous terms; a whole recent volume of *Speculum* (65.1, 1990) is dedicated to its articulation. If the texts are printed in a classicizing disguise, we will never be able to examine their language with the necessary exactness. What Bonnaz says, for example, about the insignificance of incorrect and inconsistent spelling is diametrically opposed to the truth. As is clear from the studies of József Herman (e.g. 1990), relative statistics, both comparing correct and incorrect forms in a text and comparing the separate incorrect ones, can be used as powerful evidence for the nature of Early Romance; recent studies by Erica García (e.g. 1985) show that changes in progress can be noticed precisely through changes in such relative statistics comparing the proportions of use of each variant; and as Cravens has shown in his recent acute study (1991), within texts that the author is trying to make respectable, every little error could have great significance. Yet we can see that at times Bonnaz, in his recent edition of the Rotense version of the Chronicle, has changed its spelling and morphology. Bonnaz is thus doing the same as Lucas of Tuy; as the sixteenth-century copyists of the Chronicle, who were unable to leave the text alone without "changing it to suit classical requirements" (Gil, p.59); the same as Ambrosio de Morales did when confronted with the works of Eulogio de Cordoba (thanks to which, the writings of Eulogio have little value for linguistic study); the same as all editors of Isidore of Seville's *Etymologiae*, including the most recent; and, indeed, the same as the writer of the so-called "Erudite" version (*Ad Sebastianum*) of the Chronicle of Alfonso III, which was made in the tenth century. All these editors have been classicizing a text which seems to them too "barbarous." Furthermore, we know that the tenth-century editor of the "Erudite" version of the Chronicle was not in fact correcting the actual surviving Rotense text, but another version even earlier than both of those; we can see this from the stemma, which seems now to be more or less generally agreed ("the *Crónica de Alfonso III* comes from another Leonese manuscript which was polished up before being transcribed in the Rotense manuscript," Díaz y Díaz 1979:37). The Rotense version itself has corrections and additions written in by the copyist himself, even though it is taken to be a version elaborated on the basis of an earlier one; and even this earlier version is very likely to have been already polished up from the original first draft. That is, even the most "barbarous" of the surviving versions in fact represents a fairly high rung on this centuries-long ladder of classicization, which is still being climbed.

Gómez Moreno referred to the "barbarousness" of the text, but also said that "all its defects...are valuable symptoms of spontaneity and liveliness" (1932:585). This can be accepted in part, but we cannot believe that the Rotense text is "spontaneous" in the sense of being a transcription of the spontaneous speech of its authors. It has been filled with references from the Bible and the martyrologies, with legal phrases, and the kind of literary stylistic effects that had pleased the Visigoths. These details must have been added because of a desire to raise the level of the style to one higher than the spontaneous. If we insist on thinking that all non-classical uses are by definition "barbarous," the original (lost) draft must have been one long barbarity.

The normal view that has been taken of these texts begs the question. It presupposes that the authors were indeed aiming to write Latin, conceived of as another language separate from their normal vernacular Romance. But it seems more likely that they were not trying to write "Latin" at all, neither the Classical Latin of the very distant past, nor the Medieval Latin of the unforeseeable future, but merely the most respectable style they could achieve of their own language, of their Romance vernacular. This was not easy, for they still had no other accepted way of writing than the old traditional one, for they had not yet invented either written Romance or phonetic transcription; and they were wanting to achieve, by a process of polishing and refining, a more and more respectable version; even so, in essence this is an Iberoromance text, written in a very high and occasionally tedious style, rather than a Latin text written in an extremely low style. (I merely say "Iberoromance," without wishing to be more precise; it is misleading for us to adopt more precise geographical labels for their speech before the thirteenth century, and they do not seem to have done so themselves; that is why I refrain from calling their Romance "Early Leonese" or "Early Asturian"; see Wright 1992b). In this way we can restore some professional self-respect to these Asturian writers, for they were not writing Latin badly, they were writing their Romance well, the Romance of their time and place. They were not irredeemably stupid, but intelligent professionals.

2. EARLY ROMANCE AND ROMANCE PHILOLOGY

It is worth remembering at this point how Romance Philology nowadays views the linguistic state of the Iberian Peninsula in the ninth and tenth centuries; and first we should recognize that the language they spoke cannot be described as "barbarous" in itself.

It has sometimes been suggested that both the development of the Romance languages from their origin in the spoken Latin of the Roman Empire, and their divergence from each other, were caused to a large extent by the political disintegration of the Empire. Some philologists of the first half of the twentieth century (e.g. Muller 1929) postponed this date, both for the evolution and the divergence, to the start of the seventh century. Such a late date seems improbable to historical linguists now, because we know for certain that linguistic change cannot just be stopped like that during whole centuries. Even so, unfortunately, some Latinists and historians still trust that dating. In its place, some of the philologists who work with reconstruction methods have preferred to move the date of both evolution and divergence to long before the end of the empire, or even before its start; De Dardel (1983), for example, dates the separation of Proto-Sardinian Romance from Proto-Romance in general to the second century B.C. This dating, in turn, understandably seems absurd to Latinists and historians, who see no evidence for the existence at that time of a need for interpreters between Sardinians and Romans. The result of all this has unfortunately been that the specialists in Romance historical linguistics and the specialists in Early Medieval History have stopped taking each other seriously.

But in fact it is quite easy to reconcile the two perspectives. Indeed, it is true that many Romance phonetic developments started early, but for all practical purposes the geographical divergence happened very late. Alberto Varvaro (e.g. 1991) has been able to solve this fairly clearly, taking into account the sociolinguistic nature of modern speech-communities of similarly wide geographical extension, such as Modern English, French and also Italian. All these speech communities contain within them a great deal of variation, geographical, sociolinguistic and stylistic, and when new linguistic phenomena arise—which happens all the time—they manage to fit in to the single complex mosaic. Thus we can see that many of the phonetic, morphological and syntactic developments that the philologists wish to postulate did indeed start early, before the end of the Empire, without this meaning that the existing forms that fulfilled the same function necessarily had to disappear until centuries afterwards (if at all). This is more or less what Menéndez Pidal proposed (in 1926) when he used the phrase *estado latente*, the "latent phase" of a change. Under this perspective we can postulate the existence of a single monolingual Western Early Romance speech community up to the eighth and even the ninth century. As time went by, this monolingualism became ever more complicated, but even so it does not seem that any of its speakers explicitly had the idea that difficulties in communication were so great that there must have existed separate languages, neither in a diastratic nor a diatopic sense (this conclusion has been independently reached recently by, for example, Herman 1988, Van Uytfanghe 1989, Banniard 1989). Complex, but monolingual.

In a recent book, the French medievalist Michel Banniard (1989) writes that the inhabitants of the Romance-speaking area in this period belonged to one *ensemble linguistique* (187), in which there was still a functional symbiosis between written and spoken forms of the language (197). The illiterate, for example, had nonetheless enough passive competence to understand homilies and Saints' Lives and other texts that were read aloud to them (204). This monolingual perspective preserves Muller's genuine insight, that in those centuries nobody made metalinguistic distinctions between "Latin" and "Romance," without drawing the conclusion that Muller himself drew from this, that Latin managed to remain at the start of the seventh century more or less the same as it had been in the first. There was surely never a state of linguistic immobilism. Latin, like every other language, has never been fixed in a state of stable perfection. It has kept on inexorably evolving, before the Empire, during the Empire, and ever since. It makes no sense to ask "When did Latin begin to change?" Its name may have changed, but whether we call it Indo-European, Italic, Latin, or Romance, the language has always been evolving. It is still evolving now, without our needing for that reason to describe any of the synchronic linguistic states as "barbarous."

Even though it seems absurd, however, the speech of whole communities for centuries on end has indeed been described as "barbarous." It has often been claimed that Early Romance was in itself "inferior" to the Latin of the Empire (e.g. by Salvador 1988:644-45). There is no sense in this claim, neither in general, nor with reference to phonetics, nor morphology, nor syntax nor semantics. Cultural changes had indeed taken place, naturally. For example, it is possible to deduce that the Romance-speaking communities between the fifth and eleventh centuries were in general less literate than than those of the Empire. That is, they wrote less. Even so, as Banniard points out, since they were still using biodegradable materials such as papyrus and wax tablets, they probably wrote far more than we now appreciate, without wanting to preserve it down the centuries for our benefit. They also occasionally wrote on slates, a few of which happen to survive (see e.g. Díaz y DIaz 1986; Velázquez, in Fontán and Moure 1987:135-38).

Early Romance, if and when it was written, had in practice no alternative but to exhibit - at least in the first draft of any text - more features characteristic of oral registers than are normally visible in the artificial texts of "Classical" Latin. Such oral features are in themselves neither "bad" nor "decadent." In oral contexts, every language has greater flexibility and more nuances than it has in writing. They offer chances for subtle effects of intonation, of word order, of topicalization, of the use of deictics, of pragmatic devices, of varying styles and registers, of effects based on the relationship between old and new information, of interaction with the listener or listening audience, etc. In sum, oral registers have an exuberance and a complexity which can hardly ever be achieved in writing, even by the best modern dramatists.

But all the surviving evidence is, of course, written. Written language is normally, almost necessarily, standardized. Standardization of written language nearly always involves a restriction of the options that are available in speech, choosing some from out of the extensive range of available spoken variation. The inevitable consequence of this is that many features of oral language that were not originally chosen as suitable for representation in the standard written form are bound to seem later, to Grammarians (who instinctively tend to see written standards in moral terms), to be cases of "decadence." So the features of oral language that were not chosen to be included in the standardization tend to disappear from texts, even if they continue to be alive in normal speech. This was the effect of the *Ars Grammatica* tradition; many perfectly straightforward features of normal speech were thought to have been decreed to be "bad" (by omission from the list of the "good") and were thus excluded from writing; and for this reason, as seen above, later copies of already written texts were changed on purpose to fit this norm.

The arrival of new morphological and syntactic features in Early Romance, so far as we can now perceive them, had often had the consequence of making available to the speaker greater flexibility and versatility than he had had before. For example, the new non-Classical possibility of combining verbal auxiliaries (Green 1982), on the lines of eventual Spanish constructions such as *habrían sido hechas*, or the availability of constructions including the word *se* with a semantically passive rather than reflexive function, brought with them the possibility of exploiting in speech a wider range of semantic nuances than there had been before. This was not barbarism; this was versatility. The arrival of the new alternatives enriched the resources of the language with new useful material that could be employed to create contrasts with the already existing possibilities, which often stayed in the language for centuries before falling into disuse.

After the Empire, and in the Iberian Peninsula up to the twelfth century, the techniques of writing (*Ars Grammatica*) still followed the tradition set by Donatus. This tradition had continued in Visigothic Spain through to Julián de Toledo, and survived after the invasion, both in Moslem and Christian Spain. Sometimes we are able to glimpse the existence of other, more experimental, ways of writing, used for texts of little importance such as the famous list of Leonese cheeses (the *Nodicia de kesos* of the late tenth century), but if a text was intended to be kept for centuries, they naturally cleaned up its spelling and its morphology in order to be "correct" according to the traditional standard. For at that time, as at almost any other, linguistic alternatives were thought of in moral terms; different uses were not merely seen as old or new, spontaneous or tedious, formal or informal, etc., but as "correct" or "incorrect"; and they identified "correctness" as lying in conformity with the ancient precepts. Professional writers of this Early Romance, of this sophisticated monolingual mosaic, were aiming above all for "correctness."

Unfortunately for modern philologists, "correctness" did not consist in attempts to transcribe spoken language exactly. (Nor does it now, of course.) One of the most important tasks of those who undertook to write important works was to eliminate from the initial draft of their text any feature which would not have seemed "correct" to the grammarians of the fourth and fifth centuries. Inevitably, this meant that the versatility of their speech was severely restricted in their writing. That is why these Chronicles seem to us now to have such a clumsy style; the writers believed that it was necessary to write them like that. They believed that in this way they were achieving correctness.

In those centuries, they had no alternative. It is true that later on, at least after the year 1000, vernacular morphology, phonetics and syntax were represented occasionally in France on manuscript without their archaizing disguise, and some Spanish regions, those with French contacts, can provide us with evidence that they were aware of this strange French habit. The Riojan glossers, at least, seem to have imitated it (and we should all now bear in mind the work of Bézler, 1984 and 1985, who concluded that the original of the glossed Silos manuscript must have been written after the year 1060, and of Stengaard (1991a), who shows how glosses of different types in the San Millán manuscript were used to aid oral delivery). But before the arrival of distinctive Romance writing norms in the Peninsula, they wrote well by imitating ancient practice. In the Chronicle of Alfonso III, they were writing Early Romance well.

3. ROMANCE PHONETICS AND TRADITIONAL ORTHOGRAPHY

In general, there is no reason to complain about orthographic standardization. It has a sensible practical purpose, even if orthographical traditions sometimes hide phonetic variability from our view. For example, in tenth-century Asturian texts the letter *t* could represent a word-initial [t] (as in the word written *tenere*), an intervocalic [d] or even a [đ] sound (as in the word spelled *pratum*; see Walsh, 1991), a [dz] sound (as in the word spelled *ratione*) or a [ts] sound (as in the affix written *-antia*) before a semivocalic [j], or even, word-finally, no sound at all (as in the word spelled *sunt*). When they read aloud a written text, this lack of biuniqueness caused no problem. The main practical purpose of a written form is to enable the reader to recognize the lexical unit, regardless of what the phonemes are; that is how logographic script such as that of Chinese is able to function, and to a great extent the reading of texts in the Peninsula in the tenth century worked the same way. Those who had learned to read at all had learned the usual traditional forms, and thus had no difficulty in recognizing the word written *tenet* as the one pronounced [tjéne], the written form *pratum* as representing [prađo] (or [prado]), the one written *sunt* as representing [son], etc. Those who had not learned to read at all would not have been helped in any way by the existence of a more "phonetic" type of orthography (that is, more isomorphic with the phonemes), and those who knew how to read already thereby knew how to recognize the old forms. This is what happens in modern French and English, where attempts to establish a new spelling system more closely allied to speech always fail, for such simple practical reasons. Thus, as is by now generally understood, forms written in a "correct" old way do not in themselves imply that the pronunciation has failed to change since the orthographic standardization, neither in the *Chronicle of Alfonso III* nor in modern English or Spanish works.

But we should also beware of being misled by the opposite case, when there seems to have been relative consistency in the pronunciation of a word but a variety of written forms representing it. As Alarcos Llorach (1982:25) pointed out, such variation does not mean - could not mean - that there existed exactly the same wide range of phonetic realizations as there is of orthographic. According to the apparatus criticus provided by Prelog, some words in the

Chronicle are given up to eight different spellings in the manuscripts, but we cannot deduce from this that the word was pronounced in eight different ways. For a small example, let us consider the ways in which the name of King Bermudo is written in the Rotense version. He is the syntactic subject of his two appearances in Chapter 20; we find the following forms: *Ueremudus, Ueremudo, Ueremundus* and *Ueremundo*. Prelog prints *Veremudo*, Gil *Ueremudus*, Bonnaz *Veremundus*. The Rotense manuscript itself has *Ueremudo*, and it is better to print it precisely that way, because apart from anything else we can be sure that they did not pronounce in normal speech either the [n] or the ending [-us], and the written forms that include *n* and *-us* do so merely in their determination to be "correct." The lack of uniformity in spelling is often the result of inconsistent attempts at achieving this "correctness." Many philologists nowadays have realized what is happening here, in cases where the confusion is orthographic rather than phonetic; see, for example, the two excellent studies by Puentes Romay (1986a, b) and the important article by Carmen Pensado Ruiz (1991). Pensado Ruiz investigated inconsistencies in the spelling of Leonese legal documents of this time, and deduced that these early Medieval writers were consistent at least in trying to write their own language as well as they could. The existence of spelling variation need mean no more than this. They were trying to write well, according to their rules (such as, "represent the sound [we] with the letter o"; "use inflectional affixes rather than prepositions," etc.), but they did not always succeed in applying these rules consistently.

The conclusion we can draw as regards phonetics and spelling is this: that the Latin of the Roman Empire, Early Iberian Romance, thirteenth-century Castilian, and modern Castilian also, all contain within them phonetic variation of a normal type, which is in no sense dysfunctional or problematic. There is no need for us to call tenth-century Romance phonetics "decadent" or "stammering" or "incipient" or "disintegrating" or "inferior" to that of Imperial Latin, or to that of Modern Spanish; and if the spelling was often not the same as that of the fourth century, nor yet instead a faithful transcription of their own phonetics, this cannot have been of great importance in practice.

4. MORPHOLOGY AND SYNTAX.

The same can be said of morphology and syntax: that there was a lack of isomorphism between speech and "correct" writing, but that this was not in itself a symptom of "barbarousness." It has already been shown above that the arrival of new alternatives in the speech of the late Empire gave rise to greater versatility and flexibility. Similarly, in the morphology and syntax of Early Iberian Romance there also coexisted old and new features, but this in itself did not cause problems any greater than there had been in the Empire or than there are now. This variation had, as we saw, practical advantages, particularly in speech. For example, in the tenth century we can reconstruct that there were available two "pluperfect" forms: *fiziera* (< FECERAT), the traditional form, and *avia fecho* (< HABEBAT FACTUM), the newer form created with the Romance auxiliary. At first sight, this coexistence might seem a case of decadence, or at least of confusion. But the different forms had different functions, and in this respect the medieval language turns out to have been subtler than either the modern language or that of the Empire. Chevalier (1984) argued that the forms with *avia* should be analyzed as the imperfect of the forms in *ha*, rather than the pluperfect of the present; and Lunn and Cravens (1991) have discovered that in the *Poema de Mio Cid* the two forms have different pragmatic purposes, in that *avia fecho* indicates to the listener "pay attention; this information is new," whereas *fiziera* indicates "this is old information within the discourse." This distinction has value above all in speech.

It is also now very fashionable to study apparently redundant clitic pronouns. Riiho (1988) examined these uses in an exhaustive investigation and concluded that they had no strictly grammatical function, but caused no problem in context, being a sign of the exuberance of speech rather than of decadence or confusion. Silva Corvalán (1984) analyzed them in the *Poema de Mio Cid*, concluding that they reflected oral usage, fulfilling the function of directing the attention of the listeners in an appropriate direction. Oral versatility can look like redundancy when transcribed in texts; these pronouns were symptoms of an oral register, and they also probably existed in the speech of the tenth century. But in the tenth century the writers also knew that such features should not be included in a "correctly" written text, so they did not put them in; that is, they on purpose hid from our view the "spontaneity and liveliness" that Gómez Moreno claimed to see there, because in this way they were writing their own language well, as they had been instructed to do. Thus Díaz y Díaz (1976:225) referred to the "expressive poverty" of the Rotense, but that was what they were aiming to achieve; in that way they were exhibiting discipline, rather than any lack of discipline.

The conclusion to be drawn as regards morphology and syntax is the same as that concerning phonetics; there was no morphological or syntactic collapse, nor was the speech community less efficient than it had been. The language served the needs of its users. But here, as in phonetics, the relationship between speech and writing was getting increasingly complicated. The available morphological and syntactic variants in the Romance spoken in tenth-century Asturias were, over time, coming to coincide less and less with what they were told was acceptable in writing. This problem arose when they wrote, but not when they read aloud, nor did it greatly hamper their ability to understand a text read aloud by somebody else. It seems reasonable to conclude that people could understand many constructions which they rarely or never used in their own active speech. In other words, their passive competence in understanding existing texts, in reading or in hearing them read aloud, was considerably wider than their active competence. Thus there were features of spoken morphology and syntax that rarely appeared in writing, as well as features of writing that rarely appeared in speech; but even so, in general, the traditional written forms of the language, including in texts of serious practical importance, remained comprehensible not only in Asturias but even in Carolingian France, as McKitterick (1989) has established convincingly. This also fits Banniard's pan-Romance view (e.g.Banniard 1989:190). As Green (1991) and Stengaard (1991b:5.2.1) have argued, for example, the synthetic passives could be understood on the whole in the tenth century, even if almost nobody then used them spontaneously. There always is a gap between active and passive competence; modern Spaniards understand their future subjunctive without using it, modern Frenchmen understand their preterites without using them.

In tenth-century León such discrepancies were gradually increasing. The traditional *Artes Grammaticae* concentrated most on morphology, and it was possible by consulting them to write correctly such inflections as *-ibus* or *-atur*. In the *Chronicle of Alfonso III* we find many uses of the synthetic passive that appear to be quite unnecessary; the authors would have felt proud of them, for they showed how important and serious their work was. For an example, consider "arma adsumunt, eriguntur fundiuali, abtantur funde, migantur enses, crispantur aste hac incessanter emittuntur sagitte," ch.10 (Gil, p.128). The word written *emittunt* in the earliest manuscripts of the Rotense version was turned into *emittuntur* in the "Erudite" version, and also in later copies of the Rotense itself, for the greater glory of its syntax. They had less success, though, with their nominal inflections. They seem to have known how to use these affixes in writing, without being at all sure of which was necessary when. For that reason we can find the normal vernacular form, usually derived from what was once the accusative (but which often looks like the ablative) in any syntactic position at all (as with *Veremudo* ending in *-o* in subject position, already discussed above).

5. Lexis and Semantics

In the same way, most people in these Early Romance societies could also understand many items of vocabulary that they were unlikely to use spontaneously themselves. As writers strove for "correctness," they often consciously imitated texts from the past. This is what lawyers always do, of course, but modern research has established that ancient models can often be found for the phraseology of ninth and tenth-century texts, even for phrases that seem of little significance. Bonnaz has presented several such discoveries in the notes to his edition of the *Chronicle*, for example, without it always being clear if the earlier phrase is the model or a coincidence. (Working in our post-romantic age a millennium later, we tend to feel that this carefully unoriginal technique is counterproductive.) In the *Chronicle of Alfonso III* it was not merely a question of imitating earlier Histories that served as sources; Gil has shown, for example, in his edition (ch.9), that the conversation between Pelayo and Oppa before the Battle of Covadonga follows detailed models in the Bible and in hagiography.

Neither we, nor the first readers of the Chronicle, are in a position to know whether there was any underlying truth in the details presented in this way, but that was not the point; in this way they were writing "correctly."

This is one more example of the discrepancies between speech and writing. It has no consequences in itself for our evaluation of their speech. The idea which has so repeatedly been put forward, that the Romance speakers of the time had no more than a barbarous and stammered language, seems only conceivable if we are also to suggest that for centuries on end nobody actually spoke at all. It seems to have been taken for granted in some philological traditions that everyone who lived in the Christian areas of the Early medieval Iberian Peninsula was extremely stupid, so much so that there is no need to try to construct a reasonable explanation for the nature of the texts they left behind them. Such a hypothesis does not seem attractive to the historians of the age, who can glimpse that there there were many intelligent individuals, trying successfully to overcome practical obstacles of all kinds in their lives, not merely in their writing systems. For on the whole the Christians in the Iberian Peninsula in these centuries were not suffering from total intellectual barbarousness, linguistic decadence and general stupidity. It was a time of essentially oral culture; differences between speech and writing (which exist everywhere) were growing slowly more marked, but individuals were not in general less intelligent than we are. It could be argued that the first part of the thirteenth century was the only time when it was possible to write in a style that could genuinely be called more or less "oral," without the limitations and pedantry inevitably imposed by standardization (as was also the case in France; see Fleischman, 1990).

6. THE LANGUAGE OF THE CHRONICLE

I hope to have shown by now that the language spoken in ninth and tenth-century Asturias was not in itself "barbarous." What is it then, that this much-mentioned "barbarousness" in the texts is supposed to consist of? It seems that the features that have been so identified are merely the symptoms of the writers' intense efforts to write in the way they were trained to regard as "correct": often discarding constructions normal in speech for words and phrases found in venerated ancient texts, and following the traditional spelling which had by then become almost logographic in nature. This is seriousness, not barbarousness.

But even though these texts are thus in disguise, we can see that they were written in the Ibero-Romance of their time, from details which it was not possible for them to write in the "correct" manner, or which it could not possibly have occurred to them that they needed to change. Obviously, Arabic personal names, for example, had no "correct" form. The writers had to improvise. The same applies to arabisms; Corominas (among others) has explained convincingly that the word written *mollite* (ch.25: *alium mollite nomine Alporz*) is the one that turns up later as the toponym *Muélledes*, and which is usually now rendered as *muladí*.

Semantic changes attested in these texts are also important evidence (cp. Wright 1987). Semantic changes were not mentioned in the Grammars, nor in the scribes' training. For example, in the Chronicle they used their normal vernacular word [poblarə] (which had by then the meaning which *poblar* still has, "populate"), spelling it correctly as *populare*, without realizing that centuries earlier this word had instead meant "devastate" (see Bonnaz, 135-36). Quoting Gil's edition:

> ...quum ciuitas Uiseo et suburbis eius iussum nostrum esset populatus (ch.7, p.122).

These words of the Rotense version have been slightly "corrected" in the "Erudite" version, but the editor of this is not aware of any semantic anomaly:

> ...quum Uiseo ciuitas et suburbana eius a nobis populata esset (p.123).

There are further similar uses of the same word in chapters 11 and 14, both endowed with impressive but unnecessary passive morphology. There was no problem in achieving this passive morphology; that was an established trick of their trade; nor in achieving the correct orthography, which in this case was much more straightforward for them than is that of many words in Modern French, for example; but they had no means even of suspecting the existence of the semantic change. (Both versions also used the Ibero-Romance word [despoblaron], which would later be endowed with a reformed orthography as *despoblaron*, spelling it here "correctly" as *depopulauerunt*.)

It has also been pointed out that the word written *consubrinus* has in this Chronicle the modern meaning of "nephew" rather than the original one of "cousin":

Cindasuindus rex magnifice suscepit et in coniungio consubrinam suam dedit (ch.2, p.116)

Magno uiro Egicani consubrino Bambani Regi (ch.3, p.118).

These really were nephews. But it looks as though in this case the semantic change was not totally complete. The change may have happened in the unprefixed form (which was to survive in the written form *sobrino*) because of its use to designate a cousin of a younger generation ("once removed"). An example of this can be seen in ch.20, where the word *subrinum* is used to refer to the future Alfonso II, son of King Bermudo's cousin:

Ueremudus...subrinum suum Adefonsum...sibi in regnum successorem instituit.

The same applies to semantic change in morphological affixes. For example, in Romance the passive participle was tense-neutral, but earlier it had been used specifically to refer to the past. This meant that in Romance, to form the pluperfect passive they added to the now tenseless participle of the lexical verb the pluperfect forms of the auxiliary verb, whereas earlier the Romans had added those of the imperfect. At the start of the Rotense version we see the words *sepultus fuisset* (Gil, p.114); in that century the word pronounced [fwese] (later to be written *fuese*) still carried pluperfect meaning. Earlier, to mean "had been buried" in the subjunctive, the Romans had used *esset*. In the sixteenth century, the copyist of manuscript M changed *fuisset* into *esset*, but no copyist did that before then. In the text we see the form with its Romance meaning.

The point is not that these phenomena represent the "influence" of the spoken language; they just *are* the spoken language, nothing more than that. They need no further explanation. What does need further explanation is the existence in the text of features that were probably not present in their normal speech, and the explanation for these is to be sought in the writers' neurotic need to be "correct."

CONCLUSION

How should we then describe the language of this *Chronicle*? Some commentators have said it is in "barbarous Latin"; Díaz y Díaz has even called it "ulcerated latinity" (1976:225); Stero referred to its "poverty-stricken style," etc. I prefer to call it "Romance written in a high style." Modern investigators have become used to making a conceptual distinction between Latin and Romance, but this conceptual distinction had not yet been invented at the Court of King Alfonso III. They thought they had one language only, and in my view we should agree with them (1). It may seem, though, that for this very reason it does not matter much whether we call the language of the text "Latin" or "Romance." But it is indeed important; for it affects the evaluation we make of it. Calling it "barbarous Latin" suggests that the authors were barbarous, an implication that is totally lacking if instead we call its language "Romance written in a high style." Talking of "barbarousness" would only be at all reasonable if all the Asturians at the court of Alfonso III had been stupid, incompetent and uneducated. But I do not believe, and see no reason to believe, that they were all like that, and presumably modern Asturians would not wish to think so either. They were building remarkable churches, they were preparing impressive manuscripts, they were travellers, they had a genuine interest in the past and they were planning a reconquest of the Peninsula for the future, they had an active and complex life. If we can be in a position to conclude that they were writing well the only language that they had, a multifaceted, versatile and lively language, and we can call the language of their texts "well-written Romance"—which seems to me not only more fair but also more accurate—we will be able to come to the conclusion that at least some of the Asturians at that Court were intelligent, serious and skilled professionals. That is more generous; more importantly, it is also more plausible.

Note.

1. They used the word *vulgo* (and cognate terms) to refer to the normal language of the time, without thereby making any metalinguistic synchronic distinctions, although occasionally contrasting modern and ancient usage (see Van Uytfanghe 1989, for France; Wright 1993, on the *Vita Dominici Siliensis*; etc). The only use of *vulgo* in this *Chronicle* is this, at the start of the Rotense:

...in uillam propriam uenit, cui nomen erat Gerticos, quod nunc a bulco appellatur Bamba (Gil p.114, Prelog p.5).

Moralejo translates this well (p.194): .". que ahora es llamada por la gente Bamba," "which people now call Bamba."

After preparing this lecture, I have read Collins (1990); I am delighted to see that, for completely different reasons, Collins comes to a conclusion similar to mine.

1994 POSTSCRIPT

This is a translation of the lecture given on the evening of Thursday October 25, 1990 to the conference on "Asturian as seen by the Romance Philologists" held in Oviedo University by the Academia de la Llingua Asturiana. A penultimate version had been delivered to the Annual Conference of the Historians of Medieval Iberia in Birmingham the previous month. The Spanish lecture was published as "Textos asturianos de los siglos IX y X: ¿Latín bárbaro o romance escrito?" in the Academia's journal, *Lletres Asturianes*, 41, 1991, 20-34. For this English version all the translations from other scholars are my own. I am grateful to José Luis García Arias and his colleagues for inviting me to Oviedo, even though I explicitly warned them that the paper would contain nothing about Asturian, for such geographical labels, of doubtful value even now, can be seriously misleading when applied to these early centuries.

In November 1993, I visited the magnificent exhibition in Oviedo cathedral entitled *Orígenes*. This demonstrated effectively how impressive the early medieval culture of Oviedo had been; but perhaps the most remarkable aspect of the exhibition lay in the huge numbers of people visiting it. The reevaluation of their written texts should be part of a general increasingly favorable appreciation of the culture of the late ninth century and in particular of Oviedo at that time, which is long overdue. The wider cry for genuine unemended texts is still growing; Suzanne Fleischman's excellent plenary at the 11th International Conference on Historical Linguistics in August 1993, on the early Romance texts from France, deserves to change the general practice. Without the chance survival of the early Rotense version, the process of composition of the Chronicle would be hidden from us; we can be reasonably sure that this method of composition was used for other texts whose early drafts are unfortunately now unavailable to us.

12
Sociolinguistics in Spain
(8th – 11th Centuries)

THE IBERIAN PENINSULA IN THE year 700 was a theoretically unified Visigothic state. The Visigoths had come into the peninsula in the fifth century already speaking Latin (Old Romance); even if they were still also speaking their Germanic language then, they had stopped speaking that long before 700. The extensive Jewish communities of the peninsula left a few inscriptions in Hebrew, but Hebrew was only a written language; at one time they had spoken Aramaic, but by 700 they too were Romance-speaking. Perhaps the only communities of 700 that did not speak Romance at all were the Basques, who may have covered an area that spread further to the East than the modern Basque country, and were not entirely Christianized; but even many of them were probably in practice bilingual (Basque - Romance). Writing was usually carried out on wax tablets or papyrus, which have not survived the centuries, but the seventh-century writings on slates found in Salamanca province seem to attest both literacy and numeracy in ordinary communities. Seventh-century Visigothic Spain was the most educated and literate area of the former Western Roman Empire, continuing as a society essentially based on literacy, which formed the basis of literate culture in the whole peninsula until the end of the eleventh century.

The Moslem invasions began in 711. By 718 most of the Peninsula, except the North-Western mountains, were under Moslem domination. The official language of the invaders was Arabic, but most of the military personnel were not originally Arabic-speaking, being Berbers from the Maghrib. The inhabitants of the North African coastline largely spoke Romance before the Moslems came in the seventh century, and it is a reasonable supposition that many of the Berber invaders of the Iberian Peninsula were already speakers of Romance, either as a first or a second language, and mutually intelligible therefore with the previous inhabitants. They were not necessarily all Moslem, and the Berber languages which they otherwise spoke were probably not all mutually intelligible with each other. It is not clear how long the Berber languages continued to be spoken among the communities descended from the original invaders and settlers; on the other hand, Berbers were continually immigrating, being in particular recruited by Almanzor in the late tenth century, and as time went on the originally Romance-speaking communities of the North African coastline seem to have lost their Romance to Arabic, so the later arrivals probably did not speak Romance. The court slaves, many of Slavonic descent, seem to have learnt Arabic.

In many aspects of life, as Collins has pointed out, there was continuity between the seventh century and the eighth. Romance was the main working everyday language of Al-Andalus, in fields, markets, streets, offices and homes, since the invaders were mostly men and thus mothers were mostly Romance-speakers. Many inhabitants were consequently bilingual and of mixed descent; Caliph Abd-el-Rahman II (d. 852 A.D.), for example, is said to have had 87 children, mostly by native women. The Romance spoken there is now usually called *mozárabe*, after the term which was not used then but later applied to eleventh-century exiles, but the community at the time called it [ladino] (written still as *latinus*), and the Arabs referred to it with a form borrowed from that same word. Studying this *mozárabe* now is not easy, for much of the written evidence is in the Hebrew or Arabic alphabets, but increasingly the scholarly consensus suggests that in most respects *mozárabe* was like Northern Iberian Romance. When literate Christians left Al-Andalus to work in the North as notaries or scribes (and others as carpenters and farmers), as happened often from the late eighth century, they leave us no hint in the surviving documents of any incomprehension between Asturian clients and *mozárabe* writers. It has proved possible for Galmés de Fuentes to hypothesize details of the geographical variation that must have existed in the mozarabic Romance area (from Portugal to Valencia, from Málaga to Zaragoza), but, as commentators have pointed out, much of the evidence is less clear than Galmés suggests, being in essence confined to vocabulary and such phonology as can be tentatively deduced from that.

The Romance speakers in Al-Andalus came increasingly to be Arabic-Romance bilingual, and much of the community probably remained bilingual until at least the traumatic events after 1085 (when many mozarabs had to flee before the Berber Almorávides). The nature of the relationship can be seen to have changed, however. At first the Romance-speakers continued to read and write in the old-fashioned manner of the Roman Empire, and the Cordoban ninth-century scholars seem in essence to have been educated in the tradition established by Isidore, and exemplified by Julián de Toledo in the late seventh century. Albaro's famous lament (852) that educated Christians preferred to be literate in Arabic, however, indicates the change that was under way; to begin with, bilinguals continued to be primarily literate in Romance/Latin, but eventually they preferred to be primarily literate in Arabic. The Bible and some Christian church Councils were turned into Arabic, and there is a tenth-century Christian history written in Arabic, although tombstones survive in good traditional Latinate form even into the eleventh century, and presumably it was felt that people could still read them. Van Koningveld's research established that there was a serious intellectual community of bilingual Christians probably literate only in Arabic in Toledo at and after the time of its fall to the Christians (1085). Christians in Moslem Spain were thus largely cut off from the linguistic and other reforms of the Frankish empire, but in compensation were more in touch with the Christians of the East.

It is possible that it was the venerable administrative literacy of the Christians which eventually raised the level of literacy among the Arabic-speaking community once Christian conversions to Islam became common, in the tenth century. Native Spanish-born Moslems were similarly bilingual but only ever literate in Arabic, so the sociolinguistic differences between the different religious groups were slowly disappearing as the Christians inverted the social diglossia. Arabic itself had sociolinguistic gradations unknown as yet in the mozarabic world, with dialectal variations enabling andalusíes to be identifiable from their speech in the rest of the

Moslem world, and there was increasing divergence between official (Classical) Arabic and colloquial speech. No original eighth-century composition survives from Al-Andalus, but later caliphal Córdoba shone at a serious intellectual level in many fields; books were widely read and written, and translated from Latin to Arabic, and its library was one of the largest in the Moslem world. At a simpler level, much social interaction was probably macaronic, and the Romance grammar may perhaps have simplified as a result of social circumstances; and although it may often have been unclear to a listener whether participants in a conversation were speaking Arabic with Romance loanwords in or Romance with Arabic loanwords in, the languages are sufficiently different in structure for no genuine mesolectal hybrid to be envisageable, even though bilinguals may only rarely have been 100% fluent in both. There is a hint of this insufficiency in the fact that so many Spanish lexical borrowings from Arabic took the definite article (/al-/) as well as the lexical item, for sandhi prevented the word boundary from being always phonotactically distinguishable; that is why such words tend to begin with [a-] (e.g. *alcázar, albaricoque, ajedrez, arroz, acequia*). The phonological systems are so distinct that the earliest written forms in Romance of such Arabisms often vary wildly from each other as well as from the Arabic etymon. Attempts to attribute phonological or syntactic peculiarities of subsequent Andalusian Spanish or Valencian Catalan to mozarabic have given a meager harvest, but that is probably both because the Northern forms came to overwhelm native Southern speech habits after the Reconquista, and because there were far fewer mozarabs in Moslem Spain after 1100 than there had been earlier. Attempts to view the possibly-Romance forms of the *kharjas* as evidence for mozarabic Romance are probably over-optimistic, mainly because the readings are so uncertain; some literati seem to have operated with a sociolinguistic scale with perhaps three or even four varieties of Arabic superimposed upon a prestigeless Romance basilect.

Romance and Arabic involved two alphabets, and the presence of Hebrew (only as a written language) provided a third. In theory, and perhaps in practice, any of the three languages could be written in any of the three alphabets. This is problematic for modern scholars. Perhaps it was also for the inhabitants of Al-Andalus. The best *kharja* texts, mainly Arabic but with possibly Romance components, are in the Hebrew alphabet. Hebrew was not spoken colloquially, but texts were recited in the synagogues, and Jewish scholarship flourished in Moslem Spain from the tenth century. Menachem Ibn Saruk produced an important dictionary of Hebrew at that time, when a school of learning was founded which was to lead to one of the great flowerings of Jewish cultural history, in the eleventh and twelfth centuries. The Jews were not all scholars, diplomats and businessmen; there are fairly reliable records of artisans and farmers with Jewish names, but the existence of Hebrew in reading and writing rather than in speech may perhaps have largely confined the literate aspect of Jewish culture to an élite. Recitation was taught letter by letter, such that their pronunciation was based isomorphically on the pre-existing orthography. Even for them, original composition was often in Arabic, sometimes in the Hebrew alphabet, as the Jews also changed from Romance to being predominantly Arabic speakers.

Visigothic culture continued to the north of the religious divide as well as the south. In the eighth century the independent Christians were largely confined to the Northern mountains, but after 800 they became confident enough to re-establish political capitals further south, in Barcelona (801), Pamplona (after 824), Burgos (884), and León (914); settlers went from Galicia to Coimbra; in each case the new inhabitants of the expanding city came mainly from several valleys to the North, and a sociolinguistically simpler interdialect formed, usually only perpetuating in the prestigious capital city the highest common factor of such regional diversity as already existed in the northernmost mountains (which is why the speech of the mountain valleys is even now linguistically more complex than their related dialects to the south). The continuing repopulation movements were later to reinforce mutual intelligibility several times through the Middle Ages. For much of the period under consideration, Asturias (León) was politically dominant in the North. The Basques were mostly in the separate kingdom of Navarra. There is perhaps something to be said for Menéndez Pidal's view that the influx of Christians from Al-Andalus (not necessarily from the south) from the ninth century formed the basis of an expansion in Asturian literacy.

The Romance speech was by then largely losing, for example, all nominal cases other than the originally accusative, synthetic passive and future verb forms, *ut* clauses, etc., and gaining analytic future and perfect forms created with auxiliary *habere*, new definite articles from *ille*, extended use of prepositions to compensate for the loss of nominal case, neologisms with diminutive suffixes, etc. Yet the traditional written norms were still those taught and learnt, and Astur-Leonese society still ran on a general assumption of literacy, and its lawcourts on documentation; although not many people could write, many more could read, and almost everyone (then as now) could understand texts, letters, orders, sermons, documents, prayers, Saints lives, tombstones, etc., if they were read aloud to them. Probably each village had someone, not necessarily a cleric, who could read aloud to his neighbors when necessary, and perhaps who could also write on their behalf. Legal transactions were made with the help of a notary, who might in practice belong to a local monastery. There were many small monasteries and churches, and the number of surviving documents suggests that at a practical level this still operated as a literate society. At the time of the Moslem Invasion, the Romance of the peninsula would still in general have been intelligible elsewhere; the period of relative isolation from 711 to 1020 is probably the period in which the Romance of non-Catalan Spain became generally more distinct from that of the other Romance-speaking areas, including Catalonia.

It is probably anachronistic to visualize separate dialects with clear boundaries in the Iberian Romance-speaking areas of these centuries. There were, naturally, differences between the speech habits of Romance-speakers in different places, but in the age before the thirteenth-century standardizations these were essentially statistical variations in the distribution of competing allophones or allomorphs. It is reasonable, for example, to hypothesize that in Galicia the first syllable of the word spelled *alteros* was [out-] more often than [ot-], whereas further East in Castile it was [ot-] more often than [out-], but neither of these forms were found on 100% of the occasions of the word's use in any one place, and the sociolinguistic situation was that normally found in monolingual societies everywhere; gradual geographical variation within a monolingual continuum. Texts cannot be definitively located geographically from such variants. As Alarcos Llorach pointed out, all speakers could communicate with Iberian Romance-speaking neighbors when they needed to, both from within the Christian kingdoms and further south. The Castilian Count Sancho García (reigned 995-1017) spoke eloquently to the nobles of nearby Moslem-ruled Tudela.

The evidence for Romance pronunciation of the time comes largely from backwards reconstructions based on the subsequent texts in reformed spelling (in the thirteenth century); although spelling mistakes in pre-reform documents are often interesting, they are too often inspired by misapplications of the traditional orthography to be taken as any kind of direct phonetic transcription. In their monastic schools spelling was taught then, as now, of course, one word at a time; teaching apprentice scribes to spell [ésa] as *ipsa* or *ipsam* and [óu̯tɾo] as *alter* or *alterum* was no harder than teaching Modern French apprentices to spell [ɛm] as *aime, aimes* or *aiment*. The old-fashioned morphology and grammar encountered in texts and needed for independent composition seems to have led a kind of twilight existence, in which it was generally understood passively but rarely used actively (like the Past Preterite in Modern French). When important texts had to be written, such as the official histories prepared at the Asturian court in the 880s, they went through many drafts in which such half-surviving stylistic tricks as synthetic passive verb-forms and oblique nominal cases were inserted in order to make them appear more professional. This was often achieved by imitating earlier works. Hymn-composers did the same. Even eighth-century Asturias had not seen the loss of such techniques entirely, unless the place of origin of Beato de Liébana's strikingly well-informed Commentary on the Apocalypse (c.780) has been wrongly located by modern scholarship (which is possible). Unofficial texts were not so treated, as the chance survival of the late tenth-century Leonese quartermaster's account of cheeses in the Rozuela larder shows us. As a result, the sociolinguistic nature of tenth-century Iberian Romance was unusually versatile and sophisticated in its exploitation of variants, old and new, and the surviving clumsy documentation is presented in merely an unflatteringly limp disguise. We are not now in a position to carry out technical sociolinguistic analyses of the statistics of variability in class, age, context, social network, etc., in the modern sense, but a knowledge of sociolinguistics shows us that the tenth-century Spanish Romance-speaking community was similar to that of Modern France; there was a great deal of variation in any one place, hidden from us by a traditional written norm.

The Castile-Navarra border area gives us our first surviving evidence from a writer who is consciously not trying to write correctly in the usual way. The Riojan glosses of San Millán and Silos were once ascribed to the tenth century, but are now thought to be of the eleventh, even (in the Silos case) of after 1060. Two manuscripts contain marginalia, some in an apparently reforming orthography, and often also in Romance morphology. For this purpose, at least, the usual stylistic tricks were thought inappropriate, and the purpose was probably to facilitate reading aloud (sermons and a penitential). This new way of writing can hardly have aided a native Riojan, who knew how to pronounce his own speech without such prompting, and may have been intended to help one of the many visitors from further North-East, since by 1060 the idea of writing the Occitan way was generally accepted in Catalonia and Provence, and the letter-sound correspondences would actually have been helpful then. That experiment was not apparently followed up, however. No other texts describable as Romance seem to survive from the peninsula before 1100.

Two of the Riojan glosses are in Basque, its first written examples, although there is confused evidence in a partly bilingual document from Guipúzcoa in 1055. The glosses can only have been experimental, for Basque literacy cannot be postulated for that time; any Basque who wrote was bilingual. Outside the mountainous areas where Basque still survives, Basque speakers were probably all bilingual. Theirs was a clear case of bilingual diglossia, similar in 1100 to what it had been in 100 A.D., and as usual the lower language in the pair was much more influenced than the higher : Romance influence in Basque is more pervasive than vice versa. They were not weak, however, as their crushing defeat of the Franks at Roncesvalles in 778 showed, and this independence was probably what led Basque to survive at all.

In those centuries, Aragón consisted only of a few high Pyrenean valleys, whose Romance was for geographical reasons sufficiently isolated to preserve some distinctive features, such as unvoiced intervocalic consonants. The Ebro valley to their south was still in the Moslem-ruled area. Further east, however, was Catalonia, or as it was known after 800, the Spanish March of the Frankish Empire. Catalonia had had little direct Arabic influence, and came during these centuries to be part of the French rather than the Iberian cultural sphere. It is noticeable, for example, that the isogloss that can with some legitimacy be drawn (south of the mountains) between Catalan and Aragonese corresponds roughly with the Frankish boundaries. This too was no great barrier to intercommunication. There was no real boundary between Catalan and Occitan at this time, nor for long afterwards, and Catalans were to be part of the driving force of Provençal culture. The Catalans also imported one of the major inventions of Frankish Romance culture; the conceptually separate language which we now know as Medieval Latin, used only in formal and at first exclusively ecclesiastical contexts. The use of Medieval Latin in ninth and tenth century Catalonia was probably patchy, as was the Caroline script that seems to have been imported with it, but in the early eleventh century Catalan Medieval Latin culture came to shine. The sociolinguistic implication is that a variety of diglossia between related varieties of the same language existed in eleventh-century Catalonia—as with Arabic in Moslem Spain—but not in other Iberian Romance communities. Even then, it is legitimate to wonder if they really thought Medieval Latin was entirely separate from their native Catalan, rather than still being as before a veneer to be fitted on top.

The end of the eleventh century saw many changes in Iberian sociolinguistics. The conquest of Toledo (1085) led to meetings between Arabic-speaking scholars, Jewish interpreters, Castilian clerics, French bishops, Medieval Latin-speakers from further north, joining native mozarabic-speakers and Romance speakers from elsewhere, in a city whose sociolinguistic patterning is still unclear to us; although the old idea that the mozarabic community was persecuted now seems to be groundless. The resulting prestige speech was to be another interdialect (as earlier in Burgos and later in Sevilla). The Leonese decision (in 1080) to adopt the liturgy generally used elsewhere in Europe had unexpected sociolinguistic consequences, as French clergy had to be imported to teach the new non-vernacular Medieval Latin pronunciation their liturgy required, and that imported distinction eventually led to the same Latin-Romance diglossia as already existed in Catalonia. In the twelfth century the script also Europeanized. The arrival of pilgrims from many lands, both Romance-speaking and otherwise, made Santiago a cosmopolitan and multilingual center, and Galician Romance was the first to show signs of influence from Occitan lyric. The political split of Portugal from Galicia began, although a linguistic boundary did not exist at that border (or probably anywhere else in the continuum from Galicia to Aragón) for at least another century. The arrival of the Almorávides into Moslem Spain (after 1086) ended much of the bilingual culture there as Christians came north to Toledo and elsewhere, and Moslems increasingly used Arabic alone. A whole age ended between 1050 and 1100, and the sociolinguistic state of the Iberian peninsula changed drastically with it.

1994 POSTSCRIPT

This article was published in French, as "Sociolinguistique hispanique (VIIIe - XIe siècle)," in *Médiévales* 25 (Autumn 1993), 61-70, at the invitation of Professor Michel Banniard, the volume's editor. The above is the original English text, which was translated into French for the volume.

13
Logographic Script and Assumptions of Literacy in Tenth-Century Spain

Much has been discovered in recent years about the linguistic differences between literate and non-literate societies, and historical linguists have been able to relate these discoveries to our two types of evidence about linguistic situations of the past, that is, texts and reconstructions. But some societies fall into neither category, in that they have only a small proportion of literate people but nonetheless preserve some general assumptions from a more literate past. Tenth-century Spain is such a case. Furthermore, when we try and use their surviving texts as evidence for the nature of their speech, it is probable that our analysis is hampered by the fact that their originally phonographic orthography was probably taught and learned in an essentially logographic manner (as in Modern Britain): that is, one word at a time, rather than one letter at a time.

The way that we should analyze the social assumptions that lie behind the existence of texts written ln the distant past is not at all self-evident (cp. Wright 1992c). At times writers wish to transcribe speech with some directness. For example, the earliest texts intentionally written in a Romance language, in the central Middle Ages, were prepared with morphology, syntax, vocabulary and spelling that were intended to be more or less isomorphic with at least some style of the regional vernacular. But before the invention of such specifically Romance writing methods, such language planning as there was, if any, was not based on this ideal of isomorphism with speech, and writers' intentions were nearly always in principle to attain the written features that had been deemed as correct centuries before by the late Roman grammarians. I intend to refer here, as examples of our difficulty, to texts of tenth-century North-Western Spain. These were written towards the end of the period that predates the language-planning reforms in that area, which would later lead to the existence of written Galician, Leonese and Castilian. Thus they were prepared according to an orthographical system that corresponded to a long-distant stage of the language. For nobody can doubt that the vernacular of the area had developed considerably from that of a millennium earlier. In order to work out any details of the spoken language used by those who composed this documentary evidence, therefore, we need first to consider in general terms what happens to writing systems that survive into periods when both (a) the speech with which they were originally intended to correspond has developed markedly, and also (b) the proportion of people in society who are able to write has decreased appreciably, such that the skill may have been the province only of professionals. This has hardly been studied, in fact; the acquisition of literacy into a society has been investigated by several scholars, but the social and linguistic consequences of such disparity and simultaneous professionalization remain to be assessed. And yet in some respects, this is what has happened to Modern French and Modern English (although their spelling was never entirely phonemic). The related problems have ramifications for the historical study of all levels of language, although the orthography-phonology interface is the one to be considered in this paper. Since writing is an artificial technique, whose acquisition depends on explicit instruction within an ad hoc kind of micro language planning, it is also of great importance to try to reconstruct the way in which writing and spelling were actually taught, at various places and times in the past. In the case of tenth-century North-Western Spain the near total absence of explicit evidence from any contemporary commentator means that our best available method is to deduce details of that teaching process from comparing genuinely attested (unemended) written forms with reconstructable pronunciations. Some printed versions are useless for this purpose, having been distorted ("emended") by modern editors; others are more reliable. The texts I have in mind are those such as in

Mínguez Fernández 1976, Ubieto Arteta 1976, García Leal (forthcoming). One of Mínguez's is reproduced here as an Appendix.

Tenth-century Christian Spain was a society which functioned on a basis of written texts (documents of sale such as the one reproduced here, charters, sermons, letters, Saints lives, laws, liturgy, etc.) which were intended to be read aloud. Compared with the proportions for modern societies, it seems that not many people could write; but we have to bear in mind that the chance survival of several pieces of slate from the Salamanca area on which shepherds of (probably) the seventh century noted practical details in respectable written form, onto an untypically non-biodegradable surface, suggests that the ability to write in Visigothic society was more widespread than is often now assumed. The relative proportion in society of those who could write may well have declined by the tenth century, even if we include the mozarabic immigrants often thought to have boosted their numbers. Even then, many more people could read without being able to write; and even those who could not read were not thereby cut off from the literate world, for historical research has come to suggest that most texts, however old-fashioned, seem to have been expected to be generally comprehensible when read aloud sympathetically (see e.g. McKitterick 1990, Wright 1992), as they often are to children and illiterates today. Thus the social role of the reader-aloud (*lector*) in a community was an important one. It is hardly surprising, therefore, that Isidore of Seville had recently devoted careful consideration to the habits of a good *lector*, largely on that assumption of intelligibility if the *lector* did his job well (Banniard 1976). *Lectores* could also work as scribes (see Ganz and Goffart 1990:917), so it seems reasonable to deduce that at least some of those who wrote had the needs of the reader-aloud much in mind. For example, in order to be binding, legal documents usually had to be first recorded in writing and then also read aloud by the actual scribe for confirmation by the interested parties. Several documents (such as the one in the Appendix) have near the end a first-person clause in which the first-person deixis refers to the depositor (rather than to the notary) including the words *relegente audivi* ("I heard it read aloud"): in this case, *Ego Ermildi in ac karta bendiccionis que relegente audibi manu mea* (signo) *fecit ante testibus mul[tis] tera[di]dit roboranda.* Presumably the witnesses could largely follow the oral version as well.

Tenth-Century Christian Spain (and late Early Medieval pre-Reform Europe in general) is perhaps unusual in being a society of comparatively restricted literacy, in the sense that fewer people wrote than before, which had nevertheless maintained several social assumptions from an earlier time of much wider literacy. Yet it is probably more misleading than has been previously realized to analyze the nature of that restriction in the same perspective, and using the same terms, as those with which other societies are usually characterized, in which the proportion of literate people in society is numerically similar to that of the Late Early Romance world, but has in contrast developed from total illiteracy in the relatively recent past. For example, Stock (1983), Armistead (1986) and also myself (1990-91), have made what may be an unwarranted assumption that the work of anthropologists such as Goody, on the change from pre-literacy to literacy, will necessarily be relevant to societies such as those of tenth-century Spain. In this latter case, the continuing administrative and educational infrastructure, based on an inherited assumption of textual intelligibility, which continued to be valid, could well be more relevant to our assessment of the relationship between textual evidence and speech than are the actual numbers of writers. That is, the illiterate were not cut off from literacy then in the way that they are often seen to be in societies where the literate are pioneers in a new universe. The general population of tenth-century Europe need not be patronizingly dismissed as illiterate on merely comparative numerical grounds, if by that characterization we mean that it was untouched by literate culture (cp. McKitterick's comments, 1990:2, on Stock 1983). Their society, essentially post-literate rather than pre-literate, could thus in some respects be said to be more like that of Modern English than that of the modern developing world; there is much to be said for the "idea that written language has irreversibly changed the human mind" (Frith 1983:603), and that irreversible change was not reversed by the decline in educational standards in either Modern Britain or tenth-century León.

Historical linguists need therefore to investigate, if we can, the nature and role of literacy in a society before we can reconstruct speech from texts with any certainty. This applies to all societies of the past, in fact, for writing never reflects speech exactly. In the first place, no hitherto devised writing system is in practice a complete biunique representation of phonetic output. Even the narrowest transcription of tape-recorded natural vernacular is unlikely to represent exactly in its detached written units every detail of the speed, pitch, intonation, rhythm, resonation, and frequencies in a section of continuous speech. An orthography has a different function from an acoustic spectrogram, for orthographic texts are intended to communicate meaning, but a connected text in spectrogram form would communicate nothing at all. Such a direct textual representation of the sound alone is no help in practice, because what readers want are not such phonetic details but immediate indications of what the morphemes and the words are. For in reading, everything else is secondary; the immediate practical function of reading is to recognize the words rather than the sounds. As the modern specialists in teaching reading and writing stress, we "read by eye" even if in part we "write by ear" (Sampson 1985:208; Frith 1980; Savin 1972). This is a linguistic universal, albeit of a vague kind; yet it is not the sort of universal that diachronic linguists are used to operating with, even if we subscribe to merely the weaker varieties of uniformitarian principles, because in fact although orthography and phonetics never match exactly, the closeness of the fit between speech and writing can vary widely at different places and times. This wide variation is largely the consequence of disparate manifestations of human inventiveness, sometimes institutionalized as socially purposive Language Planning. Apprentice writers are not usually taught phonetic script. That is always advanced study. Instead, apprentice writers are taught "correct" written forms of words and morphemes. Thus in order for modern historical linguists to use those written texts as evidence for the phonetic or morphosyntactic nature of contemporary speech, we need to work out, if we can, how far each writer wrote his text according to set conscious principles of what he thought he "ought" to write, and how far, if at all, he was directly trying to reproduce what he would say himself. As regards Late Early Romance, Pei and Muller and others have already been criticized extensively for expressing the latter view (sixty years ago).

There is no need to dance on their graves any more, merely to point out that, in the light of subsequently-accrued sociolinguistic expertise, the writers could hardly have been able to express their own vernacular directly.

This remark presupposes that the results of sociolinguistic research into the present have direct relevance for societies of the past. In other words, it implies the Uniformitarian hypothesis. This is not, in fact, an invention of sociolinguists; it was used first by geologists, and then by Philosophers of History (see e.g. Dray 1989). These latter have been discussing at length whether we are likely to understand events in the past better by analogy with similar and already well-understood phenomena of the present, or by detailed study of the original context. Clearly, we need to do both if we can, but at the very least those of us who are considering the sociolinguistic state of Early Romance communities should not postulate phenomena that directly contradict what we know about similar societies in the twentieth century (cp. Wright 1988). On the other hand, linguistic universals can only strictly apply to events outwith the conscious control of the language user; and Philosophers of History would mostly agree now (if not in their behaviorist phase) that to understand historical events that are even to some extent in the conscious control of the participants we need to try and get into their conscious minds. This is often, of course, impossible, in any strict sense, which is why historiography is always going to remain in large part a sequence of ifs and buts. Even so, despite the uniformitarian validity of some general principles, we need for present purposes to put to one side the search for universals, and look at the specific society that our texts come from to see what the authors thought they were doing. Different societies, different writers and different orthographical systems need to be assessed differently by the investigator.

Sometimes writers have consciously tried to reproduce speech. This has probably always been the initial intention of those who first invented (or adapted from elsewhere) writing systems for their own language. Speech, however, is a vague term. As is generally known, orthographical systems fall into two main categories. These are (a) the logographic systems, such as the one devised to transcribe Chinese, whose original intention was to signal morphemes as phonetically unanalyzed wholes; and (b) the phonographic systems, such as the Roman alphabet, whose original intention was to signal units of sound. The theoretical distinction between the two is clear. But the picture tends to become confused, because, over time, most systems become a mixture of the two. Research suggests that texts prepared with the logographic systems tend to be easier to read (by those who have learned how), but that on the other hand the phonographic systems are easier to learn to write. It is not the case that either should be regarded as intrinsically more advanced or desirable than the other (Sampson 1985; Coulmas 1989). It seems plausible to propose that readers and writers in tenth-century Spain, like those in the Modern English-speaking world, living in a society where speech sounds and the orthographic units of the traditionally "correct" written forms often fail to correlate closely, operate a system that, although it was originally phonographic (using sounds as the basic unit), has come to work, at least partly, in a logographic manner (seeing words as the basic unit). This is not meant to be seen as in any sense a process of decay or corruption. Our present system works, and the important practical matter is to operate a system that works, whether or not it has a phonographic basis. It is conceivable, for example, that future generations will laugh at our own clumsy naiveté in operating with a writing system for Modern English that makes no attempt to reproduce on paper the nature of acoustic formants. It is already the case that Korean script could be seen as more advanced than ours, in a phonographic sense, in that it includes direct representation of distinctive features. An acoustic-formant-based writing system seems as odd a concept to us as written vocalic representation would have seemed to a Sumerian, because we are all used to operating with what we have been taught. But we can infer from the work of Schmandt-Besserat (e.g. 1991) that the Sumerians' system was a sufficient and practical one for their perceived needs. So is ours now. So was that of tenth-century Spain. Chomsky and Halle made the sensible comment that (1968:49) "orthography is a system designed for readers who know the language" (and cp. Klima 1972). Orthographies are not designed to assist philologists of a millennium later. Let us assume that the strange appearance of documents such as many of those from tenth-century Spain corresponds neither to a desire to mystify, nor to endemic total stupidity and incompetence, nor to improbably precocious expertise in phonetic script (Wright 1991c, 1992), but to a practical purpose.

At a slightly later period than the one I am centrally concerned with here, several approximations to spoken usage can be seen to be intentionally made in some eleventh and twelfth-century documents in the Iberian Peninsula, at a time when the ancient systems were still in theory the only ones in use; these came to be used as the basis for the consciously isomorphic thirteenth-century standardizations of written Castilian, Catalan and Portuguese (Wright 1982: ch.5). We cannot assume, of course, as Penny has showed (1991), that the correspondences they operated with were those of modern phonetic alphabets, but this was at least a period of phonographically-inspired spelling reform.

Most texts, however, are not prepared during or just after reforms of the writing system. Indeed, even if they are, reforms are sometimes specifically directed towards *not* representing speech; as with the late eighth-century reforms at the Frankish court which eventually led to the separate concept of Medieval Latin, (Wright 1991b), aiming to revive "correct" written forms, that in fact reflected the speech of a whole millennium earlier: or several of the orthographical decisions taken in the eighteenth century by the newly established Royal Academy of the Spanish Language. The nature of a spelling system can change unintentionally as well as being consciously invented and reformed. As a result, many writing systems work in practice on both semantic and phonetic levels. In the first place, logographic systems, over time, tend to acquire phonetic components. This has, in fact, happened to Chinese script (DeFrancis 1984; Coulmas 1989:109), which nowadays aids the reader with both phonetic and semantic indicators. Conversely, on the other hand, phonographic systems, over time, become naturally more logographic as the inevitable consequence of phonetic change. This has happened to words written with the Roman alphabet in many languages, including modern English and French, and also tenth-century Spanish Romance (see the studies by Emiliano and Varvaro in Wright, ed., 1991). In Sampson's words (1985:203): "the fact that the Roman letters originally stood for segmental sounds would not in principle be any bar to constructing a purely logographic script with them". Thus in both kinds of system there is often a simultaneous appeal to recognition of both words and sounds. This fact has practical consequences for teachers. One method used in teaching reading in British schools, for example, involves the use of what are known as flashcards; the teacher says, for example, "this word is [najt]", holding up a card with the written word *night*, and with this technique the pupil is encouraged to learn the word's written form as a whole. Pupils still need to be able to recognize the individual letters, of course (Besner et al. 1984), but there is no intermediate stage of mentally allotting particular sounds to each individual letter. This is just as well, because such a process would be positively unhelpful in words such as *night*. As a consequence of this method of teaching, when reading aloud words we know, at least, the word (and its lexical entry) is always the basic unit that inspires our pronunciation, rather than the individual letter. It may even perhaps be a universal truth, concerning the consumers of ostensibly phonographic scripts, that the letter-sound correspondences are utilized in reading individually, that is, sounded out as separate entities, only when we encounter a word we do not immediately recognize as a whole. Spelling-pronunciations, therefore, are due to poor readers, those who cannot read well enough to recognize the word concerned immediately ("by eye"), and thus have to have clumsy resort to piecemeal phonographic correlation. This simple and indeed obvious deduction is, even so, diametrically opposed to that which is standardly taught in University classes on Romance Philology, in which spelling-pronunciations ("mots savants", "cultismos") are usually diagnosed as being the result of specifically erudite influence rather than of the reading incompetence that they actually attest (Wright 1992a).

Accordingly, it is worth considering the hypothesis that when people in tenth-century Christian Spain were taught to read (for they must have been taught somehow), they were indeed taught to recognize the letters, but as an aid to reading logographically; that is, the aim was to enable the apprentice reader to recognize whole, without clumsy piecemeal phonographical analysis, the written forms of at least those words that occurred commonly in their ordinary speech. That is, that the orthographic forms would have been taught as single phonetically-unanalyzed units. There is no immediately obvious way of knowing for certain if that was indeed the case, but the modern evidence suggests that it would at least have been a sensible method to use. The teacher in tenth-century Castile, as it were, might have held up a card or slate or plank or piece of bark or stone or leaf or parchment bearing the written letters I P S A and said "this is [ésa]"; held up a card inscribed S U P E R (or even perhaps its abbreviation *sup*) and said "this is [sóβre]"; held up a card with the letters P E T R U S and said "This is [pédro]". These are three words commonly found in documents, although only *ipsa* is in the one in the Appendix here. The fact that the written letter P in these three words actually corresponded in tenth-century Spain to an unvoiced bilabial plosive in P E T R U S, a voiced bilabial fricative in S U P E R, and to nothing at all in I P S A, might never have occurred to the pupils, and possibly not to the teacher either, who was not a theoretician of linguistics. In tenth-century Spain, we can reconstruct plausibly many such phonetic forms whose phonetic transcription would not have been exactly the same as their traditional "correct" orthography. Words that a scribe was likely to read and write often, such as the word reconstructably pronounced [komplógo] in 933—with possible variations—and written *conplacuit* in the text reproduced here (and also in that of 908 in Wright 1982:166-67), would have been much simpler to teach and learn as whole units, particularly for those who were only learning to read rather than also to write—which was always the case, for it seems that it was normal practice to learn to read first and to write later if at all. More general principles of individual sound-letter correspondence would only be broached for recognizing words that were less common and less easy to recognize whole. For those who are learning only to read, in any language, such correspondences are only secondary; reading has to be based on a logographic recognition of the words and morphemes when (as in Modern English) the fit between the traditionally correct orthography and the speech sound is so often awkward and indirect. Since reading in tenth-century Spain seems to have been very often reading aloud, and intended to be immediately intelligible, it was essential to have a direct procedural link from the recognition of the written shape of the lexical item, to its oral production with its normal vernacular phonetics. In practice the oral rendering of both modern English and these tenth-century texts would be greatly confused and indeed stultified by any attempt to read traditional spellings one letter at a time as if they were phonetic script. This is only common sense, and yet many Romance philologists have assumed that the reading of these texts can only have been phonographic, allotting one sound to each letter. Research evidence suggests that we do not after all read in that way, and that normal logographic reading could render the words, at least, intelligible to an unlettered audience, although the word-order might occasionally have been a problem (but see Blake 1991; and even if it was, cp the transposition techniques proposed by Stengaard 1991, Korhammer 1980).

Since writing was usually taught only to people who had already learned to read, as Riché established, writing would have been taught most practically on the basis of the already learned reading techniques. Having already learned to read, for example, the word written I P S A as [ésa], the apprentice scribe would probably have found it a comparatively simple operation subsequently to reverse the direction of inference and learn to write the word [ésa] as I P S A, still as a largely unanalyzed whole. For the apprentice, morphology, of course, produced additional complications, since logographic script based on whole words is inherently insufficient for languages with non-syllabic morphemes such as the plural-marking final [-s] of Old Spanish. We can hypothesize that the root was taught as one logographic unit, and the suffix, however brief, as another. There is some evidence for this: orthographical treatises of that age devote a great deal of energy precisely to the operation of these combinatorial techniques. For example, for a scribe to know when to add in writing a final silent letter -M to nouns and adjectives, needed extensive explicit teaching. So he received it, in, for example, Cassiodorus's *De Orthographia*, aimed at his protegés in Vivarium, Italy. In addition, the fact that many words were commonly written in the same widely accepted abbreviated form can only imply that these abbreviations were also taught as wholes (Bischoff 1990:150-68; for Spain, Millares Carlo 1929: ch.5); it is no great extension of the argument to propose the same for many words in unabbreviated form also.

An internal analysis of some written forms in tenth-century Galicia (Wright 1991a, partly based on Veiga Arias 1983 and the study of León in Pensado 1991) led me to the conclusion that the written form of a number of words was indeed taught in this way without phonetic analysis, during the teaching of writing as well as that of reading. These words probably included those commonly used in formulaic expressions; if so, this would explain why the words in question are comparatively rarely misspelled in texts. The written forms of some other words were not taught whole in this way. For the written representation of words whose integral form they had not learned, scribes had to fall back consciously on a loose piecemeal collection of rules of thumb, probably comprising both sound-letter and syllable-multigraph correspondences. The existence of the latter type of syllabic correspondence seems possible in the light of the fact that the units are syllabic rather than phonemic in the late eleventh-century *Artes Lectoriae* from South-Western France (Kneepkens and Reijnders 1979) (and the fact that modern Spanish schoolchildren are often taught that way as well). To make such an analysis, of course, modern investigators need to be able to trust editors to reproduce the textual evidence exactly as it is written. Unfortunately, there are still editors around who aim to "emend" the spellings of their originals; we still apparently need to beseech them not to do that grotesque and unscholarly disservice to academic advance (Wright 1991d). The particularly interesting cases, in the tenth-century Spanish spellings investigated, are those in which phonological features which had not changed since the days of the Roman Empire, and were thus still broadly speaking isomorphic with the traditional orthography, were nonetheless often spelled in an incorrect way; in these cases the incorrect spelling can be ascribed not to a phonetic variant (as has been a common reaction of philologists in the field) but to an inappropriate use of those rules of thumb used for writing less common words.

Since teaching people to write always involves some kind of consciously transmitted technique, it is tempting to wonder whether any general Language-Planning ideas were around in tenth-century Galicia, as they were going to be later in Alfonso the Wise's Castile or the eighteenth-century Academy. Individual monastic centers had their own spelling habits, however, and vary between each other as to which words are liable to be misspelled and which are not (cp. Pensado 1991:199). We can deduce from this that there were teachers, probably monks, who talked to each other, but not the wider standardization that would imply the presence of teacher-training colleges. The situation was thus quite different from that which prevailed in France at the same time. In France, the Carolingian reforms, intended to be uniform over the whole empire, were leading by then to a clear distinction between Latin and Romance (French) as conceptually separate languages. Yet many details remain unclear, even in France. For example, when we consider the relationship between scribal technique and reading aloud in the transitional period of the ninth century, Nelson's (1985) study of Nithard and the Strasbourg Oaths is going to have to lead French philologists back to the drawing-board, for the whole of Nithard's *History*, not just the Oaths, seems (in Nelson's persuasive analysis) to have been intended to be read aloud intelligibly to French-speakers with no great experience of higher education. How was it in fact read, with the new Medieval Latin pronunciation, or as normal Romance? What does this apparent intention imply? It continues to seem appropriate to believe that the reason why the Old French Oaths were originally prepared in the way they were (perhaps by Nithard himself, despite Nelson's tolerant skepticism of this suggestion) was in order to aid Germanic speakers who had already become used to reading aloud in the new reformed way (producing a sound for each written letter), to read the text aloud as intelligible vernacular French. For the situation in ninth-century France was confused (and probably into the tenth century as well, in many places); despite the increase in educational levels, the Carolingian Reforms had brought unforeseen complications. Language planning often does. Its effects are often catastrophic. It can be argued that the results of Alcuin's prejudices were almost entirely pernicious (cp Wright 1991c). On the other hand, further south and west, the contemporary Christian Spaniards, still fortunately unaffected by these reforms, still worked within a metalinguistically monolingual framework, which involved writing a somewhat ad hoc mixture of logographic forms and sound-letter correspondences. That makes life difficult for us, the philologists of a thousand years later, but it was a very reasonable attitude for them to take, and in keeping with the versatility, sophistication and flexibility that tenth-century Spanish Romance had in general (Wright 1991d). Philologists of the thirtieth century will have similar problems with texts from twentieth-century France.

CONCLUSION

Linguists like to think there are linguistic universals. Maybe in the event there is a diachronic universal which we can see at work here, in tenth-century Spain (but not in tenth-century reformed France). Societies that continue to function on a basis of documents generally expected to be intelligible, even when literacy is more restricted than it used to be, and that have inherited traditionally correct and originally phonographic written forms from that much earlier time of wider literacy, may always find it most practical to operate largely logographic systems of reading; and to some extent also of writing. Discovering whether this actually is a universal development is an empirical issue, which I invite specialists in other fields with comparable circumstances to consider. As a consequence of this, it is reasonable to conclude that post-literate societies are different in kind from pre-literate societies even with the same proportion of literate members.

APPENDIX

1st March 933. Ermildi sells Nina and his wife Juliana her daughter's inheritance in Ebas and Lores.
AHN, *Clero*, Sahagún. carp. 873. no. 1.

(*Christus*). In Dei nomine Domini.
Ego Ermildi.
Placuit mici bono animo et ispotania nobis benit bolu[m]tas ut binderem tibi Nina et uxori sua Iuliana ereditate de filia mia Sendina in Ebas, in Lores bel in alios lorares binias, terras, pumares bel pumifera in monte, in fonte acesu bel que recre ab omnia intecritate foras una binea que comudabi in Taberneio. Et tu dedisti nobis precium pro ipsa ereditate duas ceramenes kabiane sirguacata, quartario de cebaria, emina de bino in sub unum in setemedio

qua[n]tum nobis bene conplacuit; et de ipso precio abut te debitus non remansit. Ut in ac die bel te[m]pore abeas, teneas ac defendas tum et filis tuis bel progenie tue, tum et fi'is tuis bel progenie tue belis abere, belis donare.

Sit aliquis te inqietarem benerit pro ipsa ereditate aliquis omo de parte mea aut de subrogita persona mea qui in iudicio bindicare non potuero post nomine meo tu[n]c abeas potestate de meo adpre[n]dere ipsa ereditate dupplata qua[n]tum a te[m]pus fuerit meliorata.

Facta karta bendiccioni ipsas kalendas marcas in era DCCCC LXXI.

Regenate domno Rademiro in Legione.

Fredena[n]do Gontesalbes comite in Kastela.

Ego Ermildi in ac karta bendiccionis que relegente audibi manu mea (*signo*) fecit ante testibus mul[tis] tera[di] dit roboranda:

Agane: Dulcidius confirmat manus (*signo*); Argiso testis (*signo*); Domninus testis (*signo*); Ervigius testis (*signo*); Serenus (*signo*); Aragildus (*signo*).

Arias (*signo*) scribsit.

1994 POSTSCRIPT

This paper was delivered at the special colloquium held to mark the retirement of Professor Glanville Price, at Gregynog, the country house owned by the University of Wales, on the morning of Tuesday July 14th, 1992. Professor Price was the general editor of the *Year's Work in Modern Language Studies*, to which I contributed (with a colleague) an ever expanding section on "Spanish Language" for eleven years, and a more pleasant and efficient colleague it would be impossible to imagine. The proceedings of that superb occasion are published as *The Changing Voices of Europe*, ed. Mair Parry et al., University of Wales, 1994, chapter 8, and this paper is reproduced here with the permission of the University of Wales Press. It represents a reworking of part of the paper delivered (under the title "Approaching writing—then and now") to the Tenth International Conference on Historical Linguistics at the Free University of Amsterdam on Wednesday, 14th August 1991. The other part, less concerned with Early Iberian Romance, was eventually reworked as "La escritura—¿foto o disfraz?" in *Actas del Primer Congreso Anglo-Hispano, Vol. I: Lingüística*, Junta de

Andalucía / Castalia, 1994, pp. 225-33. The increasingly logographic nature of reading and writing in this community holds the key to many of the problems in the field, I suspect; it deserves eventually a more thorough consideration.

14
The Teaching of Orthography in Tenth-Century Galicia

Dr. Amable Veiga Arias did Romance philologists a great service with his book entitled (with unnecessary modesty) *Algunas calas en los orígenes del gallego* (1983). With this study he has begun to fill the gap that existed to the West of the field of operations of the famous *Orígenes del español* of Ramón Menéndez Pidal (1926). With the data and ideas presented in these two studies we can now begin to try to understand the problems faced by notaries and others in Early Medieval Galicia when writing. Of course, it is not easy for us to enter the minds and intellectual perspectives of a thousand years ago, but if we want to make a reasonable interpretation of the evidence of the surviving texts of the time, that is what we need to attempt: to reconstruct their "orthographic consciousness" (what Gribomont, 1963, called their "conscience philologique").

We must assume that tenth-century Galicians had no idea of what was going to happen in the future. They could not foresee the later lines of evolution of Galician Romance, nor the metalinguistic distinctions (diatopic and diastratic) that would be erected later. Nor could they then have foreseen the future political dominance of the Romance spoken in Castilla, three hundred kilometres or more to their East. Nor were they specialists in etymology. But neither were they all stupid, illiterate and uncultivated barbarians (see, for example, Sánchez Albornoz 1944, García Alvarez 1965, Wright 1991b; and for the tenth century in general, Riché 1981:ch.15, and López 1951, although these do not refer to Galicia). They spoke their own language, and operated within their own chronological context. Some people knew how to read, and had been taught therein how to recognize lexical items. Some learned to write, always after learning to read; they were still taught the old traditionally correct written forms, because there were as yet no other acceptable ones. This means that in theory, at least, they would have been reproducing in their own writing forms which they had already previously learned (in most cases) to recognize when reading. In order to write the formulaic sections of a new document, they almost certainly had textual formulae to follow, or even learn by heart (similar to those in the famous Merovingian formulary of Marculf; Riché, 1981:ch.14, reminds us that Marculf composed this in his old age *ad exercenda initia puerorum*); the formulae have considerable philological interest in themselves (cp. Uddholm 1955), but this study will concentrate on the "free" sections, whose wording had to be prepared quickly on the spot without the help of such formulae.

In the case of a common normal word, used regularly as much in Galicia in the tenth century as it had been in the second (even if phonetically different), there was no real problem. For example, when they learned to read they found out that the form written *super* was that of the common word which they pronounced [sóbre] (or even perhaps [sóβre], if we accept Walsh, 1991), and if they had to read that word aloud, they could read it in the normal phonetics without hesitation. For this reason, most Galicians of that time could have understood texts read aloud to them, even if they were illiterate, more or less the same as now; and for this reason the view of the Romance-speaking Early Middle Ages that tends to be given to us nowadays, that theirs was a community untouched by literate culture, is needlessly ungenerous. We know that notarial documents had to be read aloud to the interested parties for them to sign afterwards, thereby confirming them. For example, nine of the tenth-century documents that survive from Sahagún (printed in Mínguez Fernández 1976) have a phrase at the end explicitly including the word *audivi* (or *audivimus*): e.g., "nos supra nominati sive hunc testamentum sive cartam vendicionis quod iussimus facere et audivimus legere roboramus" (doc.299, from 979); and 21 of them have the vaguer phrasing of *cognovi* (or *cognovimus*), which also refers in practice to having heard it read aloud. There is evidence of other kinds to the effect that at this time, even within the Carolingian Empire, texts written in the traditional way could still be understood when read aloud, even if the vocabulary used did not tally closely with the words found in the listeners' ordinary active speech. Society could still work on a basis of written documentation, of a legal, ecclesiastical, administrative and hagiographical nature, etc. Theirs was still what Riché (1981:ch.6) called a "civilisation de l'écriture" (with reference to seventh-century France). On this point it is worth also consulting Alarcos 1982, Dutton 1980, Collins 1985 and 1990, Wood 1990, Banniard 1989 and 1990, McKitterick 1989, Nelson 1990, Guerreau-Jalabert 1981, Wright 1991 and 1993, etc.

On the whole, modern specialists in historical linguistics and sociolinguistics prefer to operate with the same general principles when studying the past as when studying the present. If we can accept this, we can realize that nowadays even children and illiterates can understand texts read aloud to them, and thus postulate that also in the tenth century normally most people could understand texts read aloud to them—although not necessarily perfectly, then any more than now. And almost everything then was read aloud; the so-called "mozarabic" liturgy, the homilies included in the services, the *Lives* of Saints, notarial documents, orders that came from the Court to the regional officials, even perhaps the official Histories (it seems quite likely that the *Chronicle of Alfonso III* was intended to be read aloud to the Court, for example). To achieve this, we can presume that the reader aloud had to recognize the written lexical units and pronounce them in a normal comprehensible manner. On such occasions readers aim now, and aimed then, for intelligibility. There was in most noble homes, villages, offices and military camps, etc., someone who had precisely the job (among others) of reading out any communications that turned up, and all those who had some kind of access to this person were not in fact cut off from literate culture, even if they were illiterate themselves. They could also use his professional services as a writer if the need arose.

A mere three centuries earlier, Isidore had given advice to *lectores* to read slowly and clearly enough for the listeners to follow; he assumed that thereby the text would be intelligible. Similarly, in the tenth century we can presume that a reader would already know how to recognize the word written (for example) *super* (or its abbreviated form *sup*) and automatically read it aloud as [sóbre] (or [sóβɾe]). This lexical item, pronounced as either [sóbɾe] or [sóβɾe] by everybody, and found in texts in the written form *super* (or *sup*), was part of the general common vocabulary. The fact that the usual spelling was not exactly the same as a phonetic transcription would have been had they known the International Phonetic Alphabet would not have worried them at all. They are unlikely even to have noticed the anisomorphism; the English word that has (in part) the same meaning is pronounced [əbʌv] and written *above*, but it would not occur to an English-speaker to complain about this; it is just a fact of the language, which is taught to children at school, that this ordinary word is written *above*, and there is no further problem. It is normal for the established spelling not to change, even if pronunciation does.

A few people also learned to write. It does not seem to have occurred to anyone anywhere to teach writing before reading. For that reason, they were already able to recognize the written form *super* (or *sup*) as being the same word as that pronounced [sóbɾe] or [sóβɾe], before they ever had to write it (if they ever did). It could not have been difficult in this case, then, to train the notaries to write the word later in the correct way when it was their turn to write texts of their own. Learning to produce the written form of such a common word cannot have seemed problematic to them. And so, to remain with the same example, when we find the phrase *super agro de Scaurietum* in an unpublished document of 934 from Celanova (quoted in Veiga Arias, 198), we can draw no phonetic conclusions at all from the existence of the form *super*. This written form was the correct written form, however it was pronounced; the notaries were aiming for orthographic correction as they wrote; and in this case he achieved it. (Veiga Arias tells us nothing about the abbreviations in his text, unlike the scrupulous Menéndez Pidal, but this observation is just as valid if the form in this document happens to be *sup*). The same applies to the written form *Scaurietum* in the same phrase; if indeed it is true that this is the officially correct form, in itself its use tells us nothing at all about its pronunciation, and if we wish for other reasons to postulate that it was pronounced at that time more or less in the manner indicated by the written form *Escouredo* found in a document from Penamayor of (perhaps) 1188, the existence of this other, orthographically more correct form, is no reason not to do so. In general, in any language, words spelled correctly tell us nothing about phonetics. But they may, however, be usable as evidence of the manner in which the writers were taught.

   The most frequent words are the ones usually spelled best. This is not because they are less likely to have changed phonetically, but because their written form is easier to remember. This may well seem obvious; but it is the opposite of what is often said about the Iberian Peninsula of a thousand years ago, where unevolved orthography has often been thought to be evidence of unevolved phonetics (Blake, 1987, makes this point well). It has not prevented, for example, the influence of the Aragonese spoken in the High Pyrenees being invoked to account for written forms that include intervocalic -t- -p- or -c- in some of the Riojan Glosses, which in fact corresponded straightforwardly with Romance words spoken with [d], [b], [g] (or [đ], [β], [ɣ]): e.g., Gl.Em. 2, lueco, representing [lwégo]. The correspondence [g] with /-k-/ was normal. These are "culto" forms in the obvious sense that they were written by an educated person (by definition), but no more than that. The mythical "Leonese Vulgar Latin" was invented in the twentieth century to explain something that needs no explanation at all, that is, the commonly found coexistence of correct and incorrect spelling; see Wright 1983 and 1989, Marcos Marin 1984; if, as we write, we can remember the correct spelling on some occasions but not on others, that does not mean we are speaking some other hybrid language.

   But sometimes they had to write words which were less common, or words whose "correct" spelling was not as straightforward as in the case of [soβre]~[sobɾe]. Sometimes the words did not even have a "correct" traditional form: many names of people and places, particularly those of Germanic origin, had no such form (as Menéndez Pidal pointed out, of course). Even though the orthographic form of commoner words could be learned whole as logographic units, without any conscious analysis of their phonemic structure, some tricks of the trade seem to have arisen and established themselves in a more or less conscious fashion in order to give a more correct (or more formal) appearance to words whose traditional correct form the writers either could not remember or did not exist. It seems unlikely that the notaries worked with a dictionary or other reference tome actually open on their desks. Dictionaries did not exist, and the collections of glosses (glossaries) had a quite different function, being comparatively useless in cases of orthographic uncertainty. The notaries often had to write quickly, following the dictation of their client, at a speed more suited to speech than to erudite composition. In such a case, they had recourse to tricks of their trade, which were based on the most frequent cases. There were, for example, verbs formed with the prefix [soβre-] (o [sobre]). In the *Poema de Mio Cid* we find, for example, *sobrevienta* ("surprise," 1.2281), *sobrelievo* ("I guarantee," 1.3478), *sobrepelliças* ("surplices," 1.1582). These words derive respectively from SUPERVENTA, SUPER + LEVARE and SUPER + PELLIS + -ITIA (SUPERPELLICIA, according to Menéndez Pidal). As Menéndez Pidal (1946:855-56) points out, the form of the second of these words (*sobrelievo*) is presented as *superlevare* in the *Fuero de Cuenca* XIX, 4a. They would have done the same in Galicia and in preceding centuries; derived verbs formed with the prefix [soβre-] (or [sobre]) were written as *super-*; notaries knew that, whether or not they knew the whole word, and even if they may have made spelling errors in the following root.

To investigate whether what happened in Galicia was exceptional, I shall briefly also glance here at some documents from nearby territories. In the first place, I consider the two documents from Portugal that were closely examined by Lange (1966: from São Pedro de Cete, 882, and Pedroso, 897). The second one (pp.50-52) includes: "...filjos meos iam superius nominatos...que ibi sunt auitantes uel que ibidem Dominus superduxerint et in uida sancta perseueraberint sub manus de ipse abba et de ipsa filja mea iam superius nominata...et insuper auri talenta et a rex au comite aljo tanto." It looks as though this scribe recognized the morpheme spelled *super* inside the combinations *superius*, *superduxerint* and *insuper*. The other scribe, however, seems to make a lexical distinction between *super* and *subra* (pp.4-5): "...ad ista ecclesia adque Sacrosancto altarjo quod subra taxatum est"; and possibly also between *insuper* and *insubra:* "et insubra parjent tantum et alium tanto quantum inde abstulerjt et insuper aurj talemtum post parti testamenti et coram pontificum." (Menéndez Pidal, 1926:para.45.1, mentions *iam subra dictos* from León, 962, and *subra,* from Eslonza, 1005.) The opposite is also found; the Romance word [soβrarə] (nowadays written as *sobrar*) had its etymological origin in SUPERARE, but some scribes may not have recognized it: Lange offers us (1966:145-46) *superatum* (955) and *soberado* (Coimbra, 1108), plus the toponyms *Superato* (1070) and *Sobradu* (1102) (cp. Löfstedt, 1959:58, *soperatum* "attic," from San Millán, 956).

In addition, to set up some comparisons with the lands to the East of Galicia, I have looked for comparable evidence in the documentation from tenth-century Sahagún (Mínguez Fernández 1976, Herrero de la Fuente 1988). These editors have prepared beautiful editions, but make no indications of abbreviations in the sources. In these 372 documents there are 84 cases of *super* (plus 1 of *siper*), 48 of *insuper*, 28 of *superius* (plus 1 of *superuis*), 11 of *desuper*, 1 *superfata*, 1 *supertaxatum*, 1 *superest*, and 1 *superdictum;* there are also 90 *supra,* either on its own or used as a prefix (that is, both 17 *supradict-* and 15 *supra dict-*); plus *superato* and *supratos* (= subsequent "sobrados"). There is not even a single case here with the letter *b.* In Sahagún, it looks as though they were well trained in how to write [soβre], even when it was only part of a longer word; and even if these data in fact include many cases of the abbreviated form (*sup*), that form also must have been taught to them as a whole unit.

This is the explanation, in my view, for the strange forms of [soβriɲo] (= subsequent Galician *sobriño,* "nephew") presented to us by Veiga Arias as beginning with *super-*. They must have thought it was the prefix. It was not. The correct written form of [soβriɲo] was *sobrinus.* Even so, the forms *superinis* and *superino* from a document from Xubia, 1191 (Veiga Arias, p.60, seems to imply that here it is not an abbreviation to *p̄*) are the only ones that include a letter *e* out of the 36 written cases that Veiga Arias mentions. He refers here to the "restitution of a pretonic [e]," but that seems unlikely; this letter *e* was entirely "silent," written without anyone having pronounced this word with an [e] (we should remember that there was no [e] in the original form). Out of the 20 written representations of [soβriɲo] that contain the written letter *p,* among those that Veiga Arias reproduces in his book, the other 18 do not contain an *e.* So that it is easier to understand what happened when they tried to write this word [soβriɲo], here are reproduced all the forms mentioned by Veiga Arias (pp.58-60):

6 *sobr-* (*sobrinus* 1, *sobrinum* 1, *sobrino* 2, *sobrina* 2).

2 *super-* (*superinis* 1, *superino* 1)

16 *supr-* (*suprinis* 2, *suprini* 2, *suprinos* 8, *suprino* 1, *suprinus* 2, *suprinum* 1)

10 *subr-* (*subrino* 4, *subrina* 2, *subrinis* 1, *subrinas* 1, *subrini* 1, *subrinos* 1)

1 *sopr-* (*soprina*)

1 *supl-* (*suplinum*)

Sometimes, as Veiga Arias points out, there is variation within the same document.

If these are all the forms of this word that are to be found in this documentation, which is what Veiga Arias implies, we can see that on only six occasions (out of the 36) did the notary succeed in reproducing the correct spelling of the word. They never hesitated in representing the [ɲ] as *n*, which is no surprise at all (as Dr Veiga Arias also made clear) because that was the normal spelling of this ending. It was the anxiety to be "correct" that led the other notaries to the other 5 guesses (or 4, if we ignore the metathesis of the scribe who wrote *suplinum* in a document from Oseira of 1098, and we allot this form to those with *supr-*). It is clear that they did not know the form as an integral whole, and they had to make guesses on the basis of the tricks of their trade. In this case, we are fortunate enough to be looking at a word that did not suffer, and had no reason to expect to suffer, any phonological change in its first two syllables (assuming for the moment that if it was [β], that was merely allophonic, which is, I realize, debatable): the Iberoromance development of SOBRI- to [soβri-] is what we would expect, and is indeed what happened. We cannot believe that any of the five phonemes concerned changed phonologically (except eventually the [β]), nor even indeed that there could have been many variants in its pronunciation (neither diatopic nor diastratic) that were later to disappear; and even if there had been some variation, we cannot believe that this word can ever have been pronounced with a [u] or a [p] in the speech of any Galician of a thousand years ago. This variation was merely orthographic.

There is never any variation in the spelling of the initial [s-], because there was never any alternative available. The sound had not changed before a vowel, so [sV-] was always correctly written *s*-. Before a consonant at the start of a word, it never existed in speech; some of them knew that when [s] appeared before a consonant and after word-initial [e-] they should ignore the latter in writing; that was achieved, correctly, by the aforementioned notary who wrote [eskouredo] as *Scaurietum*. Since this was merely a trick of the trade, there were times when they missed the [e] out of the written form and thereby got it wrong; that explains why we so often find the incorrect form *ste* rather than the correct *iste* in the card-index of Visigothic Latin compiled by the Latin department of the University of Santiago de Compostela; and *Spania* (rather than *Hispania*) in the "Rotense" text of the *Chronicle of Alfonso III*, for example (Gil et al., 1985).

Intervocalically, we can sometimes find -*ss*- (e.g. in *fuisset*). But in the case of our word [soβriɲo], there was no reason to encourage the notary to write anything other than *s*-, and that is what we find every time. In the same way, the [ɾ] and the [i] presented no difficulties. But the written representations to be given to the other two phonemes were not so easy to work out.

There were many words in the Romance spoken in Galicia a thousand years ago in which the sound [o] was correctly spelled with the letter *o*. [monte] was correctly written as *mons* or *monte*, for example. We know from the note that Veiga Arias dedicated to this word (1982) that they apocopated the word in the toponym *Monfero*, and were sometimes unsure as to the correct inflectional morphology to give this word (that is, the inflection appropriate to the sentence the word was in), but it seems that the vowel of the first syllable was never written with any letter other than *o*. But in other words, in order to achieve orthographical correction, it was necessary to represent the sound [o] with a letter *u* (as in *super*, representing [soβre]). They seem to have been aware of this anisomorphism, and, either assuming that it would be preferable to make a mistake through overeagerness rather than through apparent ignorance, or remembering the case of *super*, or both, 29 of the other 30 writers chose the letter *u* rather than *o* to represent the first [o] of [soβriɲo].

There were also complications with the representation of the [β]. There were many words in which a [β] or [b] was correctly written with a letter *p*, as in *super*, or *Riparia* ([riβei̯ra]: Veiga Arias, 103-04), etc.; and others in which it would have been correctly written with a *b* (as in *beber*) or a *u* (*v*) (as in *vivir*) or even *bb* (as in *abbas*). Often, in an intervocalic position, they had success in opting for a -*p*- (e.g. *Riparia*, three times) instead of the -*b*- (7 times in that case) or the -*u*- (*Riueira* is found once). In the case of [soβriɲo], on ten occasions the writer chose -*ub*- and fourteen times -*up*- or -*op*-. This is only an orthographical variation, of course, but interesting even so.

If it had merely been a question of having to choose (when writing [soβriɲo]) more or less at random between two pairs of orthographical alternatives, *u* / *o* and *p* / *b*, we would expect to be confronted with statistics something like this: 9 times -*up*-, 9 times -*op*-, 9 times -*ub*-, 9 times -*ob*-. The statistics that Veiga Arias actually offers us here are so different from these that it is reasonable to suggest that they may even be significant. In the first place, the 6 "correct" uses of *sobr*- are less than the 9 we would have expected if the notaries were merely choosing at random; so perhaps we were wrong to make the deduction made above, to the effect that these six writers did know the orthographically correct form. Maybe these were guessing just as much as the others were, but happened to guess right. A reminiscence of the written form *super* could well explain some of these forms, but is not enough to explain why the form *sopr*- is found only once and the form *subr*- ten times; it looks as though the reasons they felt for representing [-o-] as -*u*- were some ten times more powerful than those they felt for representing [-β-] ([-b-]) as -*p*-.

This discrepancy can perhaps be explained by the instructions they had been given for representing inflectional morphology correctly; written forms of nouns were so often correct if the writers represented [o] with -u- that this formalizing trick (writing u for [o]) was used, correctly, in many other words as well. (This is a guess, of course. Besides, in some areas the final vowel of these nouns might have been [-u], at least in some words that had a high vowel in the root). On the other hand, in inflections -p- was never correct; whereas in imperfect verb forms [aβa] was written correctly as -abat (-abam, etc), and the correct form of the future indicative of many verbs—a paradigm which seems to have hardly ever been written, unlike the future subjunctive—also included a -b-. In the future tenses, this letter may well no longer have corresponded to any sound at all in the Romance of the tenth century; *amabit* is likely to have in effect represented [amará]; although earlier the -b- indeed had corresponded to a [β], when the [β] of the postposed auxiliary *habeo* was still pronounced, and it may be reasonable to hypothesize a slight residual [β] even in this tenth century (that is, it could have been [amaráβe]). The same was true, mutatis mutandis, of the -*ibus* which sometimes had to be written but which (in the tenth century) was no longer used in speech, not even (I suggest) in reading aloud; I follow Politzer 1961 and Green 1991 in saying this, rather than Löfstedt 1983. Pensado (1991:198-99) noted that in her corpus the commonest suffixes were written in the orthographically correct form more often than other morphemes, although she did not find that as a consequence of this the *t* was written in other morphemes more often than *p* and *c* (the other letters usually representing unvoiced consonants). Even so, it could be that reasoning such as this (not necessarily conscious) led them to think in cases of uncertainty that *b* was more likely to be correct as the written representation of [β] than *o* was of [o]. If this was so, then the combined statistical predominance of -*ub*- over -*op*- in the forms that we have attested of our word could be explained as a consequence, either conscious or unconscious, of their training. And even if we were right, on the other hand,to see the forms written in *sobr*- as lucky guesses, we still have a ratio of 20:16 for *p:b* (56%:44%) but 29:7 (81%:19%) for *u:o*, and the second figure is still striking.

The written forms of this word in Lange (1966:129) are *sobrinis* (Celanova, 842), *sobrinas* (Livro de D. Mumadona, 982), *sobrinum*

(Livro Preto, 1005), and *subrinos, subrinum, sobrina* (1101). In the tenth-century documentation from Sahagún there are 5 *sobrino*, 1 *sobrinos*, 3 *sobrinis* (= 9 *sobr-*, 27%); 2 *subrino*, 2 *subrini*, 3 *subrinos*, 9 *subrinis*, 1 *subrineas* (??[ɲ]) (= 17 *subr-*, 51%); 1 *suprina*, 2 *suprinis*, 1 *suprimis* (= 4 *supr-*, 12%); plus 1 *superinum*, 1 *subsuprinis* and 1 *consoprinis*. These percentages are not unlike the ones from Galicia, and we can deduce that, in this case, in Sahagún as in Galicia apprentice scribes were taught the spelling *super* (or *sup*) as an integral whole, but not *sobrin-*. It might be that the reason for this was that *super* was often found in various semi-formulaic phrases, but *sobrino* was not. (There are also 5 *tio*, 1 *tios*, 1 *tiu*, 1 *tia*, representing the converse, "uncle").

What conclusion should we draw from this, then? That at least some of the scribes learned the equivalence of [soβre] and *super* (or its abbreviation) during their professional training, but they did not usually learn the equivalence of [soβriɲo] and *sobrinus*; and also that they learned the equivalences of [-β-] and [-b-] with *p* or *b*, and of [o] with *u* or *o*, as some of the formalizing tricks of their profession. That can explain the surprising statistic that in Galicia *super* was very often written correctly, despite its phonetic evolution to [soβre], and *sobrin-* was only written correctly one time in six, without ever having undergone any phonological change. There is no need to conclude that *super* was always taught in this way in every center, nor that they always learned it right; for example, I have studied elsewhere (1982:166) a tenth-century Leonese document containing the form *suber*, and Jennings (1940:63) noted the form *desuber* in a 982 document from San Vicente de Oviedo.

It is, in passing, of great interest to observe what happened to a similar word in tenth-century Sahagún: [aβadesa] (now written *abadesa*, "abbess"). The masculine *abba* "abbot" was written correctly with no problem; yet the feminine [aβadesa] was written there 7 times *abbatissa*, 2 *abbatisa*, 1 *abbatisi* (= 10 *bb*, 38%); 6 *apatissa*, 1 *apatisse*, 2 *apatisa*, 3 *appatisa*, 1 *apatesa*, 1 *apatesam*, 1 *apase*, 1 *apa* (= 16 with *p* or *pp*, 62%). It seems that they knew that the [d] (or [đ]) of this word should be written as -t-, as in so many suffixes, but, even given the analogy of *abba*, and in the absence of any prefix analogous to *super-*, the letter *p* exerted its attraction on more than half of these occasions. Here, as with *sobrino*, the word had always been pronounced with a voiced consonant (it comes from the Greek, which had β,), and we cannot envisage the existence of any [p] (and certainly not of [pp], obviously).

These data show that we cannot just trust the spellings of these times to be faithful transcriptions of anyone's speech. To quote Pensado (1991:197; my translation): "the intention of writing correct Latin removes any evidential value from archaizing forms." But the mere fact that they wrote, and did compose new texts, is a guarantee that they must have been taught how to write. It is impossible to write without having been taught how to choose spellings. We need to investigate how this training was done: every letter, every word, every phoneme, possibly every syllable, needs individual research. This is what Puentes Romay has begun to do, over a wider geographical range than this, studying the letters *b* and *v* (1986a), and, more adventurously, the representation of the reconstructable phoneme /ts/ (1986b). Puentes concludes that "some very definite tendencies can be established" (1986a:348), which could well be attributable to the way the writers had been taught. In her important study, Pensado (1991), working with a huge Leonese corpus to study the orthographic variation of *p* and *b*, *t* and *d*, *c* and *g*, discovered that some of the commonest words were never written incorrectly; for example (staying in the field of kinship terms) it is noticeable that she assures us that *pater* and *mater* were never written with a letter *d* (p.200), and we can deduce from this that if there was indeed such a list of written words learned whole, these two words must have been on that list. Pensado has not yet studied those cases (such as *sobrino* and *abadesa*) in which the correct orthography included *b* (or *d*, or *g*) but the word is sometimes found written with a *p* (*t*, *c*) which cannot ever have corresponded to an unvoiced sound. (Jennings, 1940:47-48, refers to the letter *p* of the form *suprino* in a document of 990 from Oviedo as being due to the confusion that there was in the contemporary pronunciation of the word; an absurd explanation, for there was never any such confusion. In fact, he has misunderstood a comment by Muller and Taylor 1932:45-46).

As we saw in the data from Sahagún, the difficulty experienced by Galicians as they tried to write [soβriɲo] was also felt slightly further East in writing [soβrino] (where the nasal had not palatalized). In the famous tenth-century list of cheeses from San Justo y Pastor (León) we read the form *soprino* (Menéndez Pidal 1926:24-25; Wright 1982:173). In the *Chronicle of Alfonso III*, written in Oviedo at the end of the ninth century, we read *subrinum* (Gil et al. 1985: ch.20, pp.138-39), *consubrinam* (ch.2, pp.116-17) and *consubrino* (ch.3, pp.118-19): they all turn up in the same spelling in both versions (the Rotense and the "Erudite" one of the tenth century), without having been further corrected in the Erudite version, whose editor "corrected" many other details of this kind. There is no way of knowing whether they used the lexical item [konsoβrino] in active speech at that time, but it is entirely possible; it also appears in document no.251 from Sahagún (of 967), and Isidore had used it shortly before (for its semantic change, see the notes in Bonnaz 1987, and my own assessment of the language of the Chronicle, Wright 1991b). The cheese-loving Leonese monk wrote *sopr-*, and all the Oviedo historiographers wrote *subr-*, both forms being "incorrect" in just one detail, but we can feel sure, in this case, that they all said [soβr-] or [sobr-] (both in [soβrino] / [sobrino] and in [soβre] / [sobre]).

This is a significant example, because it involves a word whose first two syllables never changed phonologically, but which were written in Galicia in six different ways (according to the data provided by Dr Veiga Arias); and another word whose first four phonemes were pronounced the same way in tenth-century Galicia (in [soβre]), but which apparently was regularly spelled in a manner both correct and unlike phonetic transcription. We cannot be sure of the statistics of this form in tenth-century Galicia, however, until all the data used by Dr Veiga Arias are available in a form accessible to those of us who do not have the good fortune to work in the beautiful city of Santiago; all those of us who live elsewhere but are interested in Galician hope that they can be published soon, because for the moment we have to be content with the brief phrases quoted in the works of Dr Veiga Arias. There are not many words like Castilian [soβrino], in which there had been no phonological change (apart from in the final inflections, of course). As we saw earlier, *montes* is another (being [móntes], or at least /móntes/, in the first century, the tenth, and still now), and, so far as I am aware, the first syllable has always been written as *mon-*, although the word was occasionally apocopated to just that in toponyms. These three letters, *mon*, are those that always appear in the forms mentioned in the *Orígenes del Español*, although we can presume that sometimes the /n/ was represented in writing with a tilde (*mō-*). The first vowel in [móntes] is the one that interests us here. It was [o], the same as in [soβriɲo], but in this case it seems that it was never written with u (***mun-*). So there were some words which they could always manage to represent "correctly" with a *u* representing the [o] (as *super*, or *sup*), and others which they could (nearly) always manage to represent "correctly" with an *o* for the [o] (such as *montes*), while there were also others which they did not know beforehand how to represent the [o] in, and thus they had to make a guess, choosing from the two possibilities offered by the correspondences they had met elsewhere (as with [soβriɲo]). These facts can be best explained by the hypothesis—which is merely a hypothesis; there is no polemic or dogma to be derived from this—that in their professional training they often had to learn by heart correct forms of frequently-used words, including those found in formulaic or semi-formulaic phrases that occurred often, learning them logographically as whole units without phonemic analysis; whereas for less common words, they had learned sound-letter correspondences that they could later use when writing quickly to dictation. This hypothesis is not at all unlikely in itself. Modern English children are taught to read, and at times also to write, with the same mixture of techniques; it is practical. So it is not particularly adventurous to suggest it also for the Galicia of a thousand years ago. I am referring here merely to the methods they used in writing their own language, so there is no need to discuss antiquated words that were found in previously written texts that they may have had to read aloud, but were otherwise outside the active competence of the tenth-century writer and not written in new texts; I have already considered the methods they seem to have used to read aloud archaic items in Wright 1982:165-73 and 1983a; Pensado (1991:191-92) also considers them.

Three words, of course, cannot prove anything. So let us consider another case, this time of words and sounds that indeed changed. The letter *t* for example, had room for more confusion than the letter *p*. As did the *p*, at the start of a word the letter *t* represented an unvoiced plosive, both in words inherited from the Empire, such as *terras* and *tauros*, and in those that had come from elsewhere, such as *taleiga*; Dr Veiga Arias presents us with three written forms of this latter word (211-12), without variation in the initial *t*-. (They knew nothing of its etymology, of course; such a distinction is only made by us). In post-consonantal position the letter *t* also represented [t] (e.g. *monte* and *portum*; Veiga Arias, 122). In these two positions, syllable-initially, there seem to have been no problems: [t] was represented with *t*. At the end of a word, this letter probably represented no sound at all, in the Romance spoken in tenth-century Galicia, although it is true that we cannot be sure of the century in which the final [đ] (written -*t*) disappeared from the end of verbal affixes. By the eleventh and twelfth centuries, at the latest, we can feel sure that there was no dental sound at the end, for example, of words such as the ones written *dicunt* or *stat*, which represented [dídzen] and [está] (*dicent* is actually attested in Sahagún, doc.258, of 970). In La Rioja, the famous eleventh-century Glosses seem to show that the final plosive fell out of use there after the plural [-n] earlier than in postvocalic position, but not even these Glosses were actually written in a manner systematically isomorphic with the phonemes. Let us suppose that at least often, and perhaps always, in "correctly" written forms from the Galician data the final letter -*t* represented no sound. It would be possible, under these circumstances, for a written final letter -*t* to be equally "silent" in other words, as for example in the forms *Eytat*, *Heitat* or *Eitit* (Veiga Arias, 123) or in *Roderiquit* or *Miguit* (mentioned in Dr. Veiga Arias 1989:13 and 24). This possibility, that such forms are "hypercorrections" of this type, is only mentioned here because it is one more of the many possibilities in such difficult cases.

In intervocalic position the letter -*t*- usually represented [đ] (or [d]); *pratum* represented [práđo]. This phoneme was also sometimes represented by the letter *d*, at the start of a word (*de* [de]) or of a syllable (-*ando* [-ando]); but there were so many morphological inflections in which [đ] (or [d]) was represented by -*t*- (e.g. [-áđes] by -*atis*, [-íđa] by -*ita*); and perhaps still [-eđoɾ] by -*itur*, if the synthetic passive was indeed still occasionally used in high-style speech—that probably they would statistically be more likely to be correct on average if they chose to represent the phoneme with the letter *t*. Meanwhile, intervocalic [-t-] was hardly ever heard; if such a word was to be written, sometimes it needed -*tt* (e.g. *gutta*), sometimes -*pt*- (e.g. *scriptos*) or sometimes -*t*- (see below).

In Castille, they had a special problem with words beginning in [ot-]. It is possible to reconstruct that there, in the tenth and eleventh centuries, the words that began that way were [otóɲo] (< AUTUMNUM), [otorɡás] (< AUCTORICARE), [ótɾo] (< ALTERUM), [otéɾo] (< ALTO + ARIUM), and—in some styles and some regions, at least; perhaps in all—[óto] (< ALTUM). That is, not a single one of the words that began with these two phonemes could be written correctly with either an initial letter *u*- or *o*-. *octo* represented [oito] at that time ([oit-], more or less as in Modern Galician), and it seems likely that *october* then represented [oit-] as well, since its first nakedly Castilian documentations, in the thirteenth century, begin with *och*-.[1] AUT > o had already lost its [-t] (see the form *au* in the quotation above from Lange, for example). The only word in the Latin of the Empire that had begun in [ot-] had been *otium* (and its derived terms, such as *otiose*), a word which did not survive in speech; if [óđjo] existed in the tenth century, which is not certain, it was written *odium*; the words that had begun in *ut*- had either disappeared from active speech (e.g. *utrum*) or seen that consonant voice ([óđɾe] < UTER), and the form written *ut* was probably rarely if ever used in active speech, although it certainly still remained in

---

[1] Corominas and Menéndez Pidal offer us the forms *ochubre* and *ochubrio* from that century, as well as *octubre* with the traditional correct spelling of *oct*- (and so, as we have seen, this latter form cannot be used as evidence for phonetics), and, later, *otubre* (from Santander, 1380 and 1419: Menéndez Pidal 1966:34); that is, that the phonetic history of "octubre" developed parallel to that of "ocho" until after the thirteenth century. In tenth-century Sahagún they always wrote this word with *oct*-; nearly always in the form *octobris*, but twice as *octubrias*. There, dates including an 8 were written in numerals (VIII) except two cases of the year 970 (era 1008), with *octaba* and *octava*; later, in the already quoted *Fuero de Valfermoso de las Monjas*, there appear *oitabas* (107), *oictavas* (198) and *octavam partem* (199) (vernacular "octava, ochavas").

the passive competence of listeners; yet it would have been said and read as a clitic with [o], or maybe [oḋ], but never [ot]. The consequence was the well known fact that the vowel [o] of words that began in [ot-] was written in all sorts of different ways (see the data in *Orígenes*, paras. 20-21), but that the [t] of these words was always written as *t*. So far as I know, we never even find it geminated into *-tt-*.

And we can now see from the studies of Dr Veiga Arias that the Galicians had a similar problem. It was not exactly the same problem, because there the normal pronunciation of the initial phonemes of such words was [ou̯t]: the three initial letters of the modern written forms *outono, outorgar, outro* and *outeiro* probably represented more or less the same sounds then as they do now. They also had stylistically-motivated variants of *alto*, and first it would be best to solve this ancient philological puzzle. The variation we find in the texts, but which on this occasion it is also justified to reconstruct in their speech, seems to imply that this word found itself at the end of the queue for the lexical diffusion of this phonetic change ([alt-] > [au̯t-] > [ou̯t-] and/or [ot-]—perhaps because it was the only one with tonic stress on that syllable—and the variation which is always found during a sound change continued right up to the twelfth-century in this case. As we know from the superb study by Malkiel (1975), in that century the multitude of available forms derived from DULCE was simplifying out to the benefit of the spoken form [dúltse], which happened to coincide with the phonetic form given to this word in Church pronunciation (the new "Medieval Latin" introduced into the peninsula at that time; cp. also Hartman 1980, Wright 1982:34-36). I suspect that in *alto* we have a similar case, in which a word had available several competing phonetic variants ([alto], [au̯to], [ou̯to], [oto]), and this phonetic indeterminacy was solved in that same twelfth century in favor of the [-lt-] which members of the Church were being taught to pronounce during their training in that century (but not before), since this is also a word used in the Christian liturgical offices. That is, the "culto" effect is not a reactionary conservative one, but a reflection of the progressive Europeanizing reforms of the twelfth century. So [alto], in Galicia as elsewhere, eventually survived as the independent lexical free morpheme, but at times [oto] or [oṷto] survived in placenames, either as a separate word or as a morpheme inside a compound word (where it may not have been recognized), both in Castille (Menéndez Pidal refers to *Villota*, in Burgos province, etc.) and in Galicia (e.g. *Montouto, Outomuro*, etc., mentioned by Dr Veiga Arias, 182) and elsewhere. *Alto* ([alto]) is indeed the genuine Galician vernacular form, as Fontanillo and Rodríguez (1985:34) point out; the written literary variant "*outo*, which has been adopted by several writers, is a literary creation, invented to be different from the Castilian..."; we need to take care not to be misled by this kind of invention.

We are used nowadays to making the diagnosis that forms (of these words) in [ou] are Galician and those in [o] are Castilian (and elsewhere). But in this case, as in most others, it does not seem in practice that the evolution was so neatly geometrical, nor obeying political boundaries with such clarity. We can easily reconstruct that there was a long time when both forms (as well as the preceding form [aṷ]) were found all along the Cantabrian range, and probably elsewhere also. A synchronic sociolinguistic study carried out in the tenth century would have discovered, I suspect, that the two phonetic forms of these words existed in both Burgos and Compostela, but that in the latter area [oṷ] was more common than [o]—80% to 20%, say—whereas in Burgos [o] was more common than [oṷ]—again 80% to 20%, perhaps. Then later, at the time of the linguistic standardizations (in the thirteenth century) it is understandable that in each area they chose (either consciously or not) to standardize the variant form most frequently used there. For this reason I am in complete agreement with Dr Veiga Arias when he says that written forms of such words in *o-* found in Galicia (such as e.g. *otero*) should not be described as "Castilianisms." Neither should forms found in Castille with the letters *ou-* be described as "Galicianisms."

It would be useful to be able to study in detail the Galician word *outro* in the tenth century, but Dr Veiga has not provided quotations of this word, so the necessary data are not immediately available. (Neither are there many attestations available of *outono* and *otoño*, < AUTUMNUS). In *Orígenes*, 20.4, Menéndez Pidal offers us the forms *altras*, from Sahagún, 1097, and *autra*, from León, 1163, and in several paragraphs considers the competition between the different written forms. On this occasion, as with *alto*, it is probably justified to postulate a connection between written variation and spoken variation. *Autra* is also found in Modern Galicia (Fontanillo and Rodríguez 1985:429). Among the Riojan Glosses we find *altra, altro, altras* and *altros*, and perhaps there was in the Rioja a spoken form including [l]; although this *l* is attributed to "cultismo" by Menéndez Pidal. (If that is indeed the explanation, we could well wonder why this supposed "cultismo" was not also written with an *e*.) In the tenth-century documents from Sahagún I only found 1 *alteros*, 1 *alteram*, 2 *alterum*, plus 1 *alterutrum* in a text that was almost certainly rewritten much later.

In theory, [o̯ṭoɾɡaɾ] should have been written as *auctoricare* ("grant"). Although it seems that this word was never found in this written form in the Empire, the two component morphemes, *auctor* and *-icare*, are venerably ancient. In Galicia, according to the data of Dr Veiga Arias (189-93), there are for this word 28 written appearances of *auct-*, four of which are also found with *-iz-* (e.g. *auctorizare*) which Dr Veiga Arias diagnoses as being a separate lexeme from *auctoricare*, without providing the semantic contexts that lead him to this conclusion; there are also 7 written with *oct-*, 2 with *aut-*, 7 with *ot-* and one with *obt-* (and, in the event, *-iz-* also: *obtorizare*). We can hardly attribute the domination of the forms in *auct-* to the possibility that in this case they had been taught the orthography of the word whole as a logographic unit, because there is not even a single case of the "correct" *-ic-*; as well as the four with *-iz-*, two are written with *-g-* (e.g. *auctorigare*) and the rest with just *-g-* (e.g. *auctorgare*). Although the syncopation process must have been completed in this word by then (Harris-Northall 1990:97-101), it is hard to believe that they can actually have been taught to write the word as *auctorgare*, and there is no need for us to come to that conclusion, since, according to the correspondences which they either knew explicitly or intuited inductively, [ɾg] could be written as *-rg-* without any problem (e.g. [laɾga], *larga*). It could be suggested that they were indeed taught how to write the complete morpheme *auctor*; this word was written this way in the *Fuero de Avilés*, for example; but it does not seem to have been a frequent word in daily notarial usage. It is also possible to suggest that there might have been an idea—less formalized than their tricks of the trade, presumably—that words beginning in [oy̯t-] (and, where appropriate, [ot-]) could be given their correct form with the letter *c*. This is how we can explain the forms of this word written with initial *oct-*; while those that began with *aut-* owe that form to the operation of the common sound-letter correspondence of [oy̯] with *au* (e.g. [koy̯t-], *caut-*); and those with *ot-* may well represent directly the sociolinguistic variant glimpsed above. There is not a single case of written *out-* for [oy̯torɣaɾ] in the data from Galicia provided by Dr Veiga Arias; neither he nor I nor anyone else doubt that it was indeed regularly pronounced [oy̯t-], and so once again we can discard the possibility that the notaries were dedicated simply to using phonetic script.

Even so, in the data from tenth-century Sahagún all we find is *auctori-*; 1 *auctorizamus*, 2 *auctorizare*, 2 *auctorizaverimus*, 4 *auctorizemus*, and (all in documents that seem to have been revised much later) even 1 *auctoricabit*, 1 *auctoricationis*, and 1 *auctoricare*. In that monastery at that time it looks as though they had been taught the spelling of this lexical unit whole. But that did not happen everywhere within León; in the *Fuero de Valfermoso de las Monjas* (of 1189), as photographed in 1983 by J. C. Villaverde Amieva and A. D. Laca, we see *otorguet* (1.57) *outorguet* (60-61), *otorgan* (119), *autorgamento* (122, var. *-miento*), *otorgant* (144) and *outorgarent* (186, 187). Lapesa (1985:54-55) relates the forms in *ou-* with mozarabic.

The only form left undiscussed in the data from Galicia, *obtorizare* (of 929), represents the same confusion among supposed prefixes that is found exactly 850 years before in the *Graffiti* from Pompeii, in which we read [oskultat] written as OBSCVLTAT instead of the correct form AVSCVLTAT. *Escuchar*, and the forms in the Glosas Silenses *scuitara* (120) and *scuita* (125), come from a postulated *SCULTARE, which lost its initial syllable via backformation because this was wrongly identified as being a prefix; wrongly, because in fact this word had originally been a compound of AURIS. This phenomenon is found in other cases also: for example, in Sahagún we can see, as well as many written forms with *aquaduct-*, those with *adque-* and *atque-*, *adqueductibus* (p.145), and *atqueductum* (p.280), similarly attesting misidentification of a prefix. The converse form *auctinuerit* (that is, written mistakenly for the correct *obtinuerit*), which Dr Veiga Arias (181) presents, guarantees that the letters *obt-* could represent the same sound at that time as *auct-*. This idea, that [ot-] and [o̯ut-] could be correctly written as *auct-*, or at least as *oct-*, was not a new one; I have discussed elsewhere (1982:63) the form, found in eighth-century Italy, *octummio* (that is, instead of *autumn-*, "autumn"); and, in fact, in the tenth century the only words that this correspondence could be correctly applied to were *auctor* and its post-classical derivative *auctoricare*.

Yet this correspondence was also applied when writing the word [o̯ute̯iro] ("hill"). If this had been written "correctly" we can only suppose that it would have been written as *altarium* (its etymological equivalent). Unfortunately, this written form was already regularly in use, to mean "altar." In the tenth-century documents from Sahagún we find 22 cases of *altario*, 31 *altariorum*, 3 *altariis*, plus 1 *altari* and 5 *altaribus*, and they all refer to altars, none to hills. It is the same in Lange 1966:4-5. It would seem from this that a spoken form [altarjo] with the meaning of "hill" never existed; *outeiro* and *otero* represent Early Medieval formations, that is, *out-* plus *-eiro* and *ot-* plus *-ero*. We can hardly expect them to have written *altarium* to mean "hill" since they already knew this written form well; for it is often used in these documents (the depositors regularly want a candle to be placed on an altar). And, indeed, Dr Veiga Arias never found the word [o̯ute̯iro] written with a letter *-l-*. There are 15 cases of *aut-*, 14 of *auct-*, 3 of *out-*, 7 of *oct-* and 2 of *ot-*. It seems unlikely that they can have been taught in Galicia to write this word as a unit with a letter *c*; these 41 forms must be the consequence of the sound-letter correspondences they intuited as being relevant to this initial syllable (and as a result, it seems even less plausible to give the logographic explanation for the form *auctorgare*).

Further East, in the documents from tenth-century Sahagún, placenames including this word were spelled with *Au-*: *Autero, Auteros, Autero Maurisco, Autero de Aquilo, Autero de Lopos, Autero de Sellas, Autero de Sendino, Auteros de Rege, Auterolo de Legione*. In a non-toponymic use, there is one case of *autero* (doc.167) but also one case of *otero* (333). It seems possible, therefore, that in Sahagún, unlike in Galicia, they were taught a single orthographic unit, *Autero*.

It looks as though all the wide orthographic variation we find in these words can be simply reduced to this: on the whole they said [ou̯t-] in Galicia, although some may well have sometimes said [ot-]; they knew that [ou̯] could at times be correctly written as *au*, but also that [ou̯t-] could at times be written correctly as *auct-*. That may be all there was to it, although possibly some writers in some centers had also learned the separate written unit *auctor* whole, without any analysis of sound-letter correspondences.

And if we come to the same conclusion for Castille, where they usually said [ot-] but we find the same wide range of written forms, we are unlikely to be far out. Menéndez Pidal considers (with reference to [otoɾgaɾ]) the written forms *auct-*, *aut-*, *obt-*, *oct-*, *at-* and *ot-*. As we saw above, there was no problem with the correspondence of [ot-] with *ot-*, and maybe they only rarely said there [ou̯t-]. Even given these six written alternatives, there is no reason at all to hypothesize the existence of six phonetic alternatives also; nor for us to call any of them "learnéd" ("culto"), nor "semilearnéd," nor "hypercorrect," nor "Latin," nor "Vulgar Latin," nor "Low Latin," nor "sporadic," nor "Church Latin," nor "Notarial Latin," nor "contaminations," nor "barbarous," nor "corrupt," nor anything else. There may in fact have existed in Castilla a variant in [a-]. In Aragón it is found written with *at*—see *Orígenes*: parr.75.2 also in Sahagún (see *Cantar de Mio Cid*:485), although it is not attested there in this form in the tenth century; and in the *Poema de Mio Cid*, lines 198, 3411 and 3645, as well as *otorgar* (that is, with *ot-*) in lines 1303, 2340, 3670. Menéndez Pidal seems in his comment to be implying that the two are separate lexical items, although no real semantic distinction is perceptible. These forms written in *at-* suggest that this syllable may well have been pronounced at times as [at-], in which the pretonic diphthong simplified by losing the semivowel [w]. So far as I know, there is no sign of this development happening in Galicia. And perhaps we should add that although some of the scribes may well have been originally mozarabic (cp. Sánchez Albornoz 1944), it is not particularly helpful here to visualize mozarabic phonetic habits as underlying this variability, since they were probably not particularly different.

By suggesting in this way that the scribes were operating with a psychological correspondence of [ou̯t-] (and [ot-]) with *auct-*, rather than merely of [ou] with *auc/oc*, as has been suggested before, we solve a problem that remains unsolved if we consider merely the diphthong in isolation without its following consonant; for it seems that all the cases of written *auc* or *oc*, in which we would wish to postulate that the letter *c* did not correspond to any sound, precede a written letter *t*, representing [t].[2] This is also true of the few occasions when we find these written letters in the middle of a word; for example, the cases of *saucto*, *sauctis* (that is, representing [sót-], "copse") presented by Menéndez Pidal (1926:para.20.3), and of *sauctos* (representing [sóu̯t-]; Veiga Arias, 186: this form is not found in the tenth-century documents from Sahagún, where there are 10 *Sauto*, two *sauto*, two *soto*, 1 *saltos*, and 1 *saltu*); or of *cocto* (that is, representing [kóto], "hunting-ground"), in which, unlike Menéndez Pidal (parr.21.1) I would prefer not to postulate a sound [u] (nor [w]) corresponding to the letter *c*. The form *alctare* (for "altar") considered by Veiga Arias (176-77) could probably be best explained in the same way, although it remains peculiar even so.

One other word deserves comment here: *tomar*. In the Middle Ages they used this word (for "take") less than *prender*, but it is a vernacular word without any doubt. Its etymon is still debated; Schuchardt (1890) suggested **tumbare, which is not impossible; Pío Rajna (1919) suggested that it could have been AUTUMARE, via **atomar, reanalyzed as *a* + *tomar*; subsequently Jud (and Corominas) expressed agreement with this etymon, but without the intervening monophthongized form of the first syllable. They preferred to believe that the whole initial syllable had been dropped in another case of backformation through erroneous identification of a prefix. In sum, then, under any proposed scenario the spoken form in Early Iberoromance was never *[otomár]; so it is not to be included in our list of words of the time which began in [ot-]. But

---

[2] In tenth-century Sahagún we find 2 *aucmentare*, 1 *aucmentaberit*, 2 *augmentare*, 1 *acmentare* and 1 *acmentum*, but no case without either *c* or *g*; we can provisionally deduce from this that in this word there may still have been some trace of the original velar consonant.

even if this was indeed the correct etymon, they do not seem to have been aware of this, for then the correct written form would have been *autum-*, but, so far as I am aware, the word has never been found spelled in this way in the Early Medieval documentation; nor even—so far as I am aware— spelled as *tum-*; as with the placenames and other words of uncertain origin (that is, uncertain to them at the time), this word must have seemed best written via the most appropriate available correspondences, in this case [t], [o] and [m] as *t*, *o* and *m-*, all helpfully unambiguous in this case, as we have seen. Malkiel (1990), in turn, prefers to propose AESTUMARE as the etymon, analyzed wrongly as AES + TUMARE, from which the second (hitherto non-existent) morpheme acquired a life of its own. All in all, though, it seems that this word does not qualify to be among those studied in detail here.

CONCLUSIONS

To understand what lies behind the written forms of the Early Iberoromance Medieval documents, we need to be able to reconstruct the phonetics of the vernacular Romance of the time and place concerned, collect together all the data that there are available (from the original manuscripts, and without making any "emendations," obviously), and then attempt to draw deductions from all this concerning how they were taught to move from phonetic forms (in so far as we have been able to reconstruct them) to the written forms (textually attested still). In this article, only those words that began with [soβr-] and in [out-] in tenth-century Galicia have been considered in any detail, together with their cognates in Sahagún and in Castilla, and we can expect that the investigation of more words will lead us to more of the techniques and tricks of the trade that they learned; for the moment, we can provisionally conclude that they learned the orthographically correct written form of some common words and inflectional affixes as complete whole units, without bothering to analyze their phonology, while they learned how to write all other words according to professional rules of sound-letter and syllable-letters correspondence.

And that is all there was to it. It is time for us to discard inappropriate and misleading concepts of a diastratic and evaluative nature such as, on the one hand, those of "cultismo," of Latinism, of "semicultismo," of hypercorrection, and of a general skill in direct phonetic transcription; at the same time, on the other hand, we should discard the concepts of linguistic barbarousness, corruption, degradation, decadence, contamination, etc; similarly, certainly before the turn of the millennium and preferably right up till the thirteenth century, let us also discard such misleading and anachronistic concepts as Galician, Leonese, Castilian (etc.), terms which were only valid at the time with a literally geographical reference, without, at that time, being used yet to distinguish between conceptually separate linguistic entities; all these concepts are modern inventions, and cloud our view. The inhabitants of the Iberian Peninsula (apart from those who spoke Arabic, Basque or Hebrew, but no Romance) formed one large Romance speech community, complex but still monolingual; they spoke in their natural evolved vernacular, and writers had to start from that basis when trying to achieve the traditionally "correct" spelling. The same sort of thing happens nowadays in modern France, England or Argentina. It is not easy to learn to write in these presentday countries, working out how to fit the vernacular pronunciations to the respected standard orthography, but many of us do indeed learn to do so; and it is one of our duties as Romance philologists to try and find out how they learned to achieve this in the Galicia of a thousand years ago.

This may all seem obvious. I have been told that it is. But even if it is, it is not what we are usually told. A common assessment of the texts of this time, diametrically opposed to the one expressed in this article, has been neatly expressed by Díaz y Díaz (1981:71; my translation):

> This reduction of Latin to the status of merely an autonomous written language used as a common "koine," without the support of being the language spoken in any community...unlike any normal written language, medieval Latin was not the stylistic elaboration of a particular spoken language..

This is the right perspective for the period after the early thirteenth century, but it seems to be exactly the opposite of what happened in the tenth century (which is the century that Díaz y Díaz is considering in this study). Written language was at that time still precisely "the stylistic elaboration of a spoken language," in the same way as the written Galician or written Castilian of the present day is the stylistic elaboration of spoken Galician and spoken Castilian. Spoken and written styles can vary considerably now one from the other, of course (for the manifestation of this in Castilian, see e.g. Klein Andreu, 1990). Latin and Romance were not at that time, even though they were going to be much later, two separate "autonomous" languages. This anachronistic mirage has merely created unnecessary problems for philological analysis; stopping believing in it will help solve them.

Dr. Veiga Arias' book is much larger than this brief study by Díaz y Díaz. It is an interesting book, intelligent, full of information and ideas. It will have become clear from my conclusion, however, that I do not share his (p. 19; my translation):

> The result will be a decisive contribution to our knowledge of Galician in its initial stammering phase ["balbuceos"], and of the survival of Latin merely as a vehicle for written communication.

On the contrary, I do not believe that the tenth-century Galicians could only "stammer" their language. I prefer to agree with Alarcos Llorach (1982), who argued that the language used in the Iberian Peninsula a thousand years ago served the inhabitants as well for communication then as the present languages do now. There is no evidence of their having made a clear metalinguistic distinction at that time between speech and writing as autonomous and separate languages. It seems hardly even possible that they could have maintained at that time such a system of diglossia, which needs always to be underpinned by educational systems of a complexity we cannot postulate for tenth-century Galicia. It is not relevant either to compare their language with that of a long time earlier (calling it a barbarous corruption of Latin) nor with that of a long time later (calling it the incipient stammerings of Galician); their language has to be studied in their own cultural context. That is what I have tried to do here.[3]

1994 POSTSCRIPT.
To mark my joining the editorial committee of the journal *Verba* (*Anuario Galego de Filoloxía*) in 1991, I was invited to write a review-article of Veiga Arias's book; that task got out of hand, but the editors of this journal are famously generous with space and were happy to publish the Castilian original of this discursive account whole as "La enseñanza de la ortografía en la Galicia de hace mil años," the initial article in *Verba*, 18, 1991, 5-25. The discovery that the data can be used and sensibly explained in the monolingual perspective makes this, in my view, the most important article in this section, although the individual assessments are in several cases merely provisional.

---

[3] But this is less immediately important than the need to have the data published. For the purposes of this article I have trusted the transcriptions of Dr. Veiga Arias, which seem in general trustworthy, but there are also signs of what may well be printing errors: for example, sometimes the same phrase from a document is quoted slightly differently on different pages; and these are able to lead our analysis astray as much as do the hypercorrecting copyists of the twelfth century. Nor is it easy to follow his interesting later article (1989), because in this article there is no bibliographical help at all to explain the origin of the quoted phrases for those who may not have his book (not even the book itself is mentioned). We need the documents published whole, so we can see all the data in context. So I end this study with a request; to help those of us interested in Galician, but not in Galicia, I humbly request that these data be published, preferably by *Verba*.

15
The Purpose of the Glosses of San Millán and Silos

The Monastery of San Millán de la Cogolla is situated in the wine-producing area of La Rioja. A party was held there in November 1977, to celebrate the thousandth birthday of the Spanish Language. More precisely, they were celebrating the existence of manuscript *Emilianense* 60, which is now in the Library of the Real Academia de la Historia, in Madrid. Twenty-one folios of this manuscript have annotations in the margin, some of them in a non-Latin form, in what could be described as Romance orthography and (sometimes) morphology. These are the famous *Glosses of San Millán* which Menéndez Pidal published at the start of his seminal *Orígenes del Español*, in 1926. Menéndez Pidal dated them to the second half of the tenth century. 977 is in the second half of the tenth century, which is why the millennium was celebrated in 1977. In the same year Olarte Ruiz published his facsimile of these folios.

If this were the right date, the glosses would come from the most interesting context of late tenth-century Rioja; the circle of the scribe Vigila and his mathematically-organized compositions, and the original home of the magnificent ecclesiastical codices now in the Library of El Escorial. But that date is not the right one. The year after that celebration, the best of all the Spanish Medieval Latinists, Manuel Cecilio Díaz y Díaz, published a short but excellent book (1978) in which he declared that there was no doubt that these glosses come from fairly late in the eleventh century, after 1020 and perhaps even 1050. It would be difficult to argue against this. But it is an ill wind; we can have another thousandth birthday party in the year 2020.

There are also other Romance-like glosses on a manuscript from the Monastery of Santo Domingo de Silos, now in the British Museum in London (Additional Manuscript 30,853). The last section of this manuscript contains a European-style Penitential, glossed in a similar way. This is also of the eleventh century, but seems to be a copy of another manuscript with the glosses already in, which could have been of an earlier date. It is possible that its original could have come from San Millán, since the Monastery at Silos was re-founded at the start of that century with the help of the monks from San Millán.

Naturally, these isolated words do not in fact attest the "birth of the Spanish Language." This has often been said, but it makes no sense; Romance had been "born" a long time earlier, as is generally realized. Neither are they symptoms of ignorance, as is also sometimes said; it is clear that they were prepared by a writer (or writers) with an impressively enterprising spirit. Another idea which has gained wide currency is that these glosses were copied out of a pre-existing glossary; this seems very unlikely to me, but other investigators have taken it seriously. I have already written about this at some length (Wright 1982:195-207), but even so wish to return to the topic here.

Díaz y Díaz suggests that these glosses were taken from existing Latin-Latin glossaries, which we know to have been in circulation at that time. Three glossaries from Silos (published by García de Diego, 1933) and two glossaries from San Millán survive from the tenth and eleventh centuries. Unfortunately for this theory, though, glossaries were normally compilations of glosses already found in other manuscripts; there is no evidence that they were regularly employed as a source for other glosses to be added later to unglossed manuscripts. In general, glossers had prime recourse to their own experience, without having open in front of them a glossary, although they probably had seen glossaries, and memories of their contents could indeed have echoed in the back of their minds as they worked. In other glossed manuscripts of the age, the glosses tend to represent an item of vocabulary which was still in vernacular use, added in order to explain antiquated vocabulary in an old text. Such glosses were otherwise normally meant to be spelled in the traditional manner still.

Although Díaz y Díaz claims to see an "undoubted source" in

the Silos Latin glossaries for 22 of these Romance glosses, even they are merely 22 out of over 300 (in the Silos manuscript), and even then there is only an exact equivalence in the written forms in two cases. And even in these two, there is room for doubt. For example, in one of the Glossaries we find the word *pudor* explained as *verecundia*, both words being spelled in the correct traditional manner. This is understandable; *pudor* was not used at that time in vernacular, and the word spelled as *verecundia* was, even though in an evolved phonetic form closer to the Modern Castilian *vergüenza*. In gloss Em.17, the *pudor* in the text is glossed as *verecundia*, written that way. But in gloss Em.76 *erubescunt* is glossed as se *bergudian* (that is, "se averguenzan," "they are ashamed"); and in gloss Sil.171, *pudoris* carries the gloss *dela vergoina*; here it is the same lexical unit, but not the same written form. The glossary can hardly be the source when the word is written in the glosses in such different forms. Indeed, only two of the 513 glosses coincide exactly with one of the more than twenty thousand words in the Silos glossaries (this *pudor* as *verecundia*, and gloss Em. 118 *iter* as *via*), and that proportion is less than we could have expected out of mere coincidence.

This theory of Díaz y Díaz's at least has the merit of being possible. Unfortunately, not even this can be said of Menéndez Pidal's suggestion that the glosses were taken from a now lost Latin-Romance glossary, of a type we do not find attested until some four hundred years later. It is not easy to believe in the existence of such Latin-Romance glossaries at that time. How were they compiled? Where would the words have come from? If they came from pre-existing glosses on other now lost manuscripts, which is the way glossaries were normally compiled, where did the glosses on these other manuscripts come from? How did these hypothesized early glossary-compilers decide what the "Romance" spelling was to be? If such glossaries had indeed existed earlier, their existence would attest to a conscious manipulation of the language and a technical mastery of phonetic detail that it seems hard to envisage for the period. Besides, there is clear internal evidence that they did not use any such Latin-Romance glossary. Some of the glosses are written in normal traditional spelling. Some words in the text have different glosses on different folios. Many words in the text are given glosses which make good sense in the context, but would seem wrong outside that context: e.g., gloss Em.59 *occupare* "parare uel aplecare"; Em.82, *offero* "dico"; Sil.163 *matrimonio* "prima junctatione"; Sil.321 *coitu* "semen." Some glosses offer an explanation rather than a synonym: e.g. Em.9 *tertius ueniens* "elo terzero diabolo uenot"; Em.85 *exacturus* "de la probatione"; Em.131 *dicit etiam* "Esajas"; Em.137 *ayt enim apostolus* "certe dicet don Paulo apostolo"; Sil.300 *eos* "akelos qui tornaren." The same word in the Romance gloss can be spelled in a variety of ways: e.g., the word evolved from Latin IACTARE (now Sp. *echar*) appears in four different forms: Em.45, *respuit* "geitat"; Sil.43 *transmiserit* "zetare corri"; Sil.53 *relictis* "jectatis"; S .102 *inici* "por jactare." It is also worth pointing out that the more traditional the orthography of the word, the easier it is to recognize what it is, whether or not it follows the phonetics closely. Four times we find in the San Millán manuscript the gloss *quomodo*, with the Romance meaning ("like," as in Sp. *como*) and the traditional spelling, but also on two occasions *quemo*: Em.25 and 50 *sicut* "quomodo"; Em.52 *uelut* "quomodo"; Em.83 *quasi* "quomodo"; Em.115 *non per speciem neque per uelamen* "quemo enospillo noke quemo eno uello." The upshot is that there is no need to look for a source at all; the glosses seem to have been prepared in a less organized way than that.

What can, then, be deduced from the way the glosses are written? In many details, they seem to be intended to follow the phonetic shape of the Romance word, even though in that way they become harder to recognize (as is the case with phonetic script nowadays). But it is not a carefully worked out script like that of the *Cantilène de Sainte Eulalie*; in general, in the Riojan glosses, we can say that a non-traditional spelling reflects evolved pronunciation, but we cannot deduce that unchanged spelling necessarily represents unevolved pronunciation. For example, the second gloss from San Millán offers *lueco* for the word *repente* in the text. That word, as usual, has the meaning of the time (in this case, the same as the modern Spanish *luego*, "next," rather than that of its etymon LOCO, which meant "[in the] place"). The written letters *u* and *e* here represented together the Romance diphthong [we], which was the outcome of the open [ɔ] of the Latin of the Empire; we are able to conclude that here the new spelling represented the evolved pronunciation, because without this they would not have thought of inventing it. But from the written letter *c* we cannot deduce that it was still pronounced there and then as [k]. It was quite normal at that time for the written letter -*c*- (intervocalically) before a letter *o* to correspond to the sound [g], and it seems almost certain that this word was then pronounced [lwego]. In the same way, the intervocalic letter -*t*- regularly represented a voiced [d], and an intervocalic letter -*p*- represented a voiced [b]. We even find the word *sabiendo* twice written in the glosses with the final letters -*to* rather than -*do* (Sil.134, 341). But this word could not possibly have been pronounced then with an unvoiced [t]; both the Latin SAPIENDO and the Romance *sabiendo* have a voiced [d]. This spelling is what is sometimes called "ultracorrection." So for the same reason it is very probable that the written letter -*p*- in *sapiento* represents a voiced [b] in these glosses. This all means that these glosses cannot be used as evidence to argue that the Romance speech of the area still had the original unvoiced intervocalic consonants; the glosses need have nothing whatsoever to do with the pronunciation in some areas of the Aragonese Pyrenees where such words still have unvoiced intervocalic consonants; the glosses are not evidence of the mythical entity "navarroaragonese," as Elcock (1975:416-22) and Lapesa (1980:ch.6) said, an entity which represents in any event a probably anachronistic view of the nature of Romance dialect boundaries.

Since it can thus hardly be maintained that the script is strictly "phonetic," the initial question becomes at once more interesting and harder to answer; what was the purpose of these attempts at a novel kind of writing? We now know something that previous investigators did not; that they are from the eleventh century, quite possibly from well into that century. They do not belong to the concentratedly Visigothic culture of the Rioja of the tenth century, but to the more open culture of the eleventh century, in which European ideas are beginning to have an influence. In the Peninsula, outside Catalonia, they still had their Visigothic liturgy, which had been standardized in the seventh century, and their Visigothic handwriting; it was only towards the end of that century that they would start to import both the Roman liturgy and the spoken "Medieval Latin" originally standardized by the scholars at

Charlemagne's court for the representation of that liturgy. (If this seems a surprising claim, it is argued in great detail in Wright 1982). In what now seem to be the relevant years for the context of the Glosses, the mid eleventh century, as in the 1970s, Northern Christian Spaniards were beginning to come out of a period of comparative isolation into the full light of wider European culture. As Lomax (1982) and Bishko (1969) have shown, for example, there were coming to León, Navarre and Castille scholars and clerics from Catalonia and France, and the numbers of pilgrims who crossed the Northern kingdoms to get to Santiago de Compostela were increasing. For these reasons, it seems quite likely that at that time aspects of European Romance culture were beginning to be known about in San Millán, Silos, Burgos and elsewhere in Castille and Navarre.

Already, one of the customs of that culture was that of sometimes writing words of their own vernacular with the morphology they had in speech and a more or less phonetic spelling (devised according to the already existing sound-letter correspondences used further North for speaking Medieval Latin). The first attempts at writing literature in Romance in Northern France and Provence, written that way in order to inspire a local Romance pronunciation in their reading aloud, happened at an earlier date than the one which we now know to be the correct date of these glosses. In Spain, on the other hand (outside Catalonia, which was part of the Provençal cultural sphere at that time) they had still not adopted that custom. Not because they were "backward"; the point was just that in Spain they did not need a separate Romance way of writing. Since spoken Medieval Latin had not yet been introduced into the Peninsula, when they read aloud a traditionally-written text they all read the words with the normal vernacular pronunciation anyway (as, for example, English speakers do automatically when reading words in traditional spelling). Dutton (1980) has already established that legal documents were read aloud in an intelligibly vernacular manner. For this reason, in the Peninsula at that time, they had had no need to invent a new spelling based on rigurous phonetic transcriptions in order to indicate that the text had to be read with Romance phonetics: they did that anyway. Meanwhile, though, after the general adoption of the Carolingian reforms, in France and Catalonia they regularly read aloud the traditional spelling of words in the new way (Medieval Latin), and only the new vernacular spelling necessarily implied that the reading aloud would be vernacular. And yet, if the Spaniards of the time had no need yet to invent a new spelling, what were they doing when they wrote these glosses? That question has not been broached (even in Wright 1982).

Here I will put forward a hypothesis. More of an imaginative scenario, in effect. The glosses could be the result of a collaborative enterprise between a Riojan (or Navarrese or Castilian) monk and a visiting monk from Catalonia or Provence. Let us hypothesize that a monk came from Catalonia or Provence to an ecclesiastical center (in the Rioja, Castille or Navarre), and that he wanted, for some reason, to read aloud intelligibly there the homilies of the San Millán manuscript or the Penitential of the Silos manuscript (which are both of a European type). At this point I neither need nor dare wonder why. His hosts would already have known how to read and explain the texts to an audience of their own time and region. They did it every day of the week. Even if the native monks might have needed glosses to explain some of the archaic vocabulary, they did not at the same time need to have them presented in an unusual spelling. The visitor, however, did not know how to read the text aloud with the phonetics of that region. There was no need to give up his intention, though; he explained to his Spanish hosts that in his country they had invented a way of writing in which all the written letters corresponded to the sounds of words of ordinary local speech. Maybe he showed them an example. "How peculiar," they would have replied, just like a modern Frenchman or Englishman who sees for the first time a phonetic transcription of a passage of his own language. But together they had a try at adapting this newly arrived idea to the spoken forms of their part of the Peninsula, so that the foreigner could later read the texts aloud there and even explain them, through the glosses, with something like intelligibility (even the two glosses in Basque). Perhaps the glosses that remained in the old-fashioned form were ones that he did not wish to read aloud; when there are two glosses to the same word in the text, one written in the old way and one in a new way, perhaps the first explained the meaning to the reader and the second told him how to explain it to the listeners. For example, in Sil.52 we find *strages* glossed by *occisiones* (which the stranger would have understood, but which did not form part of that region's vernacular) and then also by *matatas*, since the form [matadas] would have been intelligible locally. (Compare also Sil.243, *fundaberit*, glossed as *firmaret ficieret*.)

This scenario comes from the imagination rather than from scholarship, I know. But it fits what happened in earlier similar initiatives. It seems likely that the *Strasbourg Oaths* were elaborated by a Romance-speaker in France for the benefit of a Germanic-speaker who already knew how to read Medieval Latin aloud but was none too skilled in French Romance, such that he needed some kind of phonetic script in order to make his reading intelligible to the Romance-speaking listeners (regardless of whether it was actually thus intelligible or not). It seems likely that the *Cantilène de Sainte Eulalie* was elaborated by a bilingual (German-Romance) writer in order to help Germanic-speaking singers who already knew how to perform texts aloud in the new Medieval Latin way but were also none too skilled in French Romance, such that they too needed a phonetic script of some kind in order to make their sung version intelligibly Romance (if indeed it was thus intelligible); see Wright 1982:122-35. Writing any language in an approximately phonetic script is nearly always done for the benefit of those who do not know the language; if they know the language, they do not need a phonetic transcription, and will recognize the written word more easily in its usual traditional orthographic disguise. New written forms are of no use to someone who cannot read at all, so we have to assume that the destined reader already knew how to read the usual spelling. The only people who could receive any practical benefit at all from having in front of them words written in a manner approximating the phonetics of speech in the Castille-Navarre area (as is the form of many of these glosses) would be those who already knew how to read words written in the ordinary way, but not how to read them aloud with the phonetics normal in that Castille-Navarre area. Some modern novelists do something similar; they invent a roughly phonetic manner of spelling to indicate to readers from elsewhere how people speak in Venezuela, Argentina, Murcia, etc. The fact that the glosses were written in the monk's Visigothic handwriting would have been no great inconvenience for the subsequent reader, as we can tell from the fact that in the eleventh century even Cluniacs in Spain still used the Visigothic script.

There is no difficulty in suggesting Catalan or French involvement in this enterprise. Lapesa (1980:para.42) describes the eleventh century as a century of "French influence." Lomax and Bishko describe how the diocese of Palencia and some centers in the Tierra de Campos were refounded in these years by Catalans, with the blessing of the Leonese King. We know anyway that many of the earliest compositions written in a peninsular vernacular language (including the disguised vernacular found in many *fueros*), however authentically native they seem, were prepared at the stimulus of a French or Provençal prototype. Maybe the stimulus is to be found here for these glossers also.

This line of thought has led me to the theory that these Romance glosses were written by a Spaniard, to help a foreigner read and explain aloud the text in the vernacular manner of the Castille-Navarre region. However, even if this is wrong, there can no longer be any belief in the usual assessment of these glosses, as found, for example, in the preliminary pages of the facsimile edition (Olarte Ruiz 1977). The glosses are from the eleventh century. They are not from Aragon. They were not taken from a pre-existing glossary. They are the result of enterprise and initiative, possibly prepared under the stimulus of meeting an example of the Romance phonetic scripts by then used elsewhere; and it is possible that they were provided for a reader who did not know well the vernacular forms to which the written forms were designed to correspond. Of course, if this is the right scenario, it has to be admitted that they did not achieve a very clear result. Problems remain, naturally; but I hope here to have placed the frame of the picture in a more appropriate context than it has been given before. The details need more study yet.

1994 POSTSCRIPT.

The Spanish original of this paper was printed as "La función de las Glosas de San Millán y de Silos," *Actes du XVIIe Congrès International de Linguistique et Philologie Romanes*, Vol.9 (Critique et Éditions de Textes), Publications de l'Université de Provence, 1986, 209-20; it was the verbatim text of the paper given to that conference on Wednesday morning, 31st August 1983. The style is thus that of a lecture rather than of a scholarly article, but it is still worth reproducing even though the intervening years have seen the argument move on. For example, Bézler (1984 and 1985) has convincingly postponed the date of composition of the original Silos penitential (the one copied as our surviving Silos manuscript) to later than 1060, which makes the French-contact scenario even more likely (Cluniacs themselves were around by then). García Larragueta's transcription (1984) of the manuscript has no new ideas, but often aids identification of textual details. Stengaard (1991a) has established the purpose of the numerical and alphabetical signs written above many of the words in the San Millán manuscript, signs which Wolf also (1992) uses to postulate a far northern origin for the manuscript; and Cano (1992:38-41) has produced an excellent analysis of the syntax of the glosses, which I have never considered. Neither Lloyd (1987) nor Penny (1991) consider the question, unfortunately. At the Third International Conference on the History of the Spanish Language (Salamanca, November 1993), Manuel Díaz y Díaz gave an impressive update of his present assessment of the Glosses. It is, in contrast, astonishing and depressing to see how little knowledge literary scholars wish to have of these matters; for example, Walsh and Deyermond (1992) are magnificently up to date in their literary references, but it has not occurred to them that linguistic research might have progressed since 1926.

It was only after this lecture went to press that I realized the modern analogue of what I was proposing (and it still seems to me to be the best of a bad lot of available scenarios); it is the phrasebook principle. I subsequently elaborated this in an article not published in the present volume (Wright 1988a). When British travellers go abroad, they often take with them a phrasebook to help say words in the foreign language. In this book, the foreign words are spelled in two ways; once in their normal spelling, and once in a spelling which aims to reproduce what the spelling could be if the word identically pronounced happened in fact to be part of English. This technique, of spelling words in a language that the reader does not know according to the spelling system used in a language that the reader does know, is only partly successful, of course. The British traveller in Portugal wants to say "thank-you" to his friends in Portugal, opens his guidebook at *obrigado*: "oo-bree-gah-doo" (which is not, of course, in phonetic script, since that is unfortunately not yet on our national curriculum and would baffle rather than help), and says [uːbriːgaːduː]. His friends laugh, but probably understand. If they see the form written in the phrasebook, they laugh much louder. Since the result tends to sound funny, it is not surprising that in our own scenario the Riojan experiment was not regularly followed up; French visitors would not wish to cause mirth when reading from the Penitential. I included a section on this phrasebook analogy when delivering the paper again in the University of Santiago de Compostela in April 1985, and it indeed caused astonished laughter there (also using the possible example of a Spaniard learning Welsh, discovering that the word for "six" is written *chwech*, but being helped by a phrasebook version as *juej*, which in turn would look absurd to a Welsh-speaker). The point, though, that such re-spellings help foreigners but not natives, seems well worth holding on to.

These glosses are *sui generis*, largely unlike the glosses and glossaries known elsewhere in the Early Romance world, or later in the Peninsula, but the attempt, once made, began a century-long tentative grope to a new reformed writing method. In that sense, the Glosses are indeed the "birth" of something; not of the Spanish language itself, but of intelligent attempts to reform its spelling. How ironic it is, then, that those who now praise the anonymous Glossers tend to be the very same people who argue strongly (and, on the whole, persuasively) against such spelling reforms a millennium later.

Part III

Language and Texts in the Iberian Peninsula after 1080

16
The First Poem on the Cid—
the *Carmen Campi Doctoris*

The *Carmen Campi Doctoris is* a Latin poem on El Cid, composed during his lifetime. The first half of this study concerns the manuscript, the meter, the pronunciation, the vocabulary and the possibility of a vernacular source. The evidence suggests that it was composed by an ecclesiastical author for an educated audience; it does not support the theories that it is an epic or a *canto noticiero*, a journalistic folk-song. The second half of the study examines the title, the relationship of the *Carmen* to the later *Historia Roderici*, and the treatment of the three victories included. Evidence is presented in favor of a date of composition of *circa* 1083, rather than the presently accepted date of 1093-4. The conclusion is that the *Carmen* has considerable literary value, but should be used only carefully in any historical argument.

1. The Text

Since the poem is not widely accessible outside Spain, it is here reproduced as it is in the manuscript, with abbreviations resolved and punctuation inserted.[1]

---

[1] The *Carmen* has been previously edited by: E. du Méril *Poésies Populaires Latines du Moyen Age* Paris (1847) pp.284-314 (308-14); J. Amador de los Ríos *Historia Crítica de la Literatura Española* 11 Madrid (1862), New York (1970) pp.343-6; A. Bonilla y San Martín 'Gestas del Cid Campeador' BRAH 59 (1911) pp.161-257 (173-78); G. Bertoni *Il Cantare del Cid* Bari (1912) pp.197-204 (198-201); R. Menéndez Pidal *La España del Cid* 2 Vols Madrid (1929, revised 1947) pp.876-84 (880-84); H.S. Martínez *El*

1   Ella Gestorum Possumus Referre
     Paris et Pyrri, nec non et eneae,
     multi poaete plurimum laude
     que conscripsere.
	Indeed, I can tell of the victories of
	Paris, of Pyrrhus and of Æneas,
	which many poets have praised at
	great length.

5   Sed paganorum quid iuuabunt acta
     dum iam uillescant uetustate
          multa?
     modo canamus Roderici noua
          Principis bella.
	But what good will the successes of
	pagans be, since they are now of
	little value because of their great
	age? Let us now sing of the recent
	wars of the leader Rodrigo.

Tanti uictoris nam si retexere
10 ceperim cunta, non hec libri mille
     capere possent, omero canente,
          sumo labore.
	For if I began to tell of all the
	successes of so great a victor, a
	thousand books would not contain
	them, even if told by Homer with
	all his might.

Poema de Almería y la Epica Románica Madrid (1975) pp.411-15.
 The most important criticism of the *Carmen* is in du Méril, Amador, Menéndez Pidal and Martínez (pp.348-53); four brief articles by G. Cirot: 'Le *Carmen Campidoctoris*' *BH* 33 (1931) pp.144-49; 'Le rhythme du *Carmen Campidoctoris*' *BH* 33 (1931) pp.247-52; 'Le vrai Cid' *BH* 41 (1939) pp.86-9; 'Quelques mots encore sur le Cid' *BH* 41 (1939) pp.178-80; E.R. Curtius 'Der Cid Rhythmus' *ZRPh.* 58 (1938) pp.162-72; R. Menéndez Pidal 'La Epica Española y la "Literarästhetik des Mittelalters" de E.R. Curtius' *ZRPh.* 59 (1939) pp.1-9; M. Coll i Alentorn 'La Historiografia de Catalunya en el períoda primitiu' *Estudis Romanics* 3 (1951-2) pp.139-96 (180-5); J. Horrent 'Sur le *Carmen Campidoctoris*' *Studi in onore di Angelo Monteverdi* I Modena (1959) pp.334-52—reprinted with revised notes as Ch. 2 of *Historia y Poesía en torno al Cantar del Cid* Barcelona (1973), to which page references refer; M. Barceló 'Algunas Observaciones al *Carmen Campidoctoris*' *Saitabi* 15 (1965) pp.37-58; A. Ubieto Arteta *El Cantar de Mío Cid y algunos Problemas Históricos* Valencia (1973) pp.163-70. Subsequent references to the works in this note are made in abbreviated form by author's name only, or in the case of more than one work by the same author, by author's name with abbreviated form of title.

	Verum et ego parum de doctrina quamquam aurissem e pluribus pauca	And even though I learned only too little of the many things taught at school, nevertheless I am going
15	rihtmice tamen dabo uentis uela, pauidus nauta.	to set my sail before the wind into rhythmic poetry, a terrified sailor.
	Eia letando populi caterue, campi doctoris hoc carmen audite; magis qui eius freti estis ope,	Come gladly to hear this song in praise of the *Campi doctor,* crowds of people! In particular, those of
20	cuncti uenite. all come!	you who rely on his military power,
	Nobiliori de genere ortus, quod in castella non est illo maius; hispalis nouit et iberum litus quis rodericus. Rodrigo is.	He is sprung from a moderately noble family, though there is none older in Castile; Seville and the shores of the Ebro found out who
25	Hoc fuit / primum singulare bellum cum adolescens deuicit nauarrum; hinc campi doctor dictus est maiorum ore uirorum.	This was his first single battle, when as a young man he beat the man from Navarra; that was why man older than him came to call him *Campi doctor.*
	Iam portendebat quid esset facturus,	Already he was foreshadowing the deeds that he was destined to
30	comitum lites nam superatus, regias opes pede calcaturus ense capturus.	perform, for he would defeat the campaigns of counts, trample the power of kings, and capture them with his sword.
	Quem sic dilexit sancius rex terre iuuenem cernens adlata subire;	Sancho, king of that land, favored him so much when he saw the
35	quod principatum uelit illi prime cohortis dare.	young man fulfilling his duties, that he wanted to give him the command of his main troops;
	Illo nolente, sancius honorem dare uolebat ei meliorem, nisi tam cito subiret rex mortem,	he did not want it, but Sancho was preparing to give him a greater honour, when the King suddenly
40	nulli parcentem.	succumbed to death, who spares nobody.
	Post cuius necem dolose peractam,	After Sancho's death by treachery,

Rex eldefonsus obtinuit terram; cui quod frater uouerat per totam dedit castellam.	King Alfonso took control over Castile, and gave Rodrigo what his brother had promised, throughout Castile.
45 Certe nec minus cepit hunc amare ceteris plusquam uolens exaltare, donec ceperunt ei inuidere compares aule,	Moreover, he began to hold Rodrigo in no less favor, and wanted to exalt him above the others, until his peers at court began to envy him,
Dicentes regi: Domine, quid facis? 50 contra te ipsum malum operaris, cum rodericum sublimari sinis; displicet nobis.	and said to the King: "Lord, what are you doing? You are creating trouble for yourself by allowing Rodrigo to rise so high; we are worried about this.
Sit tibi notum: te numquam amabit, quod tui fratris curialis fuit, 55 semper contra te mala cogitabit et preparabit.	You should know that he will never be loyal to you, for he was your brother's courtier, and he will always be thinking and plotting evil against you."
Quibus auditis susurronum dictis, rex eldefonsus, tactus zelo cordis, perdere timens solium honoris, 60 causa timoris,	When King Alfonso had given a hearing to the words of these whispering slanderers, his heart was touched with jealousy, fearing to lose his throne of honour, something he was afraid of;
Omnem amorem in iram conuertit, occasiones contra eum querit, obiciendo per pauca que nouit plura que nescit.	he turned his favor to anger, seeking pretexts to harm him, using the few things he had been told to accuse him of many for which he had no evidence.
65 Iubet e terra uirum exulare: hinc cepit ipse mauros debellare, yspaniarum patrias uastare, urbes delere.	He ordered the hero to live in exile outside his kingdom. So he began to fight against Moors, lay waste the lands of Hispania, and destroy their cities.
Fama peruenit in curiam regis 70 quod campi doctor, agarice gentis	News came to the King's court that the *Campi doctor*, with the help of

obtima sumens, adhuc parat eis laqueum mortis.	the best of the Moors, was preparing for them the snares of death.
Nimis iratus iungit equitatus, illi parat mortem nisi sit cautus,	He was very angry, and assembled his cavalry, preparing to kill Rodrigo should he be that careless, ordering
75 precipiendo quod si foret captus, sit iugulatus.	that if he was caught his throat should be cut.

Ad quem garsiam comitem
   superbum
rex prenotatus misit debellandum;
tunc campi doctor duplicat
   triumfum
80   retinens campum;

This King sent the proud Count
García to defeat him; then the
Campi doctor triumphed again, and
was master of the field;

Hec namque pugna fuerat secunda,
in qua cum multis captus est
   garsia;
capream uocant locum ubi castra
   simul sunt capta.

for this was his second battle, in
which García and many others were
captured; this place is called Cabra;
and his camp was captured too.

85 Unde per cunctas ispanie partes
celebre nomen eius inter omnes
reges habetur, pariter timentes, /
   munus soluentes.

This is why his name is famous
amongst all the kings, throughout
all Hispania; they both fear him and
pay out money to keep his favor.

Tercium quoque prelium comisit,
90 quod deus illi uincere permisit,
alios fugans, aliosque cepit, castra
   subuertit.

He also fought a third battle, which
God granted he should win, putting
some to flight, capturing others and
sacking their camp.

Marchio namque comes
   barchinone,
cui tributa dant madianite,
95 simul cum eo alfagib ilerde iunctus
   cum hoste,

For the Marquis-Count of Barcelona,
to whom Moslems pay tribute,
together with Al-Fayib of Lérida,
who had joined him with an army,

Cesar auguste obsidebant castrum
quod adhuc mauri uocant
   almenarum,
quos rogat uictor sibi dari locum
100 mitere uictum.

were besieging the Zaragozan fort
with the Arabic name of Almenar,
when Rodrigo asked them to make
way for him to send in provisions.

Cumque precanti cedere nequirent,
nec transeundi facultatem darent,
subito mandat ut sui se arment,
   cito ne tardent.

105 Primus et ipse indutus lorica,
nec meliorem homo uidit illa;
romphea cinctus, auro fabrefacta
   manu magistra;

Accipit hastam mirifice factam,
110 nobilis silue fraxino dolatam,
quam ferro forti fecerat limatam,
   cuspide rectam.

Clipeum Gestat brachio sinistro,
qui totus erat figuratus auro,
115 in quo depictus ferus erat draco
   lucido modo.

Caput muniuit galeam fulgenti
quam decorauit laminis argenti
faber, et opus aptauit electri
120   giro circinni.

Equum ascendit quem trans mare uexit
barbarus quidam, nec ne comutauit
aureis mille, qui plus uento currit,
   plus ceruo sallit.

Talibus armis ornatus et equo,
paris uel hector melioris illo
nunquam fuerunt in troiano bello,
   sunt neque modo.

Tunc deprecatur

And when they refused to grant his request, nor let him cross their lines there, he at once ordered his troops to arm quickly, without delay;

And first he himself put on his cuirass; nobody has ever seen a better; then his sharp sword, inlaid with gold by an expert hand;

he took his wonderfully made lance, hewn out of an ash-tree from a noble wood, which had been smoothed with strong steel and made straight at the point.

He carried his shield on his left arm; it was all inlaid with gold, and on it a fierce painted dragon shone out.

He covered his head with a shining helmet that a smith had decorated with sheets of silver and fitted round with a band of electrum.

He mounted his horse which a Moor had brought from overseas, and which he had bought for a thousand gold pieces, which runs faster than the wind and jumps higher than a hart.

Arrayed with such armor and such a horse, Paris and Hector were notbetter than him in the War of Troy, nor is anyone now.

Then he prayed...[2]

---

[2] I am very grateful to Francis Cairns for his assistance with the translation. Some details require comment. 1.1: *Ella* has been seen as a contraction of *En illa* (Du Méril p.308 n.2) and emended to *bella* (Curtius

2. THE MANUSCRIPT

Latin MS 5132 of the Bibliothèque Nationale in Paris was brought to France in 1649 from Ripoll in Catalonia. Du Méril described it at length (op.cit (n.1) pp.302-8). It contains a number of items in different hands datable to the early thirteenth century; the final document, apparently added once the rest was complete, is dated 1218. The *Carmen Campi Doctoris* runs from halfway down folio 79v to two thirds of the way down folio 80v. It is written as if it were prose. It was known to be a poem, however, for the initial word of each stanza has a capital letter, and the end of most lines is marked by a full stop. The ending of the poem has been erased: that is, the last nine and a half lines on folio 80v and approximately the first nine on the following folio (80 bis). The head of the photographic service of the Bibliothèque has kindly photographed these folios for me under both infra-red and ultra-violet light, but this has not revealed any more of the original text. The break occurs about halfway through a manuscript line; a little way below the break there now begins a copy of a letter whose original is datable

---

p.162 n.1); *Illiada* (Ubieto p.165); *milia* (Cirot ' Le *Carmen*...' p.144); and *Eia* (Menéndez Pidal *La España*... p.880), which I translate. 11.15f.: 'setting sail' is a standard topos for 'starting a Latin poem' (see E.R. Curtius *European Literature and the Latin Middle Ages* London (1953) p.430). l.21: *nobiliori* means 'fairly noble,' so *maius* must mean 'older' rather than 'greater.'1.25: *singulare* means both 'notable' and 'individual.' 1.27: *maiorum* must be 'older,' not 'most.' 1.34: *adlata*, 'things brought upon one,' is possible in Classical Latin, and J.F. Niermeyer *Mediae Latinitatis Lexicon Minus* 2 Vols. Leiden (1954-8) quotes a use from 834 to mean 'things given.' Curtius emended to *ad alta* (p.167) which is unsatisfactory since the power to *exaltare* is the King's. Neither reading is certain. 1.44: *per totam* has previously been edited as one word; it is so in the ms., but so are most other prepositional phrases. 1.67: *Hispania* has varying reference in the Central Middle Ages; here it is probably the areas near the religious frontier. 1.80: *retinens campum*, not only 'winning the battle' but also 'keeping his title.' l. 100, *hoste is* normal for 'army.'11.107 and 114: *fabrefactus* and *figuratus* probably refer to armour made of iron and inlaid with gold. l.119: *electrum* is an amber-coloured alloy of gold and silver, or perhaps bronze and tin. l. 122: *nec ne is* a medieval alternative for *nec non*; the subject of *comutavit* is ambiguous; accordingly, so is the translation.

to 1190, concerning the death of the Emperor Frederick. The final word *deprecatur* is accordingly left hanging before an empty space. *deprecatur* is as clear as every previous word; the following word is no more legible than any subsequent one. The copyist of the *Carmen* did not merely stop in mid-air, for the manuscript is scratched from *deprecatur* onwards, and the following section appears therefore to have been erased for some reason connected with its content rather than merely in order to provide space. This folio came as a result to be thinner at the bottom than elsewhere. Some of the lines embryonically visible at the foot of 80v are not remains of the original material, but the writing on 80r which is perceptible as a consequence of the erasure.

Approximately eighteen lines of prose are lost; this corresponds to some eleven further stanzas. The original length of the *Carmen* was probably forty-three stanzas, and internal evidence from the surviving part is consistent with this.

The main contents of the manuscript are: part of the *Historia Hierosolymitana* of Raymund of Aguilers (now folios 1-19v); material concerning the Council of Nicaea (26-79v); a group of homilies (81r-92v); and an anonymous saint's life (93v-101r). The rest, including the last nine folios, is mainly filled with documents of interest in Ripoll, but there are also eight poems. Some are hymns; three, including the *Carmen*, are occasional poems. The first of these is a hymn of thirty-five four-line rhythmic stanzas celebrating the capture of Jerusalem, dated by Nicolau to 1099.[3] The last is a rhythmic poem in praise of Count Ramón Berenguer IV of Barcelona, ruler of Aragon, after his death in 1162, which stresses his military successes against Moslems.[4]

The *Carmen* concerns the early military career of the Castilian warrior Rodrigo Díaz (ca. 1040-1099), now known as El Cid. It recounts his early victory over a Navarrese champion (25f.), his time at the court of Sancho II of Castile (33-40); his initially promising service under the succeeding king, Alfonso VI of León and Castile

---

[3] L. Nicolau d'Olwer *L'Escola Poètica de Ripoll en els Segles X-XIII* Barcelona (1920) pp.63-6 no.50.

[4] *Ibid.* pp.36-8 no. 13.

(41-8), his subsequent exile (49-68), his victory at Cabra over a force led by García Ordóñez (69-84), and then at greater length the initial stages of a skirmish at Almenar, near Lérida, when Rodrigo, on behalf of Moslem Zaragoza, succeeded in relieving a siege imposed by the Count of Barcelona and Al-Fayib of Lérida (89-129). The poem is broken off before battle is joined.

Someone at Ripoll had the poem copied into a blank space *ca.* 1200. This was a time of crusading fervour. The Almohad Moslems of Southern Spain unexpectedly defeated a Castilian force at Alarcos in 1195; this rattled the Christian states. The subsequent years saw a concerted diplomatic effort, backed by Papal proclamation of a crusade, to create a united force of Aragonese, Castilian, Leonese and French capable of defeating any Moslem force. Eventually the Aragonese and Castilians defeated the Moslems at Las Navas de Tolosa in 1212. The only surviving manuscript of Rodrigo Díaz's vernacular epic also dates from the intervening years (1207), and it is likely that, at least in the form in which it survives, it was compiled not long before this date.[5] Horrent has shown how the Rodrigo of history has metamorphosed by the time of this epic into a *héros Chrétien*, held up as an example of successful anti-Moslem initiative for the modern generation to admire and emulate.[6] Given this atmosphere in the Northern kingdoms, it is understandable that someone who had found a poem on Rodrigo in the monastery library should have thought it worth transcribing, like the poems on Jerusalem and Ramón Berenguer IV in the same manuscript.

Despite the probable context of the *Carmen's* transcription, however, any tendency to view Rodrigo as a Christian hero has to be resisted when we assess the poem's original purpose and attitude,

---

[5] See *Poema de Mío Cid* ed. C.C. Smith, Oxford (1972); A.D. Deyermond 'Tendencies in *Mío Cid* Scholarship, 1943-1973' in *Mío Cid Studies* ed. A.D. Deyermond, London (1977) pp.13-47; on the history of the period, see A. Mackay *Spain in the Middle Ages* London (1977) Chh. 1 and 2; D.W. Lomax *The Reconquest of Spain* London (1978). On the use of the epic as propaganda after Alarcos, see J. Fradejas Lebrero *Estudios Epicos: El Cid* Ceuta (1962).

[6] J. Horrent 'Note sur le Cid, Héros Chrétien' *Revue Belge de Philologie et d'Histoire* 54 (1976) pp.769-72.

for it is generally agreed that the *Carmen* was composed during the Cid's lifetime.

3. THE PRONUNCIATION AND METER

The *Carmen* is in rhythmic sapphics. The first three lines of each stanza have eleven syllables, with a caesura after five.[7] There is paroxytonic stress, on the fourth and tenth syllables. The fourth line of each stanza has five syllables and adonic rhythm, i.e. stress on the first and fourth syllables. This rhythm often recurs in the first half of the hendecasyllables. This is typical of medieval imitations of classical meters in that the form is based on the same number of syllables per line as in the classical version, but the partial prescription of where the word stresses should fall replaces any concern with the original quantity of those syllables. This method of creating regularity in the lengths of the lines is related to the manner in which the poem was recited, read aloud or sung, by the author and performer, for rhythmic verse was designed for oral performance.[8]

One of the reforms introduced during the reorganization of the Carolingian church was the introduction of a standard pronunciation of liturgical and other official Latin, based on the linking of one specified sound to each written letter. In previous centuries, the pronunciation of rhythmic verse would have been that of the ordinary local Early Romance vernacular.[9] This still applied later to Romance speaking areas where the new pronunciation had not come

---

[7] There is no caesura in 1.74, as Cirot pointed out ('Le Rhythme...' p.250). Perhaps it is intended to be read aloud in such a way as to stress Alfonso's heavy-handed wrath.

[8] On Latin rhythmic verse in general see D. Norberg *Introduction à l'Étude de la Versification Latine Mediévale* Stockholm (1958).

[9] The still prevalent view that there was a systematic distinction between Latin and Romance pronunciation before the Carolingian reforms and the concomitant invention of 'Medieval Latin' is baseless and linguistically improbable: see R. Wright 'Speaking, Reading and Writing Late Latin and Early Romance' *Neophilologus* 60 (1976) pp.178-89; 'Semicultismo' *Archivum Linguisticum* 7 (1976) pp.13-28. I am also preparing a book on this subject.

into general use. In areas touched by these reforms, however, rhythmic Latin verse is composed according to the norms of the Carolingian reformed pronunciation. One result of this is that the method of counting syllables in a poem such as this corresponds neither with the number present in the contemporary Romance vernacular, nor with the old classical system. For example, it is different from the classical model in that there is no elision. It can be seen that this is the norm in the *Carmen:* given that there is no elision, such hendecasyllables as *magis qui eius freti estis ope* (19) and *Capream vocant locum ubi castra* (83) are regular. On the other hand, there are in rhythmic poems subsequent to the reforms none of the non-classical diphthongs to be found in the rhythmic poetry pronounced as spoken Romance vernacular. For example, lines 89 *(tertium quoque prelium comisit)* and 113 *(clipeum gestat brachio sinistro)* are also hendecasyllables, with the unstressed *i* and *e* of *tertium, prelium, clipeum* and *brachio* being given full syllabic status, as stipulated in the reformed pattern. The versification of the *Carmen* is thus entirely regular according to the Carolingian system.

This has implications for our assessment of the *Carmen.* Firstly, the author must have been taught Latin in an establishment where the reformed Latin was in use. This supports the theory that the author was from Ripoll. The reforms came to Catalonia in the ninth century, and Ripoll was the main center of Catalan culture until the twelfth. The reforms only began to be adopted further west in the late 1070s and 1080s, however, and since the *Carmen* by general consent was written before 1094 the theory that the author was Castilian is correspondingly less plausible. Secondly, the audience will also have been composed of people who had been taught this system. Given the dissimilarity in sound between the pronunciation of Carolingian Latin and the vernaculars of the time, it is probable that the *Carmen* would have been largely unintelligible to an uneducated speaker of Old Catalan.

Every line of each stanza ends in an identical syllable. This is known as 'homoteleutic' rhyme. This is not, however, a vernacular pattern, in that the final syllables in the *Carmen* are all unstressed, whereas vernacular rhyme has always required phonetic identity from the stressed syllable onwards. It is, accordingly, further evidence of an author of some sophistication.

4. THE *CARMEN* AS A HYMN

Rhythmic sapphics are commonly used for hymns within both the Carolingian and Mozarabic Spanish traditions. One of the standard hymns in the European repertory was Paul the Deacon's sapphic *Ut queant laxis resonare fibris*. In the Spanish tradition, nineteen of the two hundred and ten hymns in the Mozarabic volume of the *Analecta Hymnica* (XXVII) are in sapphics, although none uses homoteleutic rhyme.[10] So are sixty of the five hundred hymns in the post-Mozarabic volume of Spanish hymns (XVI).[11] Accordingly, the title that this poem gives itself of *Carmen* (18) may imply that it is meant to be seen as a kind of hymn. Bertoni appreciated this, and unambiguously entitled his edition *Inno del Cid*; Amador *(op.cit.* (n.1) p.213) and Cirot ('Le *Carmen...*' p.145) glimpsed that the hymnic nature of the *Carmen* might have literary consequences. These have not been followed up seriously. Martínez, in a recent discussion of the poem, believes it is a *canto noticiero*, a journalistic folk song based on current events *(op.cit.* (n 1) pp.372, 384).

This view of Martínez is hard to accept. By the late eleventh century Sapphics had become restricted to hymns. In the volumes of the *Poetae Aevi Carolini* there are forty-three sapphic poems, most of which are very short, and a majority of which are specifically hymns.[12] The only Carolingian author to have used sapphics

---

[10] Ed. C. Blume and G.M. Dreves, Leipzig (1897) Frankfurt (1961) nos. 18, 25, 27, 90, 93, 94, 95, 106, 110, 129, 131, 151, 163, 171, 174, 184, 187, 189, 208. For a study of the hymns, see J. Szövérffy *Iberian Hymnody* Wetteren (1971). J. Pérez de Urbel prints another sapphic hymn, *de VII Dominico*, BH 28 (1926) pp.318f. Cirot, 'Le Rhythme...,' p.252 said that the Catalan hymn to St. Cucufate (106) has homoteleutic rhyme; it does not.

[11] Nos 6, 7, 10, 11, 13, 50, 51, 67, 68, 69, 75, 83, 101, 103, 105, 106, 126, 156, 157, 158, 159, 160, 170, 178, 188, 189, 190, 196, 198, 245, 251, 286, 287, 288, 290, 292, 296, 297, 298, 299, 349, 359, 360, 361, 362, 383, 398, 410, 413, 431, 440, 441, 450, 471, 487, 489, 491, 493, 495, 496, 500.

[12] Vol, I pp.81f., 83f. (*Ut queant laxis*), 142-4, 144-6, 147f., 313, 349, 529, 578; Vol II pp.244f., 252, 381, 411, 412f., 415f., 418f., 603; Vol. III pp.155, 156, 163, 176, 184, 202, 208f. *(De Strage Normannorum)*, 209, 217, 219, 220, 232, 235 (all these thirteen by Sedulius Scottus), 248, 693, 727f.

often was Sedulius Scottus; his *De Strage Normannorum* is the only precedent for this *Carmen* as a sapphic poem to celebrate military success, but his work was probably unknown at Ripoll. The only Carolingian sapphic poem to use rhyme is Gottschalk's *Oratio Metrica III*. The only other work in rhythmic sapphics that precedes the *Carmen* without being a hymn is the tenth-century Italian poem which is no.23 in the Cambridge Songs.[13] The author of the *Carmen* shows no sign of being aware of any of these. On the other hand, by the eleventh century poets came to regard the form as one reserved for hymns if it was to be used at all. Fulbert of Chartres did not use it. Baudri of Bourgueil and Rodulfus Tortuarius of Fleury wrote one sapphic poem each, and they are both hymns.[14] Peter Damian composed sapphic hymns in the late eleventh century.[15] More to the point, throughout this period hymns in this form would have been inevitably familiar to anyone in the Church;[16] and as we have seen, the nature of the Latin requires for the *Carmen* both an author and an audience used to Church pronunciation.

It is therefore likely that the form of the *Carmen* would have been felt instinctively by its audience to be that of a hymn. The fact that no other surviving poem attributable to Ripoll is in sapphics led Nicolau to exclude the *Carmen* from his collection of the Latin verses from Ripoll, believing it to be Castilian. Yet not only were earlier hymns well known, but sapphics are described in Chapter

---

(Gottschalk's *Oratio Metrica III*; Vol. IV pp.256, 328, 329, 332, 337, 338, 338 again, 414, 1097f., 1099.

[13] See F.J.E. Raby *A History of Secular Latin Poetry* 2 Vols. Oxford (1967) I p.302.

[14] *Les Oeuvres Poétiques de Baudri de Bourgueil (1046-1130)* ed. P. Abrahams, Paris (1926); no.32 is a five stanza sapphic hymn to St. Catherine. None of the other 254 poems are in sapphics. *Rodulfi Tortarii Carmina* ed. M.B. Ogle and D.M. Schullian, Rome (1933). pp.393-405 contain a sapphic hymn of 79 stanzas in honour of 'Beati Mauri.'

[15] See *AH* XLVIII nos. 19, 32, 35, 38, 42, 62; LI p.242.

[16] See e.g. the remarks by M.C. Díaz y Díaz on the St. James hymn *Gaudeat cuncta pia plebs alumna*, *AH* XXVII no. 129, in *De Isidoro al Siglo XI* Barcelona (1976) pp.272-87, whose rhythmic sapphics are rightly said to be typical of medieval Spanish hymns (p.278).

XVIII of Bede's *De Arte Metrica*, which Nicolau himself established as the metrical teaching manual used at Ripoll.[17]

This *Carmen* is based on particular military events, and thus comes also into the category of 'occasional' poetry. There are other Mozarabic hymns with military themes, but the reference of the *Carmen* is untypically specific.[18] Occasional poems in other meters more conventionally suitable for narrative were quite commonly written about the stirring events of the late eleventh century. Guy d'Amiens, for example, wrote an elegiac poem on the battle of Hastings.[19] Closer to Ripoll, there was a poem of 146 fifteen-syllabled couplets with homoteleutic rhyme written to celebrate a joint Pisan and Genoan victory in Libya in 1088.[20] Pisans and Genoans had close links with North-Eastern Spain; it was a Pisan who composed the 3525 hexameters of the *Liber Maiolichinus* on the Catalan capture of Majorca from the Moslems in 1114.[21] *Iherusalem exulta*, in the same manuscript as the *Carmen*, is within the same tradition. It is probable, therefore, that this tradition was known to the author of the *Carmen*, even though sapphics are not a normal meter for such purposes. There are, however, later examples of occasional sapphics, e.g. those celebrating the victory over Moslem Granada at Río Salado in 1340.[22]

5. Vocabulary and Style

(i) Classical

Both the author and the intended audience had knowledge of classical literature. Homer could not have succeeded in praising

---

[17] Nicolau *op.cit.* (n.3) pp.3-5.

[18] See R. Messenger 'The Mozarabic Hymnal' TAPA 75 (1944) pp.103-26 (p.122). She also comments on the 'multiplication of hymns for occasional purposes' (p.119).

[19] Orderic Vitalis says that Guy had written a poem on the battle before M. y 11th. 1068. Ralph Davis has shown that this cannot be the same as the surviving poem traditionally ascribed to Guy, in 'The *Carmen de Hastingae Proelio*' EHR 93 (1978) pp.241-61.

[20] Du Méril pp.239-51.

[21] See Martínez pp.137-40 and 281-91. Majorca was recaptured in 1115.

[22] Szövérffy *op.cit.* (n.10) Ch. 15.

Rodrigo sufficiently (11). This reference, and those to the Trojan War in lines 126f. and the achievements of Aeneas in line 2, will only have a point for those who have met them before. Nicolau showed that the *Aeneid* was used as the main model for Ripoll's poetic creativity.[23]

Line 19 is crucial to any argument concerning the *Carmen's* intended audience, since it is ostensibly addressed to that audience: *magis qui eius freti estis ope*. *fretus is* very rare in Medieval Latin, and unused in the Vulgate. It has no surviving derivatives in Romance that might assist a Romance speaking audience to interpret it. It occurs seven times in Vergil, however, of which the closest precedent for its use here is *Aeneid* 9,675f.: *portam, quae ducis imperio commissa, recludunt/freti armis, ultroque invitant moenibus hostem* (they open the gate entrusted to the leader's command, trusting in their arms, and invite the enemy beyond the ramparts).[24] *ope* is similarly esoteric in a medieval context; but it too is common in Vergil and other classical authors. We can tell it was part of the learned vocabulary taught at Ripoll from its appearance in stanza six of the poem on Ramón Berenguer IV in the same manuscript: *Barchinonam, Taragonem/[Arelatem, Ta]raschonem/rexit florens ope, fama,/terrens hostes his plus flamma* (he ruled Barcelona, Tarragona, Arles and Tarascon with the strength of his military power and fame, frightening his enemy with those rather than with fire). Since line 19 of the *Carmen* is intended to catch the attention of the audience, it seems reasonable to assume that they might be expected to know the words used. That would have required a classical education.

In the scene of Rodrigo's preparations for battle (105-28), Vergilian echoes come to the fore. A comparatively straightforward historical account is here lifted onto a higher literary plane. Perhaps this is intended to suggest that at this point Rodrigo is becoming a warrior worthy of Vergilian treatment. The words *indutus, lorica* (105), *hastam* (109), *fraxino* (110), *cuspide* (112), *clipeum* (113) and

---

[23] Nicolau *op.cit.* (n.3) p.5.
[24] Vergilian statistics are critically based on H. Merguet *Lexicon zu Vergilius* Hildesheim (1960).

galea (117), are all Vergilian. In case the audience had missed this, the conclusion of the section makes it clear with the epic comparison of lines 125-8.

The author is also aware of the *encomium*; the *pauca* he has learned at school (14) include the devices to be used when praising great men, as derived from Quintilian *Institutio Oratoria* 3,7,10-18. The phrase *nobiliori de genere ortus* (21) and *adolescens* (26) are probably included as fulfilment of the instructions to mention the hero's lineage and successes of youth.

(ii) The Vulgate

Some resonances of vocabulary and style derive from the Vulgate. This does not necessarily imply that particular references are being made to biblical episodes whenever comparable words are used; it does, however, indicate that the poem was created in surroundings where such vocabulary was readily accessible.

The phrasing of the ninth stanza makes a biblical reminiscence almost inevitable, however:

> Quem sic dilexit Sancius, rex terre,
> iuuenem cernens adlata subire,
> quod principatum uelit illi prime
> cohortis dare. (33-6)

Everyone would have heard *John* 3,16: *sic enim Deus dilexit mundum, ut Filium suum unigenitum daret...* (God so loved the world that he gave his only begotten son...). Some of the audience, at least, must have noticed the resemblance. Similarly, the word *exaltare* (46) is sufficiently common in the Bible to have associated connotations. There are such uses as *Matthew* 23,12: *qui autem se exaltaverit, humiliabitur, et qui se humiliaverit, exaltabitur* (whoever exalts himself will be humbled, and whoever humbles himself will be exalted). There might be a hint in the *Carmen*, as a result of the choice of this word, that Rodrigo's elevation at Alfonso's court represented the pride that cometh before a fall. That fall is brought about by Rodrigo's political enemies, who are called *susurrones*. This is a non-Classical word. It turns up in a famous passage from *Romans* 1,29: *plenos invidia, homicidio, contentione, dolo, malignitate, susurrones, detractores, Deo odibiles, contumeliosos, superbos, elatos, inventores malorum...* (full of envy, murder, strife, deceit, malignity, they are gossips, slanderers, hateful to God, insolent, haughty, boastful, inventors of evil...). This concerns the world's inability to acknowledge God; when Rodrigo's enemies, similarly envious and inventors of evil *(invidere,* 47; *mala,* 55) are referred to by the same word, an ecclesiastical audience might well catch the reference.[25]

When the King hears a rumor that Rodrigo is plotting against him, the phrase used is *parat eis/laqueum mortis* (71 f.). This image occurs three times in the Old Testament: II *Samuel* 22,6; *Proverbs* 21,6 and the following from *Psalm* 17,6 (now *Psalm* 18,5): *dolores inferni circumdederunt me: praeoccupaverunt me laquei mortis* (the sorrows of Hell surrounded me; the snares of death caught me).

Even in the arming passage, with its Vergilian words, Biblical vocabulary is used: *romphea, fabrefacta* (107), *mirifice* (109), *dolata* (110) and *circinni* (120) are all non-Vergilian words used in the Vulgate. *gyrus* (120) and this meaning of *lamina* (118) are commoner in the Vulgate than in Classical Latin. *fabrefacta, gyrus* and *lamina,* for example, all occur in *Exodus* 28-30.[26] Within *Isaiah* 35-44 are found *lamina, circinnus,* and the phrase *tunc saliet sicut cervus claudus* (35,6) (then shall the lame man leap like a hart) which may underlie *plus cervo sallit* (124) .[27]

These are some of the cases where Biblical vocabulary may explain the choice of words in the *Carmen.* Since for other reasons we can be sure that the poem was first composed and performed in an ecclesiastical setting, these reminiscences might be intended to convey more than is immediately evident. Even so, the apparent

---

[25] The noun *susurro* appears seven other times in the Vulgate; *susurrator* and *susurrationes* once each; the verb *susurro* twice, including *Psalm* 40,8: *adversum me susurrabant omnes inimici mei* (all my enemies whispered against me).

[26] *fabrefacta,* with gold, in 28,28; *erit autem lamina semper in fronte eius* (28,38); *faciesque ei coronam aureolam per gyrum (30,3).*

[27] This continues *et aperta erit lingua mutorum.* The only Biblical *circinus* is *et in circino tornavit illud* (44,13); *aut aurifex auro figuravit illud, et laminis argenteis argentarius* (40,19).

implication that Rodrigo is being likened to Divinity in some of these passages may be illusory. Nor are the connections so close as to imply that the author had the Vulgate open at his fingertips while composing the poem. But at the least some of the vocabulary is sufficiently recherché for an audience to need both Classical and ecclesiastical training: at the most, the poet may be playing on both these to raise his subject to the status of both epic hero and warrior with divine authority *(Deus illi vincere permisit, 90)*.

(iii) Hymns

Reminiscences of Prudentius are common in Mozarabic hymns.[28] The third and fourth stanzas of the *Carmen* continue this tradition. The most striking example concerns *retexere* (to narrate): *Tanti victoris nam si retexere/ceperim cunta, non hec libri mille/capere possent (9-11)*. This usage is neither Biblical nor Classical. There are six cases in Prudentius; all are first person singular, as here; four accompany a modesty topos, as here. The closest parallel is *Apotheosis* 704f.: *milibus ex multis paucissima quaeque retexam,/summatim relegam, totus quae non capit orbis* (I shall relate very few out of the many thousand, briefly summarising, for the whole world cannot contain them); *ex multis pauca* and *capere* also reappear in the *Carmen*.[29] Prudentius laments the impossibility of telling all the miracles of Christ; the author of the *Carmen* laments the impossibility of telling all the achievements of Rodrigo. This is probably meant to inspire an erudite smile.[30]

In the *Carmen* reminiscences from Prudentius lead up to the fifth stanza, which is consciously created from an assortment of the most obvious hymnic clichés:

Eia letando, populi caterve,
Campi doctoris hoc carmen audite;

---

[28] See Messenger *op.cit.* (n.18) pp.104-7, 123.

[29] Curtius mentioned *ex multis pauca (p.106 n.1).*

[30] The other five uses of *retexo* are *Cath.* 5,81f.; *Apoth.* 741f.; *Peris.* 2,36; 258; 10,408. The sole Vergilian use, *Aeneid* 12,763, means 'weave back and forth.'

magis qui eius freti estis ope,
cuncti venite. (17-20)

letare, populi, caterve, carmen, cuncti and *venite* are recognisable formulae of the introductory lines of Mozarabic hymns. For example, *laetare* comes in the second line of one of the sapphic hymns to St. James: *mater, exsulta, nimium laetare (AH* XXVII, 131). *populi, venite* and *carmen* appear consecutively in the first stanza of the sapphic hymn to St. Marcellus:

Martyris festum rutilat beati
Ecce, Marcelli, populi, venite
Carminis Deo resonemus hymnum
Voce sub una. *(AH* XXVII, 151)

(Behold, ye people, the day breaks on the feast of the Holy Martyr Marcellus, come let us sing a hymn to God with united voice.) *huius catervae carmina* occurs in the second line of the Resurrection hymn, *AH* XXVII, 35; *cuncta* in the first line of the other sapphic hymn to St. James *(AH* XXVII, 129), *gaudeat cuncta pia plebs alumna. eia* and *audite* introduce Carolingian hymns: Norberg discusses the sequence *Eia fratres cari*,[31] four hymns that start with *audite* and four with *audi*,[32] and the Merovingian refrain *venite et audite quanta fecit Dominus*.[33] Menéndez Pidal, however, detected in *audite* a Latinization of the minstrels' *oíd*.[34] This is possible; but there is no need to postulate a connection, and even if there is one the minstrels' cliché might have been based on the hymn cliché rather than vice versa.

Martínez said that the reciter is meant to be in a market-place, summoning a heterogeneous multitude.[35] But no-one, however interested in the subject, would have understood the summons

---

[31] *Op.cit. (n.*8) p.165.
[32] *Op.cit.* (n.8) pp.113, 125, 142, 143, 146, 158, 159.
[33] *Op.cit.* (n.8) p.150.
[34] 'La épica...' p.2.
[35] p.397.

unless well-versed in Classical and ecclesiastical usage.[36] Ian Michael comments on the surprisingly cheerful and popular sound of this stanza, but being cheerful is not incompatible with being a monk, and all the evidence of vocabulary and style points to the author's being such a cheerful monk.[37]

6. Vernacular Inspiration

Menéndez Pidal, who dated the *Carmen* to *ca.* 1090, suggested that it was inspired by a vernacular poem on the same subject. Milà i Fontanals had earlier suggested that there were vernacular songs contemporary with the *Carmen*, but he dated it to the 1130s, at which time it is probable that such songs were in circulation;[38] the view that they existed in 1090 is harder to support. There undoubtedly could have been stories circulating about the events at Almenar in 1082 in the kingdoms involved (Zaragoza, Lérida, Aragon, Catalonia), and stories about the battle of Cabra in 1080 in the kingdoms involved there (León, Castile, Sevilla, Granada), and some of these stories might have been couched in verse. Yet it is hard to see so consciously latinate a poem as the *Carmen* being such a vernacular poem in disguise.

There is evidence against the existence of a vernacular counterpart as regards the events at Almenar. This episode, which is the climax of the *Carmen*, leaves no trace in the Castilian vernacular epic tradition. The obvious occasion in the *Poema de Mío Cid* for a reference to Almenar would be in lines 960-1084, when Rodrigo captures the same Count of Barcelona on a different occasion. The epic poet is aware that the Count and Rodrigo have met before: when Rodrigo was first exiled he went to Barcelona, but was sent away, for reasons that are not explained in the histories. The *Historia Roderici*, which comes from the North-East, merely says: *ille autem de regno Castelle exiens Barcinonam venit, amicis suis*

---

[36] As Colin Smith implies in his review of Martínez BHS 54 (1977) pp.144-6.

[37] I. Michael *Poema de Mío Cid* Madrid (1976) p.12.

[38] M. Milà i Fontanals *Obras Completas* VII Barcelona (1857, 1896, 1959) p.68.

in tristicia relictis. deinde vero ad Cesaraugustam venit...[39] (When he left Castile he came to Barcelona, leaving his friends sorrowing. From there he came to Zaragoza...). The epic refers to an episode that may indeed have caused this rejection, in view of the civil strife in Barcelona at this time:

> El conde es muy folon e dixo una vanidat:
> ¡Grandes tuertos me tiene mio Çid el de Bivar!
> Dentro en mi cort tuerto me tovo grand:
> firiom el sobrino e non lo enmendo mas. (960-4)

Hamilton and Perry translate this as "The Count was a hasty and foolish man and spoke without due reflection: "The Cid, Rodrigo of Vivar, has done me great wrongs. In my own palace he gave me great offence by striking my nephew and never giving satisfaction for it."[40] Here the Count is made to recall an incident otherwise unrecorded in order to provide a plausible reason for his exaggeratedly hostile response to Rodrigo's operations, but he is not even permitted to hint at a previous military humiliation which had been well known, at least in latinate circles, in the Eastern kingdoms: not only the *Carmen* but also five chapters of the *Historia Roderici* deal with Almenar. If vernacular traditions on the battle ever existed in verse, they must have been untypically ephemeral to leave no trace in the general twelfth-century corpus of Cid stories. Their existence is not needed to explain the genesis of the *Carmen*, which has sufficient motivation in the admiration felt at the successes of Rodrigo. In addition, as Barceló pointed out,[41] a vernacular song on all the events of the *Carmen* in sequence would have had in origin to be in a variety of different vernaculars. Menéndez Pidal's theories on the existence of oral vernacular poetry at this time are not disproved by the existence of a Latin poem that

---

[39] Menéndez Pidal edited the *Historia Roderici* in *La España...* pp.919-69. This is p.923 ll.23f.

[40] In the edition, with facing English translation, by I. Michael, Manchester (1975) p.73. The episode is examined in T. Montgomery 'The Cid and the Count of Barcelona' HR 30 (1962) pp.1-11.

[41] 'Algunas...' p.51.

has not been inspired by them, but the *Carmen* cannot be used any more as a serious argument in their favor. This is a Latin poem.

7. THE TITLE

The fifth stanza is the source of the title traditionally given to the poem of *Carmen Campidoctoris*. Despite the insistence of every editor in transcribing it in this manner, *campi doctor* is quite clearly two words in the manuscript on all four occasions it is used. Rodrigo was not called Cid (probably from Arabic *sidi*, "Lord") until he was Lord of Valencia (1094-99); for most of his earlier life he was known as *Campeador*, "victor." In the *Carmen* he is twice referred to simply as *victor (9, 99)* and four times as *campi doctor* (18, 27, 70, 79). Later Latin works latinize the vernacular as *campeator* or *campiator:* e.g. in the thirteenth century, Rodrigo de Toledo 6,15: *erat autem cum rege Sancio miles strenuus, dictus Rodericus Didaci Campiator* (There was with King Sancho a very active soldier called Rodrigo Díaz Campeador). Arabic historians also adopt the term. In the East the name seems to have stuck as *Campi doctus* in Latin; this is the form in the *Historia Roderici* (e.g. 920,23) where it is still two words. Martínez says that *campi doctor* was a common cliché,[42] but all comparable post-Classical uses seem to be of a later date. Du Cange defines the word *campidoctores* as *qui scientiam armorum et omnes armaturae numeros militibus tradunt* (who hand on the knowledge of arms and all the military drills to the soldiers). He quotes examples from the late Imperial period preceding the *Carmen*, but nothing later than the fifth-century Bishop Eucherius of Lyon. Niermeyer quotes two uses from the twelfth century of the form *campiductor*. Latham quotes both forms as used by John of Salisbury. The *Mittellateinisches Wörterbuch* adds nothing for the intervening centuries. It does not even appear in the *Glossarium Mediae Latinitatis Cataloniae*, whose corpus does not include the *Carmen*.[43] No example of this phrase as

---

[42] p.337 n.135.
[43] Du Cange *Glossarium Mediae et Infimae Latinitatis* Paris (1884-7); Niermeyer op.cit. (n.2); R. Latham *Revised Medieval Latin Word-List from British and Irish Sources* London (1965); *Mittellateinisches Worterbuch* ed.

two words is listed, but that is not conclusive evidence of its non-existence.

Since *campi doctor* has no metrical advantage over *campiator* it seems likely that it is used in the *Carmen* for a purpose. Tovar suggested that it might be inspired by St. Augustine's exhortation in *Sermon* 119 (4th. May): *fac bonus miles, quod tuus te docuit campidoctor* (act as a good soldier, as your *campidoctor* taught you).[44] The author might well have met the word here. *campi doctor* was suggested by Cirot to be modelled on *iuris doctor*;[45] *doctores* in general tend to be connected with the Church in some way at this time, and the word is a mark of venerability and respect. The *Carmen* stresses that after his first success even people older than him *(maiores, 27)* were moved to admire him and call him *doctor*. It may be that this young man who never seemed to lose any battles is being given the title *campi doctor* in the *Carmen* for the first time. Its implication may be both that he is teaching his opponents and contemporaries a lesson in the arts of warfare, and also, conceivably, that he has some kind of divine authorization to defeat them, since the phrase is announced in the stanza that is modelled on the formulae of hymns.

Chalon has pointed out that the first appearance in a document of *campidoctor* as one word, applied to Rodrigo, occurs in a document from Valencia dated 1098.[46] This is ample time for the name to have become current even if the author of the *Carmen* was the first to apply it to Rodrigo.

8. THE *CARMEN* AND THE *HISTORIA RODERICI*

The *Historia Roderici* is a record of Rodrigo's life written in the

---

O. Prinz and J. Schneider, Munich (1968) II fasc.1; *Glossarium Mediae Latinitatis Cataloniae* ed. M. Bassols de Climent and others, Barcelona (1960-) III (1963).

[44] A. Tovar 'Campidoctor, Campiductor, Campidoctus' *Correo Erudito* 2 (1944) pp.111f.

[45] Cirot 'Le vrai Cid' p.87. *Doctor legis* occurs three times in the Bible.

[46] L. Chalon *L'Histoire et L'Épopée Castillane du Moyen Âge* Paris (1976) pp.13-16. The document is in Menéndez Pidal *La España...* pp.866-9; the phrase, p.867 11.5 and 18.

North-East, probably Catalonia.[47] Menéndez Pidal dated it to *ca.* 1110, in view of its soberness of tone, and Michael accepts this;[48] Bonilla dated it to *ca.* 1150,[49] and Ubieto has argued from internal references that it must postdate 1144.[50] Horrent accepts this.[51] The argument from the factual atmosphere of the *Historia* is illogical; the evidence seems to support a date of *ca.* 1150 for the *Historia,* but this in no way implies that it is less to be trusted than the *Carmen* in its account of events to which the latter is approximately contemporary. As Smith has observed in passing, the author of the *Carmen* "takes what is fundamentally historical, but develops his theme with Biblical, Vergilian and other imaginative trappings";[52] the *Historia is* trying to recover the truth.

Whatever its date, the author of the *Historia* has looked for sources, and the question arises whether he found the *Carmen.* Clearly, the *Historia* has come across sources other than the *Carmen* for most of the episodes they have in common, but Barceló has shown that they have sufficient details of fact in common for it to be probable that the later author had met the poem.[53] Bonilla thought that the author of the *Historia* knew some poetic texts but decided not to use them,[54] and this could well have applied to the *Carmen;* the *Carmen* was probably in Ripoll library when the *Historia* was being prepared, and that library was an obvious place for the historian to go in search of material.

There are some linguistic indications that the historian knew the *Carmen.* For example, the phrasing of the ninth stanza of the *Carmen* seems to be echoed in the *Historia* 920, 20-2, with a

---

[47] *La España,...* p.915.
[48] *Poema...* p.12.
[49] p.170.
[50] A. Ubieto Arteta 'La *Historia Roderici* y su fecha de redacción' *Saitabi* 11 (1961) pp.241-6.
[51] *Historia...* Ch 3.
[52] C.C. Smith 'Latin Histories and Vernacular Epic' BHS 48 (1971) pp.1-19 (p.4).
[53] M. Barceló 'Una nota en torno al Destierro del Cid' *Ligarzas* 1 (1972) pp. 127-40.
[54] p. 178.

similarly idiosyncratic use of *quod: rex autem Sanctius adeo diligebat Rodericum Didaci multa dilectione et nimio amore, quod constituit eum principem super omnem militiam suam* (King Sancho so loved Rodrigo Díaz with such great affection and love that he made him leader of all his army). A more general example of possible inspiration from the *Carmen* concerns the presentation of Rodrigo's enemies at court. The details of the scene are invented, but both authors have chosen uncharacteristically to give these opponents *oratio recta;* in the *Historia* this passage stands out as unusual for this reason.

The *Historia* has found sources of much greater precision for its description of the battle at Almenar. Even so, the arming scene of the *Carmen* may have an echo in the *Historia* 926,16f.: *Rodericus autem conmoto animo iussit omnes milites suos armare et viriliter se ad bellum preparare* (Rodrigo was aroused and ordered all his soldiers to arm and prepare themselves courageously for the battle). It is possible, therefore, that the now missing dénouement of the poem might have had something thematically in common with the following section of the *Historia*, since the version the historian may have found would have been complete.

> Perrexit itaque cum exercitu suo usque ad illum locum, in quo aspexerunt se mutuo comites scilicet et Alfagib et Rodericus Didaci. Magno autem impetu facto, belligerantes et vociferantes utriusque partis direxerunt acies suas et inierunt bellum. Sed predicti comites simul cum Alfagib verterunt continuo terga, et devicti ac confusi fugierunt a facie Roderici. Occisa est quippe maxima pars eorum, pauci nempe evaserunt.
>
> Omnia eorum spolia et substantia in iure et in manu Roderici remanserunt. Comitem autem Berengarium et milites suos secum duxit captos ad castrum Tamariz, ibique misit eos in manus de Almuctaman post habitam et factam victoriam; post v vero dies dimisit eos liberos abire in patriam suam.
>
> Rodericus autem Diaz pariter cum Almuctaman reversus est ad Cesaraugustam, ibique receptus est a civibus illius civitatis cum summo honore et maxima veneratione.

> Almuktaman vero exaltavit et sublimavit Rodericum in diebus suis super filium suum et super regnum suum et super omnem terram suam, ita ut ille videretur esse quasi dominator tocius regni sui; ditavitque eum nimis muneribus innumerabilibus; et donis aureis et argenteis multis.   (926, 1 7 - 927,8)

(So he went on with his army to the place in which the Counts and Al-Faŷib on one hand and Rodrigo Díaz on the other could see each other. He made a great charge, and on both sides the combatants shouted and formed ranks and joined battle. But the Counts and Al-Faŷib at once turned tail, and beaten and in confusion they fled from Rodrigo's sight. Most of them were killed: only a few escaped.

All their booty and belongings fell into the hands and power of Rodrigo. He took Count Berenguer and his soldiers with him to the castle of Tamarite, from where he sent them to Almuktaman after his victory; after five days, Almuktaman sent them off to return freely to their own country.

Rodrigo went back with Almuktaman to Zaragoza, and there he was welcomed by the citizens of that city with the greatest honour and praise.

Almuktaman truly raised and exalted Rodrigo in those days over his son, over his kingdom and over all his land, so that he could be seen to be as if ruler of all his kingdom; he gave him countless gifts, and many presents of gold and silver.)

It is risky to deduce details of the end of the *Carmen* from this. However, *exaltavit et sublimavit* suggests that Almuktaman raised Rodrigo to the heights that Alfonso had planned for him in León, and echoes *Carmen* 46 and 51; *munera* is an echo of the money the Kings are said to have previously paid Rodrigo to keep him from attacking them in *Carmen* 88; and the final mention of gold and silver rewards also appears to be in keeping.

It seems reasonable to suppose that the historian knew the poem but only used it occasionally, preferring material of more obvious documentary authenticity when it was available. It follows therefore as a necessary consequence that the minor details that the two texts do share are less likely to be true than those that appear in the

Historia but not in the *Carmen*. The appearance of something similar in both is not to be taken as external corroboration for the authenticity of each, but as a sign that the author of the *Historia* found no source of greater security for the details in question than the *Carmen*.

9. THE FIRST COMBAT

The structure of the *Carmen is* based on three victories of Rodrigo. The first is referred to perfunctorily in 25f.: *hoc fuit primum singulare bellum/cum adolescens devicit navarrum*. The *Historia* is the only other early text to refer to this, adding only the opponent's name: *postea namque pugnavit cum Eximino Garcez, uno de melioribus Pampilone, et devicit eum* (921,3f.) (then he fought with Ximeno Garcés, one of the best of Pamplona, and beat him). It has proved difficult to locate this combat on such scanty evidence. Menéndez Pidal thought it occurred in the reign of Sancho (1065-72) ;[55] Horrent dated it to 1062-3 ;[56] the *Historia* dates it after Sancho's death at Zamora *(postea...)*. Barceló has analysed documentary evidence from Navarra and concluded that the only two possible dates for the combat are *ca.* 1064 or 1074-6.[57] Although the logic of the poem might support the earliest date for the combat, external evidence supports the later. Rodrigo is known to have been involved in a Leonese campaign against Navarra in 1074, and his signature appears on a document from San Millán on the Castile-Navarra borders dated June 16th, 1074.[58] The *Historia's* dating is therefore plausible.

Single combat, however, was not a usual method of resolving strife at this time; despite its reputable literary ancestry, historians are justified at being surprised at such a reference here. It is possible

---

[55] *La España...* pp.601-4.

[56] *Historia... p.9*. This first chapter summarizes what is known of Rodrigo's life.

[57] M. Barceló 'En torno a la Primera Lid Singular del Campeador' *Príncipe de Viana* 102-103 (1966) pp.109-26. This article shows how the tale expanded in later versions.

[58] Ibid. p.124.

that this was not in fact a single combat at all; *singulare* could mean either "notable" or "individual" or both. Rodrigo's defeat of the Navarran as presented in the *Carmen* is quite possibly an individualization of a battle; the battle of Cabra is similarly individualized into the defeat of García Ordóñez, and the battle at Almenar into the defeat of the Count of Barcelona, so if this is what the poet has done here he is at least being consistent. The use of *singulare* may thus also be a part of the rhetorical scheme that the poet is following in lines 21-32, the *encomium:* here, to recount the notable deeds of youth. The use of *adolescens* also reflects these requirements, as we have seen. This word has uncertain boundaries. Rodrigo was about thirtyfour in 1074, but Cicero called himself *adolescens* at the age of fortyfour,[59] so this is an unreliable dating criterion. Literary logic supports the existence of a single combat in 1064, of which nothing else is known anywhere else; external evidence points to a general battle in 1074. If this is right, then the author of the *Carmen* is rearranging historical truth to suit literary convenience; but there is no reason to suppose he is averse to this procedure in view of the chronological reorganization that occurs in the central section of the *Carmen*.

10. THE BATTLE OF CABRA

The *Historia* is more reliable historically than the central section of the *Carmen* (33-84), which deals with Rodrigo's career under Sancho II and Alfonso VI, his exile, and the battle of Cabra. The whole time scheme has been inverted in the *Carmen*, for in real life the battle of Cabra preceded the exile; this means that the motivation as presented in the poem is literary guesswork. The relevant historical facts are these:

1065	Fernando I of León and Castile dies, dividing his kingdom among his children, including Sancho II (Castile) and Alfonso VI (León).
1065-72	Conflict between Sancho and Alfonso. Rodrigo is a

---

[59] *defendi rem publicam adulescens. non deseram senex* (*Philippics* 2,46).

	Castilian commander.
1072	Sancho dies at Zamora in suspicious circumstances.
1072-1109	Alfonso VI is king of León-Castile. At first, Rodrigo is in Alfonso's service.
1080	Rodrigo is sent to collect tribute from Moslem Sevilla while his political enemy García Ordóñez is sent to collect it from Granada; Granada attacks Sevilla at Cabra; Rodrigo captures García, and then releases him.
1080-81(?)	Rodrigo attacks territory of Moslem Toledo, Alfonso's subject ally.
1081	Rodrigo is exiled from León-Castile; he goes to Barcelona but is sent away; he signs on as military commander in Moslem Zaragoza.
1082	At Almenar, Rodrigo captures and releases the Count of Barcelona.

In the *Carmen*, however, Alfonso retains Rodrigo (43-8), exiles him (49-65), sees Rodrigo in Toledo (66-8), hears of Rodrigo's supposed plot against him (69-72), and responds by sending García, who is defeated at Cabra (73-84). If the historian knew the *Carmen* he must have realized that the poet had only the haziest notion of events further away than the Ebro valley; the poet is happy to elaborate what he does not know.

For example, *Carmen* 43f., *cui quod frater voverat per totam/ dedit Castellam*, was interpreted by Horrent to mean that "Rodrigo gave Alfonso the crown as Sancho had wished."[60] It is odd that Sancho should have so wished, and it may be preferable to keep the previously accepted meaning that "Alfonso gave Rodrigo the command that Sancho had promised," since *cui* as a demonstrative is acceptable Latin. Horrent, however, deduced from this that the enigmatic *honorem meliorem* of lines 37f. must have been the granting to Rodrigo of some kind of status as regent in the ensuing

---

[60] J. Horrent 'La Jura de Santa Gadea' *Homenaje a Dámaso Alonso* 3 Vols. Madrid (1961) II pp.241-65 (256f.).

interregnum. Even if Horrent's translation is right, there is no certainty in the conclusion; the lines are as likely to be there for the purpose of telling the audience that Rodrigo kept his position under the succeeding king.

The poet's literary purpose in the central section is to provide Rodrigo with a successful military career before the climax at Almenar; this whole section leads to the second of the three victories, at Cabra. It is understandable then that the author of the *Historia* should have ignored most of this part of the poem in favor of more reliable sources. The conspicuous exception to this concerns Rodrigo's exile, the reasons for which seem to have been unclear to him, as they are to us. His other sources cannot have helped him greatly here, for there are no factual details presented that imply any other source than the *Carmen*. He seems to have taken the idea from the *Carmen* of a plot invented by Rodrigo's political enemies, and also the idea of presenting it as a dramatic set-piece.

> Ut autem Rex Aldefonsus et maiores sue curie hoc factum Roderici audierunt, dure et moleste acceperunt, et huiusmodi causam sibi obicientes sibique curiales invidentes, regi unanimiter dixerunt: Domine rex, celsitudo vestra procul dubio sciat, quod Rodericus hac de causa fecit hoc ut nos omnes simul in terra sarracenorum habitantes eamque depredantes a sarracenis interficeremur atque ibi moreremur. huiusmodi prava et invida suggestione rex iniuste conmotus et iratus, eiecit eum de regno suo. (923,14-22)

(When King Alfonso and the magnates of his court heard of this action of Rodrigo, they took it very badly, and the courtiers made accusations for this reason, and, envious of him, all said to the King: "Lord and King, Your Honour should know for certain that Rodrigo did this in order that all of us, whether living in Moorish lands or invading them, should be killed by the Moors and not return." The King was unjustly roused by this false and envious accusation, and angrily exiled him from his kingdom.)

In this account, the immediate cause of the exile is said to be Rodrigo's fierce campaign in Moslem Toledo in reprisal for an attack on Gormaz, which gives rise in León to the idea that Rodrigo was trying to provoke the Moslems to attack the Leonese. This is otherwise unrecorded, and the inspiration could have been *Carmen* 65-76. Here the biblical phrase *laqueum mortis* is probably chosen for literary effect rather than strict accuracy, but might have provided the author of the *Historia* with a clue when he was trying to work out the reasons for the exile. However, Barceló has concluded that Rodrigo's plot against Alfonso not only existed but might have been the real reason for the exile. This is, surely, a case in which the two texts cannot be used to support each other: Barceló assumes not only that the *Historia* has unadduced evidence other than the *Carmen* for this plot, but that the author of the *Carmen* knows what he is talking about.[61] If the *Carmen* is right, then the poet has had access to important information unknown to historians of Castile and León at that time or later, and has demonstrated a concern and aptitude for digging out unpalatable truths that contrasts with his unworried ignorance concerning other established facts known to almost everyone in León and Castile. If, on the other hand, this is invention, as is most of the rest of the section, the approach of the poet here falls into a coherent pattern.

On the basis of a few known facts, the poet has arranged a story that leads to the desired conclusion at Cabra. In the poem this battle required some prior explanation. Rodrigo fought for Castile in his first victory, yet at Cabra he was fighting García Ordóñez, known to all the original audience to be a leading commander in León-

---

[61] Barceló *op.cit.* (n.53) takes *perdere solium honoris* (59) to imply that Rodrigo planned to depose Alfonso, and *ceteris plusquam volens exaltare* (46) to imply that Alfonso had given him power to do so; Martínez is understandably sceptical (p.349 n.3). G. West 'King and Vassal in History and Poetry' *Mío Cid Studies (cit.* n.5) pp.195-208, interprets 1.59 as "to lose his authority as commander" (p.202). West discusses the Gormaz episode on p.196.

It is tempting to speculate that the *susurrones* might be modelled on the poetic commonplace of *lozengers*, who upset the path of love by playing on envy and divided loyalties. But the chronology does not support this, the vocabulary and the situation are common in reality, and the temptation deserves to be resisted.

Castile. Some of them may have come into contact with him, since his own lands were just up the Ebro valley in Nájera. García has become a villain in the legendary tradition embodied in the later *Poema de Mío Cid*, but as Colin Smith says, "clearly the Count was in history a blameless and distinguished servant of the Crown."[62] Events in León and Toledo are far enough away for the poet and his audience to be satisfied with a garbled rearrangement of them; Cabra was five hundred miles away in the mysterious south; but García was too close to be acceptable if distorted. If the logic of the poem is not to clash with the audience's knowledge, the events of these years have to be presented in a sequence which shows Rodrigo as hero and García as nevertheless a blameless and distinguished servant of the Crown. There is no hint that García was one of the *compares aule* who instigated the exile (48); he is presented as acting under the precise orders of a badly advised king (77f.). The previous attitudes and motivation of the characters in this section can be seen to owe more to the demands of literary plausibility than to those of historical accuracy; both Rodrigo and García appear as worthy warriors of Castile, even though they were fighting each other.

11. THE ORIGINAL EXTENT OF THE *CARMEN*

When Rodrigo was exiled, he went briefly to Barcelona and then hired his services to Zaragoza. The fact that he is fighting for Zaragoza is not stated explicitly in the *Carmen*, but it has to be known for the audience to understand who is on which side in lines 97-104.[63] This indicates that the *Carmen* was probably composed while Rodrigo was still in the service of Zaragoza, i.e. before the end of 1086.

The episode at Almenar arose as follows. The *zaragozanos* captured the fort of Almenar from their neighbours, Lérida; Al-Faŷib of Lérida called on the rulers of Barcelona (to whom he was a tributary vassal), Aragon, and others of the Catalan counts, to help

---

[62] *Poema...* p.167.

[63] Barceló used this as an argument for postulating a *zaragozano* author ('Algunas...' pp.47f.), but his enemies were doubtless aware of it too.

retrieve the fort. The Aragonese are not recorded as having come; other Catalan counts are said to have in the *Historia* (925,7-9), but only Al-Faŷib and Berenguer Ramón of Barcelona turn up in the *Carmen*. Rodrigo was sent there by Almuktaman of Zaragoza; according to the *Historia* he tried to negotiate a retreat by the opposing forces (926,7-12), was rebuffed, immediately decided to fight despite having very inferior numbers, and won resoundingly. The wording of both the *Historia* and the *Carmen* suggests that he may only have been hired to take in provisions, and that the decision to fight the Count when rebuffed was going beyond his original brief from Almuktaman. This would explain the ecstatic reception given him on his return to Zaragoza.

This battle looks in retrospect insignificant in comparison with the other earth-shattering events of the 1080s in Spain, yet it seems to have been the climax of the original poem. It is possible that other events might have followed Almenar in the poem (Curtius thought it probably included the rest of his life); but there is evidence to suggest that this is the last of the *nova bella* (7f.) the hymn is designed to celebrate.

In the surviving section there are three remarks that foreshadow what is to come. The first is: *Hispalis novit et Iberum litus/quis Rodericus* (23f.),[64] in which *Hispalis* looks ahead to Cabra, and the Ebro valley may include both the Navarran fight and Almenar. This reference to his fame spreading from one end of the peninsula to the other is both accurate and a neat exploitation of a literary commonplace. The second previous reference is in lines 29-32:

Iam portendebat quid esset facturus,
comitum lites nam superat [ur] us
regias opes pede calcaturus
ense capturus.

---

[64] Horrent discusses these lines in *Historia*... pp.104f.

The defeated Counts will be García and Berenguer; the kingly might probably will be the camp of the Count of Barcelona. The third of these pointers occurs in the lines that introduce the Almenar battle: *alios fugans, aliosque cepit,/castra subvertit* (91f.). It is natural to take these lines as a summary of the following events. The ten or eleven stanzas that appear to have been erased would comfortably include the Almenar battle itself and some kind of formulaic conclusion, but little else; and if this was the original pattern, the complete poem would have had a unity of structure and theme. On the other hand, were some other victory included at the end, it would need to be presented as greater than that at Almenar, and would probably have left a trace in the earlier remarks that look ahead. The case cannot be proved, but it seems likely that the Almenar episode was the climax.

12. THE DATE OF COMPOSITION

Modern scholars have disagreed on the date of composition. The most widely accepted view is now that of Horrent, who dated it to 1093-4, accepted by Ubieto, Martínez and Deyermond *inter alios*.[65] Cirot proposed 1082-4, and that has been vigorously defended by Barceló.[66] If the Almenar battle is the climax of the *Carmen*, this is an argument in favor of the earlier date. Occasional poems on military success are usually written soon afterwards. For example, the poem on the capture of Jerusalem in the same manuscript as the *Carmen* gives the impression of being composed in the ensuing celebrations: *Urbs capitur hac hora/nulla ergo sit mora/nostra sit vox canora/Jherusalem exulta!* (113-6) (the city is captured now, so let there be no delay, let our voice sing out, Jerusalem, Rejoice!). Similarly, Amador says of the Latin poem on the capture of Toledo

---

[65] A.D. Deyermond *A Literary History of Spain: The Middle Ages* London (1971) says that the *Carmen* was "almost certainly a literary epic, probably written by one of his followers in 1093-4" (p.45). B. Powell, however, in his forthcoming *Epic and Chronicle: the PMC and the Crónica de Veinte Reyes* (MHRA), argues for an even later date, on the grounds that the historical inaccuracies are symptoms of a growing legend. I am grateful to him for letting me see the typescript of this section.

[66] 'Algunas...' pp.37-45.

that it must have been composed at the time (1085).[67] Rodrigo's success at Almenar seemed dazzling at the time, but the following decade was full of military excitement, and if the *Carmen* was not composed till 1093-4, it implies a surprisingly clear memory of a minor skirmish after these outstanding events:

1084   Rodrigo defeats the Aragonese at Morella.
1085   Alfonso VI of León captures Toledo.
1086   Almorávide invasion from Morocco defeats Alfonso VI at Sagrajas.
1086-7 Rodrigo is recalled from exile by Alfonso VI.
1088   Rodrigo is exiled again; from now he fights on his own account.
1090   Rodrigo again captures Berenguer Ramón, at Tévar. The Almorávides return with a stronger force.
1092   Alfonso VI attacks Valencia, with García Ordóñez, and support from Pisan and Genoan fleets. In García's absence Rodrigo devastates García's lands in the Rioja.

Horrent argues that the *Carmen* must antedate 1094, when Rodrigo captured Moslem Valencia for himself, or else the latter would be mentioned or hinted at. This is surely right. The same argument applies to the events of 1084-92, however, which is one of the most dramatic decades in Spanish history; none of these events seem to be hinted at.[68] Is it plausible that Rodrigo's capture of the Count of Barcelona at Almenar in 1082 could have appeared more memorable in 1093 than his second capture of the same Count at Tévar in 1090? The latter, after all, was impressive enough to become a set-piece in the vernacular epic. Is it plausible that the defeat of García at Cabra in 1080 would have seemed more memorable in 1093 than Rodrigo's devastation of García's lands in 1092? The latter is known to have been a fierce campaign that roused strong feelings, from the description in the *Historia* :

---

[67] p.212.
[68] Horrent detected a reference to the ravaging of the Rioja in *Carmen* 73, but Barceló successfully discounts it ('Algunas...' pp.43f.).

ingentem nimirum atque mestabilem et valde lacrimabilem predam, et dirum et impium atque vastum inremediabili flamma incendium per omnes terras illas sevissime et inmisericorditer fecit. dira itaque impia depredatione omnem terram prefatam devastavit et destruxit, eiusque divitiis et pecuniis atque omnibus eius spoliis eam omnino denudavit, et penes se cuncta habuit. (953,6-12)

(The devastation he caused was excessively great and painful and extremely distressing, and the burning and destruction by fire was harsh and ruthless and extensive, savagely and pitilessly spread over all those lands. He ruined and ravaged all this land with harsh and ruthless devastation, completely stripped it of its wealth and belongings and all its property, and took everything off for himself.)

The language of this passage is unusually hostile to Rodrigo.[69]

Arguments about the date of composition have often hinged on the present tense of the word *vocant* in *Cesarauguste obsidebant castrum/quod adhuc Mauri vocant Almenarum* (97f.). This is an echo of the Biblical formula for introducing place-names, *qui vocatur*,[70] which is present tense as a matter of course. It occurs in the *Carmen* with no particular implications for the only other named place at which action is set, Cabra: *Capream vocant locum...* (83). However, the presence of *adhuc Mauri* has been seen to provide a clue. Menéndez Pidal argued from this wording that the date of composition must pre-date the Aragonese capture of Almenar in June 1093;[71] Horrent argued from this wording that it must post-date the capture.[72] The argument is weak either way.

Ubieto pointed out that *adhuc is* used as a near-meaningless word in contemporary documents.[73] It is also used to fill line 71 of the *Carmen, adhuc parat eis/laqueum mortis:* the point of mention-

---

[69] West discusses this at *art.cit.* (n.61) p.200.
[70] E.g. *Luke* 2,4; 7,11; 19,29; 21,37; 23,33; etc.
[71] *La España...* p.876.
[72] *Historia...* pp. 117-20.
[73] *El Cantar...* p.168 n.5.

ing this supposed plot is to provide a cause for the King's sending a punitive expedition, so *adhuc* here can hardly mean "still." If it means anything, it means "now." Accordingly, any argument based on *adhuc* as "still" is insecure. *Mauri* is probably included to heighten the irony of the reference to *Madianite* in the previous stanza, since part of the fun is that the Count of Barcelona claims lordship over Moslem Lérida but is unable to recapture a small Moslem-held fort on his doorstep. Coll suggested plausibly that it is included here because Almenar is an Arabic name, and the author is apologising for using an Arabic word in a Latin poem:[74] this line can then be translated as "the fort with the Arabic name of Almenar." The present tense of *vocant* is paralleled by an obviously historic present in the following line, *quos rogat victor sibi dari locum*, and elsewhere. Accordingly, this line cannot be used as evidence for dating the *Carmen* at all. Horrent said that the importance of this detail has escaped nobody's notice,[75] but it might have been better if it had.

Similarly, the present tense of *estis* in *qui eius freti estis ope* (19) has been interpreted as implying that Rodrigo is still alive at the time, which is probably correct. *ope is* specifically military, and too concrete for the phrase to mean merely "those who are inspired by him." Much of the narrative is in historic present, but a second person plural in historic present is implausible. *modo* (now) in 1.129 also supports this. But this need not imply that it was performed to Rodrigo or his soldiers, still less that they composed it, in view of the errors of fact. Barceló took it to imply performance within Zaragoza.[76] But if the point lies in the celebration of the defeat of the Count of Barcelona, rather than the victory of Zaragoza, then the suggested origin at Ripoll remains plausible; and as Menéndez Pidal proposed, the audience will thus be hostile to the Count.[77] Coll, however, thought that the use of the Count's full title, *Marchio namque comes Barchinone* (93), showed that the author

---

[74] p.183.
[75] *Historia...* p.117.
[76] 'Algunas...' pp. 46-8.
[77] *La España...* p.878; 'La épica...' p.6.

cannot have been hostile to him.[78] Barceló[79] and Horrent[80] agreed. It is not clear why: the use of his full titles increases the contrast with his subsequent humiliation, and it is clear from events in Catalonia at the time that this humiliation would have amused many people.

13. CATALONIA IN 1082-3

The weight of evidence has led me to suggest that the author was educated at Ripoll, and probably composed the *Carmen* there in *ca.* 1083 for an audience hostile to Berenguer Ramón II. Berenguer Ramón and his brother Ramón Berenguer II (Cabeza de Estopa) became joint heirs to the County of Barcelona after the death of Ramón Berenguer I in 1076. They argued. There was an agreement to rule alternately from 1080, but neither this nor the intervention of Pope Gregory VII calmed the argument, and when one day in 1082 Ramón Berenguer suffered a mysterious accident on a hunting expedition, it was assumed that his brother was responsible; the Count in the *Carmen* was henceforth to be saddled with the name *El Fratricida*. The *Historia* states that the latter was the Count involved at Almenar. Historians date Ramón's death to early December 1082.[81]

Menéndez Pidal and Horrent assumed that the fratricide occurred before the siege,[82] but this need not be so; Berenguer Ramón was *comes* before his brother's death, Al-Faŷib had been his personal tributary since 1080, and Ripoll was not part of the lands allotted to Berenguer in the partnership agreement of December 10th. 1080, so nobody there need have felt inhibited from celebrating his discomfiture. It might even seem more likely for the *Carmen* to antedate the fratricide, but whatever the dating of each and their chronology relative to the siege, the significant fact is that there were almost certainly a number of people at Ripoll in 1082-3

---

[78] p.184.
[79] 'Algunas...' p.40.
[80] *Historia...* p.95.
[81] L. Suárez Fernández *Historia de España. Edad Media* (Madrid) 1970 gives December 5th. (p.190); R. d'Abadal i de Vinyals *Dels visigots als catalans* 2 Vols. Barcelona (1970) gives December 6th (II p.294).
[82] *Historia...* p.23; 'La épica...' p.6.

opposed to Berenguer. The reaction to his capture at Tévar in 1090 shows that the Count's image was not to mellow into lovability, but even so the civil dissension of 1082-3 in Catalonia tends to support the earlier date. Barceló thought that Menéndez Pidal's suggestion that the author was hostile to Berenguer implied that Rodrigo was intervening in the politics of Barcelona: it does not, but perhaps he was, since the reference in the *Poema de Mío Cid* to their having argued in 1081 is quite likely to be true.[83]

In 1082 Rodrigo was a stateless maverick who had found an awkward job on behalf of an unglamorous kingdom. In the *Carmen* he is elevated to epic stature as he prepares to meet the Count of Barcelona. Despite the elaborate description of his armour, which is likely to be exaggerated, the victory at Almenar was won against the odds by superior military skill and intelligence; and Rodrigo has given another lesson, in his guise as *Campi doctor*. The Count is paraded with his full titles, and is made to look silly; the exaggeration of Rodrigo to near-epic status was, on this view, intended to increase the amusement at the outcome of the skirmish. The poet could not have foreseen that Rodrigo was destined to become an epic hero in a different country, language and genre; he would no doubt be surprised to find his work being copied a century later and studied a millennium later, since it was probably composed for the entertainment of an audience at a particular time who already knew the story.[84] Our focus is likely to be distorted by our knowledge of the later Cid legends. The coincidence of two unrelated attempts to raise Rodrigo to 'epic' status is less extraordinary if we recall that it is only because of the later legends' existence that the Latin poem was copied and survives at all. There may have been other comparable poems which perished unrecorded. Nor is the postulated amusement at Almenar unparalleled in contemporary Latin literature: the *Tractatus Garsiae* from Toledo in 1099 shows that

---

[83] 'Algunas...' pp.41f. n.33. For the distribution of land in 1080, see the maps in d'Abadal *op.cit.* (n.81) II pp.223 and 250. Nicolau refuted the idea that Ripoll was especially favored by the Counts of Barcelona *(op.cit.* (n.3) p.7).

[84] Martínez (p.372) thinks it is designed to inform those who did not know the facts, but if so it would not have succeeded.

accounts of contemporary events need not be assumed to be straight-faced.[85]

14. THE ERASURE

This view of the *Carmen's* nature may shed light on the problem raised by the erasure in the manuscript. Why was the *Carmen* deliberately cut off before its climax? The final section would have included the defeat, capture and release of the Count of Barcelona, and it is unlikely that the picture presented would have been flattering to the Count. The unfavorable impression would have been heightened by the use of a hymn form to celebrate a Christian defeat, as if the character of Berenguer was such that even his defeat at the hands of Zaragoza could be represented as a triumph of good over evil. But times have changed by 1200. The Count of Barcelona has by then become *ex officio* ruler of all Catalonia, and, since 1137, of Aragon too; his kingdom, the *Corona de Aragón*, was beginning to become a world power, and Barcelona was beginning to become one of the great Mediterranean ports. Even if the scribe who transcribed the *Carmen* could bring himself to copy rude remarks about a previous holder of the same title, a reader might easily have been sufficiently offended in the early thirteenth century to have erased the final portion of the *Carmen*. Chapter 49 of the *Historia* has similarly been deleted from its manuscript, probably because it deals with Alfonso VI's humiliation at Valencia in 1092.[86]

Another possible motive for the erasure can be seen in the *Historia's* account of Rodrigo's triumphant return to Zaragoza, when he is exalted by Almuktaman higher than his own son; such a dénouement would have been an embarrassment at a time when Rodrigo was being specifically presented as a hero of Christianity. We cannot be sure, however, that this episode was in the original.

---

[85] *Tractatus Garsiae* ed. R.M. Thomson, Leiden (1973). See also M.R. Lida de Malkiel 'La Garcineida de García Toledo' NRFH 7 (1953) pp.246-58.

[86] Menéndez Pidal *La España...* p.953.

CONCLUSION

Instead of understandable frustration at the loss of the last few stanzas, perhaps we should feel surprise that the poem has survived at all, for its literary success depended greatly on the original literary and historical context. This analysis suggests that it was composed in ca. 1083 for a sophisticated monastic audience at a time of civil war which to later eyes is of no great significance; it also shows that although the *Carmen* is a better poem than it is usually considered to be, it cannot be used as a historical document. Apart from the *Historia Roderici*, later histories and the Castilian epic seem not to know it, so it probably stayed hidden at Ripoll.[87]

Several Hispanists have looked at the *Carmen* before; the only ones to see it in a medieval Latin framework were Cirot and Curtius, but their studies were perfunotory. Du Méril misled his readers by stating it was a popular poem; Amador misled his by saying it was Castilian, with the result that Nicolau omitted it from his collection of poems from Ripoll. Menéndez Pidal made more progress than anyone, but led speculation onto a sidetrack over possible vernacular sources. Horrent's article was a summary of previous criticism. Barceló's thought-provoking work seems to be largely unknown outside Spain. Smith, Ubieto, Martínez and West have recently referred in passing to the *Carmen* in works whose focus is elsewhere. Since the *Carmen* is now generally considered to be Catalan it was ignored by Rico,[88] but since it was not included in Nicolau it was also omitted by Raby, who dismisses it in a footnote.[89] So the *Carmen* has received inappropriate treatment from Latinists and Hispanists alike. Yet being at once a hymn, an occasional poem, a poem that uses classical and ecclesiastical traditions in a constructive manner, and a poem showing energetic partisanship in current events, it has sufficient sophistication and

---

[87] M. Laza Palacio *La España del Poeta de Mío Cid* Málaga (1964) produces no evidence for his assertion (pp.35 and 68f.) that the authors of the *Poema de Mío Cid* and the Latin *Poema de Almería* (1147) had met the *Carmen*.

[88] F. Rico 'Las letras latinas del siglo XII en Galicia, León y Castilla' *Abaco* 2 (1969) pp.9-92.

[89] *Op.cit.* (n.13) II p.236 n.4.

literary value to deserve wider recognition.[90]

1994 POSTSCRIPT

This paper was first published in *Papers of the Liverpool Latin Seminar, Second Volume, 1979*, ed. Francis Cairns; ISBN 0 905205 03 0; copyright, Francis Cairns, 1979. (Published by Francis Cairns (Publications) Ltd, currently c/o The University, Leeds, LS2 9JT, UK, and reprinted by permission of the publisher). That was a longer version of a paper first delivered to the Liverpool Latin Seminar on the evening of Friday 4th November 1977. It is thus the only paper in this collection that predates *Late Latin and Early Romance*, and since it is anyway for other reasons atypical, the references are in the present volume included in the notes rather than in the global bibliography. Part of section 3 was updated in *Late Latin*, p.147, but on the whole I stand by what I said two decades ago. Some day I will return to this *Carmen* in detail. One clarification needs to be made: the date of the sole surviving manuscript of the *Poema de Mio Cid* is of course of the fourteenth century, despite the final explicit date of era 1245 (1207 A.D.); and I have had one firm change of mind: the *iberum litus* of 1.23 probably refers to Rodrigo's service at Zaragoza, and would be understood as such in the 1080s.

Surprisingly little work has been done on the *Carmen* since 1979. There is a new edition, almost without comment, published by Juan Gil in *Corpus Christianorum: Continuatio Medievalis*, no. 71, Turnholt, Brepols, 1990, pp.99-108. It is also re-edited with a useful French translation (which manages to make the stanzas sound like Biblical verses, and is not dissimilar in important details to my English version), by M. de Epalza and S. Guellouz, *Le Cid: Personnage Historique et Littéraire*, Paris, 1983, 62-67. Some comment on the c.1083 dating and proposed circumstances of composition has been favorable; e.g. Richard Fletcher, *The Quest for El Cid*, London, Hutchinson, 1990, whose lengthy appraisal includes a reconstruction of the events at Almenar and in Catalonia at that time; *Cantar de Mio Cid*, ed. Francisco Marcos Marín, Madrid, Alhambra, 1990,

---

[90] Martínez (p.348 n.2) optimistically thought that nothing new could be said on the *Carmen*. He was wrong.

pp.10-11; Geoffrey West, "Hero or Saint? Hagiographic elements in the Life of the Cid," *Journal of Hispanic Philology*, 7, 1983, 87-105 (p.91), and "Mediaeval Historiography misconstrued: the exile of the Cid, Rodrigo Díaz, and the supposed *INVIDIA* of Alfonso VI," *Medium Aevum*, 52, 1983, 286-99. Colin Smith, however, in *The Making of the Poema de Mio Cid*, Cambridge, University, 1983, pp.56-57, and "The Dating and Relationship of the *Historia Roderici* and the *Carmen Campi Doctoris*," *Olifant*, 9, 1982, 99-112, feels strongly in favor of a mid-twelfth-century dating; Brian Powell's *Epic and Chronicle: the Poema de mio Cid and the Crónica de Veinte Reyes*, London, MHRA, 1983, sees the attitudes expressed in the *Carmen* as "at the heart of the developing heroic image of the Cid" (9), considering that lines 9-12 would be too exaggerated for an eleventh-century poem, being instead "a reflection of the fame of the hero after his death" (10). Ian Michael agrees, in his review of Powell (*BHS*, 62, 1985, 128-29). On the dating I still agree with what Colin Smith has said in another context, that "no one at a later stage would have bothered to resurrect such small memories," reviewing Diego Catalán, *Siete siglos de Romancero (Historia y Poesía)*, Madrid, Gredos, 1969, in *BHS*, 48, 1971, 261-62; if, as Smith (1982) proposes, the *Carmen* took such small details from a mid-twelfth-century *Historia Roderici*, we have then the extra problem of where the *Historia* got them from. Smith (1982) and Fletcher have, however, accepted my one incontrovertible discovery: that *Campi Doctoris* is two words. So do Josep M. Nadal and Modest Prats, *Història de la llengua catalana* Vol.I: *Dels inicis fins al segle XV*, Barcelona, Edicions 62, 1982, in their useful summary on pp.160-61. Other investigators seem to disagree; Gil noticed the discovery, but preferred the one-word form for its greater similarity to *Campeador*.

The following treat the *Carmen* on literary terms alone: Marina Conti, "Sopravvivenze classiche nel *Carmen Campidoctoris*," *Apophoreta Philologica*, Vol.2 (Madrid, Estudios Clásicos, 1984), 415-21; Joseph J. Gwara, "The heroic vision of the *Carmen Campidoctoris*," *Mittellateinisches Jahrbuch*, 22, 1987, 197-211 (who seems to think it is Castilian). The brief comments in F. López Estrada, *Panorama Crítico sobre el Poema de Mio Cid*, Madrid, Castalia, 1982, pp.193-94, end as follows: "De lo que no cabe aquí duda es que el autor de este *Carmen* fue un clérigo y que lo compondría (en lo que puede presumirse por lo que queda) de acuerdo con las normas de una tradición escolar." Agreed; but the fact that this *Carmen* is not an oral poem does not in itself constitute an argument against the existence of oral poetry at the time; and, as Fletcher says (p.93), it was "clearly intended for recitation aloud."

17
Latin and "ladino" (in the eleventh and twelfth centuries)

The spoken language of the Roman Empire was called by its speakers "lingua latina." This language contained within it considerable variation of a stylistic, sociolinguistic and geographical nature, but was still a single language. It continued to be called by this name throughout the Visigothic period, and subsequently in Moslem Spain also. The word written as *latin-* was used at that time to refer to the language used in Christian communities in Spain, and was only contrasted with different languages entirely, such as Greek, Hebrew or Arabic. (The Arabs borrowed it also, referring to the native vernacular as *Latīnī*.)

This word underwent phonetic changes, naturally, and after the voicing of intervocalic plosives it was pronounced [ladino]. Subsequently, that consonant would be fricativized, as [laðino], which is still its pronunciation today. This word did not change its meaning between the fourth and thirteenth centuries; it meant "the vernacular language," in the Roman Empire, in Visigothic Spain, in Al-Andalús, in 12th-century León; and *ladino* still meant "vernacular" in Medieval Spain. In communities where other quite different languages were also used, such as Arabic or Hebrew, there came to be a natural distinction between the Moslems and Jews who were "ladinos," that is, who spoke and maybe also wrote *ladino*, and those who did not (cp. Séphiha 1985:673). The word *ladino* has never been used by anybody to refer to Medieval Latin. Medieval Latin was something else, conceptually distinct from the Romance *ladino*. This distinction needed to be invented consciously, or else it could not have existed. Sociolinguistic variation is natural, but diglossia such as this does not just turn up by itself. It has to be established, and continually thereafter reinforced, by purpose-built social and educational systems (as is explained in the elementary sociolinguistic handbooks; e.g. Silva 1988:178, Rotaetxe 1988:61). It still seems most likely that the conceptual distinction between Latin and Romance was an invention of the scholars at the Carolingian court at the end of the eighth century, when there was imposed, for the first time in a Romance-speaking area, the Anglo-Saxon method of reading texts aloud (cp. Wright 1982/89, 1991a; Cano 1988:33-65). By the eleventh century, at least some people in France made this distinction (between Latin and Romance) in a more or less clear manner. It also still seems most likely that in the Iberian Peninsula (outside Catalonia) this conceptual distinction was only introduced after the Council of Burgos of 1080, where Alfonso VI, King of León, decreed that the old "Toledan" liturgy should be dropped and the "French" one introduced instead. This liturgy had to be performed in the manner which we would now describe as "Medieval Latin," that is, pronouncing a specified sound for each written letter of the text. Pronouncing in this way seems natural to us now when reading Latin, but native speakers will never read their native language aloud like that, and in the Iberian Peninsula this unusual manner of pronouncing when reading had also to be introduced in a conscious manner. The new distinction in speech, between the ordinary Romance pronunciation and the new "Medieval Latin" one, had subsequently led on in France to the establishment of a different distinction, in writing, when at last there was established a system of writing French Romance that was clearly separate from the traditional methods; and by the thirteenth century, at the latest, similar new writing systems were being used in Spain also.

The Spanish word *latín* was probably introduced into the (non-Catalan) Iberian Peninsula during the Europeanizing reforms of the twelfth century. The French word *latin* probably evolved from the adverb LATINE, but it had already become a noun, and in Alfonsine texts the Spanish word has even acquired a plural: e.g. "La gramatica a ell offiçio de fazer las letras et componer ende las partes et ayuntar los latines...et estos latines quieren asi dezir en nuestro lenguaje de Castiella..." (*General Estoria*, 2.1.ch.36, p.57). Unfortunately, Corominas and Pascual (1980) tell us nothing about *latín* or *latino*, classifying them as Proper Names.

The Alfonsine texts sometimes make a clear distinction between Medieval Latin and Romance vernacular, although the latter is usually called *romance* or *romance castellano* rather than *ladino*: for example, "*Depositum* en latin tanto quiere decir en romance como *condesijo*" (*Partida* V.3.1). Hans-Josef Niederehe even suggests, though, that the distinction was not always clear even in the Court of Alfonso "El Sabio": "Latin and Spanish...are not always in opposition for Alfonso el Sabio...but are thought of as registers within a single language" (1987:102; my translation). There is one Alfonsine reference to Romance as being "nuestro latin," and once (*Partida* I.5, ch.37) the Castilian word *honestad* is said there to be "latin" (cp. Escavy 1985:209). If this lack of a conceptual distinction was indeed the case, then it was still in essence a continuation of the situation that had existed since the Roman Empire, with a wide range of registers and variations within a single language, as is the normal state of affairs if nobody has built a diglossic barrier. Even so, it is possible to deduce that in general there was felt to be a distinction between two languages in thirteenth-century Castile. There must have been such a feeling by the time of the Council of Valladolid of 1228 (Wright 1982/89, ch.5). Berceo felt this way, of course, and as Rico (1985) has shown, those who wrote the early "mester de clerecia" in Romance knew the genre already separately in Latin. Once it was established, this tradition (like many invented traditions) came to seem obvious, normal, natural, and indeed ancient, so much so that Dante thought that Romance and Latin had always existed as separate entities.

But in the Iberian Peninsula of the previous century, there must, at least sometimes, have been considerable confusion. The word written *latinus* is not found often in texts from that century; it could have been used then either to refer to the vernacular (representing [ladino]), as in previous centuries, or to refer to the new [latin] introduced from France. Perhaps this potential ambiguity could have been one of the reasons—among others of a more political and nationalistic type—why gradually inhabitants of the Peninsula preferred to call their vernacular by the name *romance*, or the geographical terms *castellano*, *aragonés* (etc), rather than *ladino*. The word *ladino* did not completely die out in the Christian communities, but in later years it may be that only the Moslems and Jews used it regularly still as the normal word to apply to their vernacular Romance. Thus the inductive force of this contingent statistical regularity led everyone to the idea that the fact that the word *ladino* was most commonly used to refer to the Romance spoken by non-Christians was the consequence of this being the word's literal meaning; for the result was indeed a semantic change in the word *ladino* to mean "The Romance spoken by non-Christians." This sequence would explain the remarkable semantic change that happened between the twelfth century, when the word was confined for use to refer to the native language (Early Romance) of the indigenous Christian inhabitants, all over the Peninsula, and the fifteenth century, since when it has been used to refer to the Romance spoken by non-Christians, by Moslems and Jews and also Indians in Guatemala and Peru, black slaves in Cuba, etc. The history of the two words *ladino* and *romance* after the Alfonsine period has been well studied by Alvar (1985, 1986), and needs no further discussion here.

For these reasons, it is interesting to investigate what was happening in the 12th century. Some of the texts composed in the Peninsula in that century seem to have been the work of writers from France or Catalonia, who would probably have been trained to regard their Latin as a separate language from their native vernacular (the *Garcineid*, the *Historia Compostellana*, the *Chronica Adefonsi Imperatoris*, the *Historia Roderici*, for example). It also seems a reasonable conjecture to suggest that the famous Riojan glosses were written there for the benefit of a French or Catalan visitor (Wright 1986; we now know from the studies of Bézler 1985, 1986, and Díaz y Díaz, 1983:405, that the original from which the glossed Silos manuscript was copied was composed after the year 1060). Notaries, on the other hand, did not have such an erudite training (cp. Gimeno Menéndez 1988).

At this point we meet a genuine difference of opinion between modern investigators. Faced with the notarial documents of the Kingdom of León before the thirteenth century, almost all of which were not written in a way we would regard as "correct," some modern philologists believe that the notaries concerned were incompetent bilinguals who were nevertheless expert in phonetic transcription; that is, that the notaries would have learned "Latin" as a whole separate language from their Romance, and that they would have had the intention of writing in that separate language, but that they had learned it so extremely badly that they committed a whole range of obvious and elementary errors, and yet were even so skilled at analyzing their own phonetic usage and able to provide an exact and careful phonetic transcription of what they were themselves saying, errors and all. This is the kind of analysis that is still at times seen today in studies of documents where there is a section on the orthography entitled "Phonetics," as if the spelling had necessarily been a faithful and detailed transcription of speech.

Other philologists take a different line, believing that all that the notaries of the twelfth century were trying to do was to add a "veneer" on top of their vernacular to make it look more respectable. These modern scholars thus do not need to postulate that the notaries had been on a course to learn "Latin" as a separate and distinct language, that they had even so learned it extremely badly, nor that they were even so simultaneously expert phoneticians. Emiliano (1988) presented an excellent study from this point of view to the Cáceres conference, for example. This second scenario seems the more plausible for at least the great majority of the documents of the twelfth century, including the *Fueros*. It is very similar to what was proposed by Lapesa in his most recent study (1985) of the *Fuero de Valfermoso de las Monjas* of 1189; he writes that even though this fuero seems at first sight to be written in a "mixture of Latin and Romances" (p.51), it is in fact rather a representation of the "live reality of speech" (Romance) with a "veneer of Latin added on top." Lapesa concludes like this (p.95): "the cleric...usually confines himself to giving a Latin appearance to what he has thought and almost formulated in Romance, latinizing mainly the letters, the phonetics that these correspond to, and the morphology." I would suggest omitting the word "almost" ("casi"); and "the phonetics that these correspond to" ("la fonética a que ésta corresponde"), since we have no clear evidence of what the phonetics were; and change "latin" to "formal" and "latinizing" to "formalizing," so that it can be seen to be a question of registers rather than separate languages. The consequence would be that we would conclude that, with reference to many twelfth-century documents, the writer "is trying to give a formal appearance to what he has thought and formulated in Romance, formalizing mainly the spelling and the morphology." In this way we have no need to envisage an army of incompetent bilinguals, merely writers who are trying to do no more than write. After 1250, at the latest, the notaries had two kinds of writing that they could choose between, which at that time could well have corresponded to two different languages in the mind of the writer, but in the twelfth century there was still only one respectable way to write.

So most of the Leonese notarial documents of the twelfth century are in essence similar to those of the eighth to eleventh centuries; they had an author who spoke the normal Romance vernacular of the time and place and wrote in the only respectable way there was, although Menéndez Pidal (1926) was right to point out that the level of professional training of notaries in the early twelfth century seems to have improved. It is possible to study the texts of earlier centuries from this perspective also, and thus come up with results of great interest (cp. Puentes Romay, 1986 and 1986a; Pensado Ruiz 1991, for example). Lapesa has more recently referred (1988:469-70) to "the haziness of the frontiers between Latin and Romance in the usage of the Leonese notaries of the eleventh century"; it would be possible to go even further, and say that there was no such frontier; that all that existed was Romance, whether spoken or written. The documents attest "written Romance," that is, written in the only way there was, rather than "Romance-influenced Latin" ("latín arromanzado"); and even in the twelfth century most notaries were still not learning another separate language to write in, but instead were still trying (when they wrote) to make their language respectable by adding a "veneer" on top, applied via a few provisional rules and tricks of the profession (cp. Wright 1982:240-44).

But those who still believe that twelfth-century writers must have learned "Latin" badly and phonetic transcription well, are not going to yield merely to arguments based on plausibility. It is worth looking to see what they said about this at the time. For example, in line 2677 of the *Poema de Mio Cid* we hear of a "moro latinado"; one of the Infantes de Carrión says some words in Romance to the other, and *un moro latinado bien gelo entendió*. The word *latinado* can only mean in this case specifically "who could understand spoken vernacular Romance," and it does not look as though a distinction was perceived at that time and place between two separate languages. In one of the Alfonsine prosifications of this passage, the word *latinado* is left unchanged (in the version of the *Crónica de Veinte Reyes* recently published by Powell 1983:148; folio 158a); but in the other it is prosified as *ladino* (cp. Menéndez Pidal 1945, III:729); the scholar who drew up this second version must have realized that here the point was that the "moro" could understand spoken Romance, and he thus used a different word based on the distinction which indeed had come into existence by that later period. This is the only time that the lexeme LATIN-/ *ladin-* is used in the *Poema*. (In non-linguistic contexts, this lack of a semantic distinction between *latino* and *ladino* still applied in the fourteenth century; for example, line 1228d of the *Libro de Buen Amor* mentions la *guitarra latina* in manuscript S, and *la guitarra ladina* in manuscripts G and T, both contrasted with *la guitarra morisca*.)

When abbot Peter of Cluny came to Toledo in 1142, he hired a certain "magister Petrus Toletanus," expert in the two languages, Arabic and *latina*, to translate an anti-Mohammedan treatise from Arabic. This Petrus collaborated with Peter of Poitiers (the Abbot's secretarial companion), who (according to Peter of Cluny) *verba latina impolite vel confuse plerumque ab eo prolata poliens et ordinans* produced the written text. That is, the written text is said to be have been made more polished and ordered, less crude and confused, than the oral version of magister Petrus toletanus, but they do not seem to have thought it was a question of translating the Romance spoken by the magister into Latin, but of a formalization of the register (Peter of Cluny's relevant section is reproduced in an appendix at the end of this paper). By operating this way they came up with a translation better than others of the time (Kritzeck 1964:111).

Such a distinction, based on relative formalization, is sometimes said to have been occasionally expressed for several centuries by the use of the word *vulgus* (and cognates). For example, in the *Historia Compostellana*, I.103 (Flórez 1765/1965), we find the Spanish word *galeas* (of Byzantine origin) described as a word of the *vulgus*: *magno itaque admodum sumptu, factis duabus biremibus quas vulgus*

"*Galleas*" *vocat, Irienses accito sibi altero palinuro...*; and the word *duplicia* said to be Galician (*Gallaeco vocabulo*), referring to part of the entrails of a cow: *Altera ergo die cum militibus suis inter epulas sedenti dapifer suus unum ex intestinis illius vaccae, quod Gallaeco vocabulo duplicia nuncupatur, in scutella argentea inter alia fercula apposuit*, I.2.5. This does not seem to be a word of modern Galician; perhaps an unattested *dobreza (< DUPLICIA) existed in the twelfth century, but the point is that, even if it did, that form is written in this text in its formal respectable guise, not transcribing directly any of its evolved phonetic features. (Martínez, in his book, 1975, on the *Chronica Adefonsi Imperatoris* and the *Poema de Almeria*, often makes an explicit distinction between Latin and Romance, but the author of the texts he is studying never does; cp. the next chapter).

But it is not always easy to work out what they meant in the twelfth century when they used the lexeme VULG- (*vulgo, vulgariter, vulgari locutione*, etc). In the last part of this paper, I shall present some very strange data from the *Vita Dominici Siliensis*, written at the start of that century (and edited by Valcárcel 1982). Grimaldo wrote this as far as Chapter II.39, and it was then continued by other colleagues from the monastery of Santo Domingo de Silos. They had contacts with France there; the text quotes both liturgies, the new "Roman" and the old "mozarabic" (132-33, 619-21), and dates events according to both Anno Domini and the Hispanic era (309). Most of the book narrates 124 miracles performed by Santo Domingo of Silos. In the course of this, 99 placenames are introduced with a "naming" verb, on the lines, for example, of *villa qui Penna Alba vocatur* (III.41). (*Vocatur* is the verb used 57 times, *dicitur* 22, *nuncupatur* 6, *vocat(us)* 4, *nominatur* 3, *appellatur* 3, *dict(us)* 2, *vocitatur* 1, *vocitat(us)* 1). Most of the placenames are written in a spelling that is hardly "correct" but without any explicit linguistic comment; e.g:

    I.15   vico Tordeagamor vocato
    II.29   vico que nuncupatur Ormaza
    II.49   villa qui dicitur Cuebas
    II.50   urbe que vocatur Cuellar
    III.6   vico que vocatur Taggata
    III.36   kastrum quod Alkalaten vocatur
    III.14   opido que Montego vocatur.

This last one, which refers to the place called *Montejo* (<MONTIC-ULUM), is a good example of how "incorrect" the orthography of these placenames can be. But on the following eight occasions, the placename is explicitly described as being *vulgaris*:

> I.21 villam que Mons Rubicundus vulgari locutione vocatur
> II.9 villa que vocatur Kobaense vulgari lingua
> II.45 ecclesia... que vulgari lingua dicitur Ripa Rotunda
> III.2 villa que dicitur Spinosa vulgari locutione
> III.13 villa... que Gormaz dicitur vulgari locutione
> III.20 vico Clunia vulgariter dicto
> III.35 opido que vulgari locutione Mons Rubicundus vocatur
> III.47 villa que vulgari locutione Quintanar natus.

Of these eight, only *Gormaz* and *Quintanar* (de la Sierra) look at all "Romance" in their written form. *Mons Rubicundus*, on the other hand, is a completely formalized and correct form of the vernacular placename *Monterrubio* (de la Sierra); and so is *Ripa Rotunda* as a written version of (Santa María de) *Rivarredonda*; so are *Spinosa* of *Espinosa* (de Cervera), and *Clunia* of *Coruña* (del Conde). This same Coruña is called *Clunia* without this metalinguistic qualification in I.16. As regards *Kobaense* (written in one manuscript as *pobaense*) it is not clear what the place in question is, but if Valcárcel is right in suggesting that it is a written version of *Cuevas*, the form *kobaense* seems to be neither Romance nor Latin nor formal nor vulgar nor anything more than the result of a provisional and unsuccessful attempt at formalizing the name; perhaps we can envisage that [kweβas] was given this written form *kobaense* according to the rough rules of thumb that they had learned for going from sounds to choice of letters, as follows; [k] > k, + [we] > o, + [β] > b, + [a] > a, + [s] (plural morpheme, but here confused with [-és]) > *ense* = *kobaense*. Yet the well-transcribed written form *Cuebas* for this place (II.49, cited above), unlike *kobaense*, was not there described as being *vulgaris*. These examples demonstrate that when they used the word *vulgaris* they cannot have been referring to any feature of the phonetics or of the spelling; or even, so it would seem, of the etymology, in view of the fact that all the placenames of Arabic origin are written with no metalinguistic comment at all. (For details of the toponymy, see also Ovejas 1956).

The *Miracula Beati Felicis*, probably written by the same monk Grimaldo, present us with the same problem concerning the six placenames it mentions (Flórez 1781:436-58):

> p.450: Villa quae vulgariter vocatur Cortices
> 452: Vico qui vulgari lingua Balneus dicitur
> 453: Vici qui vocatur Puras
> 454: Monte qui Aucha vocatur
> 455: De villa vocata Petrosa...quae in territorio quod vulgari nuncupatione dicitur Ulbere rivus

Two of the three placenames here described as *vulgares* are actually written with the traditional spelling: *Cortices* and *Balneus* (on the presumption that this place is *Baños*). The third is *Pedrosa del Río Urbel*; Berceo calls it *río d'Urbel* (*Vida de San Millán* 470a). Auch, however, is written as *Aucha*; in formal Latin it would have been AUSCIA; here it has almost no "veneer" at all, but is not described explicitly as being *vulgaris*.

Statistically, in the two works, the percentage of placenames written in the correct formal spelling happens to be much higher among those names that are explicitly called "vulgares" than among those which are not.

Besides these eleven placenames, in these works the only words described as "vulgares" are two non-technical names of diseases; *beruelas*, (Spanish "viruelas," < VARIOLAS), *telo* ("gout"):

> III.38 saevissima egritudine que vulgari locutione beruelas vocatur
> II.28 irruente gutta, que vulgo vocatur telo
> II.29 irruente infirmitatis molestia que vocatur telum, id est, gutta vulgari lingua
> III.21 infirmitate que vulgo telum dici solet

These forms, called "vulgares," are on two occasions written with formal correct morphology (*telum*), and twice with that of vernacular Romance (*telo*, *beruelas*); we can see from this that whatever their "vulgarity" consists of, it is entirely unconnected with either their phonetics or their morphology. It might be suggested that the point here lies in the existence of a distinction between registers: *telo* (< TELUM, "weapon") no longer survives anywhere in Romance, but it could have been used in the Rioja area in the twelfth century, to disappear soon after. But this explanation is not convincing; *gota* (< GUTTAM) was the word used to mean "gout" in Old Castilian, and St Isidore wrote (in the seventh century) that *telum* was used by doctors (that is, in a formal register) to describe rheumatic pain in the ribs *(Etymologiae* 4.6.13: *telum lateris dolor est. Dictum autem ita a medicis quod dolore corpus transverberet quasi gladius*). Meanwhile, epilepsy, popularly called *gota caduca,* is referred to as such by Grimaldo, as *gutta cadiva,* in a metalinguistic conment that lacks the word "vulgaris": I.14, *infirmitate que...congruo sibi satis vocabulo gutta cadiva vocatur*. Valcárcel explains that the "congruent" aspect of this is that epileptics fall over.

CONCLUSION

The conceptual distinction that we are used now to making between "Latin" and "Romance" was hardly felt in the non-Catalan Iberian Peninsula twelfth-century; at times it might be possible to glimpse distinctions of register or formalization, but not of bilingualism. This is similar to what Van Uytfanghe (1989) discovered in eighth-century French texts.

APPENDIX

From the letter written by Peter of Cluny to Bernard of Clairvaux concerning the translation of the *Al-Kindi* (Kritzeck 1964:212; cp.27-36, 101-07):

> Mitto uobis carissime nouam translationem nostram, contra pessimam nequam Mahumet heresim disputantem, quae dum nuper in Hispaniis morarer, meo studio de Arabica uersa est in Latinam. Feci autem eam transferri a perito utriusque linguae uiro, magistro Petro Toletano. Sed quia lingua Latina non adeo ei familiaris uel nota erat ut Arabica, dedi ei coadiutorem doctum uirum, dilectum filium et fratrem Petrum, notarium nostrum, reuerentiae uestrae ut aestimo bene cognitum. Qui

uerba Latina impolite uel confuse plerumque ab eo prolata poliens et ordinans, epistolam immo libellum multis ut credo propter ignotarum rerum noticiam perutilem futurum, perfecit.

1994 POSTSCRIPT

The Spanish original of this paper was published as "El latín y el ladino (siglos XI-XII)," *Actas do XIX Congreso Internacional de Lingüística e Filoloxía Románicas*, A Coruña, 1993, vol.5, 61-70; it was delivered to that conference at the University of Santiago de Compostela, on the morning of Tuesday September 5th, 1989, just three weeks after the Rutgers conference, also coinciding with the publication date of the translation of *Late Latin*. Much of the first part of this paper recapitulates a lecture I gave to a conference in Jerusalem on Wednesday 27 June 1984, entitled "Early Medieval Spanish, Latin and Ladino"; by September 1989, I was under the impression that the papers were not going to be printed, but now they have been, as *Circa 1492: Proceedings of the Jerusalem Colloquium "Litterae Judaeorum in Terra Hispanica,"* ed. I. Benabu, Jerusalem, The Hebrew University, 1992, 36-45. Romance is still *ladin(-)* in Sephardic communities and in the Alps, where they did not adopt a new geographically-based name at the time of the mid-medieval nationalisms. This continuity of language-naming (a question taken up in Janson 1991) supports the view of a continuity between Latin and medieval Romance (*ladino*) rather than between Imperial and Medieval Latin, and is what led József Herman, at Santiago, to tell me I should make it clearer that my investigations are into "metalinguistics"; as will be seen from the next chapter, I took that advice to heart, and since used the term extensively, including in this translation.

18
Twelfth-century Metalinguistics in the Iberian Peninsula (and the *Chronica Adefonsi Imperatoris*)

The eminent Romance philologist József Herman said recently that my studies concern metalinguistics rather than linguistics; hence the title of this paper. I have often proposed the hypothesis that the conceptual distinction between Latin and Romance was an invention of the Carolingian Renaissance, and that nobody had made such a distinction before. Herman (1991) reacts by saying that maybe nobody distinguished them before, but modern philologists and Romanists are entirely justified in looking at earlier evidence and deducing that there were indeed two recognizably distinct languages in existence before the ninth century, even if nobody actually recognized their distinctness at the time. I do not accept this view, because I believe, with many sociolinguists, that diglossia can only exist if the two languages concerned are generally thought to be different.

Paul Lloyd's view (1991) also seems reasonable to me; that for a language to have independent existence, conceptually separate from other languages, its speakers have to think themselves that it is different from all other languages. This is a very topical question in Spain now. For example, foreign Hispanists tend to feel that the Catalan of Barcelona and Valencian are not distinct enough to deserve different names; but if those who speak it really feel that Valencian is another separate language, maybe that belief should be enough to decide the question. Speech-communities are self-defining. Thus the conceptual break between the Catalan of

Barcelona and Valencian (if indeed that is what is happening now) is quite similar to the increasing break between Catalan and Occitan through the twelfth and thirteenth centuries. In the later twelfth century, the system of vernacular writing used in the Corona de Aragón was closer to the speech habits of the Northern part of the Corona than to those of the Southern part (from 1157 to 1213 Provence was ruled from Barcelona). The decision that was later taken, to invent a separate writing system more like the way they spoke in Barcelona, was one consequence of the political separation of Catalonia from Provence after the Battle of Muret (1213). These decisions are political rather than linguistic, both in the twentieth century and in the twelfth and thirteenth. The "Academia de la Llingua Asturiana" of our own time, for example, emphasizes the distinctive characteristics of the *bables* for political rather than linguistic reasons, and as usual this decision can be seen most clearly in the elaboration of a separate spelling.

The example of modern Spain shows us that types of speech that are really very similar to each other can come to be thought of as separate languages for political reasons. This decision is never taken with reference to an objective list of necessary and sufficient distinctive features that have to be satisfied before a form of speech can be considered to be a separate language entirely. Lexical distinctions, lexicalized in the names of languages as in all other words, are used as labels to pin down semantic distinctions which seem useful to the speakers, and such semantic distinctions can at times be very subtle and at other times extremely broad. Modern English, for example, presents quite a different case from that of the Modern Iberian Peninsula; the extensive variation found in English speech could easily be classified according to objective criteria as being several separate languages, but the majority of English-speakers prefer to think that we are all using a single language containing wide variation, which is why English is usually regarded as just one language. I would say that through the twelfth and thirteenth centuries, the metalinguistic situation of the Iberian Peninsula changed from being considered as more or less monolingual, as in the modern English-speaking world, to being thought of as multilingual. We know now from many recent studies (e.g. Herman 1988, Varvaro 1991, Banniard 1989, Van Uytfanghe 1989) that writers in the Pre-Carolingian Romance-speaking areas did not make explicit distinctions between Latin and Romance; and that after the Carolingian reforms introduced there at the start of the ninth century there was a distinction between two methods of reading aloud in Church, at least, and maybe in other circumstances also. But what happened in ninth- and tenth-century France still presents us with very interesting questions, which are quite similar to those of the twelfth century in the Iberian Peninsula. The distinction between Latin and the Romance vernacular of the time seems obvious now to us; but we can tell that it was not obvious to them. The distinction seems to have taken a long time to get established and be really felt to be true. The famous Council of Tours of 813 is the only one of the five Councils held that year even to mention the problem; but Alcuin, the prime mover of the reforms, had lived at Tours, and it could well be that in other centers this distinction was not yet really felt. The Council of Mainz of 847 repeated the famous Tours edict; this Council was celebrated immediately after the arrival there as archbishop of Rhabanus Maurus, former pupil of Alcuin and native speaker of Germanic; this represents one stage in the slow spread of the reform. McKitterick, for example, has recently presented evidence to show that in the Romance-speaking part of the Carolingian Empire, even in the later ninth century, writers did not normally foresee nor expect that there would be a problem in communicating a written text to illiterate listeners. The studies of Van Uytfanghe (1989, 1991) show that, in the ninth century, explicitly metalinguistic references to their language (or languages) are still often most confused and even self-contradictory. Not even the Strasbourg Oaths attest a clear distinction between two languages, any more than the strangely-written sections of gaucho speech in Güiraldes' novel *Don Segundo Sombra* (1926) attest that gaucho speech wasn't Spanish; neither do passages of phonetic transcription in a modern Spanish linguistics handbook attest some other language. It seems that the definitive attribution of the category of "different language" tends to follow (or at least accompany) the invention of a different writing technique, rather than preceding it (see Janson 1991); it could be that even in ecclesiastical contexts we can only envisage the definitive establishment of the conceptual distinction in France after the time of the experimentally-written *Cantilène de Sainte Eulalie* (late ninth-century). And even in the tenth century, it has been suggested that the Latin-Romance distinction was not made in a very clear way (Guerreau-Jalabert 1982:21, n.37). I still feel that it only really began to be intuited with any clarity in France in the eleventh century.

For the moment, in connection with the Iberian Peninsula (outside Catalonia), I am going to assume provisionally that the clear distinction between Latin and Romance could not be consciously formulated until after the arrival of the new methods of reading texts aloud that the French clerics brought with them after 1080; that is, after the arrival of what we now call with hindsight "Medieval Latin." In the twelfth-century Iberian Peninsula, as in ninth-century France, we can envisage a slow, slow spread of both the idea and the technique of the new norms of reading aloud, promoted in each case by speakers of another language (Germanic in France, French in León). By the end of the following century (the thirteenth) some more or less clear distinction can be observed in Alfonsine texts between two languages, *latin* and *romance (castellano)*. But even then, as Niederehe points out, (1987:102), "Latin and Spanish...are not always in opposition for Alfonso el Sabio...but are thought of as being registers of a single language"; that would just be a prolongation of the metalinguistic situation that held over the preceding thousand years, that is, of a single multifaceted language. But there must in fact have been many people in the Peninsula by then who felt the distinction, particularly in the Church after the Council of Valladolid (1228). But the twelfth century is still rather enigmatic. Not even the French and Catalan writers who wrote texts in the Peninsula seem to have distinguished very clearly between two languages, even though we have to presume that the distinction had become valid by then in France, Provence and Catalonia. Many of the notaries who prepared the *fueros*, for example, seem to produce texts in which Latin and Spanish Romance are hopelessly mixed (and sometimes Provençal Romance as well). At the Santiago conference (Wright 1993) I considered such texts, and proposed that their authors were not incompetent bilinguals of grotesque stupidity, which is the usual assessment, but monolingual Romance-speakers who tried to write well the only language they thought they had. In that century, there was as yet no choice. They had to write the way they had been taught. Public life in the twelfth century in the Peninsula was very complicated; considerable intelligence was required even to keep an official post; we cannot explain the ostensibly miscegenated hybrid language of the most important notarial texts simply with the hypothesis that all the writers were thick as bricks.

Here metalinguistics rides to the aid of philology. If we look at what the writers of that century say, they can tell us if they thought they were operating with one language or with two. It seems that most of them did not think that there were two languages involved but just one; and it also seems best to accept their own assessment, even though it is not in accordance with conceptual distinctions we have become accustomed to making subsequently.

The metalinguistic situation of twelfth-century León can also be compared with that of modern France. In León there were no linguists or philologists, and in modern France there are, but even so it is not normally the case that modern Frenchmen think that written French and spoken French are separate languages. They are seen as different modalities of the one language. Muller's *Le Français d'Aujourd'hui* (1985) makes it clear that the differences there are between colloquial spoken French and formal written French (in the same geographical area) are so huge that we could well be justified, if we found them in geographically separate areas, in distinguishing them as separate languages. Formal written French and colloquial spoken French are more different from each other than are, for example, Barcelona Catalan and Valencian, more than Castilian and the *bables* of Asturias, more, perhaps, than Galician and Portuguese. Even so, if we leave aside professional linguists, if you suggest to a Frenchman that here there are sufficient or even necessary conditions for considering that the language usually called French is in fact two separate languages, one spoken and one written, you will find that this seems absurd to them. The situation was similar in twelfth-century León. In the *Poema de Mio Cid*, for example, we meet a "moro latinado"; one of the Infantes de Carrión says something to the other in ordinary Romance, and *un moro latinado bien gelo entendió* (1.2677). The word *latinado* here explicitly refers to a Moslem who understood spoken Romance;

there seems to be no idea here that Latin and Romance are different languages.

The last part of this paper is going to concentrate on the evidence of the *Chronica Adefonsi Imperatoris* and the *Poema de Almeria* which forms the final part of this *Chronica*. On the basis of this evidence, I will be sceptical of several interpretations made by Salvador Martínez (1975), Gómez Redondo (1988) and others, concerning the metalinguistics of the age. Martínez often makes, in his book, the distinction between Latin and Romance, but it does not seem to be there in the actual text. (This *Chronica* was written to commemorate Alfonso VII's military expedition to Almería in 1147. It has been suggested that the author was Arnaldo, bishop of Astorga and probably a native of France, although that is really only a guess).

The noun phrase *nostra lingua* is used in this *Chronica*, but only with reference to four words: the placename *Jerez*, and the military phenomena *algaras*, *alcázares* and *celatas*. Which language is the author referring to with this expression? The first-person plural is used twice in the text to refer to the author himself: at the start of the *Poema*, *Da nobis pacem linguam prebeque loquacem* (*Poema de Almeria*, 1.2), and at the start of the second book of the *Chronica*: *ad ea quae olim christianis asperrima fuere bella tractandi veniamus*, (*CAI*, ch.96). So it could be that with the phrase *nostra lingua* the author is referring directly to a group of speakers of which he thought of himself as being a member.

It is worth looking at all the individual contexts in which the phrase *nostra lingua* appears. The case of the reference to *Jerez* is unfortunately a bit confused. There are many placenames in this History. They are often introduced with the venerable old formula *quod vocatur* (or a close variant). Some of these placenames are written in an unimpeachably traditional way; for example, *castellum quod dicitur / vocatur Aurelia* (ch.145 / ch.147), that is, the castle called [oréʒa] (now written *Oreja*); and others are written in a less acceptably traditional spelling: for example, *castellum quod dicitur Alleriz* (75), that is, Allariz (in the Province of Orense); sometimes the placenames are Arabic, such as the *flumen quod dicitur Goadalquivir* (passim; e.g., 131); but there is only one of these many placenames in which the language concerned seems to be specified, and that is *quandam civitatem opulentissimam, quam antiqui dicebant Tuccis, nostra lingua Xerez* (37). The distinction being made here is merely the chronological one that differentiates the use of the ancients (*antiqui*) from that of "our language" (sc. "now"); it is a distinction which St Isidore used to make quite regularly five centuries earlier, and is not directed towards any dichotomy within the twelfth century itself. It seems that here the author thought that the name *Tucci* would not be enough to identify the place for the reader; and this is where the confusion arises, because although indeed hè was right in that, and we know from the context that Jerez must be the place he is referring to, the town that was called *Tucci* by the Romans is not in fact Jerez at all, but the town of Martos, way over in the modern province of Jaén. (Jerez seems not to have had a Roman name). In another chapter of this same History the town is spelled as *Gerez* (*Adefonsus imperator ascendit in Gerez*, 115), without any metalinguistic comment at all (and with manuscript variants *Xarez* and *Xares*); and in the Poem that celebrates the capture of Seville in 1248 (Carande 1986) we find *Xarez* (*Et a mari Gallico, Xarez, Regis Cella,* 1.86c) and *Xaret* (*Usque mari Ispalis, Xaret captis portis,* 1.48c).

The word *algaras* is also introduced with the phrase *nostra lingua: magnae turbae militum, quod nostra lingua dicitur algaras* (36). Later it is used without this comment: *misit ante faciem suam magnas algaras in omni regione* (187); and we have to draw the conclusion from this that the language he is actually writing is the one that he calls *nostra*. The word *alcazares* is accompanied on three occasions by the phrase *nostra lingua*, but also appears without it once: *fortissimae turres quae lingua nostra dicuntur alcazares, praedictarum civitatum* (102), *super excelsam turrem quae nostra lingua dicitur alcazar* (150), without it in *imperator abiit in illa alcazar, in palatiis regalibus* (158), and *in turribus excelsis Cordubae, quas nostra lingua dicit Alcaceres* (189). Jerez, *algaras* and *alcazares* are all words of Arabic origin, and this fact inspired Martínez to his suggestion that maybe the author meant to refer to "mozarabic" with the words *nostra lingua*; which is peculiar, because Martínez himself is insistent that the author of the *Chronica* was not a Mozarab. But in fact many other words of Arabic origin are in this text, without apparently qualifying for this metalinguistic label. The word *alcaydes* appears at least twelve times, for example, all without it. The word now spelled as *alquitrán* is used with the nominating verb but without the phrase *nostra lingua* in Chapter 198 (*misit fortissimum ignem quem vocant de alcatran in illam turrem*), but its first use, a hundred chapters earlier, did not even have the nominating verb (*coeperunt mittere fortissimam ignem de alcadran in lignis*, 98); both with *alquitrán* and *alcázares*, the different manuscripts offer us many orthographic variants, so we can hardly believe that the scribes and copyists understood that here reference was being made to phonetic details requiring close transcription. Thus we cannot be satisfied with the simple solution that the phrase *nostra lingua* was needed for words of Arabic origin, although this coincidence is not accidental, as we shall see.

The fourth occurrence of *nostra lingua* is with the word *celatas*. *Celata* is a nominalization formed off the participle of *celare*, "hide," to mean "ambush"; the noun is used in the *Poema de Mio Cid* (e.g. 1.436, *Mio Cid se echo en çelada con aquelos que el trae*). The ancient word with this meaning had been *insidiae*, and in the *Chronica* this is found five times (in Chapters 4, 110, 135, 148, 178), but only in the second of these occurrences is it further specified as being *celatas*: *et miserunt insidias, quas lingua nostra dicunt celatas, in quodam loco abscondito* (*sic*, written with a letter *t*, which suggests that in this case also nothing phonetic can be intended with the word *nostra*). Now, the words in other Romance languages that are cognate with Spanish *çeladas* do not in fact have the same meaning. The French word (*salade*) and the Italian (*celata*) usually meant "the visor of a helmet." So it seems that one thing these four words have in common (*algaras, alcázares, celatas*, and also probably *Jerez*) is that they would be understood in the Iberian Peninsula but not in the other Romance-speaking areas. So it could be worth suggesting that the author was referring to a geographical (as well as a chronological) distinction with this phrase *lingua nostra* ("nowadays in the Peninsula"), without distinguishing thereby between contemporary Latin and Romance.

This is not what I said in my book (Wright 1982:228); there I suggested that this phrase *nostra lingua* was used in the *Chronica* to distinguish Spanish Romance from Medieval Latin. But further thought has led me to change my mind. I now think that with this phrase *nostra lingua* the author is referring to what we think of as being two languages but which he thought of as being one, as it were, "latino-romance." Equally vague was the word *vulgo*, which I considered in the Santiago conference through its appearances in the *Vita Dominici Siliensis* (Valcárcel 1982); the use of this word is similarly unconnected with any attempt to make clear metalinguistic distinctions. (In the *Chronica*, *vulgo* is only applied to one of the seven uses of the word *muzmutos*, used there to refer to the confederation of Berbers (Maṣmūda) that formed a large proportion of the Almohades.)

Thus I do not believe that in the Iberian Peninsula in the twelfth century there was a generalized diastratic conceptual distinction between Latin and Romance. And it seems unlikely also that there was any general diatopic conceptual distinction, between separate dialects within the Peninsula. This is not to suggest, obviously, that there were no geographically significant differences, but that the speakers of the time did not think in terms of the separately identified dialect names that are used by modern dialectologists and historians of the language. The author of the *Chronica* may well have known that some words, some lexical peculiarities, were found in the Peninsula and not in France, but it still remains to be shown that he, or any other writer of the time, used to differentiate metalinguistically between Galician, Leonese, Castilian, Navarrese and Aragonese.

With the phrase *nostra lingua*, then, was our author referring to the Latin-Romance language of the Iberian Peninsula in general, or did he have in mind a more precisely delimited geographical area? In their anthology of Medieval Latin, Fontán and Moure baldly state, without any discussion, that this author spoke Castilian ("el autor era persona de lengua castellana"; 1987:359). It is impossible to agree with this. Martínez, for example, believes that the author was of French origin and Bishop of a Leonese cathedral under a Portuguese Archbishop. Then, when mentioning El Cid in the *Poema de Almeria* the author commented: *qui domuit Mauros, comites domuit quoque nostros* (1.235). It is inconceivable that the word *nostros* is here being used to refer specifically to Castilians. Ruy Díaz (El Cid) was Castilian, and the Counts that he "tamed" were the Count of Barcelona (Berenguer Ramón II), García Ordóñez (a Leonese, owning lands in the Rioja), and—perhaps—the Infantes de Carrión, who were also Leonese. *Nostros* in this case seems to refer in general to Christians in the Peninsula, as vaguely as that.

At this point another well-known line of the *Poema de Almeria* becomes potentially relevant. Most of the *Poema* enumerates the separate constituent parts of the Christian army. The part referring to the Castilians includes the line (149) *illorum lingua resonat quasi tympanotriba* (I am following the edition made by Gil 1974; *triba* is usually interpreted as being written in error for *tuba*). This line was completely missed out of the Spanish translation made in the sixteenth century (published in Rodríguez Aniceto 1931), but in the twentieth it came to be regularly interpreted as a reference to the Castilian dialect, conceptually separate from the Leonese dialect. I suggested in the book, and this time I still think I was right, that with these words the author was referring to their tone of voice; to the proud spirit of independence of the Castilians with respect to the Leonese King, which made them speak in a loud and confident manner. In this text the author makes elsewhere no such geographical-linguistic distinction as the one suggested. The word *lingua*, for example, is used otherwise with different reference; to a fluent style in the second line of the *Poema* (already quoted: *linguam loquacem*), and in 1.47 to the very loud voice of a Bishop *lingua vociferando*. The word *resonat* is used to refer to the manly voice of Count Poncio in 1.188, *dextra ferit fortis, resonat vox, sternitur hostis*, and to the noise made by the young soldiers in the camp of Martín Fernández de Hita, *castraque Martini turba resonant iuvenili* (1.263); but in none of these lines can we glimpse a reference to isoglosses, or to which side of them these people normally lived. Perhaps there is an implicit comparison, in 1.149, with the call to the crusade, which is described as: *tuba salutaris resonat per climata mundi* (1.53). The only languages from within the Peninsula that are distinguished in the History are Arabic, Hebrew, and undifferentiated Latin-Romance: *omnes principes christianorum et Sarracenorum et Iudaeorum et tota plebs civitatis...unusquisque eorum secundum linguam suam laudentes et glorificantes Deum* (ch.157). Thus I conclude that the author may well have been aware of some minor lexical differences between the Peninsula and France, but made no metalinguistic distinction of a geographically more precise kind.

First Conclusion

The metalinguistics of this text are not precise. There are no clear conceptual distinctions made, neither diastratic, nor, so far as can be seen, diatopic, within the general ensemble of Iberian Latin-Romance, regardless of where the author came from. The clarity of the distinction which we now usually take for granted between Latin and Romance certainly has its origins in the reforms that began at the end of the eleventh century, but their spread took a long time, and only became generally applicable in the thirteenth century. So it is merely anachronistic if we, the philologists of the twentieth century, apply these distinctions to the twelfth.

Second Conclusion

It is essential to realize that this is all rather important, with far-reaching implications. It is not merely a philological question, although it is certainly important to expel the mirage of phonetic "cultismo" (learned influence) from the centuries earlier than the one examined here. We are going to have to change the way we look at the culture of the Romance-speaking world over many centuries, and refocus our perspective in a far more generous way. Modern historians are sometimes liable to write that before the thirteenth century, the congregations could "of course" not understand the sermons and the Saints Lives that were read aloud to them, that ordinary people "of course" could not follow legal documents that were read aloud to them, that illiterate soldiers had "of course" not been able to understand their written orders, that ninety per cent of the inhabitants of the Peninsula had no part at all in literate culture, because, so we are now often told, written texts always used a different language from the spoken vernacular that was all they had. And yet many of the speakers and writers of the age did not believe that there were two languages involved. We are now in a position to give back to these thousands and thousands of Iberoromance speakers their social dignity, their voice, their ears and their intelligence, that is, their practical ability to participate in society that modern historians have refused to grant them; for all that existed was one language with sociolinguistic variation, such as is found all over the world, and there were no barriers to interaction such as those that would have been caused by bilingualism (I would have said "diglossia," but at the moment this word seems to be losing any clear sense of its own). Above all, perhaps, specialists in the History of Literature ought now to stop distinguishing between forms, styles, and genres that are supposedly "Romance" and others that are supposedly "learnéd," before the thirteenth century. There was a single Christian cultural world in the twelfth-century Peninsula; multifaceted, pluralist, but not yet rigidly divided into two separate cultures, "Latin" and "Romance."

1994 POSTSCRIPT

The Spanish original of this paper was published, in slightly shortened form, as "La metalingüística del siglo XII español (y la *Chronica Adefonsi Imperatoris*)," in the *Actas del II Congreso Internacional de Historia de la Lengua Española*, ed. R. Cano et al., Vol.2, Madrid, Pabellón de España, 1992, 879-86. The paper was delivered to that Conference at the University of Sevilla on Tuesday March 6th, 1990; and prepared very soon after the Santiago one (in the previous chapter), which explains the repetition of some details. I am grateful to Professor Harvey (as so often), here for explaining the reference to *muzmutos*. It has subsequently been suggested to me that perhaps the author thought that *celada* was an Arabic word.

The winter between the Santiago and the Sevilla conference seems, in retrospect, to have been when I first realized how fundamental our reappraisal of Early Romance culture is going to have to be as a result of the monolingual perspective. Since a fundamental reappraisal is precisely what is needed in order to overcome our apparently instinctive desire to patronize the past, this is a good thing not a bad one.

19
How Old is the Ballad Genre?

In the last century there were scholars who believed that the extant ballad texts were older than the epics; this view has been untenable since the realization that the ballad texts date from the sixteenth century and the epics—however many there were—from considerably earlier. So the equation was reversed, and the ballads were said to be (in many cases) remnants of old, now-lost, epics.[1] The discovery of prosified verses in the late thirteenth-century histories, many of which seem to be simple ancestors of the subsequently attested ballads, reinforced this view. There can be certainly no doubt that some of the histories included in their source material contemporary poems (*cantares* or *canciones*) about historical events (*gesta*); but there is no compelling evidence for the proposition that these verses were all parts of long epics, and I would like to suggest here that they are more likely to be the reflections of contemporary ballads, ancestors of those that survive into the sixteenth century.

Several scholars have been implying that the ballad tradition might be old. López Estrada, referring to the earliest vernacular poems from which epics grew, said "cabe pensar, entonces, en que estos Poemas de la primera época tuviesen alguna analogía, parecido o relación con un tipo de composiciones semejantes a unos "ro-

---

[1] E.g., by A.D.Deyermond, *A Literary History of Spain: the Middle Ages* (London, Benn, 1971), p.125; and "Courtly and popular elements in Medieval Spanish Literature", in G.S.Burgess (ed.), *Court and Poet* (Liverpool, Cairns, 1981), pp. 21-42 (27-31).

mances", muy anteriores al siglo XIV, tal como propugnaba la tesis romántica de F. Wolf, expuesta para el caso español por Agustín Durán" (with a reference to Gies, pp. 99-100). Brian Powell said that he sees "no reason why some short poems could not have coexisted alongside longer works at an early date. The evidence I have adduced would suggest this". Carola Reig's book is sometimes adduced by those who believe in the existence of a long early epic on the siege of Zamora, but she only claimed that the evidence suggested the existence of short songs ("breves cantares"), with only a provisional inclination for one source over several. Going further back, Monroe and Armistead feel happy to discuss the nature of the Romance poetry that might or might not have influenced the *kharjas* with reference to ballads. Monroe has elsewhere suggested that ballads could go back to Roman times. Salvador Martínez saw a Late Latin origin for the epic, arguing sensibly for a continuity that in the event applies no less forcefully to ballads. (So, indeed, with reference to *lírica*, did Menéndez Pidal). There are brief octosyllabic religious verses attested from Moslem Spain, such as Vincent's *Carmen Poenitentiale* (printed by Gil, and called a "romance" by Simonet), a genre which goes back to Saint Augustine, and even if this does not in itself represent an orally-transmitted genre I have argued that it would be read aloud with Romance pronunciation. Alan Deyermond has been suggesting that many themes and images to be found in lyrics, but also in non-historical ballads such as *Fontefrida*, have an ancient common heritage in Pan-Mediterranean or even world-wide traditions, which implies that some of our ballads have very remote roots. In short, the existence of Spanish ballads before the fourteenth century does not seem to strike scholars in practice as a hopelessly implausible idea.[2]

---

[2] F.López Estrada, *Panorama crítico sobre el "Poema del Cid"* (Madrid, Castalia, 1982), p.205; D.T.Gies, *Agustín Durán: a biography and literary appreciation* (London, Tamesis, 1975); B.Powell, "The *partición de los reinos* in the *Crónica de veinte reyes*", *Bulletin of Hispanic studies*, 61 (1984), pp.459-71 (p.471); C.Reig, *El Cantar de Sancho II y Cerco de Zamora* (Madrid, RFE Anejo 37, 1947): "Me inclino, pues, aunque de manera provisional, por la existencia de los breves cantares de gesta primitivos. ¿Fueron uno o varios estos cantares? Esto es imposible de precisar, pero la

The meter of ballad and epic in Spain is the same, ballads in performance being no more rigidly octosyllabic than are the hemistichs of the *Poema de Mio Cid*, as can be seen from the versions in modern collections.[3] Consequently, the only formal difference between an epic and a ballad is that of length. So the question boils down to this: are we to believe that whenever the inhabitants of early and mid medieval Spain chose to sing in octosyllabic form, they were never able to stop until they had sung for well over three hours or so?

I would hope that I am here pushing at an open door; that even those who believe in a multiplicity of ancient epics will accept that at the same time smaller texts, both on the same themes as the epics and on other more lyrical ones, were often performed, both to audiences and privately while doing the washing. If such smaller performances can be envisaged, then the reconstructable passages of approximately octosyllabic verse that can be glimpsed by modern scholars in the old histories might as well, in principle, attest a number of separate ballads rather than one epic per theme in disjointed fragments (since no reconstructed passage is as long as the longest attested ballads, let alone as long as the *Poema de Mio Cid*).

---

unidad que hemos visto en la crónica nos hace pensar en una sola fuente poética" (p.41); S.G.Armistead and J.T.Monroe, "Beached whales and roaring mice: additional remarks on Hispano-Arabic poetry", *La Corónica*, 13 (1985), pp.206-42 (p.210); J.T.Monroe, "Prolegomena to the study of Ibn Quzman: the poet as jongleur", in S.G.Armistead et al. (eds), *El Romancero Hoy* (Madrid, Gredos, 1979), vol.III, pp.77-130 (pp.114-16); H.S.Martínez, *El "Poema de Almeria" y la épica románica* (Madrid, Gredos, 1975); R.Menéndez Pidal, "Cantos románicos andalusíes, continuadores de una lírica latina vulgar", *Boletín de la Real Academia Española*, 31 (1951), pp.187-270; J.Gil, *Corpus Scriptorum Muzárabicorum* (Madrid, CSIC, 1973), p.688; F.Simonet, *Historia de los mozárabes de España* (Madrid, Real Academia de la Historia, 1903), p.343; R.Wright, *Late Latin and Early Romance (in Spain and Carolingian France)* (Liverpool, Cairns, 1982), p.153 and passim; A.D.Deyermond, "Pero Meogo's stags and fountains: symbol and anecdote in the traditional lyric", *Romance Philology*, 33 (1979), pp.265-83.

[3] E.g. S.H.Petersen (ed.), *Voces nuevas del romancero castellano-leonés*, (Madrid, Gredos, 1982).

Since we know that it was possible for a number of separate ballads on the same historical theme to have existed later, it would also be possible to use Occam's razor and suggest that it is unnecessary to postulate the longer single unit at the earlier date; and even if we want to keep our oral epics we can follow López Estrada and believe that *romances*, or something very similar, predated the hypothesized epics on the same theme.

There are two works that can on formal grounds be called "epics" which survive from the Spanish Middle Ages: the *Poema de Mio Cid* and the *Mocedades de Rodrigo*. The *Cantar de Roncesvalles* is often included in the genre because of the 200 lines that accidentally survive on a loose folio, but there is no way of knowing how long that text originally was when complete. Since the meter of epics and ballads is essentially the same, that could be a fragment of an epic of 3000 lines or of a ballad of 300, so its existence is a neutral factor in the current discussion. There are other works on themes that could broadly be called "epic", such as the *Poema de Fernán González* (which probably had oral inspiration of some kind), but the two works on the Cid are the only attested epics of the time in approximately sixteen-syllabled assonating lines. The fourteenth-century *Mocedades de Rodrigo* is almost certainly a composite text. It falls naturally into several parts, each with its own rationale and coherence, but collectively heterogeneous and even self-contradictory; the likely oral antecedents of this work seem more easily understood to be several ballads rather than one oral whole (though neither supposition can be proved). The hypothetical ballad antecedents are not, of course, to be identified with any surviving sixteenth-century texts, but they can be, and have been, glimpsed in prosified form in earlier histories, as separate entities. The *Poema de Mio Cid* has also at times been thought to be an aggregation or growth of several pre-existing parts (as in the ideas of Von Richthofen[4]), but even if it is not, all scholars say that this *Poema* is unique and *sui generis* and some believe that it had

---

[4] E.g. E.von Richthofen, *Nuevos estudios épicos medievales* (Madrid, Gredos, 1970).

no direct earlier oral counterpart.[5] The *Mocedades*, the *Poemas* of the Cid and of Fernán González and the Roncesvalles fragment support the proposal that there was oral poetry in the thirteenth century and earlier, but not necessarily that it was of "epic" proportions.

The commonly-expressed view that the ballad genre cannot be dated to a time earlier than the Trastamaran wars is not, in fact, a commonly-held one; I have yet to meet a Hispanist who strongly feels that this must be true, although no doubt I soon will. For one thing, the supporters of Enrique de Trastámara would have expected to have more success from inserting their propaganda into a pre-existing tradition than from inventing a new one. They can hardly be seen as avant-garde littérateurs. But the Trastamaran wars are not very long after the Alfonsine histories, some of the composition of which is now assigned to the fourteenth century as well; so this line of thought leads to the idea that there were ballads around at the time of the composition of some of the histories. There are ballads about Alfonso X himself, which there is no reason to suggest cannot be contemporary. The *Mocedades de Rodrigo* and the Trastamaran ballads, both of the third quarter of the fourteenth century, are easier to interpret if there was an already established ballad tradition than if there wasn't; the histories give evidence of shortish poetry in the ballad/epic form; so we can cause little offence by at least considering the view that ballads—ancestors of, but not identical to, surviving ones—were sung in the mid-thirteenth century. Perhaps when Alfonso's Partida II.21.20 encouraged the singing of *cantares* (songs) about *gesta* (historical events) to soldiers at mealtimes, he was only referring to brief digestible performances rather than full-blown epics that lasted for several hours. Perhaps Ximénez de Rada heard them before inserting his few brief unconnected references to the Cid into his *De Rebus Hispaniae* of 1243. Perhaps Arnaldo de Astorga had heard ballads about the Cid in the 1140s when he described him as *de quo cantatur* (in the *Poema de Almería*)...[6]

---

[5] E.g. C.C.Smith, *The Making of the "Poema de Mio Cid"* (Cambridge, University Press, 1983).

[6] Rodericus Ximenius de Rada, *Opera* (Valencia, Anubar, 1968; reprint

When the vogue for printing ballads arrived in the sixteenth century, they were usually printed on *pliegos sueltos*, that is, as single items, rather than in cycles. Their appearance in this form was abetted by the technological advance of print and the nature of folded paper, but it does also suggest that they may have been circulating naturally as separate items, rather than as elements in cycles. As I argue in a study of the ballads currently in Press, this view is reinforced by the way in which ballads with internal consistency of their own can seem contradictory in attitude when combined with different ballads on the same topic.[7] The Rey Rodrigo ballads form a good example. In *En Ceuta está Don Julián* (*Primavera*, 4) we are told twice that Rodrigo was never seen nor heard of again after the final battle; in *Las huestes de Don Rodrigo* (*Primavera*, 5) we indeed see and hear him after the battle, in great detail. In *En Ceuta* and *Los vientos eran contrarios* (*Primavera*, 5a) it is made quite clear that Rodrigo's affair with Cava is thought to be the reason for his downfall; in *Las huestes* she is not even mentioned, nor is Julián. The first two ballads see the battle as poetic justice and divine retribution, the third as an appalling military disaster. These perspectives are central to the ballads' raisons d'être, and cannot be plausibly dismissed as superficial developments consequent on a fourteenth-century fragmentation of

---

of Madrid, 1793) has eight references to *Rodericus Didaci (Campiator*, but never *Cid*), seven of them very brief (v.1, v.23, vi.2, vi.15, vi.18, vi.20, vi.26) and one of some twenty lines on the capture of Valencia. He has heard tales about Rodrigo chasing Vellido Dolfos to the gates of Zamora (vi.18) and separately about the oath of Santa Gadea (vi.20), but nothing from the *Poema de Mio Cid* (nor indeed from the *Historia Roderici*, which suggests that, pace Smith, it was not at Salamanca). There is one brief reference in his *Historia Arabum* (ch.49). The best critical edition of the text of the *Poema de Almería* is that by J.Gil, "Carmen de Expugnatione Almariae Urbis", *Habis*, 5 (1974), pp.45-64, in whose correct line-numbering this quotation comes from line 234 (=Martínez's 1.221).

[7] R.Wright, *Spanish Ballads: a critical guide* (London, Grant and Cutler, 1991). In the present paper individual ballads are identified by first line and their number in M.Menéndez y Pelayo, *Primavera y flor de romances* (=*Antología de Poetas Líricos castellanos*, vols VIII and IX: Madrid, Biblioteca Clásica, 1899).

a former single epic. If, on the other hand, there had been a number of shorter songs in existence for several centuries, even perhaps from the eighth century (which is likelier than an epic, in my view), such differences in presentation are no more surprising than finding different attitudes in different films about the Vietnam War. Later collectors tried to form a corpus; Timoneda amalgamated *Los vientos* and *Las huestes* into an uneasy whole, for example; but there is no reason to suppose such a corpus was necessarily unitary in the centuries before printing, in the oral tradition. The only medieval compilation we can see as a corpus of oral material is the *Mocedades*, which uneasily cobbles together tales that are each of greater cohesiveness than the whole, and cannot seriously be seen as a record of an actual oral song in itself.

This problem has been noticed before, naturally. The case of the behaviour of Urraca in the siege of Zamora is particularly surprising. When Rodrigo Díaz is besieging Zamora, he is depicted in a famous ballad (¡*Afuera, afuera, Rodrigo!; Primavera*, 37) as going to interview Urraca there. She recalls when they were lovers, and Rodrigo suggests that they could be again; Urraca rejects the offer forcefully, Rodrigo being married to Ximena. The ballad is a fine one, with a strong logical interplay and succession of emotions to keep an audience interested. The reason for Urraca's presentation here as being genuinely shocked by suggestions of adultery (*mi ánima penaría*, 1.25) lies in the need within the story to find an explanation for Urraca's determination not to yield Zamora to the besieging army, and the strong personal feelings presented in the ballad achieve that end. It is, consequently, necessary to suppose that the audience knew the broad outlines of the wider plot, without it being necessary to suppose that that wider plot was an epic.

The immediately preceding ballad in Menéndez y Pelayo's *Primavera* (36), also taken from the 1550 *Silva*, is *Morir os queredes, padre*, another well-known and striking ballad. Urraca complains to her father, the dying Fernando I, that her brothers have been given kingdoms but she has been given nothing. In order for the King to be shaken into changing his mind, she is given powerful words to say: she will travel round Spain alone, giving her body freely to any Christian and to any Moslem for money. Her sentiments here, as in

¡Afuera!, have internal literary point, as well as being strong enough sex-interest to keep the audience happy. Both these ballads are excellent. But it is difficult to see how they can come from the same one source; that source must have been rather confusing, if Urraca was determinedly promiscuous at one point, genuinely shocked by the idea at another (and soon after that apparently offering her favors to the notoriously untrustworthy Vellido Dolfos as in *Primavera* 45). This problem has been solved by allotting the Urraca-Rodrigo tale to a different epic, not the Siege of Zamora epic but one related to but not identical with the *Mocedades*.[8] If we can legitimately postulate the existence of separate unconnected epics on the same historical topic, the argument in favor of the existence of several short ballads is halfway to being granted. None of them need necessarily be parts of a single greater whole, either.

The references to songs as sources in the histories are indeterminate as to their length. The two sections from the *Crónica de Veinte Reyes* that refer to songs on the early part of the life of the Cid (quoted, for example by Pattison[9]) call these *cantares* and *canciones*; *canciones* are short (or shortish) songs, and *cantares* can be of any length at all;[10] all such references to verse sources (unlike those to prose sources) seem to be in the plural, however: e.g. *et algunos dizen en sus cantares segund cuenta la estoria que este frances Bueso era primo de Bernaldo* (about Bernardo del Carpio: PCG 617, II:351a21-22); *et dizen en los cantares de las gestas que la tovo cercada VII annos: mas esto non pudo ser...* (about the Siege of Zamora: PCG 834, II:509a37-39); *et algunos dizen en sus romances et en sus cantares que el rey, quando lo sopo, que mando quel fiziessen bannos,* (PCG 655, II:375a27-29; as Garci-Gómez says, the

---

[8] S.G.Armistead, " 'The enamoured Doña Urraca' in chronicles and balladry," *Romance Philology*, 11 (1957), pp.26-29.

[9] D.G.Pattison, *From Legend to Chronicle: the treatment of epic material in Alphonsine historiography* (Oxford, Medium Aevum, 1983), p.82.

[10] See Nebrija's phrase in his *Gramática*, "cantares que llaman romances", referred to in M. Garci-Gómez, "Romance, según los textos españoles del Medioevo y Prerrenacimiento", *Journal of Medieval and Renaissance Studies* 4, 1974, 35-62 (n.38).

two terms are here used without distinction): this use of the plural, and the fact that these phrases are used mid-chapter to introduce minor details rather than major sections, seem strongly to suggest the existence of several shorter source poems for each episode rather than one long one.[11] Other references such as that in the Poema de Almería (*de quo cantatur*) are also indeterminate (as to the length and number of the songs in question). Pattison's reconstruction (pp. 105-06) of an early fourteenth-century version of the *Jura de Santa Gadea* ballad (from the *Crónica de Castilla*) is convincing; any assumption that it is a part of a longer epic is less so and unnecessary. Perhaps songs in the meter of all lengths from very short to very long existed, as Powell suggested; it is also reasonable to consider the proposition that only shorter ones (ballads) existed in genuinely non-erudite oral tradition, an idea that will appeal in particular to those who see the *Poema de Mio Cid* as a growth out of earlier shorter elements, or as an unprecedented act of original creativity, but is in itself worth considering by all (whether labelled (neo)-traditionalist or (neo)-individualist or oralist or British or whatever[12]). There has never been much evidence against the hypothesis that ballads were performed before the fourteenth century. Perhaps no scholar has seriously believed they were not, although many have written it. On balance, the evidence is favorable to the hypothesis that many brief "popular" octosyllabic verses in vernacular have been sung in Spain since Roman times, and it might even be argued that this hypothesis is sufficient to explain all the evidence that has come to be explained by the hypothesis of oral epics. If this is so, could someone please explain why—other than out of a natural respect for those who have handed on to us the currently received wisdom—we need postulate

---

[11] References are to R.Menéndez Pidal *et al* (eds), *Primera Crónica General de España* (Madrid, Gredos, 1955). See also the refreshing article by J.M.Caso González, "La *Primera Crónica General* y sus fuentes épicas", *Actas de las III Jornadas de Estudios Berceanos* (Logroño, Instituto de Estudios Riojanos, 1981), pp.33-56, who even concludes that the direct sources were prose *estorias*, some of which—e.g. *Fernán González*—might also pre-date the poems referred to.

[12] I accept none of these labels on myself; my views are my own.

genuinely oral epics (rather than ballads) at all?

1994 POSTSCRIPT

My interest in the Spanish Ballads was originally performance-based, unconnected with my interest in Latin and Romance; only gradually have I come to see that the postulated existence of a vital oral culture before the thirteenth century in the peninsula is at the same time an important aspect of our necessary reevaluation of the culture of these centuries. This article was first published in *La Corónica* 14, no.2, 1986, 251-57; the notes are reprinted neat here, and the references are thus not in this volume's general bibliography. It elicited an immediate response from Professor Armistead, as will be discussed in the next chapter. It is, incidentally, not true (as Brian Powell has pointed out) that all chronicle references to *cantares* are in the plural.

20
Several Ballads, One Epic and Two Chronicles (1100-1250)

In the initial note to his article on "British contributions to the study of the medieval Spanish epic" (*La Corónica* 15, 1987:197-212), Alan Deyermond referred to the "Wright-Armistead controversy." This use of the word "controversy" with reference to articles by myself and Professor S. G. Armistead in *La Corónica* 1986[1] is surprising, for in his article Professor Armistead expressed vehement agreement with the main point of my own: that is, that the ballad genre is almost certainly older than the fourteenth century. In Armistead's words, "Ballads undoubtedly existed early on, but we don't know much of anything about them" (n.3, p.59). Indeed, I still know of no Hispanist who strongly feels that this cannot be the case. It is perhaps true that a reader might intuit a mildly argumentative tone in some of Professor Armistead's other comments, yet the arguments in question there were not directed against myself but against "neo-individualism," *cantilènes*, "proto"-romances, Gaston Paris, Ernst Curtius, Joseph Bédier and Colin Smith. I pointed out in the original article (n.12, p.257) that I am not a "(neo-)individualist"; of the others, the only one even mentioned was Colin Smith, with whom I did not express agreement (n.5, n.6). If we must have these labels, my own University lectures on both ballads and El Cid are probably less "neo-individu-

---

[1] Wright 1986a; S. Armistead, "*Encore les cantilènes!* Prof. Roger Wright's *Proto-Romances,*" *La Corónica* 15, 1986, 52-66.

alist" than any in Britain (now that Professor Harvey has retired); I agree closely with the views recently expressed by John Miletich, concerning the partial reliance of the *Poema de Mio Cid* on a "rich tradition of Hispanic folk balladry,"[2] and have great respect for Professor Armistead's own work on the *Romancero*, referring to it approvingly both in the article (n.2) and in my own recent annotated bilingual *Spanish Ballads with English Verse Translation* (Warminster, Aris and Phillips, 1987); indeed, this edition adopts such an uncompromisingly "performance-based" approach to the ballad genre that some readers have found the notes rather startling.[3]

There is only one further clarification of detail to be made concerning this supposed "controversy"; it may well be true that the attested texts of the ballads *En Ceuta está Don Julián*, *Las huestes de Don Rodrigo* and *Los vientos eran contrarios* "all spring from chronistic accounts: *En Ceuta* is based on PCG, while *Los vientos* and *Las huestes* follow Pedro del Corral" (Armistead, p.55), but it still seems reasonable to argue that Pedro del Corral certainly, and the *PCG* probably, did not invent the tales from nowhere, and that it remains perfectly likely that the traditions they reproduce already existed, probably in octosyllabic verse.

All readers of *La Corónica* will be grateful to Professor Armistead for reponding so succinctly to the request (Wright, p.256) for elucidation on whether "we need postulate genuinely oral epics (rather than ballads) at all." In turn, Professor Armistead asked "individualists" to offer "a viable convincing alternative solution, based on specific, meticulous textual comparisons between a variety of epic chronistic and balladic texts" (p.57). Not being an "individu-

---

[2] J. S. Miletich, "Folk literature, related forms, and the making of the Poema de Mio Cid," La Corónica 15, 1987, 187-96.

[3] I am sufficiently aware of the ballad as a living "performance" genre to have performed some of the translations myself in Liverpool folk-clubs (where even the translations definitely turn out to "vivir en variantes"). It was this active interest, and the work on my edition, that inspired the article in *La Corónica*, and not, as Professor Armistead deduced, the passing comments made in my *Late Latin and Early Romance*, pp.231-33. [The *Critical Guide* (London, Grant and Cutler) mentioned in the article had been "in press" since 1984; it eventually escaped in 1991.]

alist" (not in the sense intended, at least), it is naturally not up to me to respond to this invitation. The rest of this article follows that train of thought, though, with reference to the years before 1247.

Professor Armistead states clearly and correctly that "epic poetry cannot be dissociated from the *Romancero*. Both genres are inextricably and genetically connected: the same meter, the same formulas, the same style, the same narrative themes. They are part of a single multisecular traditional process" (p.65). So much so that it is worth considering if it might be best to regard them as being the same genre. The words used to describe them (at least before 1400) seem not to make a generic distinction. This may be a special case of the situation where a clear metatheoretical distinction made by subsequent scholars was not felt at the time by the people concerned (as with Latin and Romance in Spain in the twelfth century).[4] If modern critics specializing in both genres, and of all labels, agree that on balance it is probable that both what we now call epics and what we now call ballads existed in the period 1100-1250, then considering them both as subsets of the wider genre of assonating oral octosyllables might well be illuminating. It has long been fashionable to assess Spanish ballads in the light of what we think we already know about Spanish epics, although only the unfortunately named "historical" ballads have been claimed to have a close connection, being often said to derive from epic fragments. Even then, these claims are made for the reconstructed rather than for the attested epic genre other than the *Mocedades de Rodrigo*. My original article was prepared without the benefit of reading the excellent study of this latter question by Thomas Montgomery, in which he argued that ballads of some kind must in fact have preceded the composition of the *Mocedades de Rodrigo*; this line of thought suggests that the later attested ballads derive from those earlier ballads rather than from the *Mocedades*.[5]

---

[4] For further elucidation of this idea, see many of the studies collected in Wright (ed., 1991 ; in particular that by Janson); and Wright (1993).

[5] T. Montgomery, "Las *Mocedades de Rodrigo* y los romances," *Josep Maria Solà-Solé: Homage, Homenaje, Homenatge*, Barcelona, Puvill, 1985, 119-33. Montgomery has been called "oralist." I am, as a matter of unavoidable fact, "British." And yet we agree on this!

In the present article the intention is to invert the perspective, and consider whether the probable existence of the ballad genre in the twelfth century can help us understand some of the characteristics of the *Poema de Mio Cid*. My view of the chronology of the *Poema* is still that "even if c.1140 is right as an approximate date of composition, it is unlikely to be right as the date of its first being written down...the existence of poems on the Cid in the" [12th] "century seems assured" (*Late Latin and Early Romance*, pp.231-33). Such poems might well have been octosyllabic. This is not necessarily to claim that the *Poema* itself (in its surviving version) is simply one long ballad or sequence of ballads, but that such shorter twelfth-century poems could well have been among the twelfth-century material available to whoever compiled the *Poema* as extant, however and whenever that happened; cp. Montgomery, "el poema" [de Mio Cid] "es de carácter mixto, y que si tiene autor o autores, en el sentido moderno de esa palabra, ellos se basaron en formas y materias preexistentes" (p.133). If so, the themes and attitudes of the contemporary ballads might have helped mould the nature of the *Poema* that survived.

The ballads whose twelfth-century existence seems now to be least controversial are the non-historical ones (such as *Fontefrida*). This is perhaps mildly surprising, since the existence at that time of early versions of what we now call the "historical" ballads seems likely. The ballads now called "Carolingian" are perhaps the least likely to have been in existence in twelfth-century Spain, but even in this case we know (e.g. from the *Poema de Almería*, 229-30)[6] that some of the stories were in circulation, presumably oral and unwritten, and there was no reason why a singer of that time should have felt unable to fit the themes into an octosyllabic mode. The *Roncesvalles* fragment, tantalizing as it is, might have had unwritten precursors, of a length which we cannot now determine. The *Bernardo del Carpio* episodes originally presupposed in their audience some knowledge of French tales set at that time, and although eventually the part of the tale that survives in attested

---

[6] Referring to the edition and line-numbering of Juan Gil, "Carmen de Expugnatione Almariae Urbis," *Habis* 5, 1974, 45-64.

ballads concerns his birth and inheritance, in the twelfth century the anti-French element appears to have been thematically important (as we can tell from the *Historia Silense*). Tales about Rodrigo, the last King of the Visigoths, are likely to have existed in some popular unwritten form, in which the geopolitical invasion has already turned into a personalized tale of lust and revenge. The real Fernán González and the Infantes de Lara also predate the twelfth century and seem reasonable candidates for being themes of octosyllabic verse then also, sometimes in a form that modern scholars might be prepared to call "romance"; unless we are still to believe that whenever they "chose to sing in octosyllabic form, they were never able to stop until they had sung for well over three hours or so" (Wright, p.252). However, for some reason the idea that ballads on these historical themes can necessarily only post-date their reconstructed "epic congeners," rather than also being a possible part of the postulated epic's source material (in a form ancestral to their later attestations) is an idea so wearisome to attempt to dislodge (cp. Armistead's n.26), that I shall not do so.

The following suggestions therefore concern mainly the ballads of Love and Adventure (sometimes called "novelescos"), many of which are, apparently by common modern consent, ancient in origin (although as unattested from the twelfth century as all other octosyllables). Naturally, we do not wish to imply that ballads discussed existed in the twelfth century in exactly their attested sixteenth-century form. Indeed, since the sixteenth-century collectors were far more interested in the "historical" ballads, some of the best known "novelesque" ballads were not actually attested in written form until the nineteenth or even the twentieth century. Many of those could well be in origin very old also. If so, as Jesús Cid argued,[7] the distorting effect of early printed versions can mean that recently-collected versions of ballads unattested in the sixteenth century may be closer to their early mediaeval versions than are the written attestations of those that did indeed catch the

---

[7] Jesús Antonio Cid, "Recolección moderna y teoría moderna de la transmisión oral; *El Traidor Marquillos,* cuatro siglos de vida latente," in *El Romancero Hoy: Nuevas Fronteras,* ed A. Sánchez Romeralo, D. Catalán and S. G. Armistead, Madrid, Gredos, 1979, 281-359.

eye of collectors four centuries ago.

"The themes of the ballads that are most appreciated nowadays deal with universally interesting emotions such as love, sex, duty, honor, horror and poetic justice" (Wright, *Spanish Ballads*, pp.vii-viii). These are also characteristics of the fictional parts of the *Poema de Mio Cid*. Even though the fashion for composing ballads on contemporary events has waned since the capture of Granada (although not disappeared entirely), these universal emotions probably held for twelfth-century audiences and singers as well. We can be reasonably sure that there were such singers: the only doubt concerns whether their repertoire included shortish octosyllables. Nowadays the genre is most commonly found in the mouths of women. Maybe this was always so. Certainly the genre nowadays mostly concerns the adventures of women. The women in the ballads are almost all more warm, human, intelligent, caring, enterprising and interesting than the men, which is probably both the cause and the result of the fact that it is usually women who sing them. It is tempting to agree with the feminist interpretation that in this way many ballads are implicitly subversive of traditional male authority in Spanish society (there is an excellent article by Teresa Catarella presenting this view, currently in press with the *Bulletin of Hispanic Studies*). That is one aspect of the ballad tradition that can hardly have appealed to those who were preparing a long performance exalting a male hero; and yet Alan Deyermond is arguing that Spain is an exception to the general rule that epic is men's poetry (on the grounds that most reconstructable epics are centrally concerned with sex).[8] The logic of this argument may not be entirely watertight; but the characteristics that Deyermond highlights are also central to the *Romancero*.

What are the most obvious fictional elements in the *Poema de Mio Cid*? Most notably, the marriages between the Cid's daughters and the Infantes de Carrión, and their violent dissolution. In the *Poema* the purpose of these episodes is usually not described as lying in the need for love interest so much as a plot mechanism, the

---

[8] A. D. Deyermond, "La sexualidad en la épica medieval española," *Nueva Revista de Filologia Española*, 36, 1988, 767-86.

means of the hero's final vindication. Even so, the provision of husbands for the Cid's daughters is parallelled by the invention of fictional relationships between the sexes in most ballad novelizations. Such an invention probably ensured the survival of the Rey Rodrigo figure in the tradition; Julián may have existed, and may have had a daughter at Rodrigo's court, conceivably, and she may perhaps have indeed been raped, but it is inconceivable that this could have been the cause of the actual Moslem invasion as in *En Ceuta está Don Julián* (M4 W28).[9] What seems to be the only currently surviving Cid-based ballad, *Helo helo por do viene* (M55 W50), probably survives only because of its reliance on an invented obsession felt by Búcar for one of the Cid's daughters. The lecherous archpriest in the Fernán González tale (as in *Preso está Fernán González*, M5) has a similar function there, whether fictional or not. The tale of the *Siete Infantes de Lara* depends organically on a scene where a Moorish princess takes the sexual initiative (as Deyermond stresses). Such an aspect seems necessary for any originally "historical" tale to survive in genuine oral tradition.

The marriage in the *Poema de Mio Cid* is set in motion in the same way as the Cid's own marriage is in the *Mocedades de Rodrigo* (371-81, 426-38) and its attendant ballads; the Infantes de Carrión ask the King (Alfonso) to arrange their marriage and the King agrees, as a conciliatory sign of his favor to both sides (1879-1906); Ximena asks the King (Fernando) to arrange the marriage with Rodrigo and the King agrees, to avoid open civil war, a conciliatory sign of his favor to both sides. Montgomery points out that such a plot device seems to be Pan-Indo-European (pp.121-23), even though arranged marriages were also a common method of

---

[9] See the probably over-credulous article by A. M. Howell, "Some notes on early treaties between Muslims and Visigothic rulers of Al-Andalús," *Actas del I Congreso de Historia de Andalucía: Andalucía Medieval*, Tomo I, Córdoba, Monte de Piedad, 1978, 3-14. References in the present article are (M) to their number in M. Menéndez y Pelayo, *Antología de Poetas Líricos Castellanos*, Vols VIII and IX: *Primavera y Flor de Romances* (Madrid, Biblioteca Clásica, 1899), and (M,X) to Vol. X: *Romances Populares Recogidas de la Tradición Oral* (1900); and (W) to their number in my bilingual edition.

cementing conciliatory alliances in real life.

Modern commentators agree that the Cid's attitude to his daughters is that of a loving and honourable father and family man. It is also that of a noble figure concerned about his own descent and dynasty, as the final comment in the *Poema* emphasizes ("oy los rreyes d'España sus parientes son," 3724). This is a common "novelesque" ballad theme. Many ballads in the ancient tradition tell of a princess whose love life worries her father, the King. This concern is not mere parental interference, for it was (in real life) part of a King's duty at the time to ensure a peaceful and prosperous hereditary continuation of his line. Thus a princess's love-life was of direct political importance, given the diplomatic salience of marriages used to cement alliances. The final argument used by Princess Claraniña in her appeal to save the life of Conde Claros is that his death would cause a civil war; "sus amigos y parientes / todos te querrian mal / revolver te hian guerra / tus reynos se perderán" (*Media noche era por filo*, M190 W9:385-88). The King there, hearing this, at last lets his love for his daughter override what he sees as his duty (to punish her unauthorized lover), and when it is seen that the two love each other after all a conciliatory wedding is arranged. The King in the *Gerineldos* tale reacts the same way (*Gerineldos, Gerineldos*, M,X p.161, W3). The plot of the *Poema* could hardly be contrived to include an exactly similar feature, but there is a variation on that theme, to which the final weddings are a similarly successful conclusion; in this case the men concerned are indeed villains, making love to their wives[10] and then abandoning them in pain, so the Cid fulfils his thematic role by engineering the dissolution of those marriages (which he had never wished for) and, in due course, having them married into politically more suitable families. The Cid is motivated as much by dynastic duty as by fatherly love, like the ballad King-fathers. In addition, the whole impetus and resolution of the Afrenta de Corpes episode exemplifies the "poetic justice" that is so noticeably absent from real life and thus seems so desirable in fiction (including the

---

[10] Perhaps for the first time, since their role as figures of fun at Valencia seems to be based on their supposed impotence as much as their cowardice in face of the lion.

Romancero). In short, the Infantes's marriages to the Cid's daughters, and the ensuing consequences, introduce into the tale, insofar as it can be made to seem congruous, those elements which permeate the ballad tradition in general: "love, sex, duty, honour, horror and poetic justice." If the ballad tradition existed in the twelfth century, in a novelesque tradition not too dissimilar from that subsequently attested, the existence of that tradition could explain why these elements turn up in the adapted life of Rodrigo as presented in the surviving version of the *Poema*. Not merely because they fit into generalized folk-tale schemata, but for specifically contextual Hispanic reasons.

Other common ballad themes can also lead us to see echoes in the *Poema*. The Cid acquires the "King as father" role, but there is also, of course, a genuine King in the *Poema*. Kings in ballads often have the role of being basically honourable but badly advised at the start, seeing sense at the end. This applies not only to the Kings in *Conde Claros* and *Gerineldos*, but to many others. The King who condemned the *Prisoner* to prison (*Por el mes era de mayo*, M114a W5) releases him when he hears his lament; the King who condemned Virgil to prison in *Virgil and the Virgin* (*Mandó el rey prender Virgilios*, M111 W24), then forgot about him, only to be reminded and to release him seven years later—whereupon the former Virgin marries Virgil cheerfully at the end, to tie in with that cliché also—; the King who exiles Rodrigo in the *Poema* is similarly eventually persuaded that Rodrigo is an honourable vassal and reinstates him handsomely at the end. This common ballad theme might well have provided some of the inspiration for this fictional aspect of the *Poema*, for (as West and others have shown[11]) it certainly has no source in the character of either the real Alfonso or the real Rodrigo. This theme of the reinstatement of a punished hero is also closely allied to the common ballad theme of a lost or

---

[11] G. West delivered an excellent paper [still unpublished in 1994], at the 1987 meeting of the Association of Hispanists of Great Britain and Ireland, entitled "The Cid and Alfonso VI revisited: characterization in the Cantar de Mio Cid," to which I here acknowledge a debt. See also his "Hero or Saint? Hagiographic elements in the Life of the Cid," *Journal of Hispanic Philology*, 7, 1983, 87-105.

maliciously enchanted hero returning from some kind of exile, as exemplified in those versions of *Espinelo* in which at the end Espinelo returns to his original kingdom,[12] in *a caçar va el caballero* (M151 W19), in the many variants of the Husband's return (e.g. M156 W22; M,X p.83, W23), and in the long versions of *Arnaldos* (*Quien hubiese tal ventura*, W20, which I take to be no less ancient than the more famous short ones, for reasons recounted in my *Spanish Ballads*, pp.162-66). This theme of the return to favor is basic to the structure of the *Poema*, where Rodrigo is at the end partly equated with royalty, but not to real life, in which Rodrigo died in 1099 having been out of favor with Alfonso VI again since before the capture of Valencia (1094).

These are all "motifs." Not all the motifs come from the ballad tradition, naturally. Other motifs, as several scholars have pointed out, come from sources other than preexisting oral octosyllabic verse; Visigothic Saints' lives, for example, have been seen by West[13] as inspiring the presentation of Rodrigo's resigned attitude to the initial exile and calm sadness at leaving. (The fact that the written versions of these Lives seem to us to be in "Latin" rather than "Spanish" is no bar to such Saints' Lives having popular influence on an oral genre at a time when the subsequently established Latin-Romance distinction was not felt to exist—that is, before the thirteenth century[14]). All people in the *Poema* are given characters to suit the motif they happen to be personifying at the time. So the King is sufficiently weak to be swayed by the Leonese nobles into sending Rodrigo into exile, as is required by the plot at the start (assuming the lacuna),[15] but also sufficiently strong for his authority to be unquestioned when he summons all his vassals, including the same Leonese, to the Cortes at Toledo (2975-84), as is required by

---

[12] Discussed by D. Catalán, "El romancero medieval," in *El Comentario de Textos, 4: La Poesía Medieval*, Madrid, Castalia, 1983, 451-89.

[13] Respectively the *Vita Aemiliani* (San Millán) of Braulio of Zaragoza and Bishop Masona's exile by King Leovigild in the *Vitas Sanctorum Patrum Emeritensium*.

[14] Cp. note 4 above.

[15] S. Armistead, "The initial verses of the *Cantar de mio Cid*," *La Corónica* 12, 1984, 178-86.

the plot there. Rodrigo himself acts towards Raquel and Vidas, and the Count of Barcelona, in a way that strikes at least some modern readers as inconsistent with his image in the second and third *cantares*. These two episodes are both easily analysable as variants on ballad themes, both themes being conveniently exemplified in the ballad of Rico Franco (*A caça yvan, a caça*, M119 W4). Rico Franco is "franco," i.e. from the Corona de Aragón, and (like the Count in the *Poema*) is humbled by a Castilian opponent that he thought he could easily humiliate; the Princess kills Rico Franco with his own dagger, as *Melisenda* kills Hernandillo with his (*todas las gentes dormían*, M198 W18), as the knight kills Gallarda with hers (*Estábase la Gayarda*, M,X p.124, W26), as several girls attacked by potential rapists do in nineteenth-century ballads collected by Menéndez y Pelayo (M,X:34-37), and—mutatis mutandis—as Rodrigo tricks the moneylenders through exploiting their greed in the same way as the moneylenders had hoped to profit from Rodrigo by charging interest, usury being thought to be at best deceit and at worst as bad a sin as attempted rape (Dante classed bankers in the same *bolgia* of Hell as homosexuals). This applies whether or not the tale ultimately has an Oriental origin. In such episodes the characters concerned have the nature that suits the motif. The *Poema* has a unity, of course, but it can also be analysed partly in terms of a succession of separate motifs.[16] The consistency and development of characterization that the novels of the last century have led us to look for in fiction, and which has even clouded the vision of historians marshalling historical facts, is not there in the *Poema*, in the same way as it is largely absent from real life (being a fiction).[17] Separate ballad motifs can be unconnected or inconsistent with each other while still coexisting in a longer work based in part on more than one of them, and to that extent my argument has mellowed slightly (since the 1986 article) from its scepticism as to the existence of some of the postulated lost epics on the grounds of inconsistent characterization. I share Professor Armistead's admira-

---

[16] The suggestion is not being made here that each *tirada* is a separate ballad.

[17] And from the historical development of languages; see Wright (1983).

tion for Father Ong's *Orality and Literacy* (London, 1982), including Ong's view that "logic itself emerges from the technology of writing" (p.172) and is therefore not to be expected in an oral genre.[18] My first conclusion in this present article, then, is that the *Poema* is so much moulded by preexisting features of the ballad genre that we might reasonably see it as a related part of that genre.

Brian Powell recently concluded that "short compositions would be the best explanation for various stories and other references concerning the Cid that predate the PMC"; more specifically that there was a brief one which "ended with, or shortly after, the departure from Burgos of the Cid and his followers" (p.350).[19] The final part of his life was probably also celebrated; if there were in existence several octosyllabic songs on Rodrigo, or even oral compositions in other forms, some of them seem to have been connected with the Cid's rule of and death in Valencia, as we can see from the *Poema de Almería*: "Ipse Rodericus, Meo Cidi sepe vocatus, / de quo cantatur quod ab hostibus haud superatur...Morte Roderici Valentia plangit amici" (233-34, 239).[20] The latter comment (on Valencia's mourning of Rodrigo's death) is unconnected with the *Poema*, however, so if that is part of a song it is part of a different one.

At this point, Professor Armistead's invitation to study ballad, epic and chronicle together is accepted, in connection with the most impressive of the Pre-Alfonsine chronicles. For Ximénez de Rada's *De Rebus Hispaniae* (written in the 1240s) presents us with a further puzzle. Why has the best educated writer of the age not apparently heard, nor heard of, the *Poema de Mio Cid*? I mentioned in passing (in the 1986 article) Ximénez de Rada's references to the Cid, and it is opportune to clarify here why they are of interest. For example, he has heard that Rodrigo captured a Count of Barcelona, but he misidentifies the Count as being Peter of Aragón:

---

[18] Note that Ong confirms that ballad "cycles" are not normally performed complete, all at the same performance (p.146).

[19] B. Powell, "The opening lines of the *Poema de Mio Cid* and the *Crónica de Castilla*," *Modern Language Review*, 83, 1988, 342-50 (cp. also Armistead, *op.cit.* in n.15).

[20] See n.6 above.

> Hic est Petrus qui in bello postmodum a Roderici Didaci fuit captus, sed hostis clementia continuo liberatus (VI.2)[21]; cumque versus frontariam Aragoniae pervenisset, congressus cum Rege Petro Aragoniae, obtinuit contra eum, et etiam vivum cepit, sed continuo manumisit (VI.28);

whereupon Rodrigo goes straight on to Valencia (see below). Lucas of Tuy, in the 1230s, also thought it was Peter; Lucas can hardly be Ximénez's source here, though, since all he says is:

> eodem tempore Rodericus Didaci miles strenuus pugnavit cum Petro Rege Aragonum in campo, & cepit eum (p.101, 11.5-6).

On the other hand the *Poema*, as it stands, mentions the Count almost correctly by name: "El Conde Don Remont" (975, 987, 1009, 1028, 1059, 1066) and "Rremont Verenguel" (998). He was in fact called Berenguer Ramon II in real life, "Berengarius" in the *Historia Roderici*,[22] and given his title but no name in the *Carmen Campi Doctoris* 1.93,[23] "Marchio namque comes Barchinone." Collectively, this seems to suggest that Lucas of Tuy and Ximénez de Rada had heard of the capture, but neither in its Castilian epic form nor in its Eastern form. Why not? The suggestion that the source is a brief oral version that fails to mention the Count's name is as plausible

---

[21] Lucas of Tuy, *Chronicon Mundi*, = Andreas Schott, *Hispaniae Illustratae*, vol.IV, Frankfurt, 1608, pp.1-116; Rodericus Ximenius de Rada, *Opera*, reprinted by M. D. Cabanes Pecourt, Valencia, Anúbar, 1968 (indispensable also to see D. W. Lomax, "Rodrigo Jiménez de Rada como historiador," *Actas del Quinto Congreso Internacional de Hispanistas*, Bordeaux, 1977, Vol.II, pp.587-92). References to the *Chronica Najerensis* are to the edition by A. Ubieto Arteta (Zaragoza, Anúbar, 2nd ed. 1985); cp. also W. J. Entwistle, "On the *Carmen de Morte Sanctii Regis*," *Bulletin Hispanique*, 30, 1928, 204-19; C. Reig, *El Cantar de Sancho II y Cerco de Zamora*, Madrid, CSIC, 1947, pp.31-36.

[22] R. Menéndez Pidal, *La España del Cid*, 4th ed., 1947, p.922 1.20 - p.923 1.12 and p.925 1.6.

[23] In my edition (Wright 1979) I translated this as "The Marquis-Count of Barcelona," and suggested that parading the titles is meant there to be slightly sarcastic.

as any.

There are just three references in Ximénez de Rada to Rodrigo's relationship with Sancho.

> 1. Erat autem cum Rege Sancio miles strenuus, dictus Rodericus Didaci Campiator. Hic Regem suum devictum animans persuasit, ut quoad posset, fugientem exercitum revocaret, et in aurora Legionensibus et Gallaecis improvidis adveniret (VI.15).

Lucas of Tuy also referred to this episode (the battle of Golpejera in 1071), but can hardly be Rodrigo's source:

> Sed in illis diebus surrexerat miles quidam nomine Rodericus Didaci armis strenuus, qui in omnibus suis agendis extitit victor. Hic cum iam esset magni nominis Regem Sancium adhortatus est, dicens: Ecce, inquit, Gallaeci cum fratre tuo Rege Adefonso post hodiernam victoriam quiescunt securi in tentoriis nostris. Irruamus igitur super eos primo mane illucescente die, & obtinebimus ex eis victoriam. Rex Sancius acquievit consiliis eius, et...

Both seem to be basing their account on the same tale, which does not subsequently survive as a ballad (but could have been one then). The battle of Golpejera, and the conversations Rodrigo and Sancho had during it, has a much larger starring role in the *Cronica Najerense* III.34-36, and Entwistle (p.208) suggested a poetic source for these chapters; yet even Entwistle was unable to "reconstruct" a Latin one here, so if it existed it could well have been (vernacular) octosyllabic.

Ximénez's other references could well have contemporary ballads as their inspiration:

> 2. Verum Rodericus Didaci Campiator zelo domini interfecti eum prosequitur sine mora, et fere in ipsa urbis ianua interfecit, sed velocitatem Bellidii non potuit praevenire. (VI.18)

This account is essentially a summary of *De Çamora sale Dolfos*, lines 65-76 (M46 W45). (There is no need to argue that the version printed by Escobar was exactly the same as that known to Ximénez de Rada). The *Cronica Najerense* also refers to Vellido's escape, in words that seem once again to rule out its being Ximénez's source, although based on the same tale. (Entwistle's proposal that the source was a Latin hexameter poem, which he even "reconstructed," is hard to take seriously, even though it still has devoted adherents: see *Late Latin* p.230).

> 3. Sed cum nemo vellet ab eo recipere iuramentum, ad recipiendum se obtulit solus Rodericus Didaci Campiator. Unde et postea licet strenuus, non fuit in eius oculis gratiosus. (VI.20)

It is possible that, in this case, Rodrigo might just be summarizing Lucas:

> Post haec Castellani nobiles, & Pampilonenses, cum nullus esset sibi de genere regali, quem dominum possent habere, venientes ad Regem Adefonsum, eum Regem fecerunt, hac tamen conditione interposita, ut prius iuraret, quod nunquam fuerat in consilio mortis Regis Sancii fratris sui. Cumque nullus esset, qui iuramentum à Rege auderet accipere, suprafatus Rodericus Didaci strenuus miles iuramentum à Rege accepit. Quapropter Rex Adefonsus semper habuit eum exosum. (p.100, 11.6-11)

This is essentially *En Toledo estava Alfonso*, lines 33-90 (M51 W47) (the final comment in both historians' accounts having no counterpart in the (now) better known *En Santa Gadea de Burgos*, M52 W48). And even if Ximénez is merely summarizing Lucas, what is Lucas's account based on?

The usual answer would be that they knew an epic on the siege of Zamora, roughly as its reconstructability from later chronicles (in reformed "vernacular" spelling) leads many modern scholars to think it might have been then; but if so, they left an extraordinarily large amount of material out. If, on the other hand, they had heard a few shorter compositions (ballads), the brevity of their few references to Rodrigo at Zamora is more explicable.

Ximénez de Rada's *De Rebus Hispaniae* Book IV, Chapter XXVIII (quoted previously) continues as follows:

> Et inde procedens, pervenit Valentiam, et obsedit. Cumque ad succursum Valentiae Buchar Rex Arabum cum exercitu advenisset, inito certamine, obtinuit Rodericus, et Buchar fugit vix vitae relictus, caesa tamen ex suis multitudine infinita. Et in continenti civitas se reddidit Roderico, et eam habuit, quoad vixit, et fuit in ea Hieronymus de quo diximus, in Episcopum consecratus à domino Bernardo Primate Archiepiscopo Toletano. Sed postea mortuo Roderico Didaci, fuit civitas iterum ab Arabibus occupata. Corpus autem Roderici Didaci inter insultus Arabum fuit à suis fideliter et strenue deportatum ad monasterium Sancti Petri de Cardigna, ubi hodie etiam quiescit humatum.

Lucas merely said (continuing from his comment on Peter of Aragon quoted above):

> Post haec obsedit Valentiam, & cepit eam. Deinde vicit barbarorum Regem Buchar & interfecit multa millia Sarracenorum. (p.101, ll.7-8)

These accounts seem to have no connection at all with the *Poema*. Explicitly in Ximénez, and implicitly in Lucas, Búcar escapes with his life, as he does in the ballad *Helo, helo por do viene* (M55 W50:73-75). In the *Poema*, however Búcar is cut in half vertically:

> cortól' el yelmo e, librado todo lo al,
> fata la cintura el espada llegado ha. (2423-24).

Not surprisingly, this kills him. Ximénez says that Valencia surrendered to Rodrigo after the failure of Búcar's expedition, but in the *Poema* Rodrigo has been in Valencia for a long time already (since 1.1212). Bishop Jerome, both here and briefly in VI.26, is mentioned by Ximénez as having been appointed by Bernard de Sédirac, Ximénez's distant precursor in the Archbishopric of Toledo; which is true, and would be known independently to to Ximénez de Rada (who studied well his own archives) but is not the point as presented in the *Poema*. Here the appointment is presented as Rodrigo's own initiative:

En tierras de Valencia fer quiero obispado
e dárgelo a este buen cristiano (1300-01)

and the appointer is merely allotted a generic third person plural:

A este don Jerónimo yal'otorgan por obispo,
diéronle en Valencia ó bien puede estar rrico (1303-04)

Then the rest of Ximénez's account (in VI.28) concerns events following Rodrigo's death, events not mentioned in the *Poema* (it would not be reasonable to postulate a lacuna at the end of the *Poema* as we can at the start). Ximénez's only mention of Rodrigo in his *Historia Arabum* is similar, appearing during a narrative concerning Valencia:

postea cepit eam Rodericus Didaci Campiator, et eo mortuo, eam Almoravides occuparunt (ch.49).

The marriage of the Cid's elder daughter Cristina (= the Elvira of the *Poema*) to Ramiro, Prince of Navarra, probably in 1098, is mentioned by Ximénez (*De Rebus*, V.24) during his account of the development of the Navarrese dynasty after the death in 1035 of Sancho the Great:

...Ranimirum Infantem, qui Ranimirus duxit uxorem filiam Roderici Didaci, cum Valentiae morabatur...

but the *Poema* itself cannot even be the direct source of this detail either, for (in its surviving version) it does not mention the Prince's name; the two suitors are merely "los de Navarra e de Aragon" (1.3717). And there remains the perennially startling fact that unlike the *Poema de Almería* of 100 years before (c.1147), Ximénez de Rada consistently fails to call Rodrigo "Cid."

In short, Ximénez de Rada almost certainly did not know the *Poema*, but he did know about Rodrigo, including some (probably fictional) details that happen to be attested on paper later in ballad and chronicle (and in this century in reconstructed "lost epics"). This suggests that ballads or ballad-like compositions about Rodrigo, in part perhaps connected with part of the oral tradition that preceded or underlay the *Poema* but in large part not, could well have existed in the 1240s; that is, the second conclusion of this article is that a genre whose existence at that time I suggested was "plausible" and Professor Armistead said was "undoubted" (during our supposed "controversy"), although not specifically with reference to tales about Rodrigo Díaz, may in general have been better known than the *Poema*.[24]

Since not even the "British" seriously wish to argue that the surviving *Poema de Mio Cid* was elaborated on the basis of the Alfonsine chronicles (even though some ballads are still cheerfully supposed by all to have been taken from the *Primera Cronica General*, Pedro del Corral, and Ocampo), the absence of the *Poema*'s influence from the *De Rebus Hispaniae* and the *Chronicon Mundi* cannot seriously be taken to prove that the *Poema* did not exist at that time. It might, perhaps, suggest that it was not known at Toledo or in Galicia (in the form in which it survives). Other series of ballads, or isolated ballads, starring Rodrigo Díaz probably existed in the twelfth and thirteenth centuries, and, if so, their reconstructable characteristics could perhaps form part (only part, of course) of the explanation of why the *Poema*, broadly speaking in the same genre, is as it is. In *Late Latin* (p.231) I pointed out that "there seem, in effect, to be at least five surviving strands of material deriving from him, each including material not included elsewhere"; that is, the Castilian historiography (including for these purposes the *Poema de Almería*), the Eastern historiography (including for these purposes the *Carmen Campi Doctoris*), the Zamora tales, the *Mocedades* tales, and the *Poema* itself. But it has occurred to me, since writing that, that the strands may not be all unconnected. In particular, the most surprising aspect of Rodrigo's

---

[24] There is no other reference to the Cid in Lucas of Tuy other than the three sections quoted above (98.7-12, 100.6-11, 101.5-8). Ximénez's only reference to him other than those quoted here is his first (v.1): "Didacus Flavini duxit uxorem filiam Roderici Alvari de Asturiis, viri nobilis et magnatis, et ex ea genuit Rodericum Didaci, qui dictus fuit Campiator." There is no other reference in the *Chronica Najerense* either, probably composed soon after 1174.

presentation in the *Poema*, surprising, that is, to a reader or listener more used to Rodrigo's personality as presented in the ballad tradition, is the central stress on his "mesura," level-headedness, which is allied to his loyalty to the King and to Ximena. This is in any event an unusual characteristic in "epic" heroes as a whole. In the ballad tradition as we know it from later attestations (and hence as it is in essence reconstructable for the twelfth and thirteenth centuries) this "mesura" is quite the opposite of the Cid's character. In ballads he is rash, rude, impetuous, independent. In the *Santa Gadea* tales he insults King Alfonso; in the *Mocedades* tales he insults King Fernando and even the Pope (as in the ballad *A Concilio dentro en Roma*, M34 W49); in the Zamora tales he offers to commit adultery with Urraca (*A fuera, a fuera, Rodrigo*, M37 W41); he only behaves like a respectful vassal towards Sancho after Sancho's death (in the latter part of *De Çamora sale Dolfos* and the *Santa Gadea* tales). Given that—for the purposes of our present discussion—it is not unreasonable to postulate at least some of these tales as existing in oral form in the later twelfth century, perhaps widely known, then Rodrigo's remarkable restraint and calmness and loyalty to wife and King in the *Poema* are all the more striking.

So, after my two conclusions, here is a serious suggestion. Could the "*mesurado* vassal" image have been presented in the *Poema* consciously in order to counteract the "rebellious brat" image that was already at that time threatening to dominate the Castilians' perception of their national hero?[25]

---

[25] Senior Castilians (including Archbishop Ximénez de Rada and Alfonso X) would prefer their national hero to be a John Wayne rather than a John McEnroe. The above suggestion is intended to be complementary, rather than antagonistic, to the other possible motivations that have been suggested for the *Poema*'s presentation in the form we have; such as the desires to advocate legal redress (Roman) over private vengeance (Germanic), to exalt Castille over León, to insult the inhabitants of Carrión, to attract tourists to the Cid's tomb-cult, to encourage recruits for the expedition eventually victorious at Las Navas de Tolosa, to mark Alfonso's initial Cortes in Toledo in 1207, to counterpoint the marriage of Alfonso VIII's daughter, to copy French epics, etc, or even—as is still occasionally

1994 POSTSCRIPT

Most of this article first appeared in *La Corónica* 18, no.2, 1990, 21-38. Unfortunately, it was largely unintelligible, since a complete page of typescript was omitted from the printed version (at p.26); this page was printed in *La Corónica* 19, no.2, 1991, xiii-xiv. I should also have acknowledged Brian Powell's *Epic and Chronicle: the Poema de mio Cid and the Cronica de veinte reyes*, London, MHRA, 1983, for insights concerning Ximénez de Rada's mentions of Rodrigo Díaz. Teresa Catarella's article is now out: "Feminine historicizing in the *romancero novelesco*," BHS, 57, 1990, 331-43. The article on similar lines by John K. Walsh, "Performance in the Poema de Mio Cid," *Romance Philology* 44, 1990, 1-25, came out too late for reference here, or it would have had a starring role in the notes.

---

suggested—the desire to create a satisfying literary work. Multiple causation can be as respectable in literary origins as Yakov Malkiel has taught us that it is in etymology; in oral literature particularly, where multiple authors can exploit the original composition, but even a learned individual can feel multiple stimuli.

21
The Theatrical Nature of the 'Novelesque' Ballads

For the listeners, the Spanish ballads that are usually called 'novelesque' are dependent on the context of performance alone. Those ballads that formed part of a cycle depend, for their effectiveness, on a knowledge, however fragmentary, of that cycle and its context. But nowadays people know very little either about the cycles or the history that gave rise to them in the first place, and even those modern ballads that seem to have survived from a wider context are now uprooted, deprived of their original *raison d'être*, appearing as isolated, as individual, as novelesque, as the ones which have probably always been in that situation. This is what has happened, for example, to the ballad of El Cid and Búcar, ¡*Helo, helo, por do viene!*[1] which lost its original links with other ballads and episodes, to gain other more stereotyped resonances that lead it now to be one of the most archetypically novelesque. The present day ballads that are still available to be recorded include several of this general type (princess plus lover), but almost none of the ones earlier characterizable as 'epic' or 'historical.' This means that nowadays, when to all intents and purposes the genre is always 'novelesque,' every time that a ballad is performed for others to listen to—which still happens, even now—the performer has to attract, encourage and seduce the listener with the ballad alone; (s)he has to lead us along the linear path of the plot, and present the facts in the most appropriate chronological

---

[1] I quote ballad versions as edited by Marcelino Menéndez y Pelayo, *Antología de poetas líricos castellanos*, vols VIII, IX y X (Madrid, Biblioteca Clásica, 1899-1900 (= MP)). This is MP 55.

sequence to get us to react appropriately, feel the most suitable emotions (including suspense), and identify in the right way with the participants. That is, the performer has to be at once playwright, director and several actors, and succeeds, if at all, when he creates an atmosphere of collaboration between the audience and himself as "juglar."

This theatrical and dramatic character of the ballads ought to be generally recognized; but perhaps it is not. Ballads collected nowadays are usually performed for the researcher's microphone, and although the specialist collectors have managed to find an impressive number (with a success that would have astonished the young Menéndez Pidal, for example), the use of the tape-recorder always runs the risk of spoiling the atmosphere, the directness of the emotions, the interaction between singer and listener, that make the genre entertaining in its normal context. There is on the whole nothing to be done about that; this comment is not meant to be critical of anyone. The same applies to all musical and dramatic genres; "live" concert recordings, however exciting for the original audience, tend not to have the same effect when the record is played out of that context, for we hear them in a less involved way. In recently-published collections of ballads we have the words, sometimes the music, occasionally a photo of the singer, from time to time a recording, but rarely the theatrical atmosphere which has contributed so much to the survival of the genre. When we read and study the written text of a play, we know we need to visualize the scene, the actors, the tones of voice, the effect that all these are supposed to have on the audience; and, above all, we know we need to read it slowly, following the same rhythm as a performance. Reading a play quickly, at the same speed as a novel, loses it. We are left with the plot, but little else. Yet the interesting features of a play are not normally to be found in the mere plot (if that had been the point, the author would have preferred to present the work in novel form). The point usually lies in the interactions that can be set up between the play and its audience, as it develops. The same can be said of ballad performances; furthermore, however well known a ballad is (as has often been observed) tension and suspense are often strong.

If we are not lucky enough to hear them live in a real context, we need, then, to read them slowly, with pauses, so we can envisage the effect that they can have on listeners, the range of emotions and reactions that they can arouse. As has often been pointed out, the center of interest in the Spanish ballads tends to lie in the emotions of the participants rather than the actual plot of the story, but it may not have been recognized before that this is true as a result of the theatricality inherent in the genre; because the genre's raison d'être depends on the listeners feeling for themselves the emotions of the participants of the drama being enacted. This explains the ballads much-observed reliance on "universal" emotions; so that they can be felt by all listeners, they need to be more or less universal (and timeless). That is why the themes that survive are those that involve such eternally interesting emotions as love, both psychological and physical, duty, honour, horror, and poetic justice. The emotions that interest a human audience most, of course, are those that arise from personal relations between men and women. The ballads most often heard today nearly always involve such relationships; we can see that this was also the case in the sixteenth century, when many ballad episodes derived from a source in medieval history (or pseudo-history), for in these also the emotional center is the same; the relationship (whatever we think it was) between El Cid and Urraca, for example, rather than the military details of the Siege of Zamora (MP 37). Success tends to be based on the relationship between the performer and the listener; that is why there is so much direct speech that can be acted out; that is why the music is (usually) so straightforward, since its only role is to provide the background structure; etc.

We can take as an example the long ballad that has been most studied, that of Conde Claros (*Medianoche era por filo*, MP 190). I shall quote the version from the *Silva de Romances* of Zaragoza, a version which we know was familiar to the Royal Court, and which—as Seeger argues—was probably composed there by a professional performer, who would then have been singing it to an intelligent and perceptive audience.[2] In those days, just as now, the

---

[2] *Silva de romances (Zaragoza, 1550-1551)*, ed. Antonio Rodríguez Moñino, Zaragoza, Publicaciones de la Cátedra, 1970; Judith Seeger, "The curious case of Conde Claros; a ballad in four traditions," *Journal of*

performer / actor / director of this ballad has to inspire a huge range of emotional reactions in the listeners. If he manages to do that, the performance will be a great success (and he will be exhausted).

At the start of the ballad the performer presents Conde Claros, suffering from the desire he feels for the Princess Clara Niña. When they at last meet, they greet each other: "¡Mantenga Dios a Tu Alteza!'/ "¡Conde Claros, bien vengáys!" (49-50: "God bless you, Your Highness!" "Count Claros, you re blest"). Here we have a moment of genuine potential tension; we do not yet know how the Princess is going to react, and the performer can (if he wants) prolong the moment with a pause, emphasize it with his tone of voice and posture, even act out both roles at once with facial expressions and gestures (this will depend in part on whether he is accompanying himself musically or not). Even when he is singing he can convey a great deal through tones of voice, as much in a ballad as in a play. Reading the ballad quickly, we may not notice this brief moment of theatrical tension; hearing it, we do. At once, he encourages us: "las palabras que prosigue / eran para enamorar" (51-52: "and she plays on his passion with what she says next"). There are wide opportunities for dramatic effect, of course, for the singer to take advantage of in the lines of mutual seduction that follow: "Conde Claros, Conde Claros / el Señor de Montalván,/ ¡cómo avéys hermoso cuerpo / para con moros lidiar!" (53-56: "You have, My Count Claros, My Lord Montalbán, a fine body for fighting with Moors, a fine man.")—with a slight pause at the end of line 55 he can communicate anything at all—and "mi cuerpo tengo, Señora / para con damas holgar" (59-60: "My body is best with women in bed"), up to the final words of this scene, "caça que tengo en la mano / nunca la puedo dexar" (89-90: "and a bird in the hand can't be let slip away"). By his performance, and the description of the sexual act itself (91-98), he pleases the audience; not just through their prurient interest, although in a large audience some are bound

---

Hispanic Philology, 12, 1988, 221-37; see also her superb analysis of a ballad she saw performed in Brazil on part of the same tale, in which she brings out vividly how theatrical it was (Judith Seeger, "The living ballad in Brazil: two performances," in Ruth H. Webber (ed.), *Hispanic Balladry Today*, New York, Garland, 1989, 175-217).

to react just on that level, but also because the emotions felt in love are the deepest. All the audience will have felt them, in fantasy if not in reality; the men will be identifying with the Count and the women with the Princess (particularly at a performance in the Royal Court). This ballad shows the tolerant, understanding and humane attitude to love and sex that is normal in the ballads as a whole, and which seems sensible to most people (even if it is sometimes best for them not to admit it).

This is not the end of the drama. It has hardly even begun. We have many more emotions to feel yet. Fear, straightaway, when the Count realizes that the huntsman was watching them (105-20), and anger when the huntsman refuses to keep quiet about it ("el caçador sin ventura," 121: "a curse on the huntsman"); this section is most effective at the end, with the repetition of the words that seemed on first appearance to be assuring us that this is a love story with a happy ending: "de la cintura abaxo / como hombre y mujer se han" (97-8 & 139-40: "from the waist downward joined woman with man"). These words, now performed with a different tone of voice and with different consequences in context, provide another chance to cause a shudder to run through the audience. The fury of the King, who believes this to be a case of rape, inspires horror in us, as he kills the huntsman who betrayed them, but we can also understand it: Kings, in this ballad as in the case of the father of the Princess who seduces Gerineldos, and in many others, are not mere busybodies interfering in the private lives of their daughters, because in their case the peace and happiness of the whole kingdom can depend on contracting a beneficial marriage (as the Princess herself recalls later, 363-88); thus here, as in all the best dramas, we see human beings in emotional conflict, and we can sympathise with them all. The presentation is thus theatrical rather than narrative or poetic or thematic. Later we are due to feel compassion for the Count as he is put in chains (155-62) and then prison (163-70); these were more lifelike misfortunes, of course, for everyone in a medieval audience than they would seem now. When so many people beg the King not to punish the Count, our sympathy and fear increase, and our understanding of the King's obstinacy decreases accordingly. This is really the moral to be drawn from the tale: that Kings should listen before deciding (a traditional moral; it was that of the *Libro de los engaños*; but it would have had a direct motivation if performed at court); and we experience this almost as participants ourselves.

The King decrees that rapists should die, a decision which might as a general remark appeal to those listening, both to the King and to the ballad, although we happen to know that this was in no sense an act of rape. At this point the Archbishop represents us, the listeners, as he goes down to the prison to speak to the Count: "las palabras que le dize / dolor eran de escuchar" (233-34: "it's painful to speak but still harder to listen"), for both the audience and the Count. The famous lines of the Archbishop, "que los yerros por amores / dignos son de perdonar" (237-38: "for mistakes made by lovers should be forgiven"), and the even more famous words of the Count, "quien no ama a las mugeres / no se puede hombre llamar" (253-54: "those who do not love women cannot be called men") are uttered in the hope of arousing applause; that is, they have a dramatic purpose rather than a merely thematic one. The words of the page (259-74) articulate the reaction that is required of the audience, deserving similar applause. This is why it was this part of the ballad that performers particularly enjoyed singing without introduction or dénouement (as in MP, Appendix 55), being its emotional and dramatic center, even though it hardly forwards the plot at all.

Next we have to share the despairing dignity of the Count (275-86), and the sadness of the page (287-92; the formulaic phrase "bien oyréys lo que dirá" (292), although it is a cliché, serves to remind the listeners that we are too are closely involved in this drama); the horror of the Princess (297-310), and inmediately her extreme desperation as she tries to get close to the Count in the crowd (saying that she would give up her own life to save his, 335-36); the anguish and uncertainty of his escort, and the disconcerted reaction of the King when he realizes that his daughter is prepared to sacrifice her life for the man he took to be her rapist. The highly histrionic emotions of the almost judicial dialogue between the King and the brave Princess are reminiscent of the lawcourt scene in the *Poema de Mio Cid*; within a theatrical genre, of necessity oral in nature, words directly performed by the singer will touch the audience more directly than any description from an omniscient narrator. The audience hold our breath for a minute while the King and his court consider what to do for the best, and release it with thankful applause when we hear the juglar sing that the King pardons them and blesses their marriage. The aim of everything that has happened between the mutual seduction scene and the marriage has been to give us an aesthetic experience of a theatrical type. This ballad could easily last for half an hour; the time depends largely on practical decisions taken by the performer; but there is nothing boring here, despite its using the same assonance throughout (in *á*) largely involving infinitives.

This may all be obvious. Diego Catalán, for example, in a recent study,[3] refers to the "concepción dramática de los romances tradicionales" ("the dramatic conception of the traditional ballads"), which "dramatizan la narración" ("dramatize the narration"), to motifs that only exist "en el nivel dramático" ("on the dramatic level"), and to the "narrativas poéticas dramatizadas del *Romancero*" ("poetic narratives dramatized in the Ballads")—I agree with all these comments, of course—but without seeming to refer, with these words, to the theatrical interaction that I am wishing to underline here. For even texts that we think we know very well can surprise us when they leave the context of the printed page and operate as alive entities in a theatrical context of dramatic performance. I know this from my own experience as "juglar." Several years ago I was asked to prepare an edition of old ballads with English verse translation (and extensive notes), which eventually came out in 1987.[4] It was only afterwards that it occurred to me to sing some of the translations to an English folk-club audience, adapted to music of a traditional English-language type; and I am still capable of being surprised by dramatic aspects of texts that I thought I knew well. For example, in the ballad "Death Concealed"

---

[3] Diego Catalán, "The artisan poetry of the Romancero," in *Hispanic Balladry Today* (see n.2), 1-25.

[4] Roger Wright, *Spanish Ballads with English Verse Translations*, Warminster, Aris and Phillips, 1987 (= RW). This contains 71 ballads; the Conde Claros ones are RW 9 and 10. Translations in this article come from these versions.

(*Muerte Ocultada*),⁵ the moment of greatest resonance in the audience usually turns out to be the line "lo negro bien te estaría" (30, "so black will suit you there"), rather than the ending, because it is here that the listeners foresee the circumstances that will lead to the revelation of the secret (that the King is dead). In the ballad of *Rosa Florida* the most dramatic moment seems not to lie in the most obviously comic lines ("o tenedes mal de amores / o estáys loca sandía," 25-26: "you must be in love, or you're losing your head") but in Rosa's enigmatic reference to her sister's body ("si no es el de mi hermana / que de fuego sea ardida," 37-38; "apart from my sister's, cursed may she be"). These lines had previously struck me as being at best peculiar, and I had even considered omitting them as not being relevant, but now I see why they have survived within a version of the ballad that otherwise makes absolutely no reference at all to this sister: they entertain the audience, and humanize the Princess. And in the ballad *Mariana*, who poisons her former lover just before his marriage to someone else, the recipe ("Tres onzas de solimán...," 15; "Three ounces of fearsome corrosive...") has a dramatic effectiveness that I had not foreseen: it always startles, surprises and amuses, so much so that its later repetition (1.33) is also enjoyed. That is not all: Mariana invites Alonso to drink from the poisoned bottle, and when he replies "Bebe primero, Mariana, / que asi está puesto en estilo" (23-24: "But it's only polite, Mariana, for you to drink yours before mine"), a shiver genuinely goes round the audience. Even so, the theatrically central point turns out to be lines 29-30 "con la fuerza del veneno / los dientes se le han caído" ("and the poison is sharp and so rapid his teeth fall right out on the floor"), in mid-ballad, after which the audience stay on the same level; the listening women admire Mariana (all remembering, if only unconsciously, some man they would like to have treated like that) and the men feel sorry for Alonso (all remembering a woman who got that angry with them, without such fatal consequences).

I have never abused the patience of my colleagues by reciting

---

⁵ *La muerte ocultada*, MP vol.X p.110, RW 11, (and cp. Beatriz Mariscal de Rhett (ed.), *La muerte ocultada*, Madrid, Gredos, 1984-85); *Rosa Florida*, MP 179, RW 17; *Mariana*, MP vol.X p.98, RW 7.

them all of *Conde Claros*, and cannot entirely foresee which other theatrical moments might turn up in addition to the ones sketched out above. It seems reasonable to believe that it was indeed performed whole some time in the Middle Ages, in a form more or less similar to the later one which we here have actually attested. In general, it is possible to believe that ballads of this length were indeed sung even in the early Middle Ages. It is likely that if oral epics existed in the Peninsula in the twelfth century, they were much shorter in length than the surviving version of the *Poema de Mio Cid*. I have recounted elsewhere my reasons for believing that the Spanish ballad genre is older than the handbooks of literary history tend to imply, and that the ballad genre is even more likely than the epic genre to have existed in the Peninsula in that century; later I further suggested that the *Poema de Mio Cid* already belonged in the twelfth century to the ballad tradition, and that at that time nobody made the distinction which we make now, between ballad and epic, so it is merely anachronistic for us to project the modern distinction back to that time[6]. This hypothesis can explain several aspects of the "novelization" of the *Poema*. I would here like merely to add that for years Hispanists have been establishing the dramatic nature of the *Poema*, without realizing what the consequences of this insight are. For scholars have often insisted that it is very surprising not to to find works of drama in Medieval Spain (apart from a very few well-known exceptions)[7] but indeed they exist; there they are, in the ballad collections. Granted, they are presumed to be one-man shows, in which the "juglar" acts all the roles as well as being the director, but they certainly form part of the dramatic genre. This was even more the case in an age without radio or television, when people's evening entertainment often came from repeating, singing or hearing ballads, many of the early ones being distant ancestors of those attested from the

---

[6] "How old is the ballad genre?" *La Corónica*, 14, 1986, 251-57; "Several ballads, one epic and two chronicles (1100-1250)," *La Corónica*, 18, 1990, 21-38.

[7] E.g. C.B. Kirby, "Consideraciones sobre la problemática del teatro medieval castellano," in L.N. Uriarte Rebaudi (ed.), *Studia hispanica medievalia*, Buenos Aires, Ergon, 1987, 61-9.

sixteenth century. The loss of these quasi-theatrical contexts is what threatens the modern survival of the genre rather than any change in literary taste; the theatrical aspects of the ballads provide most of their personal, social and aesthetic value. Unlike the modern literary critic, the audience did not have in mind any of the other literary aspects of the genre: their historical origins, the details of the universal motifs of folklore, the connections with stories recounted elsewhere, their poetic value, etc. These aspects were there, of course, but do not explain the attraction of the genre in its own time. It was, and still is, a theatrical oral genre, whose existence depends on its effectiveness as drama rather than anything else more intrinsically appropriate to literature in writing. In written form, the ballads tend to bore modern students of Spanish literature. Sung, less so. In the same way, Golden Age "Comedias" have a different effect on stage from in the book.

In this way we rediscover the supposedly lost genre of medieval Spanish drama. We can also explain another phenomenon that sometimes appears surprising to modern critics; the fact that a high proportion of the lines of the Golden Age plays are actually in the ballad form. This would have caused no surprise at the time. In the plays, the genre is mostly used when a single actor is recounting events on stage, in his own little "one-man" performance, of a ballad type the audience were already used to hearing. That is why the ballad form was used in even the most complex dramas of the Golden Age; theatricality had always been the essence of the ancient ballad tradition.

1994 POSTSCRIPT.

The Spanish original of this article appeared as "El dramatismo del romancero novelesco," in *Homenaje a Hans Flasche*, ed. by Karl-Hermann Körner and Günther Zimmermann, Stuttgart, Franz Steiner Verlag, 1991, 409-16; the notes were as above, and the references are thus not also in the Bibliography. Professor Flasche seems indestructible, and he entirely deserved this excellent Homage volume for his eightieth birthday; unfortunately, Professor Körner died unexpectedly as the volume appeared. This was a great shock; I would like here to record my gratitude for the encouragement Professor Körner gave me on many occasions. The oral ballad genre is the only genre that resists periodization, since it is essentially immune to fashion, and has probably not changed greatly for a millennium or more. It thus may not be an accident that Judith Seeger's studies seem so satisfying; she is in essence not a literary critic but an anthropologist, and is thus more able to see it as it is. In the Early Middle Ages, the Early Iberoromance period of the present collection, the ballad could well have been the dominant entertainment genre.

...and they lived happily ever after

References.

This list contains all the references in the volume except those from chapters 16 and 19-21, which have their own.

Abbreviations

ALMA = *Archivum Latinitatis Medii Aevi* (*Bulletin Du Cange*).
BHS = *Bulletin of Hispanic Studies*.
BRAE = *Boletín de la Real Academia Española*.
BSLP = *Bulletin de la Société de Linguistique de Paris*.
FMLS = *Forum for Modern Language Studies*.
MLR = *Modern Language Review*.
NRFH = *Nueva Revista de Filología Hispánica*.
RFE = *Revista de Filología Española*.
PBLS = *Proceedings of the Berkeley Linguistic Society*.
PMLA = *Proceedings of the Modern Language Association*.
RLR = *Revue de Linguistique Romane*.
TPS = *Transactions of the Philological Society*.
ZRPh = *Zeitschrift für Romanische Philologie*.

Adams, James N. 1990. "The Latinity of C. Novius Eunus." *Zeitschrift für Papyrologie und Epigraphik* 82, 227-47.

Adams, Kenneth W. J. 1970. "Juan Ruiz's manipulation of rhyme: some linguistic and stylistic consequences." *Libro de Buen Amor Studies*, ed. by G. B. Gybbon-Monypenny, 1-28. London: Tamesis.

Agard, F. B. 1984. *A Course in Romance Linguistics*, Vol. 2: *A Diachronic View*. Washington, D. C.: Georgetown University Press.

Alarcos Llorach, Emilio. 1973. "*Libro de Buen Amor* 432d: ¿ancheta de caderas?" *Actas del I Congreso Internacional sobre el Arcipreste de Hita*, 171-74. Barcelona: Seresa.

———. 1982. *El español, lengua milenaria*. Valladolid: Ámbito.

Alfonso el Sabio. 1957. *General Estoria*, Vol.II. Ed. by A. G. Solalinde et al. Madrid: CSIC.

Alvar, Manuel. 1980. "*Tienllas* (Berceo, *Mil.* 246a, 273c)." *Festschrift für Harri Meier*, 22-26. Bonn: Bouvier.
———. 1986. "Acepciones de *ladino* en español." *Homenaje a Pedro Sainz Rodríguez*, Vol.II, 25-34. Madrid.
——— and Alvar, C. 1985. "La palabra *romance* en español." *Estudios románicos dedicados al Profesor Andrés Soria Ortega*, Vol.I, 17-25. Granada: Universidad.
Ariza Viguera, Manuel. 1989. *Manual de filología histórica del español*. Madrid: Síntesis.
Armistead, Samuel. 1986. "*Encore les cantilènes!* Prof. Roger Wright's proto-romances." *La Corónica* 15, 52-66.
Bailey, Charles J. 1973. *Variation and Linguistic Theory*. Washington.
Baldinger, Kurt. 1980. *Semantic Theory*. Oxford: Blackwells.
Banniard, Michel. 1976. "Le lecteur en Espagne wisigothique d'après Isidore de Séville; de ses fonctions à l'état du langue." *Revue Augustinienne* 21, 112-44.
———. 1985. "Vox agrestis: quelques problèmes d'élocution de Cassiodore à Alcuin." *Trames* 7, 195-208.
———. 1986. "*Iuxta uniuscuiusque qualitatem*: l'écriture médiatrice chez Grégoire le Grand." *Colloques internationaux du CNRS: Grégoire le Grand*, 477-88. Paris: CNRS.
———. 1989. *Genèse culturelle de l'Europe: V-VIIIe siècle*. Paris: Le Seuil.
———. 1992. *Viva Voce: communication écrite et communication orale du IVe siècle au IXe siècle en Occident Latin*. Paris: Etudes Augustiniennes.
Baüml, Franz H. 1980. "Varieties and consequences of medieval literacy and illiteracy." *Speculum* 55, 237-65.
Bergh, Birger. 1967. *Revelations of St Bridget: Book 7*. Uppsala: University Press.
———. 1981. "A Saint in the making: St Bridget's Life in Sweden (1303-49)." *Papers of the Liverpool Latin Seminar* 3, 371-84.
Besner, D. et al. 1984. "Wholistic reading of alphabetic print: evidence from the FDM and the FBI." *Orthographies and Reading*, ed. by L. Henderson, 121-35. New Jersey: Erlbaum.
Bézler, François. 1984. "Pour une revision de la date des Gloses de Silos." *Recherches Ibériques Strasbourg* 2.2, 1-10.
———. 1985. "Pénitence chrétienne et or musulman dans l'Espagne du Cid." *Recherches Ibériques Strasbourg* 2.3, 68-90.
Bimson, Kent D. and Thurman, Robert C. 1980. "Body language: a study of semantic shifts in body parts." *Orbis* 29, 182-201.

Bischoff, Bernhard. 1990. *Latin Palaeography: Antiquity and Middle Ages*, translated by D. O'Cróinin and D. Ganz. Cambridge: Cambridge University Press.
Bishko, Charles J. 1968-69. "Fernando I y los orígenes de la alianza castellano-leonesa con Cluny." *Cuadernos de Historia de España* 43-44, 31-135 and 45-46, 50-116.
Blake, Robert. 1987. "New linguistic sources for Old Spanish." *Hispanic Review* 55, 1-12.
―――. 1991. "Syntactic aspects of Latinate texts of the Early Middle Ages." *Latin and the Romance Languages in the Early Middle Ages*, ed. by R. Wright, 219-32. London: Routledge.
Bly, Peter A. 1978. "Beards in the *Poema de Mio Cid*: structural and contextual patterns." *FMLS* 14, 16-24.
Bonfante, G. 1951. "Note sui nomi della *guancia* e della *mascella* in Italia." *Biblos* 27, 371-96.
Bonnaz, Yves. 1987. *Chroniques asturiennes (fin IXe siècle)*. Paris: CNRS.
Borrego Nieto, Jesús. 1981. *Sociolingüística rural*. Salamanca: Universidad.
Bowman, Alan K. & J. David Thomas. 1983. *Vindolanda: The Latin Writing Tablets*. London: Britannia.
Bullough, David. 1985. "*Aula Renovata*: the Carolingian court before the Aachen Palace." *Proceedings of the British Academy* 71, 267-301.
Bynon, Theodora. 1977. *Historical Linguistics*. Cambridge: Cambridge University Press.
Cano Aguilar, Rafael. 1988. *El español a través de los tiempos*. Madrid: Arco.
―――. 1991. *Análisis filológico de textos*. Madrid: Taurus.
Cañas Murillo, Jesús, ed. 1978. *Libro de Alexandre*. Madrid: Nacional.
Carande Herrero, Rocío. 1986. *Un poema latino a Sevilla de 1250*. Sevilla: BTS.
Castro, Américo. 1936. *Glosarios latino-españoles de la Edad Media*. Madrid: RFE.
Chevalier, J. C. 1984. "Du plus-que-parfait." *Cahiers de Linguistique Hispanique Médiévale* 9, 5-47.
Chomsky, Noam. 1981. *Lectures on Government and Binding*. Dordrecht: Foris.
――― and Halle, Morris. 1968. *The Sound Pattern of English*. New York: Harper and Row.
Clanchy, Michael. 1979. *From Memory to Written Record*. London: Arnold.
Clavería Nadal, Gloria. 1991. *El latinismo en español*. Barcelona: Universitat Autònoma.
Codoñer, Carmen. 1983. "Rasgos configuradores de un estilo popular." *Serta Philologica F. Lázaro Carreter*, Vol. I, 109-18. Madrid: Cátedra.

Coleman, Linda and Kay, Paul. 1981. "Prototype semantics: the English word LIE." *Language* 57, 26-44.
Coleman, Robert. 1987. "Vulgar Latin and the diversity of Christian Latin." *Latin vulgaire - latin tardif,* ed. by J. Herman, 37-52. Tübingen: Niemeyer.
Collins, Roger. 1985. "*Sicut lex Gothorum continet*: Law and Charters in Ninth- and Tenth-Century León and Catalonia." *English Historical Review* 100, 489-512.
———. 1989. *The Arab Conquest of Spain (710-797)*. Oxford: Blackwells.
———. 1990. "Literacy and the laity in Early Medieval Spain." *The Uses of Literacy in Early Mediaeval Europe* ed. by R. McKitterick, 109-33. Cambridge: Cambridge University Press.
Comrie, Bernard. 1981. *Language Universals and Linguistic Typology*. Oxford: Blackwells.
Corominas, Juan. 1961. *Breve diccionario etimológico de la lengua castellana*. Madrid: Gredos.
Corominas, Juan and Pascual, José A. 1980-91. *Diccionario crítico etimológico castellano e hispánico*, 6 vols. Madrid: Gredos.
Corriente, Federico. 1980. "Notas de lexicología árabe." *Vox Romanica* 39, 183-210.
Cotarelo Valledor, Armando. 1933. *Alfonso III el Magno*. Madrid: Academia de la Historia.
Coulmas, Florian and Ehlich, K. (eds). 1983. *Writing in Focus*. Berlin: Mouton.
Coulmas, Florian. 1989. *The Writing Systems of the World*. Oxford: Blackwells.
Craddock, Jerry R. 1989. Review of Agard 1984. *Romance Philology* 42, 314-22.
Cravens, Thomas D. 1982. "Cross-language evidence in etymology: the origin of *Testa* as 'head' in Romance." *Neuphilologische Mitteilungen* 83, 53-60.
———. 1987. "The syllable and phonological strength: gradient loss of gemination in Corsican." *Papers from the 7th International Conference on Historical Linguistics,* ed. by A. Giacolone Ramat et al., 163-78. Amsterdam: John Benjamins.
———. 1988. "Consonant strength in the Romance dialects of the Pyrenees." *Advances in Romance Linguistics,* ed. by D. Birdsong and J.-P. Montreuil, 67-88. Dordrecht: Foris.

———. 1991. "Phonology, phonetics and orthography in Late Latin and Romance: the evidence for early intervocalic sonorization." *Latin and the Romance Languages in the Early Middle Ages*, ed. by R. Wright, 52-68. London: Routledge.
Cremona, Joe. 1959. "Historical semantics and the classification of semantic changes." *Hispanic Studies in Honour of I. González Llubera*, 129-34. Oxford: Dolphin.
Cressy, D. 1980. *Literacy and Social Order*. Cambridge: Cambridge University Press.
Crystal, David and Davy, Derek. 1969. *Investigating English Style*. London: Longmans.
De Dardel, Robert. 1983. *Esquisse structurale des subordonnants conjonctionnels en Roman Commun*. Geneva: Droz.
———. 1987. "Limites et possibilités de la reconstruction syntaxique." *Linguisticae Investigationes* 11, 337-56.
Dees, Anthonij. 1980. *Atlas des formes et des constructions des chartes françaises du 13e siècle*. Tübingen: Niemeyer.
DeFrancis, J. 1984. *The Chinese Language: Fact and Fantasy*. Honolulu: Hawaii University Press.
De Witte, A. J. J. n.d. *De Betekeniswereld van het Lichaam*. Utrecht.
Díaz y Díaz, Manuel C. 1965. "El latín de la liturgia hispánica." *Estudios sobre la liturgia mozárabe*, ed. by J. Rivera Recio, 55-87. Toledo: Diputación Provincial.
———. 1976. *De Isidoro al Siglo XI*. Barcelona: Albir.
———. 1978. *Las primeras glosas hispánicas*. Barcelona: Universitat Autònoma.
———. 1979. *Libros y librerías de la Rioja altomedieval*. Logroño: Instituto de Estudios Riojanos.
———. 1981. "El cultivo del latín en el siglo X." *Anuario de Estudios Filológicos* 4, 71-81.
———. 1983. *Manuscritos visigóticos en la monarquía leonesa*. León: San Isidoro.
———. 1986. "Algunos aspectos lingüísticos y culturales de las pizarras visigóticas." *Myrtia* 1, 13-25.
———. (In press). "Sobre las glosas protohispánicas." *Actas del III Congreso Internacional de Historia de la Lengua Española*.
Diccionario Histórico de la Lengua Española. I: *a - alá*. 1972. Madrid: Real Academia Española.
Diez, F. 1975. *La poésie des troubadours*. Geneva: Slatkine (reprint of 1845 ed., Paris: translation of *Die Poesie des Troubadours*, 1826, Zwickau: Schumann).

Dionisotti, Carlotta. 1982. "On Bede, Grammars and Greek." *Revue Bénédictine* 92, 111-41.
Dray, William H. 1989. *On History and Philosophers of History.* Leiden: Brill.
Dutton, Brian, ed. 1971. *Gonzalo de Berceo: Milagros de Nuestra Señora.* London: Tamesis.
───. 1980. "Legal formulae in medieval literature." *Medieval, Renaissance and Folklore Studies in honor of John Esten Keller,* ed. by J. R. Jones, 13-28. Newark: Juan de la Cuesta.
Dworkin, Steven N. 1982. "From 'temple' to 'cheek': Old Spanish *tienlla* reconsidered (with side-glances at *carriello* and *sien*)." *Romance Philology* 35, 375-85.
───. 1985. *Etymology and Derivational Morphology: the Genesis of Old Spanish Denominal Adjectives in -IDO.* Tübingen: Niemeyer.
───. 1989. Review of Agard (1984). *Hispanic Linguistics* 2, 357-67.
Elcock, William D. 1961. "La Pénombre des langues romanes." *Revista Portuguesa de Filologia* 2, 1-19.
Elcock, William D. 1975. *The Romance Languages,* 2nd ed. London: Faber.
Emiliano, Antònio. 1988. "Contribuição grafemática para o estudo do leonês medieval: análise da variável grafémica [ie] nos Foros de Alfaiates." *Actas del I Congreso Internacional de Historia de la Lengua Española,* ed. by M. Ariza et al., 103-14. Madrid: Arco.
───. 1991. "Latin or Romance? Graphemic variation and scripto-linguistic change in Medieval Spain." *Latin and the Romance Languages in the Early Middle Ages,* ed. by R. Wright, 233-47. London: Routledge.
Entwistle, William J. 1936. *The Spanish Language.* London: Faber.
Ernout, Alfred and Meillet, Antoine. 1951. *Dictionnaire etymologique de la langue latine.* 3rd ed. Paris: Klincksieck.
Escavy Zamora, Ricardo. 1985. "El contenido lexicográfico de las Partidas." *La lengua y la literatura en tiempos de Alfonso X,* 195-210. Murcia: Universidad.
Fasold, Ralph W. 1984. *The Sociolinguistics of Society.* Oxford: Blackwells.
Ferguson, Charles A. 1959. "Diglossia." *Word* 15, 325-40.
Férotin, Marius, ed. 1912. *Le Liber Mozarabicus Sacramentorum.* Paris.
Fillmore, Charles. 1975. "An alternative to checklist theories of meaning." *PBLS* 1, 123-31.
Fleischman, Suzanne. 1982. *The Future in Thought and Language: Diachronic Evidence from Romance.* Cambridge: Cambridge University Press.
───. 1990. "Philology, Linguistics and the Discourse of the Medieval Text." *Speculum* 65, 19-37.

Flórez, Henrique. 1765/1965. *Historia Compostellana* (= *España Sagrada*, Vol.20). Madrid: Real Academia de la Historia.
———. 1781. *España Sagrada*, Vol.33. Madrid: Antonio Marín.
Floriano Cumbrero, A. 1951. *Diplomática española del período astur*, 2 vols. Oviedo: Universidad.
Fontaine, Jacques. 1959. *Isidore de Séville et la culture classique dans l'Espagne wisigothique*. Paris: Etudes Augustiniennes.
———. 1972. "Fins et moyens de l'enseignement ecclésiastique dans l'Espagne wisigothique." *La Scuola nell'Occidente Latino dell'Alto Medioevo* (= Centro Italiano di studi sull'alto Medioevo, *Settimane di studio* 19), 145-202. Spoleto: Presso de la Sede del Centro.
———. 1981. "De la pluralité a l'unité dans le 'latin carolingien'?" *Nascita dell'Europa ed Europa Carolingia: un equazione da verificare* (=Centro Italiano di studi sull'alto medioevo, *Settimane di Studio* 28), 765-818. Spoleto: Presso de la Sede del Centro.
Fontán, Antonio and Moure Casas, Ana. 1987. *Antología del latín medieval*. Madrid: Gredos.
Fontanillo Merino, E. (ed). 1985. *Diccionario de las Lenguas de España*. Madrid: Anaya. (Redactor gallego: M. Rodríguez Alonso).
Franco, Fabiola. 1985. "A deeper look at the grammar and some implications of SER and ESTAR + locative in Spanish." *Hispania* 68, 641-48.
Frith, Uta (ed). 1980. *Cognitive Processes in Spelling*. London: Academic Press.
———. 1983. Review of Scribner and Cole (1981). *Journal of Pragmatics* 7, 603-06.
Gaeng, Paul A. 1984. *Collapse and Reorganization of the Latin Nominal Flection as Reflected in Epigraphic Sources*. Potomac: Scripta Humanistica.
Ganz, David. 1987. "The preconditions for Caroline Minuscule." *Viator* 18, 23-44.
——— and Goffart, Walter. 1990. "Charters earlier than 800 from French collections." *Speculum* 65, 906-32.
García, Erica. 1985. "Quantity into quality: synchronic indeterminacy and language change." *Lingua* 65, 275-306.
———. 1986. "Cambios cuantitativos en la distribución de formas: ¿causa o síntoma de cambio semántico?" *Papers of the 8th Conference of the International Association of Hispanists* Vol.I, 557-66. Providence, RI: Brown University Press.

―――. 1990. "Reanalysing actualization and actualizing reanalysis." *Historical Linguistics 1987: Papers from the 8th International Conference on Historical Linguistics*, ed. H. Andersen and K. Koerner, 141-59. Amsterdam: John Benjamins.

García Alvarez, M. R. 1965. "Los libros en la documentación gallega de la alta edad media." *Cuadernos de Estudios Gallegos* 20, 292-329.

García de Diego, Eduardo. 1933. *Glosarios latinos del monasterio de Silos*. Murcia: Universidad.

García Larragueta, Santos. 1984. *Las Glosas Emilianenses*. Logroño: Instituto de Estudios Riojanos.

García Leal, Antonio. 1994. *El latín de la diplomática asturleonesa (775-1032)*. Oviedo: Universidad.

Gil, Juan. 1973. "Para la edición de los textos visigodos y mozárabes." *Habis* 4, 189-234.

―――. 1974. "Carmen de Expugnatione Almariae Urbis." *Habis* 5, 45-64.

―――, Moralejo, José-Luis & Ignacio Ruiz de la Peña. 1985. *Crónicas asturianas*. Oviedo: Universidad.

Gimeno Menéndez, Francisco. 1988. "Aproximación sociolingüística a los orígenes del español." *Actas del I Congreso Internacional de Historia de la Lengua Española*, ed. by M. Ariza, A. Salvador and A. Viudas, 1183-92. Madrid: Arco.

Goddard, Keith A. 1980. "Loan-words in Spanish. A reappraisal." *BHS* 57, 1-16.

Godman, Peter. 1985. *Poetry of the Carolingian Renaissance*. London: Duckworth.

Goebl, Hans. 1983. "Parquet polygonal et treillis triangulaire: les deux versants de la dialectométrie interponctuelle." *RLR* 187-88, 353-412.

Goetz, Georg, ed. 1894. *Corpus Glossariorum Latinorum*, Vol.5. Leipzig.

Goffart, Walter. 1987. "From *Historiae* to *Historia Francorum* and back again: aspects of the textual history of Gregory of Tours." *Religion, Culture and Society in the Early Middle Ages*, ed. by T. F. X. Noble and J. J. Contreni, 55-76. Kalamazoo: Medieval Institute.

Gómez Moreno, Manuel. 1932. "Las primeras crónicas de la Reconquista." *Boletín de la Academia de la Historia* 100, 562-628.

Gómez Redondo, Fernando. 1988. "Relaciones literarias entre la historiografía latina y las crónicas latinas del siglo XIII." *Actas del I Congreso de la Asociación Hispánica de Literatura Medieval*, 305-20. Barcelona: PPU.

Goody, Jack, ed. 1968. *Literacy in Traditional Societies*. Cambridge: Cambridge University Press.

―――. 1987. *The Interface between the Written and the Oral*. Cambridge: Cambridge University Press.

Graff, H. J. 1979. *The Literacy Myth*. New York: Academic Press.
Green, John N. 1982. "Vers une théorie du renouvellement morphologique. Nouvelles perspectives sur la 'voix impersonelle'." *Actes del XVI Congrès International de Lingüística i Filologia Romàniques* Vol.II, 85-93. Palma: Universidad.
———. 1991. "The collapse and replacement of verbal inflection in Late Latin / Early Romannce: how would one know?" *Latin and the Romance Languages in the Early Middle Ages*, ed. by R. Wright, 83-99. London: Routledge.
Gribomont, J. 1963. "Conscience philologique chez les scribes du Haut Moyen Age." *La Bibbia nell'Alto Medioevo*, 601-30. Spoleto: Centro Italiano di Studi sull'Alto Medioevo.
Guerreau-Jalabert, Anita. 1981. "La 'Renaissance carolingienne': modèles culturels, usages linguistiques et structures sociales." *Bibliothèque de l'École des Chartes* 139, 5-35.
——— (ed.). 1982. *Abbo Floriacensis: Quaestiones Grammaticales*. Paris: Les Belles Lettres.
Hall, Robert A. Jr. 1950. "The reconstruction of Proto-Romance." *Language* 26, 6-27.
———. 1974. *External History of the Romance Languages*. New York: Elsevier.
———. 1976. *Proto-Romance Phonology*. New York: Elsevier.
———. 1983. *Proto-Romance Morphology*. Amsterdam: John Benjamins.
———. 1986. "From bidialectalism to diglossia in Early Romance." *Language in Global Perspective*, ed. by B. F. Elson, 213-22. Dallas: Summer Institute of Linguistics.
Harris, Roy. 1986. *The Origin of Writing*. London: Duckworth.
Harris-Northall, Raymond. 1990. *Weakening Processes in the History of Spanish Consonants*. London: Routledge.
Hartman, Stephen L. 1980. "La etimología de *dulce*: ¿realmente una excepción?" *NRFH* 29, 115-27.
Harvey, Anthony. 1990. "Retrieving the pronunciation of Early Insular Celtic scribes: towards a methodology." *Celtica* 21, 178-90.
Herman, József. 1965. "Aspects de la différentiation territoriale du Latin sous l'Empire." *BSLP* 60, 53-70.
———. 1988. "La Situation linguistique en Italie au VIe siècle." *RLR* 52, 55-67.
———. 1989. "Accusativus cum infinitivo et subordonée à *quod, quia* en latin tardif - nouvelles remarques sur un vieux problème." *Subordination and Other Topics in Latin*, ed. by Gualtiero Calboli, 133-52. Amsterdam: John Benjamins.
———. 1990. *Du latin aux langues romanes*. Tübingen: Niemeyer.

———. 1991. "Spoken and written Latin in the last centuries of the Roman Empire. A contribution to the linguistic history of the Western Provinces." *Latin and the Romance Languages in the Early Middle Ages*, ed. by R. Wright, 29-43. London: Routledge.

Herrero de la Fuente, Marta. 1988. *Colección diplomática del Monasterio de Sahagún (1000-1073)*. León: San Isidoro.

Hobsbawm, Eric. 1983. "Inventing traditions." *The Invention of Tradition*, ed. by E. Hobsbawm and T. Ranger, 1-14. Cambridge: Cambridge University Press.

Householder, Fred. 1973. "On arguments from asterisks." *Foundations of Language* 10, 365-76.

Hook, David. 1979-80. "'Que lo coma el escuerço' (*Libro de Buen Amor* 1544c)." *La Corónica* 8, 29-32.

Hurford, James. 1987. *Language and Number*. Oxford: Blackwell.

Iglesias, Angel. 1981. "Eponimia: motivación y personificación en el español marginal y hablado." *BRAE* 61, 297-348.

Isidoro de Sevilla. 1982. *Etimologías; edición bilingüe preparada por José Oroz Reta, con introducción general por Manuel C. Díaz y Díaz*. Madrid: Biblioteca de Autores Cristianos.

Itkonen, Esa. 1978. "The significance of Merovingian Latin to linguistic theory." *Linguistic Studies in Classical Languages* 5, 9-64.

Janson, Tore. 1991. "Language change and metalinguistic change: Latin to Romance and other cases." *Latin and the Romance Languages in the Early Middle Ages*, ed. by Roger Wright, 19-28. London: Routledge.

Jeffers, Robert J. and Lehiste, Ilse. 1979. *Principles and Methods for Historical Linguistics*. Cambridge, Mass: MIT Press.

Jennings, Augustus C. 1940. *A Linguistic Study of the Cartulario de San Vicente de Oviedo*. New York: Vanni.

Kahane, Henry R. 1941. "Designations of the cheek in Italian dialects." *Language* 17, 212-22.

Kasten, Lloyd A. and Nitti, John. 1978. *Concordances and Texts of the Royal Scriptorium Manuscripts of Alfonso X, El Sabio*. Madison: Hispanic Seminary of Medieval Studies.

Kavanagh, J. F. and Mattingly, I. G. (eds). 1972. *Language by Ear and by Eye*. Cambridge, Mass: MIT Press.

Kay, C. and Samuels, M. L. 1975. "Componential analysis in semantics: its validity and applications." *TPS*, 49-81.

Kelly, Susan. 1990. "Anglo-Saxon lay society and the written word." *The Uses of Literacy in Early Mediaeval Europe*, ed. by R. McKitterick, 36-62. Cambridge: Cambridge University Press.

Klein Andreu, Flora. 1990. "Speech priorities." *The Pragmatics of Style*, ed. by L. Hickey, 73-86. London: Routledge.

Klima, E. S. 1972. "How alphabets might reflect language." *Language by Ear and by Eye*, ed. by J. F. Kavanagh and I. G. Mattingly, 57-80. Cambridge, Mass: MIT Press.
Kneepkens, C. H. and Reijnders, H. F. 1979. *Magister Siguinus: Ars Lectoria*. Leiden: Brill.
Koerner, Konrad. 1989. *Practicing Linguistic Historiography*. Amsterdam: John Benjamins.
Kohler, Eugen. 1954. "Le Sens large du vocabulaire espagnol." *Romania* 75, 498-511.
Korhammer, M. 1980. "Mittelalterliche Konstruktionschilfen und A.E. Wortstellung." *Scriptorium* 37, 18-58.
Kritzeck, James. 1964. *Peter the Venerable and Islam*. Princeton: Princeton University Press.
Labov, William. 1972. *Sociolinguistic patterns*. Philadelphia: University of Pennsylvania Press.
Lang, Henry R. 1887. "The face and its parts in Spanish proverb and metaphor." *PMLA* 3, 58-83.
Lange, Wolf Dieter. 1966. *Philologische Studien zur Latinität westhispanischer Privaturkunden des 9.-12 Jahrhunderts*. Leiden: Brill.
Lapesa, Rafael. 1980. *Historia de la Lengua Española*, 8th ed. Madrid: Gredos.
———. 1985. "El Fuero de Valfermoso de las Monjas." *Homenaje a Alvaro Galmés de Fuentes*, Vol.I, 43-98. Oviedo: Universidad.
———. 1988. "Notas etimológicas y semánticas." *Hommage a Bernard Pottier*, ed. by J. L. Benezech, Vol.II, 469-76. Paris: Klincksieck.
Lass, Roger. 1980. *On Explaining Language Change*. Cambridge: Cambridge University Press.
Law, Vivian. 1982. *The Insular Latin Grammarians*. Ipswich: Boydell and Brewer.
———. 1987. "Grammars and language change: an eighth-century case." *Latin vulgaire–latin tardif*, ed. by J. Herman, 133-44. Tübingen: Niemeyer.
Lehrer, Adrienne. 1974. *Semantic Fields and Lexical Structure*. Amsterdam: North Holland.
Levine, Kenneth. 1986. *The Social Context of Literacy*. London: Routledge.
Lewis, Charlton T. and Short, Charles. 1962. *A Latin Dictionary*. Oxford: Oxford University Press.
Lindsay, William M., ed. 1962. *Etyimologiae sive Origines of Isidore of Seville*, 3rd ed. Oxford: Oxford University Press.
Lomax, Derek W. 1982. "Catalans in the Leonese Empire." *BHS* 59, 191-97.
López Pereira, Juan E. 1983. "Latín medieval y filología hispánica. A propósito de *civiliter, celata y virtus*." *Verba* 10, 155-68.

Lloyd, Paul M. 1987. *From Latin to Spanish*, Vol I. Philadelphia: American Philosophical Society.

———. 1991. "On the names of languages (and other things)." *Latin and the Romance Languages in the Middle Ages*, ed. by R. Wright, 9-18. London: Routledge.

Löfstedt, Bengt. 1959. "Zur lexicographie der mittellateinischen urkunden Spaniens." *ALMA* 29, 5-89.

———. 1983. Review of Wright 1982. *Vox Romanica* 42, 259-63.

López, R. S. 1951. "Still another Renaissance?" *American Historical Review* 57, 1-21.

Lüdtke, Helmut. 1968. Geschichte des Romanischen Wortschatzes. Freiburg: Rombach.

———. 1986. "Explicación del doble resultado de los grupos CL- / PL- / FL- en la Península Ibérica." *Lletres Asturianes* 21, 7-16.

———. 1988. "Metafonía y neutro de materia." *Actas del I Congreso Internacional de Historia de la Lengua Española*, ed. by M. Ariza et al., 61-69. Madrid: Arco.

Lunn, Patricia V. and Cravens, Thomas D. 1991. "A contextual reconsideration of the Spanish -*ra* 'indicative'." *Categories of the Verb in Romance: Discourse Pragmatic Approaches*, ed. by S. Fleischman and L. Waugh, 147-63. London: Routledge.

Lyons, Christopher. 1986. "On the origin of the Old French strong-weak possessive distinction." *TPS*, 1-41.

———. 1992. "El desarrollo de las estructuras posesivas en el español temprano." *Actas del Primer Congreso Anglo-Hispano*, Vol.I, ed. by R. Penny, 215-24. Madrid: Castalia.

Lyons, John. 1968. *Introduction to Theoretical Linguistics*. Cambridge: Cambridge University Press.

Macdonald, Gerald J., ed. 1973. *Antonio de Nebrija: Vocabulario de Romance en Latín*. Madrid: Castalia.

Macpherson, Ian. 1975. *Spanish Phonology*. Manchester: Manchester University Press.

Maiden, Martin. 1991. "On the phonological vulnerability of complex paradigms: beyond analogy in Italo- and Ibero-Romance." *Romance Philology* 44, 284-305.

Malkiel, Yakov. 1945. "The etymology of Hispanic *que(i)xar*." *Language* 21, 142-83.

———. 1947. "Spanish *cosecha* and its congeners." *Language* 23, 389-98.

———. 1970. "Typographic experimentation." *Romance Philology* 24, 328.

———. 1975. "En torno al cultismo medieval: los descendientes hispánicos de DULCIS." *NRFH* 24, 24-45.

———. 1979. "Problems in the diachronic differentiation of near-homophones." *Language* 55, 1-36.
———. 1979a. "Three isolated ideograms: the ampersand, the dagger and the asterisk." *Romance Philology* 33, 356.
———. 1983. "Alternatives to the classic dichotomy 'Family Tree versus Wave Theory'." *Language Change*, ed. by I. Rauch and G. F. Carr, 192-256. Indiana: Indiana University Press.
———. 1987. "Integration of phonosymbolism with other categories of language change." *Papers from the 7th International Conference on Historical Linguistics*, ed. by A. Giacolone Ramat et al., 373-406. Amsterdam: John Benjamins.
———. 1989. "The hypothetical base in Romance etymology." *Theory and Practice of Romance Etymology*, 1-100. London: Variorum.
———. 1990. "Les avatars de l'explication étymologique de (esp. port.) tomar." *RLR* 213, 33-59.
Manoliu, Maria. 1974. "I nuovi problemi della lessematica." Iordan, Iorgu and Manoliu, Maria, *Linguistica Romanza*, 459-86. Padova: Liviana.
Marcos Marín, Francisco. 1979. *Reforma y modernización del español*. Madrid: Cátedra.
———. 1984. "Latín tardío y romance temprano." *RFE* 64, 129-45.
——— and Sánchez Lobato, J. 1988. *Lingüística aplicada*. Madrid: Síntesis.
Martínez, H. Salvador. 1975. *El "Poema de Almería" y la épica románica*. Madrid: Gredos.
Matthews, Peter H. 1982. *Do Languages Obey General Laws?* Cambridge: Cambridge University Press.
McCluskey, Raymond. 1989. "The genesis of the *Concordia* of Martin of León." *God and Man in Medieval Spain*, ed. by D. Lomax and D. Mackenzie, 19-36. Warminster: Aris and Phillips.
McEvedy, Colin and Woodcock, John. 1967. *The Penguin Atlas of Ancient History*. Harmondsworth: Penguin.
McKitterick, Rosamond. 1989. *The Carolingians and the Written Word*. Cambridge: Cambridge University Press.
———, ed. 1990. *The Uses of Literacy in Mediaeval Europe*. Cambridge: Cambridge University Press.
McManus, Damian. 1984. "*Linguarum Diversitas*: Latin and the vernaculars in Early Medieval Britain." *Peritia* 3, 151-88.
Meier, Harri. 1987. "Nuevas acotaciones al Diccionario Etimológico de Corominas/Pascual." *Verba* 14, 5-74.
———. 1989. "Etapas de la etimología románica." *Actes du XVIIIe Congrès International de Linguistique et Philologie Romanes*, Vol.VII, ed. by D. Kremer, 37-46. Tübingen: Niemeyer.

Menéndez Pidal, Ramón. 1926. *Orígenes del español*. Madrid: Espasa-Calpe (7th ed., 1972).
———. 1944-46. *Cantar de Mio Cid: Texto, Gramática y Vocabulario*, 3 Vols, 2nd ed. Madrid: Espasa-Calpe.
———. 1966. *Documentos Lingüísticos de España*, 2nd ed. Madrid: CSIC.
Michael, Ian. 1988. Review of Wright 1982. *MLR* 83, 925-26.
Millares Carlo, A. 1929. *Paleografía española*. Barcelona: Labor.
Milroy, Lesley. 1980. *Language and Social Networks*. Oxford: Blackwells.
Milroy, Lesley and Milroy, James. 1985. "Linguistic change, social network and speaker innovation." *Journal of Linguistics* 21, 339-84.
Mínguez Fernández, José M. 1976. *Colección diplomática del Monasterio de Sahagún (siglos IX y X)*. León: San Isidoro.
Moore, Terence and Carling, Christine. 1982. *Understanding Language: Towards a Post-Chomskyan Linguistics*. London: MacMillan.
Moralejo Laso, A. 1978. "Para la etimología de la palabra *jerigonza*." *Revista de Filología Española* 60, 327-31.
Muljacic, Zarko. 1988. "Emergence et genèse des langues romanes." *Actes du XVIIIe Congrès International de Linguistique et Philologie Romanes*, Vol.V, ed. by D. Kremer, 186-91. Tübingen: Niemeyer.
Muller, Bodo. 1985. *Le Français d'aujourd'hui*. Paris: Klincksieck.
Muller, Henri F. 1929. *A Chronology of Vulgar Latin*. Halle: ZRPh.
———. and Taylor, Pauline. 1932. *Chrestomathy of Vulgar Latin*. New York.
Mullett, Margaret. 1990. "Writing in Early Mediaeval Byzantium." *The Uses of Literacy in Early Mediaeval Europe*, ed. by R. McKitterick, 156-85. Cambridge: Cambridge University Press.
Nelson, Dana A., ed. 1979. *El Libro de Alixandre*. Madrid: Gredos.
Nelson, Janet L. 1985. "Public *Histories* and private history in the work of Nithard." *Speculum* 60, 251-93.
———. 1990. "Literacy in Carolingian Government." *The Uses of Literacy in Early Mediaeval Europe*, ed. by R. McKitterick, 258-96. Cambridge: Cambridge University Press.
Niederehe, Hans-Josef. 1985. "Alfonso el Sabio y la fisionomía lingüística de su época." *La lengua y la literatura en tiempos de Alfonso X*, 415-33. Murcia: Universidad.
———. 1987. *Alfonso X, El Sabio, y la lingüística de su tiempo*. Madrid: SGEL.
Noble, Thomas F. X. 1990. "Literacy and papal government in Late Antiquity and the Early Middle Ages." *The Uses of Literacy in Early Mediaeval Europe*, ed. by R. McKitterick, 82-108. Cambridge: Cambridge University Press.

Norberg, Dag. 1958. *Introduction à l'étude de la versification latine*. Stockholm: Almqvist and Wiksell.
Oelschlager, Victor R. B. 1940. *A Medieval Spanish Word-List*. Madison: University of Wisconsin Press.
Olarte Ruiz, J. B. 1977. *Glosas Emilianenses*. Madrid: Ministerio de Educación y Ciencia.
Ong, Walter J. 1982. *Orality and Literacy*. London: Methuen.
Orr, John. 1948. "Linguistic Geography as a corrective to etymology." *TPS*, 81-91.
Ovejas, M. 1956. "Toponimia de las obras de Berceo." *Berceo* 11, 297-318, 445-62.
Pagliuca, William and Mowrey, Richard. 1987. "Articulatory evolution." *Papers from the 7th International Conference on Historical Linguistics*, ed. A. Giacolone Ramat et al., 459-72. Amsterdam: John Benjamins.
Pattison, David G. 1975. *Early Spanish Suffixes*. Oxford: Blackwells.
Pei, Mario. 1932. *The Language of the Eighth-Century Texts in Northern France*. New York.
Pellegrini, A. and Yawkey, T. (eds). 1984. *The Development of Oral and Written Language in Social Contexts*. Norwood, NJ: Ablex.
Penny, Ralph J. 1969. *El habla pasiega*. London: Tamesis.
———. 1978. *Estudio estructural del habla de Tudanca*. Tübingen: Niemeyer.
———. 1980. "Do Romance nouns descend from the accusative?" *Romance Philology* 33, 501-09.
———. 1991a. *A History of the Spanish Language*. Cambridge: Cambridge University Press.
———. 1991b. "Labiodental /f/, aspiration and /h/-dropping in Spanish: the evolving phonemic value of the graphs *f* and *h*." *Cultures in Contact in Medieval Spain*, ed. by D. Hook and B. Taylor, 157-82. London: Kings College.
Pensado, Carmen. 1991a. "How was Leonese Vulgar Latin read?" *Latin and the Romance Languages in the Early Middle Ages*, ed. by R. Wright, 190-204. London: Routledge.
———. 1991b. "Un reanálisis de la '*l* leonesa'." *Linguistic Studies in Medieval Spanish*, ed. by R. Harris-Northall and T. D. Cravens, 63-88. Madison: Hispanic Seminary for Medieval Studies.

Petrucci, Armando. 1972. "Libro, scrittura e scuola." *La Scuola nell'Occidente Latino dell'Alto Medioevo* (= Centro italiano di Studi sull'alto Medioevo, *Settimane di studio* 19), 313-37. Spoleto: Presso de la sede del Centro.
———. 1986. "Alfabetismo ed educazione grafica degli scribi altomedievali, Secc. VII-X." *The Role of the Book in Medieval Culture*, Vol.I, ed. by Peter Ganz, 109-31. Turnhout: Brepols.
Pharies, David A. 1986. *Structure and Analogy in the Playful Lexicon of Spanish*. Tübingen: Niemeyer.
Pinkster, Harm. 1991. "Evidence for SVO in Latin?" *Latin and the Romance Languages in the Early Middle Ages*, ed. by R. Wright, 69-82. London: Routledge.
Politzer, Robert L. 1961. "The interpretation of correctness in Late Latin texts." *Language* 37, 209-14.
Powell, Brian. 1983. *Epic and Chronicle: The "Poema de Mio Cid" and the "Crónica de Veinte Reyes."* London: MHRA.
Prelog, Jan. 1980. *Die Chronik Alfons III*. Frankfurt: Lang.
Puentes Romay, José A. 1986a. "Acerca de la grafía del latín altomedieval." *Euphrosyne* 14, 97-112.
———. 1986b. "Notas sobre la grafía de los documentos latinos altomedievales." *Verba* 13, 343-48.
Rabin, Chaim. 1985. "Massorah and *Ad Litteras*." *Hebrew Studies* 26, 81-91.
Ramón Trives, Estanislao. 1979. *Aspectos de semántica lingüístico-textual*. Madrid: Istmo.
Rajna, Pio. 1919. "Discussioni etimologiche: *tomar*." *RFE* 6, 1-13.
Riché, Pierre. 1981. *Instruction et vie religieuse dans le Haut Moyen Age*. London: Variorum.
———. 1989. *Écoles et enseignement dans le Haut Moyen Age*, 2nd ed. Paris: Picard.
Richter, Michael. 1983. "À quelle époque a-t-on cessé de parler latin en Gaule? A propos d'une question mal posée." *Annales* 38, 439-48.
Rickard, Peter. 1974. *A History of the French Language*. London: Hutchinson.
Rico, Francisco. 1978. *Nebrija frente a los bárbaros*. Salamanca: Universidad.
———. 1985. "La clerecía del mester." *Hispanic Review* 53, 1-23, 127-50.
Ridruejo, Emilio. 1988. "El cambio sintáctico a la luz del funcionalismo coseriano." *Energeia und Ergon*, Vol.II, ed. by H. Thun, 121-33. Tübingen: Narr.

Riiho, Timo. 1979. *POR y PARA: estudio sobre los orígenes y la evolución de una oposición prepositiva iberorrománica*. Helsinki: Societas Scientiarum Fennica.
———. 1988. *La redundancia pronominal en el iberorromance medieval*. Tübingen: Niemeyer.
Rodríguez Aniceto, C. 1931. "El poema latino 'Prefacio de Almería'." *Boletín de la Biblioteca Menéndez y Pelayo* 13, 140-75.
Romaine, Suzanne. 1982. *Sociohistorical Linguistics*. Cambridge: Cambridge University Press.
Rosen, Carol. 1987. "Star means bad: a syntactic divertimento for Italianists." *Italica* 64, 443-76.
Rotaetxe Amusategi, Karmele. 1988. *Sociolingüística*. Madrid: Síntesis.
Rothwell, William. 1972. "Medieval French and modern semantics." *MLR* 57, 25-30.
———. 1980. "Lexical borrowing in a medieval context." *Bulletin of the John Rylands Library* 53, 118-43.
———. 1981. "Historical semantics and the structure of Mediaeval French vocabulary." *Language, Meaning and Style: Essays in Memory of Stephen Ullmann*, ed. by T. E. Hope et al., 145-55. Leeds: Leeds University Press.
Sabatini, Francesco. 1965. "Esigenze di realismo e dislocazione morfologia in testi preromanzi." *Rivista di Cultura Classica e Medievale* 7, 972-98.
———. 1983. "Prospettive sul parlato nella storia linguistica italiana." *Italia linguistica: Idee, Storia, Strutture*, ed. by F. A. Leoni et al., 167-201. Bologna: Il Mulino.
Saltarelli, Mario. 1980. "Syntactic Diffusion." *Papers from the 4th International Conference on Historical Linguistics*, ed. by E. Traugott et al., 183-91. Amsterdam: John Benjamins.
Sampson, Geoffrey. 1979. *Making Sense*. Oxford: Oxford University Press.
———. 1985. *Writing Systems: a Linguistic Introduction*. London: Hutchinson.
Samuels, M. L. 1973. *Linguistic Evolution*. Cambridge: Cambridge University Press.
Sánchez Albornoz, Claudio. 1944. "Nota sobre los libros leídos en el Reino de León hace mil años." *Cuadernos de Historia de España* 1-2, 222-38.
Sánchez Alonso, B. 1941. *Historia de la historiografía española*. Madrid: CSIC.
Sánchez Belda, Luis (ed). 1950. *Chronica Adefonsi Imperatoris*. Madrid: CSIC.
Saussol, José-María. 1977. *Ser y estar. Orígenes de sus funciones en el Cantar de Mio Cid*. Sevilla: Universidad.

Savin, H. B. 1972. "What the child knows about speech when he starts to learn to read." *Language by Ear and by Eye*, ed. by J. F. Kavanagh and I. G. Mattingly, 319-26. Cambridge, Mass: MIT Press.
Schlieben-Lange, Brigitte. 1982. "Sociolinguistique et linguistique romane." *Actes del XVIe Congrés International de Lingüística i Filología Romàniques*, Vol.I, 209-15 & 223-24. Palma de Mallorca: Universidad.
Schmandt-Besserat, Denise. 1991. *Before Writing*. Austin: Texas University Press.
Schon, Donald A. 1967. *Invention and the Evolution of Ideas*. London: Tavistock.
Schuchardt, Hugo. 1890. "Span. port. *tomar*." *ZRPh* 14, 180.
Schulte-Herbruggen, H. 1978. "Polisemia y cambio semántico: *verde* y *verdugo*." *Verba* 5, 47-61.
Scribner, S. and Cole, M. 1981. *The Psychology of Literacy*. Cambridge, Mass: Harvard University Press.
Séphiha, Haim V. 1985. "Judeo-espagnol calque et islamo-espagnol calque." *Homenaje a Alvaro Galmés de Fuentes*, Vol. I, 665-74. Oviedo: Universidad.
Silva Corvalán, Carmen. 1984. "Semantic and pragmatic factors in syntactic change." *Historical Syntax*, ed. by J. Fisiak, 555-74. Berlin: Mouton.
———. 1988. *Sociolingüística: teoría y análisis*. Madrid: Alhambra.
Sinclair, H. 1987. "Language: a gift of nature or a home-made tool?" *Noam Chomsky: Consensus and Controversy*, ed. by S. Modgil and C. Modgil, 173-80. New York: Falmer.
Smith, Colin C. 1977. *Estudios cidianos*. Madrid: Planeta.
Sofer, J. 1930. *Lateinisches und Romanisches aus den Etymologiae des Isidorus von Sevilla*. Gottingen.
Spitzer, Leo. 1924. "Esp. *carrillo*, Port. *carrilho* 'joue'; esp. *carrillera* 'machoire'." *RFE* 11, 316.
Stengaard, Birte. 1991. *Vida y muerte de un campo semántico*. Tübingen: Niemeyer.
———. 1991a. "The combination of glosses in the *Códice Emilianense* 60 (*Glosas Emilianenses*)." *Latin and the Romance Languages in the Early Middle Ages*, ed. by R. Wright, 177-89. London: Routledge.
Stero, Miguel. 1946. "El latín de la Crónica de Alfonso III." *Cuadernos de Historia de España* 4, 125-35.
Stock, Brian. 1983. *The Implications of Literacy: Written Language and Models of Interpretation in the Eleventh and Twelfth Centuries*. Princeton: Princeton University Press.
Stubbs, Michael. 1980. *Language and Literacy*. London: Routledge.
Tagliavini, Carlo. 1972. *Le origini delle lingue neolatine*, 6th ed. Bologna: Patron.

Tannen, Deborah. 1982. "Oral and literate strategies in spoken and written narratives." *Language* 58, 1-21.
Traugott, Elizabeth and Romaine, Suzanne. 1985. "Some questions for the definition of 'style' in socio-historical linguistics." *Folia Linguistica Historica* 6, 7-39.
Trudgill, Peter. 1974. *The Social Differentiation of English in Norwich.* Cambridge: Cambridge University Press.
——— and Chambers, J. K. 1980. *Dialectology.* Cambridge: Cambridge University Press.
Ubieto Arteta, Antonio. 1976. *Cartulario de San Millán de la Cogolla.* Valencia: Anúbar.
Uddholm, Alf. 1955. "Les traits dialectaux de la langue des actes mérovingiens et le formulaire de Marculf." *ALMA* 25, 47-69.
Ullmann, Stephen. 1957. "Historical semantics and the structure of the vocabulary." *Miscelánea Homenaje a A. Martinet,* Vol.I, 289-303. La Laguna: Universidad.
———. 1967. *Semantics: an Introduction to the Science of Meaning.* Oxford: Blackwells.
Valcárcel, Vitalino. 1982. *La "Vita Dominici Siliensis" de Grimaldo.* Logroño: Diputación Provincial.
Valdeavellano, Luis. 1952. *Historia de España* Vol.I. Madrid: Revista de Occidente.
Van der Leeuw, S. and Torrence, R. (eds). 1989. *What's New?* London: Unwin.
Van Reenen, Pieter and Van Reenen-Stein, Karin (eds). 1988. *Distributions spatiales et temporelles, constellations des manuscrits.* Amsterdam: John Benjamins.
Van Uytfanghe, Marc. 1976. "Le latin des hagiographes mérovingiens et la protohistoire du français. État de la question." *Romanica Gandensia* 16, 5-90.
———. 1977. "Latin mérovingien, latin carolingien et *rustica romana lingua*: continuité ou discontinuité?" *Revue de l'Université de Bruxelles,* 65-88.
———. 1984. "Histoire du latin, protohistoire des langues romanes et histoire de la communication." *Francia* 11, 579-613.
———. 1985. "L'Hagiographie et son publique à l'époque merovingienne." *Studia Patristica* 16, 54-62.

———. 1989. "Les expressions du type *quod vulgo vocant* dans des textes latins antérieurs au Concile de Tours et aux Serments de Strasbourg: témoignages lexicologiques et sociolinguistiques de la 'langue rustique romaine'?" *ZRPh* 105, 28-49.

———. 1991. "The consciousness of a linguistic dichotomy Latin-Romance in Carolingian Gaul: the contradictions of the sources and of their interpretation." *Latin and the Romance Languages in the Early Middle Ages*, ed. by R. Wright, 114-29. London: Routledge.

Van Wartburg, Walther. 1952. *La fragmentación lingüística de la Romania*. Madrid: Gredos.

Varvaro, Alberto. 1984. "Omogeneità del latino e frammentazione della Romània." *Latino volgare, latino medioevale, lingue romanze*, ed. by E. Vineis, 11-22. Pisa: Giardini.

———. 1987. "Il giudeo-spagnuolo prima dell'espulsione del 1492." *Medioevo Romanzo* 12, 155-72.

———. 1991. "Latin and Romance: fragmentation or restructuring?." *Latin and the Romance Languages in the Early Middle Ages*, ed. by R. Wright, 44-51. London: Routledge.

Veiga Arias, Amable. 1982. "Dos calas en los orígenes del gallego." *Verba* 9, 319-23.

———. 1983. *Algunas calas en los orígenes del gallego*. Vigo: Galaxia.

———. 1989. "Patronímicos en -z y otros estudios de onomástica gallega." *Verba* 16, 5-30.

Verschueren, Jef. 1981. "Problems of lexical semantics." *Lingua* 53, 317-51.

Versteegh, Kees. 1984. *Pidginization and Creolization: The Case of Arabic*. Amsterdam: Benjamins.

———. 1986. "Latinitas, Hellenismos, Arabiyya." *Historiographia Linguistica* 13, 425-48.

Vilches Acuña, Roberto. 1954. *Semántica española*. Buenos Aires: Kapelusz.

Vives, Juan (ed.). 1946. *Oracional Visigótico*. Barcelona.

Waldron, R. A. 1967. *Sense and sense development*. London: Andre Deutsch.

Wallach, Luitpold. 1959. *Alcuin and Charlemagne*. Ithaca, NY: Cornell University Press.

Walsh, John K. and Deyermond, Alan D. 1992. "*Locus* and literature in the Spanish Middle Ages." *Journal of Hispanic Research* 1, 35-52.

Walsh, Thomas J. 1991. "Spelling lapses in early medieval Latin documents and the reconstruction of primitive Romance phonology." *Latin and the Romance Languages in the Early Middle Ages*, ed. by R. Wright, 205-18. London: Routledge.

Wanner, Dieter. 1986. "On the persistence of 'imperfect grammars': clitic movement from Late Latin to Romance." *Papers from the 7th International Conference on Historical Linguistics*, ed. by A. Giacolone Ramat et al., 575-90. Amsterdam: John Benjamins.

Werth, Paul. 1973. "Accounting for semantic change." *Historical Linguistics*, ed. by J. M. Anderson and C. Jones, 377-415. Amsterdam: North Holland.

Wolf, Hans-Jürgen. 1992. *Glosas Emilianenses*. Hamburg: Buske.

Wood, Ian. 1990. "Administration, law and culture in Merovingian Gaul." *The Uses of Literacy in Early Mediaeval Europe*, ed. by R. McKitterick, 63-81. Cambridge: Cambridge University Press.

Wright, Roger. 1976. "Semicultismo." *Archivum Linguisticum* 7, 13-28.

———. 1979. "The first poem on the Cid: the *Carmen Campi Doctoris*," *Papers of the Liverpool Latin Seminar* 2, 213-48. [=Chapter 16]

———. 1980. "Linguistic reasons for phonetic archaisms in Romance." *Papers from the 4th International Conference on Historical Linguistics*, ed. by E. Traugott et al., 331-37. Amsterdam: John Benjamins.

———. 1982. *Late Latin and Early Romance in Spain and Carolingian France*. Liverpool: Francis Cairns.

———. 1983. "Unity and diversity among the Romance languages." *TPS*, 1-22.

———. 1983a. "La no existencia del latín vulgar leonés." *Incipit* 3, 1-7. [=Chapter 10]

———. 1985. "Indistinctive features, facial and semantic." *Romance Philology* 38, 275-92. [=Chapter 7]

———. 1986. "La función de las Glosas de San Millán y de Silos." *Actes du XVIIe Congrès International de Linguistique et Philologie Romanes*, Vol.IX, 209-19. Marseilles: Université de Provence. [=Chapter 15]

———. 1986a. "How old is the Ballad genre?" *La Corónica* 14, 251-57. [=Chapter 19]

———. 1987. "The study of Semantic Change in Late Latin (Early Romance)." *Papers from the 7th International Conference on Historical Linguistics*, ed. A. Giacolone Ramat et al., 619-28. Amsterdam: John Benjamins. [=Chapter 6]

———. 1988. "La sociolingüística moderna y el romance temprano." *Actes du XVIIIe Congrès International de Linguistique et de Philologie Romanes*, Vol.V, ed. by Dieter Kremer, 11-18. Tübingen: Niemeyer. [=Chapter 2]

———. 1988a. "Latín tardío y romance temprano (1982-88)." *RFE* 68, 257-69.

———. 1989. *Latín tardío y romance temprano*. Madrid: Gredos. (Translation of Wright 1982).

———. 1990. "Semantic change in Romance words for 'cut'." *Historical Linguistics 1987: Papers from the 8th International Conference on Historical Linguistics*, ed. by H. Andersen and K. Koerner, 553-61. Amsterdam: John Benjamins. [=Chapter 8]

———. 1990-91. "Several ballads, one epic and two chronicles (1100-1250)." *La Corónica* 18, 21-38 and 19, xiii-xiv. [=Chapter 20]

———, ed. 1991. *Latin and the Romance Languages in the Early Middle Ages*. London: Routledge.

———. 1991a. "The conceptual distinction between Latin and Romance: invention or evolution?." in *Latin and the Romance Languages in the Early Middle Ages*, ed. by R. Wright, 103-13. London: Routledge. [=Chapter 3]

———. 1991b. "Textos asturianos de los siglos IX y X: ¿latín bárbaro o romance escrito?" *Lletres Asturianes* 41, 20-34. [=Chapter 11]

———. 1991c. "La enseñanza de la ortografía en la Galicia de hace mil años." *Verba* 18, 5-25. [=Chapter 14]

———. 1991d. "On editing 'Latin' texts written by Romance-speakers." *Linguistic Studies in Medieval Spanish*, ed. by R. Harris-Northall and T. D. Cravens, 191-208. Madison: Hispanic Seminary of Medieval Studies. [=Chapter 9]

———. 1992. "Complex monolingualism in Early Romance." *Linguistic Perspectives on the Romance Languages*, ed. by W. J. Ashby et al, 377-88. Amsterdam: John Benjamins. [=Chapter 1]

———. 1992a. "Early medieval Spanish, Latin and Ladino." *Circa 1492: Proceedings of the Jerusalem Colloquium "Litterae Judaeorum in Terra Hispanica,"* ed. by I. Benabu, 36-45. Jerusalem: Hebrew University.

———. 1992b. "La metalingüística del siglo XII español (y la Chronica Adefonsi Imperatoris)." *Actas del II Congreso Internacional de Historia de la Lengua Española*, ed. by M. Ariza et al., 879-86. Madrid: Pabellón de España. [=Chapter 18]

———. 1992c. "La escritura; ¿foto o disfraz?" *Actas del Primer Congreso Anglo-Hispano* Vol.I: *Lingüística*, ed. by R. Penny, 225-33. Madrid: Castalia.

———. 1993. "El latín y el ladino (siglos XI-XII)." *Actas do XIX Congreso Internacional de Lingüística e Filoloxía Románicas*, Vol V, ed. by Ramón Lorenzo, 61-70. La Coruña: Barrié de la Maza. [= Chapter 17]

———. 1993a. "Sociolinguistique hispanique (VIIIe-XIe siècles)." *Médiévales* 25, 61-70. [=Chapter 12]

Zauner, Adolf. 1903. "Die Romanischen Namen der Korperteile." *Romanische Forschungen* 14, 339-530.

Zumthor, Paul. 1984. "Un trompe-l'oeil linguistique?" *Romania* 105, 171-92.

Index

Abbreviations 123
Abd-el-Rahman II 156
Admonitio Generalis 28
Admyte 124
Affixation 85
Alarcos 231
Alcuin 28, 118-119, 177, 279
Alfonso X 100, 119, 125, 266-267, 271, 280, 294, 296, 317
Alphabets 170-180
Alvaro of Cordoba 116, 157
Ambiguity 76-77
Anglo-Saxon 111-112, 118, 266
Annales Regni Francorum 120
Arabic 68, 82, 150, 155-159, 163, 257, 265, 273-274, 282-288
Aragon 221-264
Artes Grammaticæ 10, 70, 109-126, 128, 142, 148
Artes Lectoriæ 176
Asterisks 45-64
Asturias 135-154, 278, 281
Augustine 243

Ballads 289-329
Barbarism 135-154, 181, 206
Basque(s) 155, 159, 162, 215
Beato de Liébana 161
Bede 112, 234
Berceo 82, 94, 97-98, 102, 132, 274
Bernard de Sédirac 314
Bernardo del Carpio 296, 302
Bible 80, 83, 97, 138, 157, 236-240, 243-243, 256
Boniface 25

Bridget (St) 82-83

Cæsarius of Arles 3, 110
Cantar de Roncesvalles 292, 302
Carmen Campi Doctoris 221-264, 311, 316
Carmen Poenitentiale 290
Cassiodorus 110, 175
Catalonia 38, 43, 71, 105, 116, 118, 160, 162-164, 213, 221-264, 268, 277-281
Celtic 94
Chindaswinth 86, 151
Chinese 170, 172
Chronica Adefonsi Imperatoris 119, 268, 272, 277-288
Chronica Najerensis 311-313, 316
Chronicle of Alfonso III 119, 124-125, 135-154, 183, 189, 194
Chronicon Mundi 311-318
Cid (Rodrigo Díaz) 221-264, 285-286, 294-295, 399-318, 321
Clitic pronouns 146-147
Comedias 328
Communication 4, 18, 155-164
Council of Coyanza (1055): 123
Council of Mainz (847) 279
Council of Nicæa 228
Council of Tours (813) 3, 279
Council of Valladolid (1228): 121, 267, 280
Counts of Barcelona 221-264, 309-310
Crocodiles 80, 83
Crónica Albeldense 135

Crónica de Castilla 297
Crónica de Veinte Reyes: 271, 296
Cultismos 173, 200, 203, 206

Dante 79-80, 119, 309
De Litteris Colendis 28
De Orthographia (Bede) 112
De Orthographia (Cassiodorus) 175
De Rebus Hispaniæ 293-294, 310
Differentialism 199
Diglossia 2, 17, 22, 27-29
Donatus 25, 41, 109, 142
Dormice 57
Drag-chain 78, 99
Drift 93

Early Romance 2
Editing 109-126
Einstein 24
Etymology 45-64
Eugenius of Toledo 116
Eulalie (Cantilena) 29, 212, 280
Eulogius of Cordoba 116, 120, 137
Evolution 21-30

Falklands-Malvinas War 133
Features 74-94
Fleury 121
Frames 74-94
French 14-15, 59, 79, 89, 98-100, 151, 281-282
Fuero de Avilés 200
Fuero de Cuenca 186
Fuero de Valfermoso de las Monjas 124, 197, 201, 269-270
Fueros 123, 217

Galicia 125, 164, 176, 181-208, 272
García Ordóñez 247-256, 286
Generalization 96
Germanic-speakers 109-126, 177, 185

Gestalt theory 75, 93
Glossaries 209-219
Glosses (Riojan) 6, 9, 19-20, 82, 123, 143, 162, 196, 201, 209-219, 268
Glosses (Goetz's) 86
Glosses (Castro's) 84, 87
Gout 276
Grammatica 109-126
Greek 267
Gregory the Great 3, 26
Grimaldo 271-276

Hebrew 68, 155-159, 265, 286
Historia Arabum 315
Historia Compostellana 268, 271-272
Historia Hierosolymitana 228
Historia Roderici 118, 221-264, 268, 294, 311
Historia Silense 303
Hrabanus Maurus 94, 279
Hymns 232-234
Hyponymy 95-106

Ildefonso of Toledo 116
Indo-European 49
Inscriptions 16
Intelligibility 6
Invention 21-30
Isidore of Seville 2, 13, 20, 40, 70-72, 80-81, 86-87, 90, 110, 116-117, 124, 137, 275
Isoglosses 91

Jawbones 80-86
Julian of Toledo 110, 116, 142, 157

Kharjas 158-159, 290

"Ladino" 265-275

INDEX

Language Planning 21-30, 169, 176-177
Las Navas de Tolosa 229, 317
Lateran Council (1215) 121
Legal language 127-134
"Leonese Vulgar Latin" 127-134, 185
Lérida 229, 240-254
Lexicon 49-54, 95-106
Liber Maiolichinus 234
Libro de Alexandre 83, 100
Libro de Buen Amor 92, 271
Libro de los engaños 323-324
Literacy 4, 70, 141, 155-208
Liturgy 14, 47, 72, 81-82, 116, 183, 213, 272
Logographic script 165-180
Lucas of Tuy 125, 137, 311-318

Martin of Leon 124-126
Metalinguistics 31-44, 53, 265-288
Miracula Beati Felicis 274-275
Mocedades de Rodrigo 292-293, 296, 301, 305, 316-329
Moslem Spain viii, 42, 115, 142, 155-159, 229, 249-252, 265, 296
Mozarabs 156-157, 232, 239, 283
Muret 278

Nebrija 82, 84, 87, 90, 296
Nodicia de kesos 124, 143, 161
Numerals 24-25

Orthography 54, 128, 144-45, 181-219

Palencia 121, 217
Pedro del Corral 300, 316
Peter of Cluny 271, 275-276
Phonetic Script 54-64
Phrasebook principle 218-219
Pliny 86

Poema de Almería 282-288, 293-294, 289, 302, 310, 315-316
Poema de Fernán González 292-293, 305
Poema de Mio Cid viii, 66, 86, 97-98, 100-101, 146, 229, 240-243, 252, 262, 270-271, 281-283, 291-294, 297, 318, 324, 327
Pompeii 9, 201
Proto-Romance 2-9, 31-44, 46, 51, 65, 84
Prototypes 74-94
Prudentius 238-240

Quintilian 236

Reconstruction 5, 31-44, 66, 69, 139
Río Salado 234
Romances 289-329

Sahagún 178-179, 187-205
San Millán 121, 143, 162, 187, 209-219, 247
Sapphics 230-234
Sardinian 13, 33, 97-98
Sedulius Scottus 233
Semantic Change 65-106, 150-152
Siete Infantes de Lara 307
Silos 143, 162, 209-219, 272-276
Slates 9, 141, 155, 167
Sociolinguistics 12-20, 35, 113, 140, 155-64, 170, 265-268
Specialization 96
Spectrograms 169
Spontaneity 138, 147
St Amand 121
Standardization 25, 28
Strasbourg Oaths 18, 29, 46, 177, 216, 281
Strength hierarchies 23-24
Substratum 33
Sumerians 23, 171

Superordinates 95-106

Theatre 321-331
Toledo 121, 157, 163, 251-253, 256-257, 273
Tractatus Garsiæ (Garcineid) 261-262, 270
Translation viii
Treaty of Cabreros viii
Trees 13, 32-37

Ueremudo 145
Universals 21
Ut queant laxis 232

Valencia 255, 260, 277-278, 281, 294, 308, 311, 314
Varro 48
Vellido Dolfos 296, 312-313
Virgil 235-240, 244

Vigila 209
Vindolanda 9
Visigoths 111
Vita Æmiliani 308
Vita Dominici Siliensis 119, 153, 272-276, 285
Vitas Sanctorum Patrum Emeritensium 308
Vulgate 235-240
"Vulgo" 153, 271-276, 285

Writing 22, 25

Ximénez de Rada (Rodrigo de Toledo) 242, 293-294, 310-318

Zamora 249, 290, 295-296, 312-313, 316-317, 321
Zaragoza 229, 240-241, 246-262